QUANTITATIVE METHODS
for Accounting and Business Studies
Third Edition

GORDON BANCROFT

Business Manager of Accounting
University of Derby

GEORGE O'SULLIVAN

Principal Lecturer in Statistics
University of Central England in Birmingham

The McGraw-Hill Companies

London · New York · St Louis · San Francisco · Auckland · Bogotá · Caracas
Lisbon · Madrid · Mexico · Milan · Montreal · New Delhi · Panama · Paris
San Juan · São Paulo · Singapore · Sydney · Tokyo · Toronto

Published by
McGRAW-HILL Publishing Company
Shoppenhangers Road, Maidenhead, Berkshire, SL6 2QL, England
Telephone 01628 23432
Fax 01628 770224

British Library Cataloguing in Publication Data

Bancroft, Gordon
    Quantitative Methods for Accounting and Business Studies. – 3Rev. ed
    I. Title   II. O'Sullivan, George
    519.5024658

    ISBN 0–07—707731–8

Library of Congress Cataloging-in-Publication Data

Bancroft, Gordon.
    Quantitative methods for accounting and business studies/Gordon Bancroft and
George O'Sullivan. — 3rd ed.
        p. cm.
    Rev. ed. of: Maths and statistics for accounting and business studies. 2nd ed. 1988.
    Includes bibliographical references and index.
    ISBN 0–07–707731–8
    1. Commercial statistics.   2. Business mathematics.
I. O'Sullivan, George.   II. Bancroft, Gordon. Math and statistics for accounting and
business studies.   III. Title.

HF1017.B29   1993
519—dc20   93-10243
                                                                              CIP

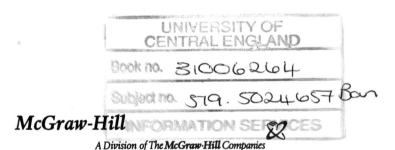
McGraw-Hill INFORMATION SERVICES

A Division of The McGraw·Hill Companies

Reprinted 1997

Typeset by Interprint Ltd, Malta, and printed and bound in Great Britain at the University Press,
Cambridge

Printed on permanent paper in compliance with ISO Standard 9706

CONTENTS

PREFACE

This book has developed from many years of teaching quantitative methods to the first-year syllabus of the major professional accountancy bodies. An important feature of the text is that it is structured around the solutions of many past examination questions of these professional bodies. Other examination questions are also given as exercises for the reader.

This third edition of the textbook aims to update the information of the second edition, published in 1988. This is achieved by:

1. taking account of new syllabus requirements of accountancy professional bodies;
2. using up-to-date examination questions;
3. incorporating recent developments in statistical computing.

Although much of the text has been completely revised it retains the structure and style of the earlier editions and hence should continue to be an ideal text for self-study or teaching purposes.

The first chapters of this book develop the mathematical foundations that are needed for the remainder of the text. However, the larger portion of this text describes the principles and methods of statistics, applying them to financial or business problems. The final four chapters of the text introduce the basic concepts of a range of commonly-used optimization and planning models that are used in business. These models have been introduced to the foundation stage of the accountancy professional examinations in recent years.

Although this book is suitable for first-year degree students in accountancy and business, it is primarily designed for the examinations of the professional accountancy bodies. It also covers the quantitative requirements of BTEC courses in business and finance.

ACKNOWLEDGEMENTS

We should like to express our gratitude to the following professional bodies for their permission to reproduce past examination questions.

The Chartered Institute of Management Accountants (CIMA)
The Chartered Association of Certified Accountants (ACCA)

Where examples and exercises include material from such examination questions, the name of the body and the date of examination paper are shown at the end of the question. Such a reference does not mean that the question is complete or appeared in the paper concerned in exactly the form of our example or exercise. Where data from an examination question is used in the main body of the text, there is a statement that the data are from a particular body and examination paper concerned. All solutions and comments relating to questions are entirely our own and make no reference to model answers produced by or on behalf of the professional bodies.

We acknowledge the cooperation of MINITAB by allowing us to use MINITAB commands and reproduce output where applicable. The address of MINITAB Data Analysis Software is: 3081 Enterprise Drive, Stage College, Pennsylvania, USA (Telex: 881612). MINITAB is a registered trademark. We also thank the LOTUS Development Corporation for allowing us to make reference to the LOTUS 123 package and Prentice Hall International for giving their permission to reproduce output from the Quantitative Systems for Business Plus package developed by Y. L. Chang and R. S. Sullivan.

INTRODUCTION

1.1 MATHEMATICS AND STATISTICS IN FINANCE

It is an important role of the accountant to make decisions based on information concerning the financial state of a business. By its very nature, financial information is quantitative and therefore the accountant requires knowledge of those procedures designed to analyse such numerical information. Thus it is essential for anyone in the financial sphere to possess a clear understanding of mathematics and statistics. It is the aim of this text to provide the necessary background knowledge in these subjects to those readers who intend to pursue a career in business or finance.

In Chapters 2, 4, and 5 we develop the mathematical foundations that are essential to the remainder of the text. This includes the topics of algebra, graphs, matrices, and calculus and will be of interest to those readers who have not met these topics before and also to those who have not studied them for some time. In Chapter 3 we deal with an important business application of mathematics, financial arithmetic, where we investigate problems involving compound interest, discounting, and investments. This chapter is of great importance to the accountant, as there is often the need to calculate the results of a possible investment. The reader will discover that only a limited mathematical knowledge is necessary for such important calculations.

The middle, and greater portion, of this book describes the methods and applications of probability and statistics. Theoretically, there is a relationship between the roles of accountancy and statistics. Instead of having results from a survey or a scientific experiment, the accountant has tabulations of financial information. Instead of scores or lengths, the accountant usually measures information in monetary units.

Despite this link with accountancy, it is only in the last twenty to thirty years that statistics has been accepted by the accountancy profession. It is in the area of sampling for auditing where the increased use is most noticeable. In the past, auditors usually selected their samples judgementally, that is, in a purely subjective manner. However, there is no way of measuring the accuracy or precision of such a sample. This is not the case with statistical sampling. It is a considerable advantage that a predetermined accuracy can be met by a statistical sample, but not from a judgement sample.

In Chapters 19–22 we introduce a range of mathematical models which are commonly used in business. The modelling techniques used in these chapters should give assistance to the planning of any business organization. In Chapter 19 we look at a range of optimization models, linear programming, transportation and assignment. In Chapter 20, on network analysis, network models are examined which are concerned with the planning and management of projects. Chapter 21 looks at models concerned with the planning and control of inventory—an important aspect of any business organization. Finally, in Chapter 22 we examine the principles of simulation models. Simulation is a method of approach which has been applied to a large number of business functions—notably capital investment, queuing and inventory control.

With the development of the computer and microcomputer it is clear that the role of the accountant is changing. He is becoming less involved with the processing of financial data and more involved with the decision-making process of the firm. Hence it is important that all accountants have a sound understanding of objective quantitative procedures.

1.2 DESCRIPTIVE AND INFERENTIAL STATISTICS

In many statistical texts a distinction is made between descriptive statistics and inferential statistics. The term *descriptive statistics* is confined to the presentation of information in an understandable form. This term is distinct from the term *inferential statistics*, which deals with the methods of analysing the data so that conclusions can be made concerning the population from which the data was drawn.

Given a large amount of numerical information, a statistician would try to arrange it in a form that makes it easy to read and understand. This may include the classification and presentation of the data in a table of frequencies, or, in order to convey its meaning more directly, the data may be presented as diagrams or graphs. Measures, such as proportions or averages, may then be calculated. The first stage of the statistical function, which includes the organization, presentation, and summarization of data, falls within the domain of descriptive statistics. We deal with this aspect of statistics in Chapters 7–11. Before we can extract useful information from data, we first have to collect it. There are many ways in which this can be done and these methods are described in Chapter 6.

An important reason why statistics has increased in importance in recent years is that methods and techniques have been devised to aid the decision-making process in business. This often involves making forecasts, estimations, or conclusions about some larger set of data than that actually observed. Inferential statistics of this kind is described in Chapters 15–18. Basic to the understanding of inferential statistics is the study of probability, which is described in Chapters 12–14.

To illustrate the distinction between descriptive and inferential statistics, we introduce the following example:

A large company enters into many thousands of financial transactions each year. An executive from the finance department has been asked to investigate how many of these transactions exceed £1000. The executive checks 500 of them and discovers that 75 exceed this value.

As long as the company is only interested in the 500 values observed, it is dealing with descriptive statistics. If, on the other hand, the company now wishes to make a statement about all of the transactions, then it enters the realm of inferential statistics. In effect, the company is generalizing about all of the values when it has information about only some.

1.3 COMPUTER PACKAGES

Before the advent of the computer and microcomputer the accountant and statistician also had to be skilled in arithmetic. For every statistical analysis, say, a large number of calculations had to be carried out and checked manually before any conclusions could be presented. However, nowadays computers can perform these calculations in a few seconds so that the statistician can concentrate on the analysis and presentation of conclusions from the analysis. Familiarity with the computer is an essential skill for anyone using mathematical techniques or statistical methods.

There is, of course, no reason why statisticians or accountants should not write their own computer programs each time they want to carry out an appropriate analysis. However, there are a number of statistical and accounting packages that have been very successfully written by a number of experts. So using a package rather than writing your own programs allows you to concentrate on the statistics or accounts rather than on the computing technicalities.

There are a number of packages available to mathematicians and statisticians. These packages can be divided into two types: batch and interactive. The older type of package tends to be batch operated. This type of operation involves the situation where the data and the statistical instructions are entered into the computer as a complete job and the statistician has then to wait for the results to be returned to him before continuing with the analysis. Many established statistical packages are of this type and are well used. Such examples include SPSS (statistical package for the social sciences), BIOMED (a package developed for biomedical work), and GENSTAT (a general statistical package). These packages are now becoming outdated with the high-powered personal computers that can store large data sets and perform high-speed operations on these data sets.

More recently developed packages tend to be of the interactive type. These allow a statistician to enter instructions one at a time and after each instruction the computer gives an immediate response. This type of package has the advantage that the statistician can take account of the response from one instruction to help him decide which future instructions to use. It can also point out an erroneous instruction without it wasting very much time. Examples of interactive packages are MINITAB (a package developed at Pennsylvania State University) and SPSSPC (which is SPSS adapted for personal computers).

In some chapters of this text we describe how MINITAB might be used to solve certain statistical problems. Now MINITAB is, in fact, written in FORTRAN, but there is no need to know FORTRAN in order to use it. All that is needed is to type in MINITAB commands. MINITAB's command language is fairly straightforward and provides a very good introduction to other statistical packages. It is not our intention to give instruction in any detail on how to use MINITAB (the student handbook published by MINITAB is excellent) so much as to show the sort of output that MINITAB will produce relevant to the topic being considered. The instruction on how to obtain such output can be obtained from the student handbook or from the on-line help facility.

In addition, spreadsheets (such as LOTUS 1-2-3 and Quattro) are often used to carry out basic statistical calculations on relatively small data sets. In Chapter 7 we make reference to these spreadsheets when drawing pie charts, bar charts and other graphs. These spreadsheets are examples of business software packages that produce graphs at the touch of a button. Also there is an increasing number of management science packages which carry out the techniques and algorithms associated with the range of mathematical models introduced in Chapters 19 to 22. There is no doubt that the use of such packages allows more time to be spent on the formulation of problems and interpretation of solutions. This text refers to the package QSB+ (Quantitative Systems for Business Plus) which can be used on all personal computers.

Before leaving this section we should point out that there are dangers in the thoughtless use of statistical packages. Given that it is relatively easy to carry out many statistical analyses, there is a great temptation to do just this. This tends to generate a large amount of pointless printout and is quite likely to lead to the discovery of a relationship for which the data, by chance, appears to provide evidence. This is a very dangerous practice. A statistical package should be regarded as a tool for simplifying the laborious calculations and not as a replacement for thought.

1.4 APPROXIMATION AND ERROR

Many numbers used in business are not totally accurate but are approximations and hence subject to a type of error. This error may not be due to a fault in the calculations but may have arisen because completely accurate figures were either unnecessary or else impossible. In this section we look at ways in which error arises and how it is manipulated.

If Mr X has a large win on the football pools amounting to £252 743.67p it is quite likely that this will be reported in the national press as £250 000. From the reader's point of view this latter figure gives a good idea of the size of the win; it provides a good approximation to the actual win. This type of approximation is often carried out with large numbers, or with numbers that have a lot of digits, 375.237 952 say. In the pools example the win has been rounded to the nearest 10 000, or is correct to two significant figures (as there are two digits to the left of the zeros). So often does approximation take place that you will find very few statistical statements that are absolutely accurate. Which of the following statements would you expect to see reported?

'The output of coal is 527 365 tonnes per day'

or

'The output of coal is 527 thousand tonnes per day'

This great use of approximation means that we must be very careful about drawing conclusions from such data.

Example 1.4.1 The following table shows the distance, in miles, between major cities within Great Britain. The distances are given to the nearest mile and are measured along the normal AA recommended route.

London				
118	Birmingham			
153	184	Cardiff		
211	135	236	Liverpool	
78	130	118	237	Southampton

(a) Determine the distance between the following pairs of cities when rounded to the nearest 10 miles
  (i) Cardiff and Southampton
  (ii) London and Cardiff
  (iii) Birmingham and Liverpool

(b) What is the distance between London and Liverpool rounded to one significant figure?

ANSWER

(a) (i) The distance between Cardiff and Southampton is 118 miles which is nearer to 120 miles than 110 miles, so the answer is 120 miles.
   (ii) 153 miles is closer to 150 miles than 160 miles, so the answer is 150 miles.
   (iii) The distance between Birmingham and Liverpool is 135 miles, which is exactly half-way between 130 miles and 140 miles. Convention states that if this happens then the number should be rounded up rather than down. This gives an answer of 140 miles.
(b) The numbers 200 and 300 both have one significant figure (one number to the left of the zones) and the distance 211 miles is nearer to 200 than 300. The answer is 200.

Suppose we read that the consumption of ceramic goods in West Germany is 20 million tonnes, it is quite likely that this figure has been rounded to the nearest 1 million tonnes, say. This information could also be expressed in the form:

$$\text{Consumption of ceramic goods} = 20 \text{ million} \pm 500\,000 \text{ tonnes}$$

where 20 million is the *estimate* of consumption (in tonnes) and 500 000 is termed the *maximum absolute error*. Typically an estimate with a maximum absolute error takes the form

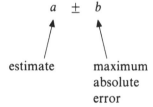

It might also be convenient to express the error in the West German consumption of ceramic goods by

$$20 \text{ million} \pm 2.5 \text{ per cent}$$

as 500 000 is 2.5 per cent of 20 million. Here the maximum error is expressed in relative, or percentage, terms. A maximum *relative error* expresses the maximum absolute error as a percentage of the estimate and is calculated using

$$\text{Maximum relative error} = \frac{\text{maximum absolute error}}{\text{estimate}} \times 100 \text{ per cent}$$

In practice we often need to perform calculations using numbers where error is present. There are two rules for determining the size of the maximum error when undertaking calculations involving approximate numbers.

RULE 1 When two approximate values are added or subtracted, the maximum absolute error in the result is obtained by adding their maximum absolute errors.

RULE 2 When two approximate values are multiplied or divided, the relative error in the result is obtained by adding their relative errors.

We illustrate these rules in the following example.

Example 1.4.2 A company is preparing future production plans for a new product. Research findings suggest that next year the company could make and sell 10 000 units ($\pm$ 20 per cent) at a price of £50 ($\pm$ 10 per cent), depending on size of order, weather, quality of supply, discounts and so on.

The variable costs of production for next year, given these data, are also uncertain but have been estimated as follows:

Type	Costs £	Margin of error (%)
Materials	150 000	$\pm$ 2
Wages	100 000	$\pm$ 5
Marketing	50 000	$\pm$ 10
Miscellaneous	50 000	$\pm$ 10

Find the range of possible error in next year's revenue, costs of production, contribution and contribution per unit, in each case stating your answer both in absolute (actual) and in relative percentage terms. (CIMA Stage 1: Nov. 1990)

ANSWER There are six pieces of information given which are all subject to error. The table below shows the estimate, maximum relative error, and maximum absolute error for each of these pieces of information.

	Estimate	Maximum relative error (%)	Maximum absolute error
Number of units sold	10 000	20	2000
Price per unit	50	10	5
Materials	150 000	2	3000
Wages	100 000	5	5000
Marketing	50 000	10	5000
Miscellaneous	50 000	10	5000

(a) The estimate of revenue is number of units sold × price per unit

$$= 10\,000 \times 50 = £500\,000$$

Rule 2 can now be used to find the maximum possible error. The maximum relative error for revenue, the product of numbers sold and price, is

$$(20 + 10) = 30 \text{ per cent or £150 000 in absolute terms.}$$

(b) The estimate of costs of productions is

$$150\,000 + 100\,000 + 50\,000 + 50\,000 = £350\,000$$

From rule 1, the maximum absolute error is

$$(3000 + 5000 + 5000 + 5000) = £18\,000, \text{ or } 5.1 \text{ per cent.}$$

(c) The estimate of contribution is revenue − costs = £150 000.
The maximum absolute error is 150 000 + 18 000 = £168 000 or 112 per cent.

(d) The estimate of contribution per unit is $\dfrac{150\,000}{10\,000}=£15$

The maximum relative error is $112+20=132$ per cent, or £19.80 in absolute terms.

It must be pointed out that the two rules for determining maximum relative error, or maximum absolute error, provide good approximations. More accurate answers can be achieved by using the minimum and maximum values.

Exercise 1.4.1 A manufacturer of cricket bats is planning future production. For a particular year materials are expected to cost £30 000, but this is subject to an error of ±10 per cent, depending on source of supply, quality, and discounts. Wages and salaries are estimated to be £50 000 ±5 per cent, depending on pay increases and the amount of part-time summer working. The manufacturer plans to produce 3000 bats (to the nearest hundred), with an ex-factory selling price of £40 (to the nearest pound).

You are required to find the rate of possible error in:

(a) costs of production;
(b) income from sales;
(c) contribution;
(d) contribution per cricket bat.

In each case state your answer both as absolute and relative errors.

TEST EXERCISES

1.1 The nominal selling prices (in pounds), and the number of units sold, of the four products produced by a company during 1985 were as follows:

Product	Units sold	Selling price (£)
A	212 400	4.20
B	220 900	5.70
C	162 500	8.40
D	95 700	10.30

If the numbers of units sold is taken as being rounded to the nearest 100 (i.e. to within an error of ±50) and the prices actually charged as being correct to within plus or minus 10 pence, calculate the total sales revenue for the year with its associated absolute error.

1.2 Accountants use a variety of aids to assist in statistical calculations, including the following:

  (i) desk/hand calculators;
 (ii) mathematical and statistical tables;
(iii) computers.

(a) What are the advantages and disadvantages of each of these aids?
(b) Explain briefly how you would use either a calculator or a computer to produce the equation of a regression line.

1.3 The revenue from the sale of Q units at a unit price of $£P$ is $£PQ$. If the estimated revenue from next week's sales is quoted as ±20 per cent, and the price is quoted as ±10 per cent, the number of units sold, Q, is liable to what size of error?

(CIMA Stage 1: May 1990)

2

GRAPHS AND EQUATIONS

2.1 THE STRAIGHT LINE

A method of charging with which you will be familiar from household bills is that of a fixed standing charge or rental plus a further charge per unit of the commodity consumed.

Thus an electricity bill for a particular quarter might involve a standing charge of £4.50 plus a further charge of 4p per unit of electricity consumed. So if 500 units of electricity were consumed the total bill would be

$$£4.50 + £0.04 \times 500 = £4.50 + £20 = £24.50$$

while if 700 units were consumed the total bill would be

$$£4.50 + £0.04 \times 700 = £32.50$$

In general, we have that

$$\text{Total bill(£)} = 4.50 + 0.04 \times \text{number of units consumed} \qquad (2.1)$$

Similarly, a quarter's telephone bill might involve a rental charge of £17.00 plus a further charge of 4.5p per metered unit. So if 200 units were metered for the quarter the total bill would be

$$£17.00 + £0.045 \times 200 = £17.00 + £9.00 = £26.00$$

In general, we have that

$$\text{Total bill(£)} = 17.00 + 0.045 \times \text{number of metered units} \qquad (2.2)$$

Equations (2.1) and (2.2) are both examples of *linear* (or *straight line*) equations. To see why this expression is used consider first Eq. (2.1). Take a selection of different numbers of units consumed and calculate the corresponding total bill in each case as in Table 2.1.

Table 2.1

Number of units consumed	100	200	300	400	500	600	700
Total bill(£) = 4.50 + 0.04 × no. of units		8.50	12.50	16.50	20.50	24.50	28.50	32.50

Next plot these pairs of figures on graph paper having the horizontal axis calibrated by number of units consumed and the vertical axis calibrated by total bill. The curve joining the plotted points is then what is meant by the *graph* of total bill against number of units consumed. As will be seen from Fig. 2.1 this graph is a *straight line*.

Exercise 2.1.1 For the quarter's telephone bill involving a rental charge of £17.00 plus a further charge of 4.5p per metered unit, plot a graph of total bill against number of metered units considering numbers of units from 150 to 450 in steps of 50.

The answer to the exercise is also a straight line. So we see that whatever the particular values of the fixed charge and the charge per unit the graph of total bill against number of units will always be a straight line. Thus if

$$\text{Total bill} = a + b \times \text{number of units consumed}$$

for *any* two numbers a and b, then the graph is a straight line.

Another important application of the straight line idea is to a firm's production costs for a product. These costs can be regarded as a fixed cost plus a cost per unit produced, called the variable cost per unit. Thus

$$\text{Total cost} = a + b \times \text{number of units produced}$$

where a is fixed cost and b is variable cost.

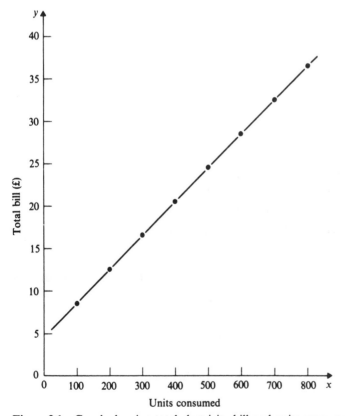

Figure 2.1 Graph showing total electricity bill and units consumed.

From a mathematical point of view all these cases are the same and they can all be represented by the single equation:

$$y = a + bx$$

This is the *general equation of a straight line*. The x and y, plotted on the horizontal and vertical axes respectively, can represent whatever variables are relevant to the particular application being considered, with x representing the 'independent' variable and y the variable 'dependent' upon it. For example, x could represent the charge per unit while y is the total bill, or x could represent the variable cost per unit while y is the total cost.

Exercise 2.1.2 Plot the graph of $y = 5 - 2x$

using x values $-3, -2, -1, 0, 1, 2, 3$.

Note that a is the value of y when $x = 0$. Thus it is the value of y at the place where the straight line crosses the y-axis.

> a is called the *intercept* on the y-axis
> b is the amount by which y changes when there is a one unit increase in x.

e.g. the change in the total bill when one extra unit is consumed, or the change in total cost when one extra unit is produced.

In terms of the graph, b represents the *gradient*. A large b means a big change in y for a unit change in x and hence a steep line. A small b means a small change in y for a unit change in x and hence a line which is not steep. Note that a negative b means that y *decreases* as x increases and so the line slopes downwards, as in the last exercise above.

Example 2.1.1 A straight line graph has intercept 4.5 and passes through the point where $x = 4$ and $y = 6.5$. What is the gradient?

ANSWER Denote the gradient by b. Then the equation of the line is $y = 4.5 + bx$. Since it passes through the point $x = 4$, $y = 6.5$ we have $6.5 = 4.5 + 4b$. So $4b = 2$ and it follows that $b = 0.5$. The gradient is 0.5. When x increases by 1, y increases by 0.5.

Exercise 2.1.3 A straight line has gradient 5 and passes through the point where $x = 3$ and $y = 12$. What is the intercept on the $y -$ axis?

2.2 SIMULTANEOUS EQUATIONS

Consider again the electricity tariff arrangement in Sec. 2.1 involving a fixed charge per quarter of £4.50 and a further charge of 4p per unit consumed. Using the notation above for straight lines the electricity bill was

$$y = 4.50 + 0.04x$$

Suppose that for the benefit of high usage customers the electricity board operates an alternative tariff involving a fixed charge per quarter of £9.50 plus a further charge of 3.5p for each unit consumed. On this tariff the bill would be

$$y = 9.50 + 0.035x$$

The question of interest to the consumer is that of how many units must be consumed in order for the second tariff to become preferable.

Figure 2.2 shows both the straight lines plotted on the same scale and axes. We see from this diagram that at the point where $x = 1000$ and $y = 44.50$ these lines cross. So this point lies on both lines. The pair of values $x = 1000$, $y = 44.50$ satisfies both equations *simultaneously*.

The number of units which must be consumed in order for the bill to be the same under both tariffs is 1000 units. If this number of units is consumed, the resulting bill is £44.50.

The intersection point of the two lines could be calculated from their equations without the need for drawing. For this purpose it is usual to write the equations with all the variable terms on the left-hand side and the constants on the right. So we have:

$$y - 0.04x = 4.50 \tag{2.3}$$

$$y - 0.035x = 9.50 \tag{2.4}$$

These equations, for which we are seeking values of x and y which satisfy both, are called *simultaneous equations*.

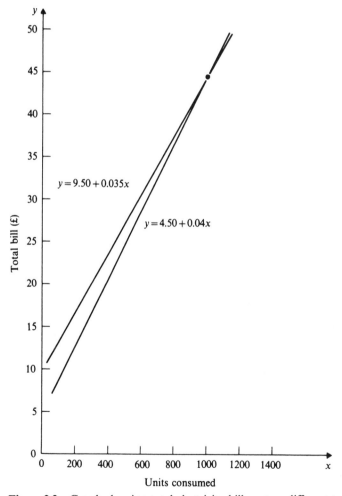

Figure 2.2 Graph showing total electricity bill on two different tariffs.

The steps available for calculating solutions are:

1. to multiply any equation through by any constant;
2. to add or subtract equations in order to eliminate variables.

For this example step 1 is unnecessary since subtraction of one equation from the other will immediately eliminate y and enable a solution to be found for x.

Subtracting Eq. (2.3) from Eq. (2.4) gives

$$0.005x = 5$$

So

$$x = 5/0.005$$
$$= 1000$$

Having found x, its value can be substituted into either of the equations to obtain y. Equation (2.3) gives

$$y = 4.50 + 0.04 \times 1000 = 4.50 + 40 = 44.50.$$

Hence the pair of values $x = 1000$, $y = 44.50$ which we saw from the graph.

Example 2.2.1 Solve the following pair of simultaneous equations

$$8Y = 18X + 3$$
$$2Y = 2X - 5$$

ANSWER Writing these equations with the variables on the left we have:

$$18X - 8Y = -3 \qquad (2.5)$$

$$2X - 2Y = 5 \qquad (2.6)$$

Taking $4 \times (2.6)$ gives:

$$8X - 8Y = 20 \qquad (2.7)$$

Then Eq. (2.5) − Eq. (2.7):

$$10X = -23$$

Hence

$$X = -2.3$$

Substituting in Eq. (2.5): $-41.4 - 8Y = -3$

So

$$-8Y = 38.4$$

Hence

$$Y = -4.8$$

The pair of values solving the equations is $X = -2.3$ and $Y = -4.8$

Exercise 2.2.1 Where do the following lines intersect?

$$2Y = 92 + X$$

$$Y = 88 - 3X$$

A $(-1,91)$ B $(12,40)$ C $(52,12)$ D $(12,104)$ E $(12,52)$

(CIMA Stage 1: Nov. 1990)

The following examples illustrate important uses of the idea of linear and simultaneous equations.

Example 2.2.2 There is a steady, weekly demand for 100 units of a product when the price is £80. If the price is increased to £85 the demand falls to 75 units. The fixed costs of the company selling the product are £2500 and the variable costs are £40 a unit.

Find the equation of the demand function that links price, P, to the quantity demanded, Q, assuming it to be linear.

(CIMA Stage 1: Nov. 1990)

ANSWER Usually the quantity of a product that is demanded will decline as the price of that product increases. A *demand function* is, as stated in this question, an equation relating quantity demanded to price charged. (Conversely, the quantity a supplier is willing to provide can be expected to increase as price rises. An equation relating quantity supplied to price is called a *supply function*.)

We are told to assume here that the demand function is a linear equation. So suppose it is

$$P = a + bQ$$

Then we have from the data given $80 = a + 100b$ (2.8)

and $85 = a + 75b$ (2.9)

Subtracting Eq. (2.9) from Eq. (2.8) $-5 = 25b$

Hence $b = -0.2$

Substituting in (2.8); $80 = a - 20$

Hence $a = 100$

The demand equation is $P = 100 - 0.2Q$

The negative value for b indicates a downward sloping line, as indicated above. For a supply function the gradient would be found to be positive.

Example 2.2.3 A company makes its product at a variable cost of £5 per unit, and sells it for £7 per unit. The company's fixed costs are £10 000 per month. Calculate the break-even quantity.

ANSWER Break-even analysis involves finding the quantity which must be produced and sold in order for total revenue to be exactly equal to total cost, so that neither a profit nor a loss is made.

In this example suppose the company makes and sells x units.

Then total revenue is $\qquad\qquad$ $TR = 7x$

while total cost is $\qquad\qquad$ $TC = 10\,000 + 5x$

So break-even occurs when $\qquad$ $7x = 10\,000 + 5x$

Hence $\qquad\qquad\qquad\qquad$ $2x = 10\,000$

$\qquad\qquad\qquad\qquad\qquad$ $x = 5\,000$

To break even the company needs to produce and sell 5000 units. It is left as an exercise for the reader to plot the lines $y = 7x$ and $y = 10\,000 + 5x$ on the same scale and axes and to note the cross-over point at $x = 5000$.

Example 2.2.4 Under a profit sharing scheme a company agrees to pay to its employees 10 per cent of its profit after tax has been paid. Tax on profit is at a rate of 50 per cent but the company does not have to pay tax on what it distributes to the employees under the profit sharing scheme. The profit in a particular year is £1 000 000.

(a) Find the amount paid in tax.
(b) Find the amount paid to the employees.

ANSWER In this question the amounts paid in tax and to the employees are interlinked. The relationships between them can be expressed using simultaneous equations which can then be solved. (The principle used here has application in cost accounting for finding the overheads to be apportioned to interlinked service departments in an organization.)

ANSWER Let tax be T and let amount paid to employees be E.

Then $\qquad\qquad\qquad\qquad$ $T = 0.5(1\,000\,000 - E)$

$\qquad\qquad\qquad\qquad\qquad$ $E = 0.1(1\,000\,000 - T)$

Hence $\qquad\qquad\qquad$ $T + 0.5E = 500\,000$ $\qquad\qquad$ (2.10)

$\qquad\qquad\qquad\qquad$ $0.1T + E = 100\,000$ $\qquad\qquad$ (2.11)

$\qquad\qquad$ $2 \times (2.10): 2T + E = 1\,000\,000$ $\qquad\qquad$ (2.12)

$\qquad\qquad$ $(2.12)-(2.11): 1.9T = 900\,000$

Hence $\qquad\qquad\qquad$ $T = 900\,000/1.9 = 473\,684$

Substituting in (2.12): $\qquad\qquad$ $E = 1\,000\,000 - 947\,368 = 52\,632$

The employees receive £52 632 and the tax payment is £473 684.

Exercise 2.2.2 It has been estimated that quantity demanded in a particular situation is related to price by the relationship

$$Q = 19.5 - 2P$$

Similarly, it has been estimated that the quantity supplied is related to price by

$$Q = -18 + 3P$$

where Q represents quantity and P represents price. Determine the equilibrium price and quantity:

(i) by solving the above as a pair of simultaneous equations;
(ii) graphically.

Exercise 2.2.3 A company makes its product at a variable cost of £3 per unit, and sells it for £8 per unit. The company's fixed costs are £12 000 per month. Calculate the break-even quantity.

2.3 THE QUADRATIC CURVE

All the graphs considered so far in this chapter have been straight lines, having equations of the form

$$y = a + bx$$

Another type of graph with which it is often necessary to deal is one having an equation of the form

$$y = ax^2 + bx + c$$

Such a graph is called a *quadratic curve*.

(The transition from a as the constant term in the linear expression to being the coefficient of the squared term here is unfortunate, but it is so standard as to forbid any alteration in our treatment.)

Quadratic expressions commonly occur in business and accounting problems in situations where revenue per unit or cost per unit is related in a linear way to the number of units produced or sold. In such a case the total revenue or total cost has the form of a quadratic curve.

Example 2.3.1 A firm producing dining chairs to order has fixed costs of £320 per week and a cost per chair of £$(0.1x + 2)$ where x is the number of chairs produced in the week. Plot a graph showing the total weekly cost for numbers of chairs ranging from 0 to 100.

ANSWER The total cost is

$$y = (0.1x + 2)x + 320$$

i.e.

$$y = 0.1x^2 + 2x + 320$$

The graph of this function can be plotted in exactly the same way as the graph of a linear function was plotted in Sec. 2.1. That is to say by taking a selection of values of x, calculating the corresponding values of y, plotting the pairs of values and joining the points together. The joining must be done using as smooth a curve as possible.

x	0	20	40	60	80	100
x^2	0	400	1 600	3 600	6 400	10 000
$0.1x^2$	0	40	160	360	640	1 000
$2x$	0	40	80	120	160	200
320	320	320	320	320	320	320
y	320	400	560	800	1 120	1 520

The graph obtained from this table is shown as Fig. 2.3. This is a section of a quadratic curve.

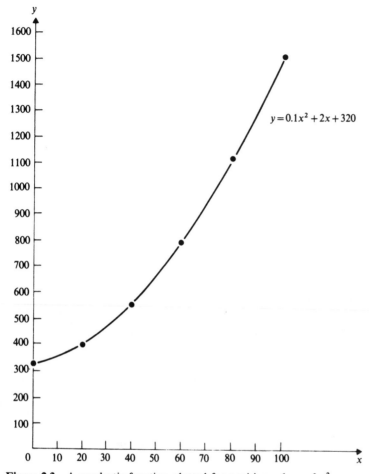

Figure 2.3 A quadratic function plotted for positive values of x^2.

To obtain a more complete picture of the *curve* we need to consider also some negative values for x, even though these have no practical meaning in terms of the example. If we take some negative values of x and plot the curve from $x = -120$ through to $x = 100$ we obtain the graph shown in Fig. 2.4. The lowest point of the curve is seen to be at $x = -10$.

Example 2.3.2 A company making lawnmowers is able to obtain revenue £$(-1.5x + 240)$ per lawnmower where x is the number of lawnmowers sold per week.

Plot a graph showing the total weekly revenue from lawnmower sales for a number of lawnmowers ranging from 0 to 160.

ANSWER Total revenue is

$$y = (-1.5x + 240)x$$

i.e.

$$y = -1.5x^2 + 240x$$

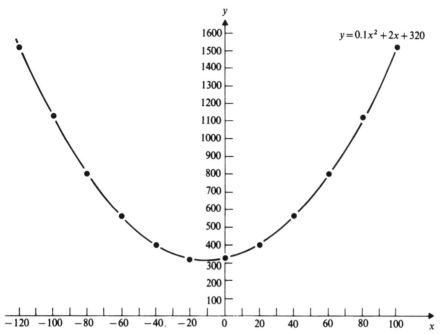

Figure 2.4 Graph of a quadratic function with positive x^2 coefficient.

x	0	20	40	60	80	100	120	140	160
x^2	0	400	1 600	3 600	6 400	10 000	14 400	19 600	25 600
$-1.5x^2$	0	−600	−2 400	−5 400	−9 600	−15 000	−21 600	−29 400	−38 400
$240x$	0	4 800	9 600	14 400	19 200	24 000	28 800	33 600	38 400
y	0	4 200	7 200	9 000	9 600	9 000	7 200	4 200	0

The graph obtained from this table is shown as Fig. 2.5.

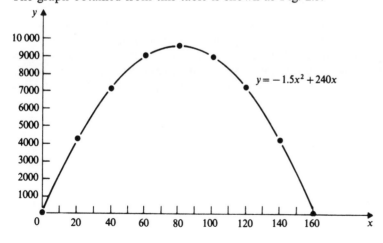

Figure 2.5 Graph of a quadratic function with negative x^2 coefficient.

Graphs having the shapes of those in both Fig. 2.4 and Fig. 2.5 are sometimes referred to as *parabolas*.

The two examples illustrate a number of points about the quadratic curve $y = ax^2 + bx + c$.

1. The constant term c determines the value of y at the point where the curve crosses the y-axis. Thus in Example 2.3.1 where c was 320 the curve crossed the y-axis at $y = 320$, while in Example 2.3.2 where c was zero the curve crossed the y-axis at $y = 0$.
2. The sign of a determines which way up the curve appears. Where a is positive, as in Example 2.3.1, the curve has a minimum point. Where a is negative, as in Example 2.3.2, the curve has a maximum point.
3. The minimum or maximum point of the curve occurs where

$$x = -b/2a$$

Thus in Example 2.3.1 the minimum was at $x = -2/(2 \times 0.1) = -10$. In Example 2.3.2 the maximum was at $x = -240/[2 \times (-1.5)] = 80$.
4. What is often of most interest is finding the values, if any, of x for which y is zero. That is to say solving the *quadratic equation* $ax^2 + bx + c = 0$. For the curve in Example 2.3.1 (Fig. 2.4) we see that there are no such values, while for the curve in Example 2.3.2 (Fig. 2.5) there are solutions at $x = 0$ and at $x = 160$.

Exercise 2.3.1 Plot the graph of $y = x^2 - 9x + 18$.

(a) Note that the intercept on the y-axis, the orientation of the curve and the value of x at the minimum point are all as suggested in points 1–3 above.
(b) Find from your graph the values of x for which $y = 0$.

There are many situations where it is necessary to solve a quadratic equation and the graphical method is not, in practice, an efficient way to do it.

There are basically two methods for solving a quadratic equation: by *factorization* or by use of the *quadratic formula*. The first of these is quicker and neater if it can be applied, and use of the formula should be regarded as a last resort.

To illustrate the factorization method consider solving the equation $2x^2 - 5x + 2 = 0$.

Factorization involves expressing the left-hand side as a product of two terms, each of which has the form $a + bx$, i.e. is linear in x. In order for such a product to be zero one or other of the two factors in the product must be zero. Hence we obtain two linear equations to solve for x. The two solutions are the x values at the points where the curve crosses the x-axis.

With practice it becomes possible to be able usually to 'spot' the two factors when they exist and immediately to write down the factorized form. But we shall consider below a systematic method for obtaining the factors which is rather long-winded but will always work if the factors exist.

For the example here the factorized form of the equation is

$$(x - 2)(2x - 1) = 0$$

This can be confirmed by expanding out the brackets.

Hence the solutions are given by

$$2x - 1 = 0, \text{ i.e. } x = 0.5$$

and

$$x - 2 = 0, \text{ i.e. } x = 2$$

Thus if the curve $y=2x^2-5x+2$ were drawn, it would be found to cross the x-axis at $x=0.5$ and $x=2$.

To see how the factorized form can be arrived at, proceed as follows. Find two numbers whose sum is the coefficient of x (in this case -5) and whose product is the product of the constant term and the coefficient of x^2 (in this case $2\times2=4$). (If such a pair of numbers cannot be found, the factorization method must be abandoned and the formula tried.) The appropriate numbers for this case are -1 and -4.

Next rewrite the equation with the x term broken down using the two numbers. For this case we obtain $2x^2-x-4x+2=0$.

Then take from the first pair of terms and from the second pair of terms separately the largest possible factor. Note that in some cases the largest common factor for the second pair will be 1. For this example the factors are x and -2 respectively, giving:

$$x(2x-1)-2(2x-1)=0$$

Because of the way the x term was broken down, this process will always result in two terms having the bracketed part as a common factor. In this case the common factor is $(2x-1)$.

Removing this factor completes the factorization:

$$(x-2)(2x-1)=0$$

Example 2.3.3 Solve $6x^2+13x-5=0$.

ANSWER Two numbers having sum 13 and product -30 are 15 and -2. Write the equation as $6x^2+15x-2x-5=0$.

Taking the highest factors from the first pair and the last pair:

$$3x(2x+5)-1(2x+5)=0$$

Taking out the bracket as a common factor:

$$(3x-1)(2x+5)=0$$

So the solutions are given by

$$3x-1=0, \text{ i.e. } x=1/3$$

and

$$2x+5=0, \text{ i.e. } x=-2.5$$

Exercise 2.3.2 Solve $8x^2-26x+11=0$.

Exercise 2.3.3 If $4x^2-6=2x$, and $x>0$, then x equals

(A) 1; (B) 1.5; (C) 2; (D) 3; (E) none of these.

(CIMA Stage 1: Nov. 1991)

In cases where the constant term c is zero the factorization is particularly simple. For instance, in Example 2.3.2 we saw the graph of $y=-1.5x^2+240x$. It can be seen immediately that x is a factor of both $-1.5x^2$ and of $240x$ so the quadratic equation $-1.5x^2+240x=0$ can be instantly factorized as $x(-1.5x+240)=0$. Hence the solutions are $x=0$ and $x=240/1.5=160$ which we saw from the graph in Fig. 2.5.

If the x term bx is missing from an equation to be solved, the standard method of factorization explained above should be attempted, beginning with the seeking of two numbers whose sum is *zero* and whose product is the product of a and c.

Next consider the equation

$$x^2 - 6x + 9 = 0$$

When this is factorized we have

$$(x - 3)^2 = 0$$

so for this case there is only one solution, namely $x = 3$. In graphical terms this means that the quadratic curve $y = x^2 - 6x + 9$ just touches the x-axis at one point rather than cutting it at two.

If factors cannot be found, either because there are none or because we are not clever enough to find them, then solutions can be sought using the quadratic formula. This says that the equation $ax^2 + bx + c = 0$ has solutions

$$x = \frac{-b \pm \sqrt{b^2 - 4ac}}{2a}$$

One solution corresponds to the positive sign in the numerator and one to the negative.

Example 2.3.4 Solve $3x^2 + 5x - 15 = 0$.

ANSWER It is not possible to spot two numbers having sum 5 and product -45 so the formula is needed, which says that the solutions are

$$x = \frac{-5 \pm \sqrt{25 - 4 \times 3 \times (-15)}}{6}$$

$$= \frac{-5 \pm \sqrt{205}}{6} = \frac{-5 \pm 14.318}{6}$$

The positive sign gives $x = 1.553$ and the negative sign gives $x = -3.220$. These are the values of x at which the quadratic curve $y = 3x^2 + 5x - 15$ cuts the x-axis.

Exercise 2.3.4 Solve $13x^2 + 7x - 8 = 0$.
Note that if the quadratic formula is applied to the equation

$$x^2 - 6x + 9 = 0$$

then the expression $b^2 - 4ac$ inside the square root is zero and both solutions are the same.

In Example 2.3.1 we considered the curve $y = 0.1x^2 + 2x + 320$ and saw in Fig. 2.5 that it does not cross the x-axis at all. Hence the quadratic equation $0.1x^2 + 2x + 320 = 0$ has no solutions. This fact would manifest itself if we tried to use the formula to solve $0.1x^2 + 2x + 320 = 0$ by our finding that $b^2 - 4ac = 4 - 4 \times 0.1 \times 320 = 4 - 128 = -124$ is less than zero. In terms of everyday arithmetic no square root exists for a negative number and so we cannot calculate $\sqrt{b^2 - 4ac}$ for such a case as this and hence no solutions can be found.

Thus use of the formula will always be conclusive in the sense of either finding solution(s) where solution(s) exist or otherwise telling us there are none.

Exercise 2.3.5 Consider again the chair manufacturer whom we met in Example 2.3.1. His total weekly cost function was found in the answer to that example to be $y = 0.1x^2 + 2x + 320$ where x was the weekly number of chairs produced.

Suppose he can obtain a revenue of £14 for each chair he produces. Find the numbers of chairs for which break even will be achieved (i.e. total weekly revenue is exactly equal to total weekly cost). Solve this:

(a) graphically by drawing the graphs of

$$y = 0.1x^2 + 2x + 320$$

and
$$y = 14x$$

on the same scale and axes and finding the value of x where they cross.

(b) algebraically by reducing $0.1x^2 + 2x + 320 = 14x$ to a quadratic equation in standard form and using factorization.

2.4 LOGARITHMIC AND EXPONENTIAL FUNCTIONS

Before the advent of electronic calculators, logarithms provided a convenient and very commonly used method for carrying out involved multiplications and divisions. The procedure for a multiplication, for example, is to look up the logarithm of the numbers to be multiplied together, add the logarithms and then look up the anti-log of the sum. Thus the multiplication process is replaced by the (simpler) addition process.

Example 2.4.1 Find 3.832×427.5 using logarithms.

Answer

$$\log 3.832 = 0.5834$$
$$\log 427.5 = 2.6309$$

The sum of these two logarithms is 3.2143 and anti-log $3.2143 = 1638$. So the method tells us that $3.832 \times 427.5 = 1638$.

The procedure works because in looking up the logarithm of a number we express that number as a power of some agreed figure called the *base*. In the tables that were most commonly used for logarithm calculations the base employed was 10. So the above example is saying

$$3.832 = 10^{0.5834} \text{ and } 427.5 = 10^{2.6309}$$

Hence

$$3.832 \times 427.5 = 10^{0.5834} \times 10^{2.6309}$$

But powers of the same number are multiplied together by adding the powers. Hence it follows that the required product is

$$10^{0.5834 + 2.6309} = 10^{3.2143}$$

Similarly, division of one number by another could be carried out by finding the difference of their logarithms and looking up the anti-log of the result.

Although electronic calculators have now virtually eliminated the use of logarithms for carrying out the sort of calculation described above, the logarithm idea remains important and relevant in a variety of situations. Indeed, most calculators include a facility for finding logarithms. In Chapter 7, for example, we shall meet semi-logarithmic graphs for presenting certain types of data. In time series, a multiplicative model can be converted to an additive model by means of logarithms; and in regression, variables which are multiplicatively related can be converted to variables which are additively related by taking logarithms. Logarithms also have application in the matter of *learning curves*. When a new process is instituted, the production per unit time or per unit cost in the early stages of the process will be smaller than later on when those operating the process have gained experience of it. Thus the productivity increases rapidly in the early stages and then levels out, and the general form of the graph of productivity against time will be that of the *logarithmic curve* $y = \log x$, shown in Fig. 2.6.

Such a graph can be plotted in the same manner as we plotted straight lines and quadratic curves in Secs. 2.1 and 2.3, respectively, i.e. by taking a selection of values of x, calculating the corresponding values of y, plotting the points, and joining them together by a smooth curve. Note that $\log x$ cannot be calculated for a negative value of x as there is no power to which 10 can be raised so as to give a negative number. Although logarithms to base 10 were the most commonly used for calculation purposes and are well tabulated, the same principles apply whatever the base. If any base other than 10 is employed, that base is written as a subscript to the word 'log'. If there is no subscript the base is understood to be 10.

The only logarithmic base other than 10 which is in common use is base e. This number (its value is 2.718 28) is useful as a base for logarithms because of certain properties concerned with differentiation (see Chapter 5). It frequently appears in solutions to differential equations, and is seen in Chapter 14 in connection with the Poisson distribution.

Logarithms to base e can be referred to using the subscript notation $\log_e$ but they are sufficiently important to warrant a special notation: ln. They are sometimes referred to as *natural logarithms* or *Naperian logarithms* after John Napier, the Scottish mathematician who invented them. Most modern calculators enable calculation of logarithms to both base 10 and base e.

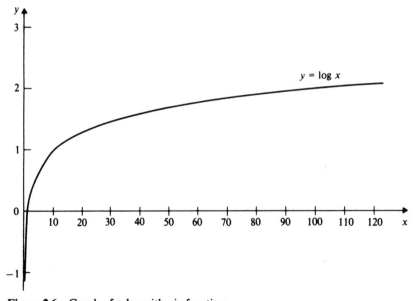

Figure 2.6   Graph of a logarithmic function.

Changing base merely multiplies all values of a logarithmic function by a constant so the basic shape of the curve $y = \ln x$ is the same as that of $y = \log x$ shown in Fig. 2.6.

An *exponential curve* in the most general sense is any curve having an equation of the form $y = a^x$ where a is a constant.

Exercise 2.4.1 Plot the curve $y = 2^x$ for values of x from -4 to $+4$.

Most calculators have a facility for raising a number a to a power x.

The exponential curve is the *inverse* of the logarithmic curve. Thus, for instance, $y = 2^x$ means that $x = \log_2 y$. That is to say, the exponential function is the anti-log function.

However, the term *exponential function* is almost always used in a more restricted sense referring to e as the constant raised to power x. Thus $y = e^x$. It is the anti-log function for logarithms to base e. This function can be looked up in tables and is available on most calculators. Figure 2.7 shows the curve $y = e^x$.

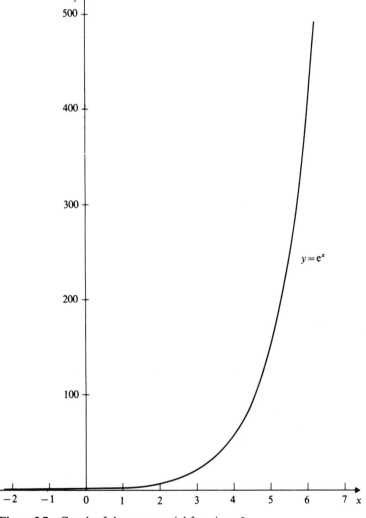

Figure 2.7 Graph of the exponential function e^x.

The exponential function is sometimes referred to as the growth function. It is relevant in modelling populations where rate of growth is proportional to current population size. A financial application of the exponential function will be seen in Chapter 3 when compound interest with continuous compounding is considered.

TEST EXERCISES

2.1 It has been estimated that quantity demanded in a particular situation is related to price by the relationship

$$Q = 100 - 2p$$

Similarly, it has been estimated that quantity supplied is related to price by

$$Q = -20 + 8p$$

where Q represents quantity and p represents price.
Determine the equilibrium price and quantity:

(a) by solving the above as a pair of simultaneous equations;
(b) graphically.

2.2 A company makes its product at a variable cost of £3 per unit and sells the product for £6 per unit. The company's fixed costs amount to £12 000 per month.

(a) Draw a graph showing total monthly revenue against quantity sold and showing also total monthly costs against quantity produced.
(b) Caculate the break-even quantity.
(c) Indicate the break-even quantity on your graph in relation to the total revenue and total cost functions.

2.3 A man staying in England for three months and needing to travel fairly extensively has to make a decision on how best to obtain use of a motor car.
The best hire arrangements he can discover are as follows:

(a) A hire charge of £225 per month payable at the end of each month plus a charge of 5p per mile travelled, payable at the end of the hire period.
(b) A hire charge of £150 per month payable at the end of each month plus a charge of 10p per mile travelled, payable at the end of the hire period.

His ability to purchase a car is limited by the outlay he is able to make. He considers the best opportunity available to him in this direction would be to buy a car for £1500 which he thinks he will be able to sell at the end of three months for £700. In addition, he expects the car to cost him £260 in maintenance charges, which he thinks he can put off paying until the end of the three months.
What is the best course of action for the man to take if:

 (i) he expects to cover 4000 miles;
 (ii) he expects to cover 6000 miles;
(iii) he expects to cover 8000 miles?

Illustrate your answer by drawing, on the same scale and axes, graphs of total cost against miles travelled for each of the three schemes available.

2.4 A manufacturer is faced with the following demand function:

$$2Q + P - 10 = 0.$$

He believes that the supply function is:

$$P^2 - 8Q - 5 = 0$$

where P denotes price in pounds, and the quantities demanded and supplied are in thousands.

(a) Draw a graph showing the demand function and the supply function.
(b) Use simultaneous equations to calculate the equilibrium price and quantity.

2.5 A manufacturer is faced with the following demand function:

$$Q = \ln 99 - \ln P$$

He believes that the supply function is:

$$Q = \ln(P - 2)$$

where P denotes price in pounds, and the quantities demanded and supplied are in thousands.

(a) Plot a graph showing the demand function and the supply function, using in each case P values 3, 6, 9, 12 and 15.

(b) Calculate the equilibrium price and quantity by solving the equation

$$\ln (P - 2) = \ln 99 - \ln P$$

3

FINANCIAL ARITHMETIC

3.1 COMPOUND INTEREST

The subject of compound interest is concerned with the growth of an investment over a period of time when earnings as they are received are added to the sum invested. The most basic problem which we can consider is that of finding the value after a specified time of a stated initial sum at a known interest rate.

Example 3.1.1 A sum of £2000 is invested for eight years at an annual interest rate of 9 per cent. To what value will the sum have grown by the end of this time if all interest is added to the investment as it is earned at the end of each year?

ANSWER The interest earned in the first year is £2000 × (9/100). This is then added to the investment so that the sum earning interest in the second year is £2000 + £2000 × (9/100). This can be more tidily written as £2000 × (1 + 0.09).

So the total value at the end of the year is seen to be equal to the total value at the start multiplied by a factor of (1 + 0.09). Applying this to the second year we see that the value of the investment at the end of that year will be £2000 × (1 + 0.09) × (1 + 0.09) which is £2000 × $(1 + 0.09)^2$.

By the same reasoning we see that the value of the investment at the end of year 3 will be £2000 × $(1 + 0.9)^3$.

Continuing in this way we find that the required value of the investment at the end of eight years will be £2000 × $(1 + 0.09)^8$. This is £2000 × $(1.09)^8$ = £2000 × 1.9926 = £3985.

In general we consider an initial sum P_0 invested for n periods at an interest rate of r per cent per period. By the reasoning used in the answer to Example 3.1.1 we see that by the end of period 1 this will have grown to $P_0(1 + r/100)$.

To make the notation less cumbersome we shall adopt the standard convention of representing $r/100$ by the single letter i, so that the end of year 1 value appears as $P_0(1 + i)$. After two periods the value will be $P_0(1 + i)^2$.

Continuing in this way we obtain the general formula for basic compound interest which says that the value after n periods is

$$P_n = P_0(1 + i)^n$$

Exercise 3.1.1 A sum of £2300 is invested at an annual rate of interest of 8 per cent. Interest is compounded annually. To what value will the investment have grown after six complete years?

Appendix 2 includes a table of *compound interest factors* for a range of values of the interest rate per period and the number of periods of investment. The compound interest formula can be rearranged to facilitate the finding of i, n or P_0 given the values of all the other quantities.

Example 3.1.2 What annual rate of compound interest would be necessary in order for £750 to grow to £1264 by the end of five years?

ANSWER We have $1264 = 750(1 + i)^5$.

Hence $\qquad (1 + i)^5 = 1264/750 = 1.685$

So $\qquad 1 + i = 1.685^{0.2}$

Most modern calculators will evaluate this expression to give $1 + i = 1.11$. Hence it follows that $i = 0.11$, and so $r = 11$ per cent. This problem could be solved from the table once the value 1.685 had been obtained, by looking along the $n = 5$ row and finding the number in that row closest to 1.685. The r value for the column concerned would be the required interest rate.

Exercise 3.1.2 What annual rate of compound interest would be necessary in order for £3700 to grow to £7800 by the end of seven years?

The *reducing balance method* for depreciation is an application of the compound interest formula with a negative percentage rate. Thus instead of an initial investment which grows by a constant percentage each year, we have an asset whose initial value declines by a constant percentage each year. If the rate of depreciation is r per cent per year and we represent $r/100$ by i, then the value P_n after n periods of an asset initially worth P_0 is, by the same reasoning as for compound interest,

$$P_n = P_0(1 - i)^n$$

Appendix 2 includes a table of *depreciation factors* for a range of values of the interest rate r and the number of periods n.

Example 3.1.3 Find the book value at the end of five years of an asset costing £27 000 which is depreciated at 10 per cent per year.

ANSWER The value after five years is

$$£27\,000 \times (1 - 0.10)^5 = £27\,000 \times 0.5905 = £15\,943$$

The factor 0.5905 could have been found from the 10 per cent column and the five years row of the table of depreciation factors.

Exercise 3.1.3 Find the book value at the end of seven years of an asset costing £36 000 which is depreciated at 9 per cent per year.

Finally in this section we consider the effect on the compound interest situation of the frequency with which compounding takes place. The more frequently compounding occurs, the faster is the rate of growth of the investment. The limiting case, representing the fastest possible growth rate, is where compounding takes place continuously. The compound interest formula for this limiting case is

$$P_n = P_0 \, e^{in}$$

Example 3.1.4 The sum of £7000 is invested at 12 per cent per annum compound interest. Find the value of the investment at the end of five years if interest is compounded (a) annually, (b) monthly, (c) continuously.

ANSWER
(a) Value after five years $= £7000 \times (1 + 0.12)^5 = £12\,336$.
(b) Value after five years $= £7000 \times (1 + 0.01)^{60}$ since 12 per cent per annum paid monthly can be treated as 1 per cent per month. Hence the value after five years is £7000 × 1.8167 = £12 717.
(c) Value after five years $= £7000 \times e^{0.12 \times 5} = £7000 \times e^{0.6}$. Hence the value after five years is £7000 × 1.8221 = £12 755.

Exercise 3.1.4 An asset initially worth £8500 is depreciated by the reducing balance method using an interest rate of 10 per cent per annum. Find:

(a) the book value after six years if depreciation is done annually;
(b) the book value after six years using continuous depreciation;
(c) the time required for book value to fall to £5000 on annual depreciation;
(d) the time required for book value to fall to £5000 if continuous depreciation is used.

3.2 PRESENT VALUES AND PROJECT EVALUATION

Using the compound interest formula to find P_0 in terms of P_n, i and n is an important procedure in investment appraisal. Problems which involve using the formula in this way are called net present value (NPV) problems.

Solving for P_0 gives $P_0 = P_n/(1 + i)^n$, or

$$P_0 = P_n (1 + i)^{-n}$$

This tells us the amount of money which if invested now (i.e. at the present time) would yield amount P_n after n periods as a result of investing it at the given interest rate. This idea is sufficiently important for tables of *present value factors* $(1 + i)^{-n}$ to be published for a range of values of the interest rate r and number of periods n. Such a table appears in Appendix 2. Note that the values in this table are the reciprocals of the corresponding values in the table of compound interest factors.

Example 3.2.1 What is the present value of £40 000 due to be paid in 25 years time if the interest rate is 9 per cent per year?

ANSWER We have $P_n = £40\,000$, $n = 25$, and $i = 0.09$. Hence $P_0 = £40\,000 \times (1 + 0.09)^{-25} = £40\,000 \times 0.116 = £4639$. Alternatively, the table of present value factors could have been used to find the factor 0.116 by looking in the $n = 25$ row and the $r = 9$ per cent column.

Exercise 3.2.1 The present value of £50 000 receivable three years from now, assuming a rate of interest of 9 per cent, is (to the nearest £)

(A) £38 500;   (B) £42 000;   (C) £63 000;   (D) £64 935;   (E) £126 500

(CIMA Stage 1: Nov. 1989)

The net present value (NPV) method for project evaluation

When investment in a project is undertaken it is usual for most, though not generally all, of the outlay to be required immediately, whereas income from the project will come at various times in the future. In order, therefore, to decide whether investment in the project is worth while, it is necessary to take into account the reduction in value of all the future cash flows because of the delay in their occurrence. One way of doing this is to assume an interest rate and work out the sum of the present values of the future flows. If the net present value (NPV) of the inflows exceeds the NPV of the outflows then the project is worth investing in; otherwise it is not.

Example 3.2.2 A company plans to buy equipment for £100 000, half of which is due on delivery, with the balance due exactly one year later. The year-end cash inflows are expected to be £25 000 per annum, for five years. After exactly five years the equipment will be sold for £10 000.

If the company has to borrow at 14 per cent per annum, analyse whether it is a worthwhile purchase.

(CIMA Stage 1: Nov. 1991)

ANSWER This problem can be tackled by finding the NPV for all the cash flows on the assumption of a 14 per cent annual rate. If the NPV is negative, the outflows exceed the inflows in NPV terms and the purchase is not worth while. If the NPV is positive, the inflows are larger and the purchase should be undertaken.

The calculations can conveniently be set out in a table:

End of year	Cash flow (£)	PV factor	Present value (£)
0	(50 000)	1.0000	(50 000)
1	(25 000)	0.8772	(21 930)
2	25 000	0.7695	19 238
3	25 000	0.6750	16 875
4	25 000	0.5921	14 803
5	35 000	0.5194	18 179
			(2 835)

Since the NPV is negative, indicating an overall outflow of £2835, the conclusion is that the purchase of the equipment is not worth while.

Exercise 3.2.2 An office services bureau is planning to purchase computing equipment costing £7000 with a life of five years. In the first year of the life of the equipment there is no maintenance charge as the equipment is covered by guarantee. In subsequent years the equipment may be covered by an annual maintenance contract which costs 10 per cent of the purchase price. This payment must be made before the annual contract comes into action. The revenue from the equipment is estimated to be £2000 in the first year, increasing by £500 every year for the life of the equipment.

The current minimum rate of return acceptable to the company is 16 per cent.

(a) Is the project viable at this rate of interest?
(b) The company is about to be taken over, the new finance director uses a minimum return of 24 per cent. Would the project still be considered viable?

(ACCA Level 1: Dec. 1988)

The internal rate of return (IRR) method for project evaluation

Another method for project evaluation, instead of calculating net present value based on a given interest rate, is to determine the rate of interest which would give the investment an overall net present value of zero. This rate of interest is called the internal rate of return (IRR) and the investment can be considered worth undertaking only if funds cannot be used in some other way which gives a higher rate of interest than the IRR.

One approach to tackling such problems, sometimes referred to as the method of interpolation, begins with a guess as to a suitable rate of interest. The NPV using that rate of interest is then calculated as in Example 3.2.2 above. (The initial guess can be arrived at by finding the gross percentage profit for the project in money terms and averaging this over the number of years involved. This will generally give an underestimate so it is multiplied by factor of 1.5 to give the rate for the first NPV calculation.)

If the result for the initial guess is a negative NPV, then a lower rate should be tried with a view to obtaining a positive figure. If the initial result is a positive NPV, then a higher rate should be tried. Having obtained a positive figure and a negative one, the IRR, which corresponds to a zero figure, can be estimated between them.

The method, which will be the only feasible one for many IRR problems, is illustrated in the following example.

Example 3.2.3 A firm is considering investing in a project which has a life of four years. The capital cost is £1000 and during the first year of its life the equipment is covered by warranty. At the end of the first year a warranty payment of 15 per cent of capital cost is payable. This covers the second year of operation. The firm intends to extend the warranty, for the same cost, at the end of each year to cover the rest of the life of the project. The income from the project is estimated to be £500 for each year of the project.

(a) Find the net present value of the project at 15 per cent.
(b) Find the internal rate of return of the project. Use an interest rate of either 10 or 25 per cent.
(c) What is the difference between the internal rate of return method of evaluating an investment and the net present value method? (ACCA Level 1: June 1990)

ANSWER The table below sets out the calculations for parts (a) and (b). The 15 per cent figure given in part (a) is the initial estimate for the IRR. It conforms to the estimation method indicated above in that capital cost is £1000 and income is, roughly, $4 \times (£500 - £150) = £1400$ so profit over four years is £400, giving an annual percentage rate of

$$0.25 \times (£400/£1\,000) \times 100 = 10 \text{ per cent}$$

Multiplying this by 1.5 then gives 15 per cent.

This choice for part (b) is 25 per cent because 15 per cent led to a positive NPV.

End year	Cash flow (£)	15% fac	NPV(£) at 15%	25% fac	NPV(£) at 25%
0	(1000)	1.0000	(1000)	1.0000	(1000)
1	350	0.8696	304	0.8000	280
2	350	0.7561	265	0.6400	224
3	350	0.6575	230	0.5120	179
4	500	0.5718	286	0.4096	205
			85		(112)

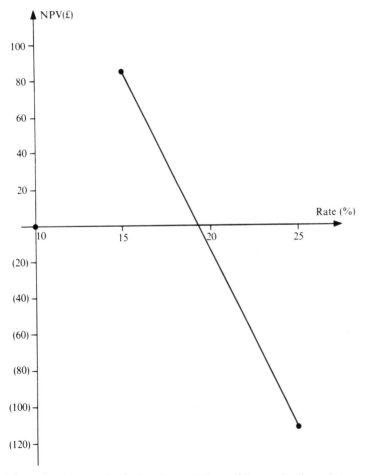

Figure 3.1 Graph for finding Internal Rate of Return by linear interpolation.

(a) The answer is £85, as seen in the table.
(b) The interpolation to find the IRR can be carried out graphically as indicated in Fig. 3.1. This involves drawing a graph having interest rate on the horizontal axis and net present values on the vertical axis.

The value £85 is plotted against 15 per cent and the value −£112 is plotted against 25 per cent. A line is then drawn to join these points and the IRR is the rate where this line crosses the horizontal axis since this corresponds to a net present value of zero.

The procedure can be set out as a calculation as follows:

$$\text{IRR} = 15\% + \frac{85}{85+112} \times (25\% - 15\%) = 15\% + 0.4315 \times 10\% = 19.3\%$$

(c) The net present value method assumes or estimates that a certain interest rate will hold, and bases decisions on the net present value of cash flows which results from that assumption. The internal rate of return does not depend on having a value for the rate but seeks to find the rate which will achieve a specified NPV, namely zero. Not having to estimate or assume a rate is an advantage, but the IRR method does still assume that a constant interest rate will prevail throughout the life of the project. A further advantage of the IRR method is that it gives as its answer an interest rate which can be compared with rates of return available from other possible ways of investing funds. We give now an example where an explicit solution for the internal rate of return can be found.

Example 3.2.4 A company has the opportunity of investing in a project which involves an immediate investment of £5000 and is expected to produce cash inflows of £3500 at the end of year 1 and £2500 at the end of year 2. Find the internal rate of return.

ANSWER This problem can be solved using an equation for i because there are only two time periods involved. The effect of this is to give a quadratic equation. More time periods would lead to an equation of higher degree (for which there is no such simple solution).

Let the required rate of interest be r, and, in the usual notation, denote $r/100$ by i. Then we have

$$5000 = 3500(1+i)^{-1} + 2500(1+i)^{-2}$$

Hence

$$5000 - 3500(1+i)^{-1} - 2500(1+i)^{-2} = 0$$

Multiplying through by $(1+i)^2$ and dividing by 500 we obtain

$$10(1+i)^2 - 7(1+i) - 5 = 0$$

Thus

$$10 + 20i + 10i^2 - 7 - 7i - 5 = 0$$

i.e.

$$10i^2 + 13i - 2 = 0$$

This is a quadratic equation which must be solved using the quadratic formula. We obtain

$$i = (-13 \pm \sqrt{169+80})/20 = (-13 \pm \sqrt{249})/20 = (-13 \pm 15.7797)/20$$

A negative value for i has no practical meaning, so the required value is given by $i = 2.7797/20 = 0.1390$, i.e. an interest rate of 13.9 per cent.

The following exercise brings together the two approaches to the IRR method illustrated in Examples 3.2.3 and 3.2.4.

Exercise 3.2.3 A capital project costs an initial £1000 and cash inflows and outflows over its two year life are as given below:

Year	Cash in	Cash out
1	£800	£100
2	£800	£200

(a) Using discount rates of 14 and 22 per cent find the internal rate of return of this project.
(b) If the net cash in year 1 is called $D(1)$ and the net cash in year 2 is called $D(2)$ then the theoretical internal rate of return is given by r in the following equation.

$$D(1)(1 + r/100) + D(2) - C(1 + r/100)^2 = 0$$

where C is the capital cost of the project.
Solve this equation for $(1 + r/100)$ using the data above and find the value(s) of r.
(c) Comment on the difference between the theoretical solution for the internal rate of return and the solution you found using the interest rates of 14 and 22 per cent.

(ACCA Level 1: June 1988)

3.3 COMPOUND INTEREST WITH INCREMENTS

The situation considered in this section is one where there is not only an initial investment P_0 which earns interest, but where also, from the end of year 1 onwards, further constant amounts w are added at the end of each year.

The value of the investment at the end of year 1, after interest has been earned and the increment invested is

$$P_0(1 + i) + w$$

Similarly, at the end of year 2, the value of the investment is

$$P_0(1 + i)^2 + w(1 + i) + w$$

At the end of year 3 we have

$$P_0(1 + i)^3 + w(1 + i)^2 + w(1 + i) + w$$

Continuing in this way to the end of year n we have

$$P_n = P_0(1 + i)^n + w(1 + i)^{n-1} + w(1 + i)^{n-2} + \cdots + w(1 + i) + w$$

In reverse order the series corresponding to the increments is

$$W = w + w(1 + i) + w(1 + i)^2 + \cdots + w(1 + i)^{n-3} + w(1 + i)^{n-2} + w(1 + i)^{n-1} \tag{3.1}$$

Viewed in this way it is seen to be a geometric series with initial term w and common ratio $(1 + i)$. Those familiar with such series will be able immediately to write down an expression for

its sum, arriving at Eq. (3.2) below. For those not so familiar, the sum can be derived as follows:
Multiplying both sides of (3.1) by $(1+i)$ gives

$$(1+i)W = w(1+i) + w(1+i)^2 + \cdots + w(1+i)^{n-2} + w(1+i)^{n-1} + w(1+i)^n \qquad (3.2)$$

Then $(3.2)-(3.1)$ gives $iW = w(1+i)^n - w$. So $W = w[(1+i)^n - 1]/i$. Hence

$$\boxed{P_n = P_0(1+i)^n + w[(1+i)^n - 1]/i} \qquad (3.2)$$

Example 3.3.1 An investment of £800 is made to which £120 will be added at the end of each
year for the next 12 years.
 Find the accumulated sum assuming an annual interest rate of 9 per cent.

ANSWER $£800 \times 1.09^{12} + £120 \times (1.09^{12} - 1)/0.09$

$\qquad = £800 \times 2.8127 + £120 \times 20.1407$

$\qquad = £2250 \qquad + £2417 \qquad = £4667$

Exercise 3.3.1 An investment of £30 000 is made at the beginning of a year at 5 per cent per
annum compound interest. A sum of £2000 is then withdrawn at the end of each subsequent
year for five years. Find the sum remaining at the end of the fifth year after the withdrawal.
 Appropriate use of formula (3.2), of which the basic compound interest formula can be
considered a special case where $w=0$, provides the solution to a variety of problems.

Sinking funds

A sinking fund is an arrangement whereby an organization decides to set aside a fixed sum of
money at regular intervals with a view to using it to replace equipment. It can be regarded as
a special case of Eq. (3.2) where the initial investment P_0 is equal to each of the subsequent
increments w. Also there will not be an increment w at the end of the whole period, when the
money is to be spent. Thus the value of the sinking fund after n years is

$$S = w(1+i)^n + w[(1+i)^n - 1]/i - w$$

This can be simplified to give the result that the value of the sinking fund at the end of year n is

$$\boxed{S = w(1+i)[(1+i)^n - 1]/i}$$

Example 3.3.2 A sinking fund is operated by saving £800 each month for five years at an interest
rate of 12 per cent per year. Find the value of the fund at the end of the five years.

ANSWER Value after five years

$$= £800 \times 1.01 \times [1.01^{50} - 1]/0.01$$
$$= £800 \times 1.01 \times 81.6697 = £65\,989$$

Exercise 3.3.2 A finance director estimates that his company will need to spend £2.5 million on
re-equipping in five years' time. He decides to establish a sinking fund starting now, and assumes
an interest rate of 9 per cent per annum. Find the necessary size of each *quarterly* payment to
the fund.

Debt repayments

Our second application of the compound interest with increments formula (3.2) is to constant repayments problems. Here P_0 is an initial negative investment, say $-M$, since it is the total amount borrowed (e.g. a mortgage) and the w's are the regular amounts repaid. The final P_n is to be zero since the amount repaid must exactly cancel out what was initially borrowed. Thus

$$0 = -M(1+i)^n + w[(1+i)^n - 1]/i$$

So

$$w = [M(1+i)^n i]/[(1+i)^n - 1]$$

Hence

$$\boxed{w = M \times \{i/[1-(1+i)^{-n}]\}}$$

The term $\{i/[1-(1+i)^{-n}]\}$ is called a *capital recovery factor* and can be used to find the size of each repayment needed. Included in Appendix 2 is a table of capital recovery factors for various interest rates and values of n. This table can also be used to find the number of years needed to complete repayment for a given repayment size and rate of interest.

Example 3.3.3 A £50 000 mortgage is arranged now for 15 years at a rate of interest of 10 per cent. Interest is compounded on the balance outstanding at the end of each year. The loan is to be repaid by 15 annual instalments, the first being due after one complete year. You are required to find the gross annual instalments.

(CIMA Stage 1: Nov. 1989)

ANSWER The repayment size is $w = £50\,000 \times \{0.1/[1 - 1.1^{-15}]\}$
$$= £50\,000 \times \{0.1/0.7606\}$$
$$= £50\,000 \times 0.1315$$
$$= £6574$$

(The factor 0.1315 used to multiply the £50 000 could have been found from the 10 per cent column and 15 period row of the capital recovery factor table in Appendix 2.)

Exercise 3.3.3 A 25-year mortgage of £50 000 is to be repaid by 100 equal quarterly payments in arrears. Interest at a nominal annual rate of 16 per cent is charged each quarter on the outstanding part of the debt. How much are the quarterly repayments, and what is the effective annual rate of interest?

(CIMA Stage 1: Nov. 1990)

Annuities

Thirdly, we consider the application of the compound interest with increments formula (3.2) to annuities. Here a fixed sum of money is paid now in return for regular income over a specified number of years into the future. The size of the regular amount to be received each year is specified and the formula allows us to find the amount which must be paid to obtain this income. This is called the value of the annuity.

In the formula (3.2) we put $P_n = 0$ since the value of the investment after the last payment has been received will be zero. If the amount received each year is A, we put $w = -A$ and then the required value V of the annuity will be given by

$$0 = V(1+i)^n - A[(1+i)^n - 1]/i$$

Rearranging this to give an expression for V we obtain

$$V = A \times \{[1 - (1+i)^{-n}]/i\}$$

The term $\{[1 - (1+i)^{-n}]/i\}$ is called an *annuity factor* or alternatively a *cumulative present value factor* since it gives the sum of the present values of a series of equal amounts of money relating to a sequence of points in time. There exist published tables of annuity factors for various interest rates and values of n. However, the values in such tables are merely the reciprocals of the corresponding values in the table of capital recovery factors given in Appendix 2, as the reader will appreciate by comparing the two formulae.

Example 3.3.4 How much is it worth paying for an annuity of £3000 a year for 10 years, payable twice a year in arrears, assuming an interest rate of 9 per cent per annum and ignoring taxation?
(CIMA Stage 1: Nov. 1988)

ANSWER The value of the annuity is £3000 $\times \{[1 - 1.045^{-20}]/0.045\}$
$$= £3000 \times \{0.5854/0.045\}$$
$$= £3000 \times 13.0079$$
$$= £39\,024$$

(The annuity factor for this example could not have been found from Appendix 2 as 4.5 per cent is not tabulated. Note, however, that the value 13.0079 lies between 12.462 for 20 periods at 5 per cent and 13.590 for 20 periods at 4 per cent.)

Exercise 3.3.4 Find the value of an annuity of £1000 paid at the end of each year for the next 12 years assuming an interest rate of 11 per cent per annum.

Note, finally, that there is a special case of an annuity called a *perpetuity*. In this case the payments go on FOR EVER. Thus the value of n in the expression for the value of the annuity becomes infinite and hence $(1+i)^{-n}$ is zero.

The value, therefore, of a perpetuity is $V = A/i$ where A is the value of each payment to be received and i is the proportional interest rate.

TEST EXERCISES

3.1 A company has to repay a loan of £1 million in exactly four years from now. It is planned to set aside nine equal amounts of £X every six months, first one now, each attracting interest at a nominal rate of 12 per cent per annum, but compounded twice a year. What should £X be?
(CIMA Stage 1: Nov. 1991)

3.2 An investment quadruples in eight years. The annual percentage compound interest rate is closest to
(A) 15; (B) 19; (C) 22; (D) 37; (E) 50.
(CIMA Stage 1: Nov. 1990)

3.3 An asset is purchased for £50 000 and will have a residual value of £2000 at the end of its useful life of ten years. Using the reducing balance (constant percentage) method of depreciation the asset's book value after five years will be closest to
(A) £10 000; (B) £14 000; (C) £19 000; (D) £22 000; (E) £26 000.
(CIMA Stage 1: Nov. 1990)

3.4 An asset, purchased for £100 000, is expected to have a useful life of ten years with a saleable value then of £10 000. Assuming a 'reducing balance method' of depreciation the asset value after five years will be valued (to the nearest £1.00) at

(A) £25 119;   (B) £31 623;   (C) £45 000;   (D) £59 049;   (E) £63 096.

(CIMA Stage 1: Nov. 1988)

3.5 A job carries a monthly salary of £1000, payable in arrears. The net present value now of next year's salary, assuming an annual rate of interest of 12 per cent is

(A) £8900;   (B) £9470;   (C) £10 370;   (D) £11 260;   (E) £12 000.

(CIMA Stage 1: May 1989)

3.6 A government advertises a Savings Bond as 67 per cent guaranteed growth after five years. This is equivalent to an annual compound interest rate (to two decimal places) of

(A) 2.32 per cent;   (B) 8.92 per cent;   (C) 10.80 per cent;   (D) 13.40 per cent;   (E) 13.68 per cent.

(CIMA Stage 1: May 1988)

3.7 A project under consideration requires an initial investment of £10 000 and is expected to produce an income of £6000 at the end of each of years 1 and 2.

(a) Use NPV calculations to estimate the internal rate of return by the interpolation method.
(b) Find a value for the internal rate of return by solving an appropriate quadratic equation.
(c) Compare your answers to parts (a) and (b).

4

MATRICES

4.1 INTRODUCTION

Matrices are purely notation. There is in principle nothing we can do using matrices which we could not do without them. However, the notation is extremely economical and therefore powerful, and many problems which can be stated simply in matrix form would be extremely cumbersome without matrices. In particular, matrix notation lends itself readily to computerization.

A matrix is simply an array of numbers in brackets. For example,

$$A = \begin{pmatrix} 7 & 3 & 13 \\ 9 & 7 & 4 \\ 6 & 8 & 2 \\ 5 & 4 & 8 \end{pmatrix}$$

is a 4×3 (four by three) matrix since it has four rows and three columns. In general a matrix with m rows and n columns is an $m \times n$ matrix or a matrix of order $m \times n$. The numbers in the array are called the elements of the matrix. Consider the following example.

Example 4.1.1 The following data relate to the retail trade in category z:

Table 1 Number of different grades of employees

| Grade | Type of outlet | | |
	Branch of multiple store	Supermarket	Independent
Supervisors	1	5	nil
Cashiers	4	10	2
Storekeepers	3	15	1

Table 2 Number of outlets in different areas

Outline	Midlands	Other areas
Branch of multiple store	36	104
Supermarket	18	75
Independent	25	30

Present the data in Tables 1 and 2 in a matrix format.

ANSWER If the data in Table 1 is written as

$$A = \begin{pmatrix} 1 & 5 & 0 \\ 4 & 10 & 2 \\ 3 & 15 & 1 \end{pmatrix}$$

they are now presented in matrix form. Note that it is most important to keep each element in its correct position, so that it can be immediately seen, for example, that the number of cashiers (second row) needed at a supermarket (second column) is 10.

Usually matrices are represented by capital letters, as in the case above. Matrix A has three rows and three columns and can be described as a 3×3 matrix. The data in Table 2 can be presented in the form

$$B = \begin{pmatrix} 36 & 104 \\ 18 & 75 \\ 25 & 30 \end{pmatrix}$$

which is 3×2 matrix.

In the special case $n = 1$ the matrix reduces to a single column. For example

$$x = \begin{pmatrix} 5 \\ 4 \\ 17 \\ 12.8 \end{pmatrix} \quad \text{or} \quad y = \begin{pmatrix} 8 \\ 3 \\ 14 \end{pmatrix}$$

A matrix of this kind is called a column vector. A column vector is represented by a lower-case letter either in bold print or underlined.

Exercise 4.1.1 Present the information

	Skilled	Unskilled
Factory A	200	150
Factory B	50	80
Factory C	100	120

in matrix format and state the order of the matrix.

4.2 MATRIX ARITHMETIC

(a) Addition and subtraction

If necessary, two matrices can be added or subtracted if they are of the same order. If addition can be performed, it is done by adding the respective elements of the matrices concerned. For example

$$\begin{pmatrix} a & b \\ c & d \end{pmatrix} + \begin{pmatrix} u & v \\ w & x \end{pmatrix} = \begin{pmatrix} a+u & b+v \\ c+w & d+x \end{pmatrix}$$

Example 4.2.1 Find

$$\begin{pmatrix} 1 & 2 \\ 3 & 4 \end{pmatrix} + \begin{pmatrix} 1 & 3 \\ 4 & 2 \end{pmatrix}$$

ANSWER

$$\begin{pmatrix} 1+1 & 2+3 \\ 3+4 & 4+2 \end{pmatrix} = \begin{pmatrix} 2 & 5 \\ 7 & 6 \end{pmatrix}$$

Exercise 4.2.1 Find

$$\begin{pmatrix} 2 & 3 \\ 0 & 5 \end{pmatrix} + \begin{pmatrix} 1 & 4 \\ 3 & 0 \end{pmatrix}$$

Consider a warehouse which is currently holding stocks of nails and screws, as described in Table 4.1.

Table 4.1

	Nails	Screws
Size A	80	96
Size B	40	72
Size C	50	104

As a warehouseman believes that these stocks are too low he puts in an order with a supplier for the quantities shown in Table 4.2.

Table 4.2

	Nails	Screws
Size A	150	120
Size B	144	150
Size C	144	120

The numbers in store immediately after the delivery of the new stock can be calculated using matrix addition.

$$\begin{pmatrix} 80 & 96 \\ 40 & 72 \\ 50 & 104 \end{pmatrix} + \begin{pmatrix} 150 & 120 \\ 144 & 150 \\ 144 & 120 \end{pmatrix} = \begin{pmatrix} 230 & 216 \\ 184 & 222 \\ 194 & 224 \end{pmatrix}$$

This indicates that the level of stock at the warehouse is now 230 size A nails, 184 size B nails, 194 size C nails, 216 size A screws, 222 size B screws, and 224 size C screws. Now suppose the warehouse receives an order for these screws and nails as described in Table 4.3.

Table 4.3

	Nails	Screws
Size A	36	60
Size B	72	60
Size C	48	60

In this case, the stock levels decrease so we use matrix subtraction.

$$\begin{pmatrix} 230 & 216 \\ 184 & 222 \\ 194 & 224 \end{pmatrix} - \begin{pmatrix} 36 & 60 \\ 72 & 60 \\ 48 & 60 \end{pmatrix} = \begin{pmatrix} 194 & 156 \\ 112 & 162 \\ 146 & 164 \end{pmatrix}$$

This final matrix gives the stock levels after the order has been sent out.

Exercise 4.2.2 Find

$$\begin{pmatrix} 2 & 5 \\ 0 & 4 \end{pmatrix} - \begin{pmatrix} 1 & 2 \\ 2 & 5 \end{pmatrix}$$

Exercise 4.2.3 Find $A + B$ if

$$A = \begin{pmatrix} 4 & 9 \\ 7 & 2 \\ 3 & 5 \end{pmatrix} \text{ and } B = \begin{pmatrix} 2 & 9 \\ 5 & 8 \\ 1 & 3 \end{pmatrix}$$

Exercise 4.2.4 The chief materials used in the manufacture of three carpet designs called 'Floral Dance', 'Blue Danube', and 'Square Peg' are wool and acrilan. The numbers in the table below give the quantities of wool and acrilan and the labour and machine times required for each unit broadloom length of carpet type.

	Wool	Acrilan	Labour (hours)	Machine time (hours)
'Floral Dance'	1.0	2.0	0.7	1.0
'Blue Danube'	0.5	2.4	0.6	0.9
'Square Peg'	1.2	1.5	0.5	1.1

(The quantities of wool and acrilan are given in 10-kilogram units.)

It has been proposed that the designs of these three carpets be slightly changed, but the same names retained. The extra amounts of wool, acrilan and times required will be as follows:

	Wool	Acrilan	Labour (hours)	Machine time (hours)
'Floral Dance'	+0.2	−0.2	+0.1	+0.1
'Blue Danube'	0	+0.1	+0.1	−0.1
'Square Peg'	+0.1	−0.2	+0.2	+0.2

Use matrix addition to determine the new requirements for the three carpet designs.

(b) Multiplication by a number

In order to multiply a matrix by a number we multiply each individual element by that number. For example,

$$k\begin{pmatrix} a & b \\ c & d \end{pmatrix} = \begin{pmatrix} ka & kb \\ kc & kd \end{pmatrix}$$

Suppose a warehouse receives two identical orders as shown in Table 4.4.

Table 4.4

	Nails	Screws
Size A	36	60
Size B	72	60
Size C	48	60

The total reduction in stocks at the warehouse can be calculated by multiplying the matrix

$$\begin{pmatrix} 36 & 60 \\ 72 & 60 \\ 48 & 60 \end{pmatrix}$$

by 2 to give

$$2\begin{pmatrix} 36 & 60 \\ 72 & 60 \\ 48 & 60 \end{pmatrix} = \begin{pmatrix} 2\times36 & 2\times60 \\ 2\times72 & 2\times60 \\ 2\times48 & 2\times60 \end{pmatrix} = \begin{pmatrix} 72 & 120 \\ 144 & 120 \\ 96 & 120 \end{pmatrix}$$

Therefore the two orders comprise, in total, 72 size A nails, 144 size B nails, 96 size C nails, 120 size A screws, 120 size B screws, and 120 size C screws.

Exercise 4.2.5 If

$$A = \begin{pmatrix} 1 & 2 \\ 3 & 4 \end{pmatrix} \text{ and } B = \begin{pmatrix} 1 & 3 \\ 4 & 2 \end{pmatrix}$$

find $2A + 3B$.

(c) Multiplication of matrices

Consider two matrices **A** and **B** . The matrix product **AB** is defined if and only if the number of columns of **A** is equal to the number of rows of **B**. The matrices are then conformable for the product **AB**.

To see how the product is calculated when it does exist, consider the following example.

$$A = \begin{pmatrix} a_1 & a_2 & a_3 \\ b_1 & b_2 & b_3 \end{pmatrix} \qquad B = \begin{pmatrix} x_1 & y_1 & z_1 \\ x_2 & y_2 & z_2 \\ x_3 & y_3 & z_3 \end{pmatrix}$$

A has three columns and **B** has three rows so the matrices are conformable for the product **AB**. The product matrix **AB** will be of order 2×3.

$$AB \times \begin{pmatrix} a_1 x_1 + a_2 x_2 + a_3 x_3 & a_1 y_1 + a_2 y_2 + a_3 y_3 & a_1 z_1 + a_2 z_2 + a_3 z_3 \\ b_1 x_1 + b_2 x_2 + b_3 x_3 & b_1 y_1 + b_2 y_2 + b_3 y_3 & b_1 z_1 + b_2 z_2 + b_3 z_3 \end{pmatrix}$$

We pair the elements in each row of **A** with the corresponding elements in each column of **B**. Note that **B** has three columns but **A** has only two rows so the matrices are not conformable for the product **BA**. So clearly we cannot in general have **AB** = **BA** since it is not necessarily true that both products exist. Even if both do exist they are not likely to be equal.

In general, if **A** has order $m \times n$ and **B** has order $n \times p$ then they are conformable for the product **AB** and the product has order $m \times p$. They will not be conformable for the product **BA** unless $p = m$. If this condition is met, then this product will have order $n \times n$.

Example 4.2.2

$$A = \begin{pmatrix} 2 & 1 \\ 1 & 7 \\ 5 & 3 \end{pmatrix} \qquad B = \begin{pmatrix} 1 & 3 & 6 \\ -1 & 2 & 4 \end{pmatrix}$$

Find **AB** and **BA**.

ANSWER

$$AB = \begin{pmatrix} 2-1 & 6+2 & 12+4 \\ 1-7 & 3+14 & 6+28 \\ 5-3 & 15+6 & 30+12 \end{pmatrix} = \begin{pmatrix} 1 & 8 & 16 \\ -6 & 17 & 34 \\ 2 & 21 & 42 \end{pmatrix}$$

$$BA = \begin{pmatrix} 2+3+30 & 1+21+18 \\ -2+2+20 & -1+14+12 \end{pmatrix} = \begin{pmatrix} 35 & 40 \\ 20 & 25 \end{pmatrix}$$

Example 4.2.3

(a) A zoo car park charges £1 for a motorcycle, £2 for a car and £10 for a coach. Write down these data as a column matrix **C**.

(b) The number of vehicles using the car park last weekend is given by the matrix **V**, where

$$V = \begin{matrix} & Motor \\ & cycle \quad Car \quad Coach \\ \text{Saturday} & \begin{pmatrix} 84 & 337 & 38 \\ \text{Sunday} & 62 & 291 & 43 \end{pmatrix} \end{matrix}$$

      (i) Which of the products **CV** and **VC** can be evaluated?
      (ii) Let this product be **Y**. Evaluate **Y** and state its meaning.
(c) To become cost-effective the car park must generate more revenue at weekends. It has been suggested that three options be considered.
      (i) Increase the charges by 50 per cent for both days.
      (ii) Double the charges for Saturdays.
      (iii) Double the charges for Sundays.

The matrix **X** is defined so that the product **XY** gives the actual revenue for last weekend *and* the hypothetical revenue which might have obtained for each of the three possible options.

Write down the matrix **X**, evaluate **XY** and interpret your result.

                                                          (CIMA Stage 1: Nov. 1987)

ANSWER

(a) The zoo car park charges can be summarized in the column matrix

$$C = \begin{pmatrix} 1 \\ 2 \\ 10 \end{pmatrix}$$

    a 3×1 column matrix.

(b)   (i) The matrix **V** is a 2×3 matrix, having two rows and three columns.
          Only the product **VC** can be evaluated, because the number of columns of matrix **V** equals the number of rows in matrix **C**, the outcome being a 2×1 matrix.

    (ii)

$$Y = VC = \begin{pmatrix} 84 & 337 & 38 \\ 62 & 291 & 43 \end{pmatrix} \begin{pmatrix} 1 \\ 2 \\ 10 \end{pmatrix}$$

$$= \begin{pmatrix} 84(1) + 337(2) + 38(10) \\ 62(1) + 291(2) + 43(10) \end{pmatrix} = \begin{pmatrix} 1138 \\ 1074 \end{pmatrix}$$

This matrix, **Y**, gives the daily takings at the car park — £1138 on Saturdays and £1074 on Sundays.

(c) The rows of matrix **X** have to represent,
      (i) the total revenue last weekend,
      (ii) the revenue if both are increased by 50 per cent
    (iii) Saturday's charges are doubled
    (iv) Sunday's charges are doubled.

Hence

$$X = \begin{pmatrix} 1 & 1 \\ 1.5 & 1.5 \\ 2 & 1 \\ 1 & 2 \end{pmatrix}$$

and

$$XY = \begin{pmatrix} 1 & 1 \\ 1.5 & 1.5 \\ 2 & 1 \\ 1 & 2 \end{pmatrix} \begin{pmatrix} 1138 \\ 1074 \end{pmatrix} = \begin{pmatrix} 2212 \\ 3318 \\ 3350 \\ 3286 \end{pmatrix}$$

The revenue last weekend was £2212. For the three options the revenue would be

(i) £3318,
(ii) £3350,
(iii) £3286.

So, provided there is no change in the number of each sort of vehicle using the car park at weekends, doubling the charges on Saturdays maximizes the takings. This assumption may be unrealistic.

Exercise 4.2.6 Determine the matrix multiplication.

$$\begin{pmatrix} 1 & 3 & 1 \\ 2 & 4 & 2 \end{pmatrix}\begin{pmatrix} 1 \\ 2 \\ 5 \end{pmatrix}$$

(CIMA Stage 1: May 89)

Exercise 4.2.7

$$\mathbf{X} = \begin{pmatrix} 2 & 0 \\ 0 & 2 \end{pmatrix} \qquad \mathbf{Y} = \begin{pmatrix} 5 & 6 \\ 7 & 8 \end{pmatrix}$$

Find the product **XY**.

(CIMA Stage 1: Nov. 89)

4.3 MATRIX PROPERTIES

(a) Equality

Two matrices are equal if and only if all their respective elements are equal. For example,

$$\begin{pmatrix} a & b \\ c & d \end{pmatrix} = \begin{pmatrix} 4 & 2 \\ 3 & 7 \end{pmatrix}$$

means that $a=4$, $b=2$, $c=3$, and $d=7$.

(b) The transpose of a matrix

If the rows and columns of a matrix **A** are interchanged, the resulting matrix is called the transpose of **A** and is denoted by **A′**. For example,

$$\mathbf{A} = \begin{pmatrix} a & d \\ b & e \\ c & f \end{pmatrix} \qquad \mathbf{A}' = \begin{pmatrix} a & b & c \\ d & e & f \end{pmatrix}$$

A matrix which remains unchanged after transposition is said to be symmetric. For example

$$\mathbf{A} = \begin{pmatrix} 1 & 4 \\ 4 & 7 \end{pmatrix} \quad \text{has } \mathbf{A}' = \begin{pmatrix} 1 & 4 \\ 4 & 7 \end{pmatrix} \text{ and so is symmetric.}$$

(c) Zero matrices and identity matrices

A zero matrix is a matrix having every element equal to zero. For example,

$$\begin{pmatrix} 0 & 0 \\ 0 & 0 \\ 0 & 0 \end{pmatrix} \quad \text{and} \quad \begin{pmatrix} 0 & 0 & 0 & 0 \\ 0 & 0 & 0 & 0 \end{pmatrix}$$

are zero matrices. Zero matrices have a role in matrix work analogous to the number zero in ordinary arithmetic in that no matrix is altered by addition or subtraction of a zero matrix, and multiplication by a zero matrix will always result in a zero matrix. A respect in which it differs is that two non-zero matrices can be multiplied together to give a zero matrix. For example,

$$\begin{pmatrix} 1 & 1 \\ 3 & 3 \end{pmatrix} \begin{pmatrix} 4 & -7 \\ -4 & 7 \end{pmatrix} = \begin{pmatrix} 0 & 0 \\ 0 & 0 \end{pmatrix}$$

An identity matrix is a square matrix (i.e. number of rows = number of columns) having every element equal to zero except on the leading diagonal (i.e. top left to bottom right) where there are ones. Thus,

$$\begin{pmatrix} 1 & 0 \\ 0 & 1 \end{pmatrix} \begin{pmatrix} 1 & 0 & 0 \\ 0 & 1 & 0 \\ 0 & 0 & 1 \end{pmatrix} \begin{pmatrix} 1 & 0 & 0 & 0 \\ 0 & 1 & 0 & 0 \\ 0 & 0 & 1 & 0 \\ 0 & 0 & 0 & 1 \end{pmatrix}$$

are examples of identity matrices.

An identity matrix has a role in matrix work analogous to the number one in ordinary multiplication in that no matrix is altered if it is multiplied by an identity matrix. For example,

$$\begin{pmatrix} 1 & 0 \\ 0 & 1 \end{pmatrix} \begin{pmatrix} 2 & 3 & 7 \\ 5 & 2 & 8 \end{pmatrix} = \begin{pmatrix} 2 & 3 & 7 \\ 5 & 2 & 8 \end{pmatrix}$$

and

$$\begin{pmatrix} 2 & 3 & 7 \\ 5 & 2 & 8 \end{pmatrix} \begin{pmatrix} 1 & 0 & 0 \\ 0 & 1 & 0 \\ 0 & 0 & 1 \end{pmatrix} = \begin{pmatrix} 2 & 3 & 7 \\ 5 & 2 & 8 \end{pmatrix}$$

An identity matrix is always denoted by the symbol **I** and it is left to the context to show what is the order of the particular identity matrix concerned. Even in the same equation the symbol **I** can have different orders on different occasions. If in the example above we wrote

$$\mathbf{C} = \begin{pmatrix} 2 & 3 & 7 \\ 5 & 2 & 8 \end{pmatrix}$$

the results can be summarized as:

$$\mathbf{IC = C = CI}$$

In the first term **I** is a 2×2 matrix and in the last term **I** is a 3×3 matrix.

(d) Matrix inverses

In talking about matrix inverses we are concerned only with square matrices as no other sort of matrix can have an inverse. Not even every square matrix has an inverse: a square matrix which does not have an inverse is said to be singular.

The inverse A^{-1} of a square matrix A is the matrix which satisfies the relation

$$AA^{-1} = A^{-1}A = I$$

Inverse matrices have a role in matrix work analogous to reciprocals in ordinary arithmetic. For example, 0.25 is the reciprocal of 4 because $4 \times 0.25 = 4 = 1$. It is the number by which 4 must be multiplied to give the result 1. The existence of matrix inverses makes possible the solution of matrix equations. Suppose, for example, we have the equation $AX = B$, where the elements of A and B are known and we want to find the elements of X.

There is no such thing as 'division by A', but what we can do, if A has an inverse, is multiply both sides of the equation by A^{-1}. This gives

$$A^{-1}AX = A^{-1}B$$

Hence

$$IX = A^{-1}B$$

So

$$X = A^{-1}B$$

This is equivalent in ordinary arithmetic terms to solving the equation $4x = 5$ by multiplying both sides by 0.25, the reciprocal of 4, to obtain

$$0.25 \times 4x = 0.25 \times 5$$

$$1x = 1.25$$

$$x = 1.25$$

Example 4.3.1 Verify by multiplication that the inverse of the matrix

$$\begin{pmatrix} 3 & 1 \\ 3 & 4 \end{pmatrix} \text{ is } \frac{1}{9}\begin{pmatrix} 4 & -1 \\ -3 & 3 \end{pmatrix}$$

ANSWER

$$B = \frac{1}{9}\begin{pmatrix} 4 & -1 \\ -3 & 3 \end{pmatrix} \text{ is the inverse of } A = \begin{pmatrix} 3 & 1 \\ 3 & 4 \end{pmatrix} \text{ if}$$

$$AB = I$$

$$AB = \begin{pmatrix} 3 & 1 \\ 3 & 4 \end{pmatrix}\begin{pmatrix} 4 & -1 \\ -3 & 3 \end{pmatrix}$$

$$= \frac{1}{9}\begin{pmatrix} 3 & 1 \\ 3 & 4 \end{pmatrix}\begin{pmatrix} 4 & -1 \\ -3 & 3 \end{pmatrix}$$

$$= \frac{1}{9}\begin{pmatrix} 12-3 & -3+3 \\ 12-12 & -3+12 \end{pmatrix} = \frac{1}{9}\begin{pmatrix} 9 & 0 \\ 0 & 9 \end{pmatrix}$$

$$= \begin{pmatrix} 1 & 0 \\ 0 & 1 \end{pmatrix} = I$$

So B is the inverse of A.

Exercise 4.3.1 Verify by matrix multiplication that the inverse of the matrix

$$\begin{pmatrix} 3 & 2 & 1 \\ 1 & 1 & -1 \\ 2 & -3 & 4 \end{pmatrix} \text{ is } \frac{1}{14} \begin{pmatrix} -1 & 11 & 3 \\ 6 & -10 & -4 \\ 5 & -13 & -1 \end{pmatrix}$$

4.4 CALCULATING MATRIX INVERSES

We consider in this section how to find the inverses of 2×2 and 3×3 matrices. Anything larger than this would not normally be inverted by hand but would be entrusted to a computer.

As a first step we must introduce the idea of the determinant of a 2×2 matrix.

The determinant of the matrix $\begin{pmatrix} a & b \\ c & d \end{pmatrix}$ is denoted $\begin{vmatrix} a & b \\ c & d \end{vmatrix}$ and is calculated as $ad - bc$.

Thus a determinant is simply a number.

The inverse of a 2×2 matrix is found by interchanging the elements on the leading diagonal, altering the signs of the other two terms and dividing by the determinant. Thus

$$\begin{pmatrix} a & b \\ c & d \end{pmatrix}^{-1} = \frac{1}{(ad - bc)} \begin{pmatrix} d & -b \\ -c & a \end{pmatrix}$$

Example 4.4.1 Invert the matrix

$$\begin{pmatrix} 3 & -1 \\ 5 & 4 \end{pmatrix}$$

ANSWER The determinant is $3 \times 4 - (-1)5 = 12 - (-5) = 17$. So on interchanging and changing signs as required we have

$$\begin{pmatrix} 3 & -1 \\ 5 & 4 \end{pmatrix}^{-1} = \frac{1}{17} \begin{pmatrix} 4 & 1 \\ -5 & 3 \end{pmatrix}$$

Exercise 4.4.1 Invert the matrix

$$\begin{pmatrix} 8 & 12 \\ 2 & 4 \end{pmatrix}$$

Inversion of a 3×3 matrix is more lengthy but is again based on determinants of 2×2 matrices.

Example 4.4.2 Invert the matrix

$$\begin{pmatrix} 3 & 2 & 1 \\ 1 & 1 & -1 \\ 2 & -3 & 4 \end{pmatrix}$$

ANSWER The first step is to form a new 3×3 matrix whose elements are the determinants of the 2×2 matrices formed by eliminating the row and column containing the element concerned in the original matrix. Also a minus sign is given to all of these other than those in the corners and the one in the middle. So we have

$$\begin{pmatrix} \begin{vmatrix} 1 & -1 \\ -3 & 4 \end{vmatrix} & -\begin{vmatrix} 1 & -1 \\ 2 & 4 \end{vmatrix} & \begin{vmatrix} 1 & 1 \\ 2 & -3 \end{vmatrix} \\ -\begin{vmatrix} 2 & 1 \\ -3 & 4 \end{vmatrix} & \begin{vmatrix} 3 & 1 \\ 2 & 4 \end{vmatrix} & -\begin{vmatrix} 3 & 2 \\ 2 & -3 \end{vmatrix} \\ \begin{vmatrix} 2 & 1 \\ 1 & -1 \end{vmatrix} & -\begin{vmatrix} 3 & 1 \\ 1 & -1 \end{vmatrix} & \begin{vmatrix} 3 & 2 \\ 1 & 1 \end{vmatrix} \end{pmatrix}$$

$$= \begin{pmatrix} 4-3 & -(4+2) & -3-2 \\ -(8+3) & 12-2 & -(-9-4) \\ -2-1 & -(-3-1) & 3-2 \end{pmatrix} = \begin{pmatrix} 1 & -6 & -5 \\ -11 & 10 & 13 \\ -3 & 4 & 1 \end{pmatrix}$$

The elements of this matrix are called the cofactors of the original matrix.

The second step is to find the determinant of the original matrix. The determinant of a 3×3 matrix is found by taking any row or column, calculating for each element its value times its cofactor, and adding all these together. Using the first row here we have $3 \times 1 + 2 \times (-6) + 1 \times (-5) = -14$.

Then the third and final step is to transpose the matrix of cofactors and divide by the determinant.

Hence

$$\begin{pmatrix} 3 & 2 & 1 \\ 1 & 1 & -1 \\ 2 & -3 & 4 \end{pmatrix}^{-1} = \frac{1}{(-14)} \begin{pmatrix} 1 & -11 & -3 \\ -6 & 10 & 4 \\ -5 & 13 & 1 \end{pmatrix} = \frac{1}{14} \begin{pmatrix} -1 & 11 & 3 \\ 6 & -10 & -4 \\ 5 & -13 & -1 \end{pmatrix}$$

A commonly used application of matrices is in the solution of simultaneous equations. Suppose we wished to solve the simultaneous equations:

$$4x + 2y = 80$$
$$3x + 5y = 95$$

These equations can be written in matrix form:

$$\begin{pmatrix} 4 & 2 \\ 3 & 5 \end{pmatrix} \begin{pmatrix} x \\ y \end{pmatrix} = \begin{pmatrix} 80 \\ 95 \end{pmatrix}$$

Suppose we let

$$A = \begin{pmatrix} 4 & 2 \\ 3 & 5 \end{pmatrix}, \quad X = \begin{pmatrix} x \\ y \end{pmatrix}, \quad B = \begin{pmatrix} 80 \\ 95 \end{pmatrix}$$

then the equations take the form

$$AX = B$$

so

$$X = A^{-1}B$$

(see Sec. 4.3). In this situation

$$\mathbf{X} = \begin{pmatrix} 4 & 2 \\ 3 & 5 \end{pmatrix}^{-1} \begin{pmatrix} 80 \\ 95 \end{pmatrix}$$

$$= \frac{1}{14} \begin{pmatrix} 5 & -2 \\ -3 & 4 \end{pmatrix} \begin{pmatrix} 80 \\ 95 \end{pmatrix}$$

$$= \frac{1}{14} \begin{pmatrix} 210 \\ 140 \end{pmatrix} = \begin{pmatrix} 15 \\ 10 \end{pmatrix}$$

$$\begin{pmatrix} x \\ y \end{pmatrix} = \begin{pmatrix} 15 \\ 10 \end{pmatrix} \text{ or } x = 15 \text{ and } y = 10$$

Example 4.4.3 Bracelets sell for £4 at a warehouse, then jewellers offer 200 of these each day. For each increase of £0.10 in the selling price, a further five bracelets are supplied to the warehouse. When bracelets sell for £10 each, then there is a demand of 100 at the warehouse. For each decrease of £0.30 in the selling price, another 10 are sold.

(a) Determine supply and demand equations for this product.
(b) Find the equilibrium value of the demand, q, and the market clearing price, p.

ANSWER From the initial information, the supply equation is $p = 0.02q$ and the demand equation is $p = -0.03q + 13$.
    These equations can be written in the form

$$p - 0.02q = 0$$
$$p + 0.03q = 13$$

or in matrix form

$$\begin{pmatrix} 1 & -0.02 \\ 1 & +0.03 \end{pmatrix} \begin{pmatrix} p \\ q \end{pmatrix} = \begin{pmatrix} 0 \\ 13 \end{pmatrix}$$

$$\begin{pmatrix} p \\ q \end{pmatrix} = \begin{pmatrix} 1 & -0.02 \\ 1 & +0.03 \end{pmatrix}^{-1} \begin{pmatrix} 0 \\ 13 \end{pmatrix} = \frac{1}{0.05} \begin{pmatrix} 0.03 & 0.02 \\ -1 & 1 \end{pmatrix} \begin{pmatrix} 0 \\ 13 \end{pmatrix}$$

$$= 20 \begin{pmatrix} 0.26 \\ 13 \end{pmatrix} = \begin{pmatrix} 5.2 \\ 260 \end{pmatrix}$$

The equilibrium value is $q = 260$ and $p = £5.20$.

Exercise 4.4.2 Solve the two equations

$$y = 5x - 4$$
$$x = y + 4$$

using matrices.

Finally in this chapter it should be pointed out that matrices can be easily manipulated when using a computer. There are very many packages available that can, for example, find the inverse of a 10×10 matrix. The MINITAB package, which has already been described in this text, contains the following commands which may be of use:

ADD matrix **M** to matrix **M**, put result into **M**

INVERSE of matrix **M**, put inverse into **M**

MULTIPLY matrix **M** by scalar **K**, put product into **M**

MULTIPLY matrix **M** on the right by matrix **M**, put product into **M**

TRANSPOSE matrix **M**, put transpose into **M**.

TEST EXERCISES

4.1 A stockbroker sold one of his customer's 100 shares of stock A, 50 shares of stock B, 75 shares of stock C, and 25 shares of stock D. These shares cost £1.20, £2.00, £1.00, and £0.80 per share, respectively. Use vectors to represent the shares purchased and the prices, such that the product of the two vectors will give the total cost of the stocks. Calculate the total cost.

4.2 A manufacturer can produce YIPS, YAPS, and ZAPS. To produce one YIP he needs two units of A and six units of B. To produce one YAP he needs three units of A and one unit of B. To produce one ZAP, one unit of A and two units of B are required. Construct a parts matrix using parts as column headings.

An order is received for six YIPS, two YAPS, and seven ZAPS. Would you use a row or a column vector to represent this order?

Use matrix multiplication to compute the total number of parts required.

Given that the cost of one unit of A is £2 and one unit of B is £3, express the costs as a vector and hence obtain the total cost of the order.

4.3 Find the inverses of the following matrices:

(a) $\mathbf{A} = \begin{pmatrix} 8 & 5 \\ 3 & 2 \end{pmatrix}$ (b) $\mathbf{B} = \begin{pmatrix} 4 & -6 \\ 2 & -2 \end{pmatrix}$

ELEMENTARY CALCULUS

5.1 DIFFERENTIATION AND INTEGRATION

Differentiation

In Chapter 2 we considered the graphs of various mathematical functions. In particular, we considered quadratic functions. The simplest function of this type is $y = x^2$ and the graph of this function is shown in Fig. 5.1.

Seven points are shown on this graph between $x = -3$ and $x = 3$. At point A the value of y is seen to be decreasing rapidly as x increases. The graph has a large negative *gradient*, where the gradient of a graph is defined to be the amount by which y changes per unit increase in x when x increases by a small amount.

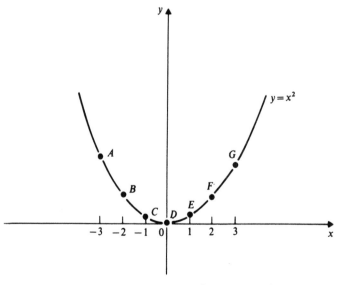

Figure 5.1 Graph of the function $y = x^2$.

At points B and C the gradient is still negative but becomes less steep as we move from A through B to C. At point D the gradient is zero. Then at point E there is a small positive gradient and this becomes larger as we move through F to G.

If the graph were plotted on graph paper and the gradient measured accurately at the seven points, the values shown in Table 5.1 would be found.

Table 5.1

Point	A	B	C	D	E	F	G
Gradient	-6	-4	-2	0	2	4	6

Next consider the function $y = x^3$ whose graph is shown in Fig. 5.2.

Again seven points are indicated between $x = -3$ and $x = 3$. There is a large positive gradient at point A which becomes smaller as we move through points B and C until it is zero at point D. Then it increases through points E and F until it is large and positive again at point G. If this graph were plotted on graph paper and the gradient measured at the various points the values shown in Table 5.2 would be found.

Table 5.2

Point	A	B	C	D	E	F	G
Gradient	27	12	3	0	3	12	27

Differentiation is the name given to the process by which an expression for the gradient of a function is obtained from the original function.

In the case of $y = x^2$ the gradient value at any point, as will probably have been deduced from the table of values given earlier, is found by calculating the value of $2x$ at that point.

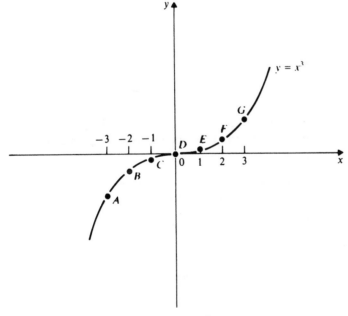

Figure 5.2 Graph of the function $y = x^3$.

In calculus work the gradient is denoted by the special symbol dy/dx (read as "dee y by dee x") and so for this case the gradient function is $dy/dx = 2x$.

Differentiation is the process taking us from $y = x^2$ to $dy/dx = 2x$. In the case of $y = x^3$ the gradient function is $y = 3x^2$. The reader should confirm that the values given in the relevant table above are found by calculating $3x^2$ for the various values of x.

So differentiating $y = x^3$ gives $dy/dx = 3x^2$. Similarly, differentiating $y = x^4$ would give $dy/dx = 4x^3$ and differentiating $y = x^5$ would give $dy/dx = 5x^4$.

In general, if $y = x^n$ for *any* value n, then $dy/dx = nx^{n-1}$

We shall call this differentiation rule 1.

Multiplying the original function by a constant leads merely to multiplying the resulting gradient function by the same constant.

So if $y = ax^n$ for any values a and n, then $dy/dx = anx^{n-1}$

We shall call this differentiation rule 2.

Example 5.1.1 Differentiate $y = 5x^2$.

ANSWER If $y = 5x^2$, then $dy/dx = 5(2x) = 10x$.

Example 5.1.2 Differentiate $y = 8x^4$.

ANSWER If $y = 8x^4$, then $dy/dx = 8(4x^3) = 32x^3$.

Exercise 5.1.1 Differentiate $y = 7x^5$.

Exercise 5.1.2 Differentiate $y = 9x^8$.

Next consider the function $y = 17$. This has the graph shown in Fig. 5.3. The gradient of this graph at the points A, B, C, and D shown, and at any other points, is seen to be zero. (Note that there is nothing special about the value 17.)

So we see that if $y = a$ for any constant a, then $dy/dx = 0$

We shall call this differentiation rule 3.

In fact, rule 3 can be seen to be a special case of rule 2 because $y = a$ could be written $y = ax^0$ since anything (other than zero) raised to power zero is 1. Then applying rule 2 gives

$$dy/dx = a(0x^{-1}) = 0$$

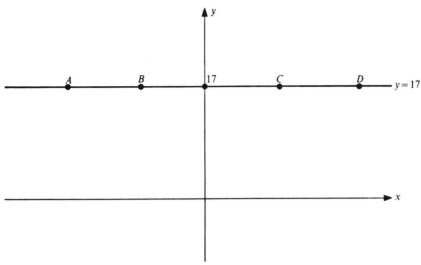

Figure 5.3   Graph of the function $y=17$.

Suppose u and v are functions of x and that their gradient functions are represented in standard notation by du/dx and dv/dx

> Then if $y=u+v$, differentiation gives $dy/dx=du/dx+dv/dx$
>
> We shall call this differentiation rule 4.

Example 5.1.3 Differentiate $y=x^2+x^3$.

ANSWER If $y=x^2+x^3$, then $dy/dx=2x+3x^2$.

Example 5.1.4 Differentiate $y=3x^2+5x+7$.

ANSWER If $y=3x^2+5x+7$, then $dy/dx=6x^1+5x^0+0=6x+5$.

Exercise 5.1.3 Differentiate $y=9x^4+4x^3+8x^2+12x+1$.

Exercise 5.1.4 Differentiate $y=10x^5+6x^4+2x^2+5$.

Example 5.1.5 Using the rules of differentiation, find dy/dx for the function $y=3x^3+2x^2+4x-8$ and evaluate the gradient of the curve at the point (1, 1) (i.e. the point where $x=1$ and $y=1$).

ANSWER If $y=3x^3+2x^2+4x-8$, then $dy/dx=9x^2+4x+4$. Hence when $x=1$, we have $dy/dx=9+4+4=17$ so the gradient at (1, 1) is 17.

The exponential function $y=e^x$ has certain properties concerned with differentiation. If $y=e^x$, then $dy/dx=e^x$. That is to say, the gradient at any point on the curve $y=e^x$ is equal to the value of y at that point.

Another useful result concerns the logarithmic function to base e which we encountered in Chapter 2. Namely, if $y=\ln x$, then $dy/dx=1/x$.

Exercise 5.1.5 For each of the following functions, find dy/dx and evaluate the gradient of the graph of the function at the point indicated.

(a) $y = 5x^2 - 3x - 4$ at $(2, 10)$.
(b) $y = 4 + 2/x$ at $(-1, 2)$ (Hint: Write $1/x$ as x^{-1} and use rule 1).
(c) $y = 7/x^2$ at $(1, 7)$ (Hint: Write $1/x^2$ as x^{-2} and use rule 1).
(d) $y = 5 \ln x$ at $(1, 0)$.

Integration

Integration can be thought of as the reverse process to differentiation. Thus if we are asked to *integrate* a function we are expected to find a function having the given expression as its gradient function. The integral of a function z of x is denoted by preceding it by an elongated letter S and following it by the symbol dx. Thus:

$$\int z \, dx$$

Example 5.1.6 Integrate the function $z = x^5$.

ANSWER We are looking for a function which when differentiated will give x^5.

We know from the above that if we differentiate x^6 we obtain $6x^5$ which is what we want apart from the 6. So we need to divide by 6 to start with in order to eliminate this. Thus the integral would appear to be $(1/6)x^6$.

However, even this is not quite the whole story because of the fact that any constant when differentiated gives result zero. So any constant added to $(1/6)x^6$ will give a function which is an integral of x^5.

We say that

$$\int x^5 \, dx = (1/6)x^6 + c$$

where c is an 'arbitrary' constant, meaning that it could have any value.

Graphically, this is saying that the graph of $y = (1/6)x^6$ has gradient function x^5, but this graph could be slid up and down parallel to the y-axis by any amount whatever and would thereby give another graph having the same gradient function.

In general, we can see by the same reasoning as above that for *any* power n (other than $n = -1$) of x we have

$$\int x^n \, dx = (1/[n+1])x^{n+1} + c$$

where c is an arbitrary constant.

Note that if n is -1 we have one of the special cases considered earlier, namely

$$\int (1/x) \, dx = \ln x + c$$

where c is an arbitrary constant.

For the other special case considered, the exponential function, note that we have

$$\int e^x = e^x + c$$

where c is an arbitrary constant.

Exercise 5.1.6 Find $\int 3x^8 \, dx$.

The integrals considered so far are what are called *indefinite integrals*. The answer is always a function whose identity is uncertain to the extent of an arbitrary constant.

There exist also *definite integrals*. These are found by evaluating the function found by the indefinite integration process at two specified values of x and then finding the difference of the two values. The differencing process will cancel out the arbitrary constant and so the answer for a definite integral will always be just a *number*.

The lower limit of the definite integral is written at the bottom of the integral sign and the upper limit is written at the top. When the indefinite integral has been found it is written in square brackets with the lower limit of integration at the bottom of the closing bracket and the upper limit at the top of the closing bracket. The indefinite integral is then evaluated for each of these values and the appropriate subtraction carried out.

Example 5.1.7 Find $\int_1^3 x^2 \, dx$

ANSWER $\int_1^3 x^2 \, dx = [(1/3)x^3 + c]_1^3 = \{(1/3) \times 27 + c\} - \{(1/3) \times 1 + c\}$
$$= 9 + c - (1/3) - c = 26/3.$$

Exercise 5.1.7 $\int_0^2 (\frac{1}{2}x^2 + x) \, dx$ equals:

(A) 3; (B) $3\frac{1}{3}$; (C) 4; (D) 8; (E) none of these.

(CIMA Stage 1: May 1988)

5.2 MAXIMUM AND MINIMUM VALUES

Maximum and minimum are familiar terms in daily life. The maximum value of a set of invoices is the amount on that invoice which is greater than all the other invoices, while the minimum value is the amount on that invoice which is smaller than all the others. It would be necessary in this case to examine each invoice and to decide whether it was larger or smaller than any other. This would be tedious but possible. When looking for the maximum or minimum value of a continuous mathematical function, examining every value taken by the function would be not only tedious but actually impossible. Differentiation provides us with a way of proceeding in this situation.

Let us examine the gradient of the curve shown in Fig. 5.4 at the four points shown as A, B, C, and D.

At A the gradient dy/dx is negative. As we proceed to B, dy/dx is still negative but is smaller in magnitude. At C the value of dy/dx has become positive and it increases to a larger positive value as we proceed to D.

For the gradient to be negative at A and B, but positive at C and D, there must be some point between B and C (at $x = a$) where the gradient is zero. We see in Fig. 5.4 a *minimum turning point* at $x = a$.

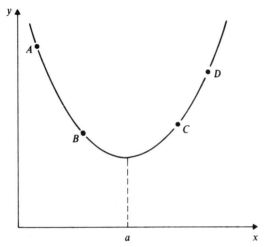

Figure 5.4 Graph showing a minimum point of a function.

Applying the same reasoning to the curve shown in Fig. 5.5 we see that this diagram shows a *maximum turning point* at $x=a$.

We see from Figs 5.4 and 5.5 that the feature common to a minimum point and a maximum point is that at either of them the gradient dy/dx is zero. This fact can be used to identify maximum and minimum turning points of functions by, as a first step, finding all values of x for which $dy/dx=0$.

Example 5.2.1 For the function $y=x^3-6x^2+9x-4$ find the values of x for which $dy/dx=0$.

ANSWER $dy/dx=3x^2-12x+9$. So the zero gradient points are found from $3x^2-12x+9=0$. This quadratic equation can be solved using the method of Chapter 2 to give

$$3(x-3)(x-1)=0$$

So $dy/dx=0$ when $x=1$ and when $x=3$.

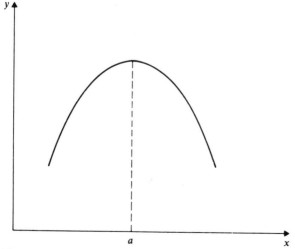

Figure 5.5 Graph showing a maximum point of a function.

Not every value of x for which $dy/dx=0$ gives a maximum or minimum point. It is possible to have a situation such as that shown in Fig. 5.6 where $dy/dx=0$ at $x=a$ but $x=a$ is neither a maximum nor minimum point of the function.

Having found all the x values which give $dy/dx=0$, we need to sort out which are maximum points, which are minimum points and which, if any, are neither.

One way of seeking to decide what exactly is happening at a point $x=a$ where $dy/dx=0$ is to evaluate dy/dx for x a little smaller than a and for x a little larger than a.

Consider Fig. 5.7 where in each of the three diagrams b is a figure slightly smaller than a and c is a figure slightly larger than a.

In Fig. 5.7(a) dy/dx is negative at $x=b$ and positive at $x=c$ so we have a minimum point.

In Fig. 5.7(b) dy/dx is positive at $x=b$ and negative at $x=c$ so we have a maximum point.

In Fig. 5.7(c) dy/dx is positive at $x=b$ and again positive at $x=c$ so we have neither a maximum nor a minimum. The same conclusion would hold if dy/dx were negative at $x=b$ and at $x=c$. This method will always enable us to distinguish the kind of point we have but care must be taken to choose b and c close to a to ensure that the diagnosis is correct.

An alternative, less tedious, method for determining the nature of turning points, which will work in most problems, is to differentiate dy/dx again to obtain the so-called *second derivative* d^2y/dx^2 (read as 'dee two y by dee x squared'.) This is the gradient of the gradient function.

So for a case like Fig. 5.7(a) where the gradient changes from negative to positive as we move through $x=a$ we can expect the gradient function to have a positive gradient and hence d^2y/dx^2

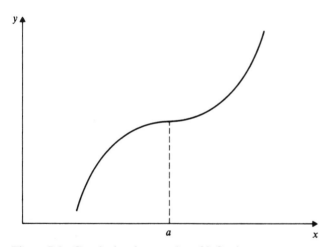

Figure 5.6 Graph showing a point of inflection.

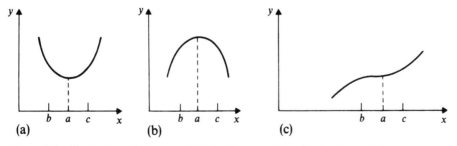

Figure 5.7 Illustration of the second derivative condition for turning points.

to be positive at $x=a$. In a case like Fig. 5.7(b) where the gradient changes from positive to negative as we move through $x=a$ we can expect d^2y/dx^2 to be negative at $x=a$.

Thus the procedure we can use is as follows:

Differentiate a second time to obtain d^2y/dx^2

Evaluate d^2y/dx^2 for the x values which make $dy/dx=0$

If d^2y/dx^2 is positive, conclude we have a minimum point

If d^2y/dx^2 is negative, conclude we have a maximum point

If d^2y/dx^2 is zero this test fails. It may indicate that we have a situation like Fig. 5.7(c). This would be true for the function $y=x^3$ at $x=0$ which we saw in Fig. 5.2.

It is, however, possible to have a minimum point, as in $y=x^4$ at $x=0$, or a maximum point, as in $y=-x^4$ at $x=0$. What is happening in these cases is that although we have situations like Figs. 5.7(a) and 5.7(b), respectively, the gradient is changing so slowly at $x=a$ that the second derivative does not differ from zero. Higher-order derivatives would have to be used to resolve the matter by this sort of approach.

If you should need to deal with a problem where $d^2y/dx^2=0$ at the turning point, the simplest method is to abandon the second derivative approach when this is discovered and revert to examining dy/dx for x just less than a and for x just greater than a.

Example 5.2.2 Consider the function $y=x^3-6x^2+9x-4$. For each of the values of x for which $dy/dx=0$ decide whether the function has a minimum value, a maximum value or neither.

ANSWER We saw in the answer to Example 5.2.1 that the function $y=x^3-6x^2+9x-4$ has $dy/dx=0$ when $x=1$ and when $x=3$; $dy/dx=3x^2-12x+9$ so $d^2y/dx^2=6x-12$.

Hence when $x=1$ we have $d^2y/dx^2=6-12=-6<0$, so $x=1$ is a maximum point.
When $x=3$ we have $d^2y/dx^2=18-12=6>0$, so $x=3$ is a minimum point.
When $x=1$ we have $y=1-6+9-4=0$.
When $x=3$ we have $y=27-54+27-4=-4$.

Exercise 5.2.1 For the function $y=4x^3+3x^2-36x+6$, find the values of x for which $dy/dx=0$.

Decide for each of these values whether it corresponds to a minimum point, to a maximum point or to neither.

Exercise 5.2.2 Your firm is considering launching a new product. A marketing comparison with other similar products has led your marketing department to believe that the amount of the product sold will vary over time according to the following equation:

$$q=-\tfrac{1}{3}t^3-t^2+168t$$

where q is number of units sold at time t (months).

(a) Using differential calculus:
  (i) find the point in time when maximum sales can be expected;
  (ii) show that this is a maximum.
(b) For values of t of $0,3,6,9\ldots21$ tabulate the corresponding amount of sales.
(c) Using the figures found in part (b) plot sales against time, showing the point of maximum sales.

(ACCA Level 1: Dec. 1989)

5.3 FINANCIAL APPLICATIONS OF CALCULUS

There are many situations in business and finance where one variable changes in response to changes in another variable. In productivity theory output might change in relation to changes in man-hours employed, or in the theory of the firm costs may change in response to output changes. These are just two instances of what is termed *marginal analysis* in economic theory. For example, marginal productivity measures the rate of change of output as employment changes, and marginal cost measures the rate of change of cost as output changes. We now consider the theory of the firm in more detail.

Suppose that the total cost of producing x units of a commodity is represented by a function of x which we shall call C. We might, for example, have $C = 500 + 3x$ where £500 is the fixed cost and there is a further cost of £3 incurred for each unit actually produced. This latter is the *variable cost*.

The *marginal cost* function, denoted MC, is the rate of change of cost as output changes and so is the gradient of the total cost function. For the case $C = 500 + 3x$ we have

$$MC = dC/dx = 0 + 3 = 3$$

In this particular case MC is constant, but more generally where C contains higher powers of x, MC will itself be a function of x. Another important function is the *average cost* function which is defined by

$$AC = C/x$$

Example 5.3.1 For the total cost function $C = 50 + 4x + x^2$ find

(a) the fixed cost;
(b) the variable cost;
(c) the marginal cost;
(d) the average cost.

ANSWER

(a) The fixed cost is the cost of producing zero units, so it can be found by putting $x = 0$ in the expression for C. We see that fixed cost $= 50$.
(b) The variable cost is the remaining part of the total cost, which varies with the quantity produced. Thus we have variable cost $= 4x + x^2$. In this case there is not just a fixed cost per additional unit, but as the quantity produced increases the cost per unit also increases giving the squared term in the expression for variable cost.
(c) The marginal cost is $MC = dC/dx = 4 + 2x$.
(d) The average cost is $AC = C/x = (50 + 4x + x^2)/x = 50/x + 4 + x$.

Similarly, from the total revenue function R we can find the *marginal revenue* function $MR = dR/dx$ and the *average revenue* function $AR = R/x$. Average revenue is also represented by the symbol p since it is the *price* per unit.

Price p as a function of x expresses the link between price and quantity demanded and is referred to as the *demand function*.

Example 5.3.2 A small factory producing a single product has weekly fixed costs of production of £2112 and weekly variable costs of £$(52 + 0.75x^2)$, where x is the quantity produced. The capacity of the factory is about 600 units.

Past experience suggests that the product's price and quantity are linked by the following demand equation:

$$p = 200 - 0.25x \quad (p, x > 0)$$

where $p = £$price/unit and $x = $ quantity sold.

(a) Find the level of production at which *revenue* is maximized.
(b) Find any break-even points.

(CIMA Stage 1: May 1988)

ANSWER

(a) Revenue is $R = $ price $\times$ quantity $= (200 - 0.25x)x$
$$= 200x - 0.25x^2$$
Hence $dR/dx = 200 - 0.5x$

So $\quad dR/dx = 0 \qquad$ when $0.5x = 200$ and $x = 200/0.5$

i.e. when $\quad x = 400$

Revenue is maximized when 400 units are produced and sold.

(b) Break even occurs when cost = revenue

$$\text{So } 52x + 0.75x^2 + 2112 = 200x - 0.25x^2$$

$$\text{Hence } x^2 - 148x + 2112 = 0$$

$$\text{This factorizes to } (x - 16)(x - 132) = 0$$

Break even occurs when the quantity produced and sold is either 16 units or 132 units.

Now profit, π, is the difference between total revenue and total cost. That is to say $\pi = R - C$.

A common objective for a firm to pursue is for it to seek to maximize profit. This involves finding x so as to make $d\pi/dx = 0$. By differentiation rule 4 we have

$$d\pi/dx = dR/dx - dC/dx$$
$$= MR - MC$$

So $d\pi/dx = 0$ means that $MR - MC = 0$.

Thus when profit is maximized, marginal revenue is equal to marginal cost.

Figure 5.8 shows a total revenue curve and a total cost curve at a profit maximizing output level $x = a$.

We note that at $x = a$ the vertical distance of the revenue curve above the cost curve is a maximum and that the gradients of the revenue and cost curves, which are the marginal revenue and marginal cost respectively, are equal.

Example 5.3.3 A manufacturer of a new patented product has found that he can sell 70 units a week direct to the customer if the price is £48. In error, the price was recently advertised at £78 and, as a result, only 40 units were sold a week. The manufacturer's fixed costs of production are £1710 a week and variable costs are £9 per unit.

(a) Show that the equation of the demand function linking price (P) to quantity demanded (X), assuming it to be a straight line, is $P = 118 - X$.

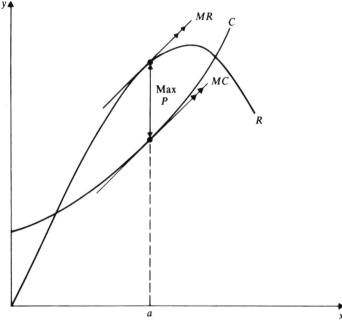

Figure 5.8 Graph showing revenue and cost curves whose profit is maximized.

(b) Find where the manufacturer breaks even.
(c) Recommend a unit price which would maximize profit, and find the quantity demanded and profit generated at that price.

(CIMA Stage 1: May 1990)

ANSWER

(a) Suppose the relationship is $P = a + bX$
Then we know from the information given that $48 = a + 70b$ (1)
and $78 = a + 40b$ (2)

(1)−(2): $-30 = 30b$ so $b = -30/30 = -1$
Substituting in (1): $48 = a + (-70)$ so $a = 48 + 70 = 118$
Hence the demand function is $P = 118 - X$

(b) Revenue is $R = PX = (118 - X)X = 118X - X^2$
Cost   is $C = 1710 + 9X$
So break even occurs when $1710 + 9X = 118X - X^2$
Hence $X^2 - 109X + 1710 = 0$
This factorizes to give $(X - 90)(X - 19) = 0$
So break even occurs where the manufacturer produces and sells either 19 units or 90 units.

(c) Profit is $\pi = R - C = 118X - X^2 - 1710 - 9X$
$= -X^2 + 109X - 1710$
$d\pi/dX = -2X + 109$
So $d\pi/dX = 0$ when $2X = 109$ and so $X = 54.5$.

Profit is maximized where the numer of units produced and sold is 54.5. The corresponding unit price is $118 - 54.5 = 63.5$ and the profit generated is

$$-54.5^2 + 90 \times 54.5 - 1710 = -2970.25 + 5940.5 - 1710 = 1260.25$$

Exercise 5.3.1 Your firm has recently started to give economic advice to your clients. Acting as a consultant you have estimated the demand curve of a client's firm to be $AR = 200 - 8x$, where AR is average revenue (£) and x is output.

Investigation of the client firm's cost profile shows that marginal cost is given by $MC = x^2 - 28x + 211$, where MC is marginal cost (£). Further investigation has shown that the firm's costs when not producing output are £10.

(a) If total cost is the integral of marginal cost find the equation of total cost.
(b) If total revenue is average revenue multiplied by output find the equation of total revenue.
(c) Profit is total revenue minus total cost. Using the methods of differentiation find the turning point(s) of the firm's profit curve and say whether these point(s) are maxima or minima.
(d) Marginal revenue is the first derivative of total revenue. Find the equation of marginal revenue.
(e) On the same scale and axes sketch the marginal cost and marginal revenue curves.

(ACCA Level 1: June 1991)

[Note that in part (a) of this question the process of going from total cost to marginal cost by differentiation is reversed using integration to go from marginal cost to total cost.]

Price elasticity of demand is an important concept in economic theory. It is used to measure the responsiveness of demand for a commodity to changes in its price. It is defined as:

$$\text{Elasticity of demand} = \frac{\text{proportionate change in demand}}{\text{proportionate change in price}}$$

So if demand is denoted by x and price by p, this can be written:

(change in x/original demand x)/(change in p/original price p)

which can be rearranged to become:

(original price p/original demand x) × (change in x/change in p)

If we take the limiting case where the change in p is considered to be very small, then (change in x/change in p) becomes the rate of change of x with respect to p, i.e. dx/dp, and we have the so-called *point elasticity of demand* $E = (p/x)(dx/dp)$. Alternatively, since it is more usual to have p expressed in terms of x rather than vice versa, the earlier expression could be rearranged slightly before proceeding to the limit as:

$$(\text{original price } p/\text{original demand } x) \times \frac{1}{(\text{change in } p/\text{change in } x)}$$

Taking the limiting case of very small changes now gives an expression for the point elasticity of demand as

$$E = (p/x)(1/(dp/dx))$$

Example 5.3.4 The demand for a product is given by $p = 384 - 2x^2$ where x is the quantity demanded (in thousands) and p is the price per unit. Determine the price and quantity for which revenue is a maximum. Calculate the point price elasticity of demand at this quantity.

ANSWER $R = px = 384x - 2x^3$. So $MR = dR/dx = 384 - 6x^2$ which is zero when $x = 8$. $d^2R/dx^2 = -12x$ which is negative when $x = 8$ so this value corresponds to maximum revenue.

The maximum is $384 \times 8 - 2 \times 512 = 256$. $dp/dx = -4x$ so the required point price elasticity of demand is

$$E = (p/x)(1/(dp/dx)) = ([384 - 2 \times 64]/8)(1/[-32]) = (256/8) \times (-32) = -1$$

The point price elasticity of demand is -1.

This can be interpreted to mean that if there is a 1 per cent increase in price then demand can be expected to fall by 1 per cent.

[It is actually *always* the case that elasticity is unity when revenue is maximized. Putting $R = px$, differentiating with respect to x and putting $dR/dx = 0$ leads to $(p/x)(1/(dp/dx)) = -1$ though full proof of this requires 'differentiation of a product' which is not covered in this book.]

Exercise 5.3.2 Your firm has undertaken an investigation for a client company and has discovered that his total cost curve TC is given by

$$TC = 140 + 5x^2$$

where x is output.

Investigating the demand for the company's product showed that the demand for output was related to price by the following equation:

$$P = 100 - 5x$$

where P is price and x is output.

Total revenue is price multiplied by output. Profit is total revenue minus total cost.

(a) Find the equation of profit.
(b) Using differential calculus find the output of the company that maximizes profit.
(c) If marginal revenue is the first derivative of total revenue with respect to output, find the equation of marginal revenue.
(d) For values of output $0, 2, 4 \ldots$ to 20 prepare a table of average revenue, marginal revenue and total revenue, and plot these values on a suitable graph.
(e) If elasticity of demand is given by $(P/x)(1/[dP/dx])$ find the elasticity of demand when profit is maximized.   (ACCA Level 1: Dec. 1990)

Although our applications have concerned cost, revenue and profit functions, there are many other areas where economic relationships exist between functions and their derivatives. Table 5.3 shows some of these relationships which are important in business and finance.

Table 5.3

y	x	dy/dx
Cost	Output	Marginal cost
Revenue	Output	Marginal revenue
Profit	Output	Marginal profit
Wealth	Time	Income
Capital	Time	Investment
Output	Time	Growth rate
Output	Labour employed	Marginal productivity
Imports	National income	Marginal propensity to import
Savings	National income	Marginal propensity to save
Consumption	National income	Marginal propensity to consume

TEST EXERCISES

5.1 If $y = 3x^2 - 2x + 8$, what is the slope of the line when $x = 3$?
(A) 13; (B) 16; (C) 20; (D) 24; (E) none of these.

(CIMA Stage 1: Nov. 1991)

5.2 $Y = 3X^2 - 7X + 2$. The slope of the function Y when $x = 3$ is:
(A) 8; (B) 11; (C) 13; (D) 18; (E) none of these.

(CIMA Stage 1: Nov. 1989)

5.3 $Y = 3X^2 - 420X$. Read the following statements.

(a) There is a local minimum for Y when $X = 70$.
(b) There is a local maximum for Y when $X = 70$.
(c) The graph of Y cuts the X axis in one place only, where $X = 140$.

Which is true?
(A) (a) only; (B) (b) only; (C) (c) only; (D) (a) and (b) only; (E) (b) and (c) only.

(CIMA Stage 1: Nov. 1988)

5.4 Consider the function $y = (1/3)x^3 + 2x^2 - 5x$. Find the values of x for which the gradient function dy/dx is zero and use the second derivative d^2y/dx^2 to decide whether each of these points is a maximum point or a minimum point.

5.5 For a project under analysis it has been found that the revenue function is $R = 50x$ and that the cost function is $C = 2x^2 + 200$, where x is the number (in thousands) of units produced and sold. Find:
(a) the marginal revenue function;
(b) the marginal cost function;
(c) the marginal profit function;
(d) the output level which maximizes profit;
(e) the maximum profit;
(f) the range of output for which there is a profit.

5.6 An economist in a company producing specialist screws reckons that for this line the weekly revenue and cost functions (in pounds) are:

$$\text{Total revenue} = 14x - x^2$$
$$\text{Total cost} = x^3 - 7.5x^2 + 65$$

where x is the number of screws produced in the week in hundreds.

(a) Find the profit function.
(b) Using values of x from $x = 0$ to $x = 8$, plot the total revenue function and the total cost function on the same graph.
(c) On a different graph, but using the same range of values of x, plot the profit function.
(d) Use differentiation to find the number of screws per week which the company should produce in order to maximize profit. (Express this answer to the nearest complete screw.)
(e) Calculate the maximum profit and indicate your result on both the graphs that have been drawn.
(f) Estimate from the graph drawn in answer to (b) the profit which would be made if the company produced that number of screws per week which maximized revenue.

5.7 Your firm has hired an economist as a consultant. The economist has estimated that your firm's marginal cost curve is $MC = 2x$, where MC is marginal cost in pounds and x is output.

The economist has also estimated that your firm's marginal revenue curve is $MR = 30 - 4x$, where MR is marginal revenue in pounds.

He also concludes in his report that when output is zero total cost is £4 and states that marginal cost is the first differential of total cost.

(a) Find the equation of total cost.
(b) If marginal revenue is defined as the first differential of total revenue find the equation of total revenue.
(c) Profit, π, in pounds is defined as $\pi = TR - TC$. Using differential calculus find the profit maximizing output.
(d) If average revenue is total revenue divided by output find the equation of average revenue.
(e) Sketch marginal revenue, average revenue and marginal cost on the same axes.

(ACCA Level 1: June 1990)

DATA COLLECTION AND SAMPLING

6.1 SAMPLE SURVEYS

Modern society seems to be preoccupied with numerical information. Television and news-papers are constantly providing numerical information about various aspects of our lives. For example, we hear or read that 8 out of 10 dog owners prefer Bonzo; 12 per cent of adults invest in unit trusts; or 25 per cent of large companies have cash flow difficulties. There is no doubt that society is now better informed about all aspects of life, and it is therefore essential that the providers of such information have an objective and unbiased basis on which to report their findings. Hence the need for a scientific method on which to obtain sample information.

We provide the following examples where sample surveys have been widely used.

1. Monitoring the quality of manufactured goods on a production line. The inspection of all products can be expensive and unnecessary so it is important to formulate a good quality-control scheme.
2. Accountants need to carry out audits on companies which will require the inspection of accounts. If the accountant is dealing with a large company then it may be necessary to take a sample of these accounts.
3. Public opinion polls often provide information on political or social issues.
4. Market research is often carried out prior to the introduction of a new product.

The first two examples are described in detail in Chapter 18. In all of the situations, the size of the underlying population can be very large. If all items of such a population are examined we are conducting what is called a census. The advantage of a census is that it should give us a completely accurate view of the population. However, it is often impractic-able and usually costly. Hence it makes sense to study only a portion or sample of the population.

In order to illustrate the advantages of sampling we look at a specific example.

Example 6.1.1 Suppose we wish to know the average wage earned by adults in a small town. Why might it be more suitable to take a sample rather than study every member of the population?

ANSWER There are several reasons why we may wish to sample rather than conduct a complete census. We deal with these individually.

1. It is clearly cheaper to sample a small portion of the population than it is to view the whole population. This economy may arise out of lower postage costs or smaller transport costs, depending on the way that the survey is to be conducted.
2. A census is time-consuming. This is important if the information is required quickly so that a conclusion can be drawn at an appropriate time.
3. In a census information is required from every member of the population. However, the entire population may not be available, possibly because not every member of the working population can be contacted, but more likely because some adults would refuse to disclose the required information. (If a sample was taken, great care would be needed to ensure that it was not biased.)
4. However, the most important reason for sampling is that total accuracy is probably not required. It may be that a fairly small sample yields enough information to get the required accuracy. This is true in many surveys. Indeed in many situations it may be argued that samples yield more accurate information than a census. For example, an audit clerk who is asked to investigate a very large number of financial transactions may make mistakes due to tiredness and lack of concentration. This may be eliminated if the clerk were to perform a more thorough investigation of a smaller sample.

The above reasons for sampling can all be generalized for most survey situations.

6.2 METHODS OF SELECTING A SAMPLE

When taking a sample we hope it has similar features to the underlying population, and thus provides a balanced reflection of it. There are several methods of sampling that have been advanced, and many are widely applied. Basically, the methods of sampling can be classified into two broad headings:

1. probability sampling.
2. judgement sampling.

In judgement sampling the sampler decides in advance on the factors that will determine whether or not a member of the population is included in the sample. In probability sampling every member has a known chance of selection in the sample. It is only probability sampling that allows us to obtain estimates with known probabilities of error.

Before selecting a sample, an investigator should, where possible, establish a sampling frame. This is a list of all persons or items in the population. For example, if we required information from United Kingdom adults, then the Electoral Register may be used to generate the sampling frame. Alternatively, if we required information from students at a college, then enrolment lists may form the basis of the sampling frame. Similarly, transaction files may contain all the orders placed in a given financial year. However, there are many populations for which no sampling frame exists; typical examples include

1. the customers at a supermarket;
2. adult smokers in the United Kingdom.

Sampling methods may well be chosen on the basis of whether or not a sampling frame exists.

The main methods of probability sampling are now described.

(a) Simple random sampling

This is the most basic form of probability sampling; it is widely used in its own right and is easy to operate from a statistical viewpoint. It also serves as the basis for other, more complicated, sampling schemes, as we shall see later.

The particular feature of simple random sampling is that it gives every possible set of n members of the population an equal probability of being chosen when a sample is selected. Such a sample is usually obtained by drawing members from the population one at a time without replacement, so that at each stage every remaining member of the population has the same probability of being chosen.

Randomness does not mean just choosing haphazardly; it is not enough for the investigator to pick members 'at random' because inevitably he or she will incorporate unconscious bias. The choice of individual observations in the sample is best achieved by the use of random number tables.

Example 6.2.1 An auditor wishes to choose a sample of 50 invoices from a total of 600 received during a financial year. Explain how the sample should be chosen.

ANSWER We must carry out the selection of the sample in such a way that every member of the population has the same chance of appearing in the sample.

Let us first of all number the invoices from 001 to 600. We then need to obtain a table of random digits. Set out below is part of a typical random number table.

27055	02606	43347	65384
59506	75440	90826	53652
15770	03281	58124	09533
20322	82000	52830	93540
38773	67687	45541	54976
30545	74383	22814	36752
00708	21816	39615	03102
33104	81206	00112	53445
72459	66136	97266	26490
82429	90288	61064	26489

We now choose the starting point of the random number tables. (If we have not used the table before, we should start at the beginning of the table.) As the total number of invoices is 600, a three-digit number, we divide the table up so that the digits appear in threes; e.g. 270, 550, 260, 643, 347, 653, 845, etc. We mark off 50 such random numbers and select those members of the population bearing these numbers. Note that if the same number appears more than once, we treat it as a blank. Similarly any number greater than $N = 600$ should be treated as blank.

We use the given random digits to illustrate this procedure.

270	✓
550	✓
260	✓
643	✗ (treated as blank)
347	✓
653	✗ (treated as blank)
845	✗ (treated as blank)
950	✗ (treated as blank)
675	✗ (treated as blank)
440	✓

The first five invoices selected are those numbered 270, 550, 260, 347, and 440. A further 45 invoices need to be selected in this way. The next time we use the table of random digits, we would start at the last one previously selected.

(b) Systematic sampling

The practicality of the simple random sampling procedure depends on the existence of a sampling frame and also on the size of the population. A good approximation to simple random sampling is systematic sampling. For example, if we wished to select a sample of size 25 from a population of size 1000 then we calculate

$$k = \frac{\text{population size}}{\text{sample size}} = \frac{1000}{25} = 40$$

and select every kth item from the population list. Suppose our randomly chosen number between 1 and 40 is 31, then the sample would consist of the numbers 31, 71, 111, 151, ... Systematic sampling provides a simple method for sample selection and is widely used in practice. An advantage of this method of sampling is that it can be used where no sample frame exists (but the items do exist); for example, every 20th customer to enter a shop might be chosen. However, with this method of sampling care must be taken to avoid regularities.

(c) Stratified sampling

Although the accuracy of sample results can be increased by increasing the sample, this can also increase costs. One way of increasing accuracy without increasing the sample size is by using stratification. This procedure ensures that the sample adequately represents all sections of the population. The procedure is best illustrated by an example.

Example 6.2.2 Suppose we wish to select a sample of 400 employees from a moderately large company to determine its attitude to a new 'productivity' scheme of payment. We decide that the two major factors which would affect their views would be their degree of skill and their sex. The company records show that the workforce has the following breakdown.

	Male	Female
Skilled	2400	330
Semi-skilled	1290	660
Unskilled	300	1020

Indicate how such a sample can be taken to ensure that it is representative of the population.

ANSWER A sample obtained by simple random sampling (and also systematic sampling) may look unrepresentative; for example, it may be that the sample contains no women workers even though there is a substantial number of women among the 6000 workers. All that can be said in these circumstances is that an unlikely sample has come up.

One way of making a sample more representative is by means of *stratified sampling*. Stratification simply means that before any selection takes place, the population is divided into a number of strata – then a random sample is selected within each stratum. If the number of units selected from each stratum is proportional to the number in the stratum, then the procedure is called proportionate stratified sampling. Otherwise it is disproportionate stratified sampling.

In proportionate stratification the sampling fraction is the same for each stratum, i.e.

$$\frac{\text{size of sample from a stratum}}{\text{total size of stratum}} = k \text{ say, for each stratum}$$

In the above example we have six strata. If we require a sample of 400 employees the sampling fraction is

$$\frac{\text{sample size}}{\text{population size}} = \frac{400}{6000} = \frac{1}{15}$$

Hence from each stratum we require a sample of size $1/15 \times$ (stratum size); for example, from the skilled male stratum we take a sample of size $2400/15 = 160$. In the same way we obtain the sample sizes from each stratum:

	Male	Female
Skilled	160	22
Semi-skilled	86	44
Unskilled	20	68

It should be emphasized that in stratified sampling the people from each stratum are selected randomly. This distinguishes it from quota sampling, which we describe later. The procedure of stratified random sampling is frequently used in practice. It is preferable that the stratification is based on some criterion relevant to the subject under investigation. For example, if it was required to test opinions of the Government by a door-to-door enquiry it would be necessary to ensure that some views were conducted in known Conservative areas and some in known Socialist regions.

(d) Cluster sampling

Cluster sampling refers to the procedure whereby the items in the sample are not chosen individually but in groups (or clusters). For example, if it was necessary to obtain a sample from a large town, it would be convenient if the sample consisted of households from the same street, or in certain areas of the town. Hence the population is split into, say, 1000 areas each containing 10 dwellings and a number of these areas are chosen at random. The great advantage of this type of sampling is the saving in time and cost. Many interviews can take place within a short space of time with a minimum of travelling.

It is advantageous, when using the cluster sampling method of selection, for the items in each cluster to be dissimilar. If the n elements in each of the m clusters were very different we would have a sample of $n \times m$ items. On the other hand, if the elements in each sample were similar, then we have, in effect, a sample of only m different items.

Cluster sampling is used because it requires relatively little administrative effort and it is less costly than other sampling methods. Another important reason why cluster sampling is used is that there may be no alternative. A typical example is one in which we wish to select a large sample of workers in a particular industry. It is likely that we can compile a list of employers but not a list of their workers. In this situation the only way we may be able to obtain a sample is to select the firms at random and ask the employers to contact their workers on our behalf.

(e) Multistage sampling

In market research it is usually necessary to draw conclusions about the whole country. This means that we have a very large and widespread population of interest. Now to travel over the entire country is costly and tedious and it would certainly be more convenient if the sample can be restricted to certain smaller areas of the country. Again we use an example to illustrate the principles.

A national survey is proposed to ascertain the likely readership of a new journal. In this situation the population of interest consists of all households in the country. It would be very costly and time-consuming to take a random sample of households for this sample. It is more sensible to use an extension of the cluster sampling procedure. Suppose we proceed as follows.

First, we randomly select a sample of counties (for example, Kent, Dorset, and Staffordshire). Second, we subdivide each of these selected counties into smaller regions from which further samples are selected randomly. Again these regions may be split into smaller units (streets, say) and a further random selection made, and so on for as many stages as required. At each stage we randomly choose three or four elements, so that we are finally left with several households which are not too isolated from other households in the sample. This process is called multistage cluster sampling.

We now turn, briefly, to methods of judgement sampling. The major disadvantage of this type of sampling is that we can obtain no estimate of accuracy of our results. A sampling method which comes under the heading of judgement sampling is quota sampling.

(f) Quota sampling

This method of sampling is closely related to stratified random sampling and is widely used in both opinion surveys and market research. Where it differs from stratified random sampling is in the fact that the samples are not chosen randomly from the strata. Typically, strata are defined, the sample stratum size needed for proportional allocation are calculated from overall stratum sizes in the population, and then the actual choice of elements within the strata is left to the individual interviewers.

Example 6.2.3 The following table shows the breakdown of a college population into categories of sex, age, and course.

	Age	
	Under 20	20 and over
Course 1		
Male	75	90
Female	60	63
Course 2		
Male	124	32
Female	86	29
Course 3		
Male	73	44
Female	59	30
Course 4		
Male	77	59
Female	90	59

(a) It is required to construct a quota sample of 70 individuals which fully reflects the distribution of these three characteristics in the population. Calculate the numbers in each category of the quota sample.

(b) Suppose that it was decided that both age and sex are no longer of importance in the survey. How would your quota sample of 70 be affected?

(c) What is the major criticism of a quota sample.

ANSWER

(a) We reflect the population by obtaining a sample in which the number of elements in the sample is proportional to the population size. Here the population size is 1050, so the sample fraction is

$$\frac{70}{1050} = \frac{1}{15}$$

Therefore we divide each number in the above table by 15 and round to the nearest whole number to obtain the following sample sizes.

	Age	
	Under 20	20 and over
Course 1		
Male	5	6
Female	4	4
Course 2		
Male	8	2
Female	6	2
Course 3		
Male	5	3
Female	4	2
Course 4		
Male	5	4
Female	6	4

The necessary information is now collected by instructing the interviewers to fill the quotas for the different cells. Instead of selecting the sample at random the interviewer tends to select those that are easiest to find until he or she has the number of respondents required for each category.

(b) If age and sex are no longer of importance we merely combine the classes in our quota table to give

Course 1	19
Course 2	18
Course 3	14
Course 4	19

(c) From a theoretical viewpoint the non-randomness of quota sampling is a great weakness. Samples drawn in this way are open to a great risk of becoming distorted. Some experts argue that the inevitable bias renders this method of sampling useless. However, we should point out that many market researchers and administrators, who actually have to conduct surveys, defend the method on the grounds of simplicity, cheapness, speed, and the fact that there is no need for a sampling frame and therefore no real problems caused by non-response.

Exercise 6.2.1 A retail shop has commissioned a market research firm to undertake a survey and the shop manager has asked you to explain the following terms contained in the market research firm's proposal.

Briefly explain the terms and say what measures of location and dispersion it would be appropriate to use in any analysis of the samples:

(a) a random sample;
(b) a quota sample;
(c) a cluster sample.

(CIMA Stage 1: June 1989)

6.3 QUESTIONNAIRES

The method of collecting information and the design of questionnaires are two important factors to be considered when conducting a survey.

(a) Method of collection

The two principal methods of gathering information for surveys are postal questionnaires and interviews. Each of these has its merits and which is best to use depends on the circumstances of the survey.

The postal questionnaire is much less costly to operate than the personal interview. The cheapness may in some situations be a decisive argument in favour of the questionnaire, especially if resources are limited or the population is widely scattered. Alternatively we can increase the size of the sample in order to make the results more reliable. As well as being fairly cheap, questionnaires allow information to be gathered reasonably quickly. We can usually expect most of the replies to arrive within a fortnight of the questionnaires being sent out. Questionnaires have the additional advantage that there is no interviewer to affect the respondent's answers. The way a question is asked could influence the respondent's answer.

Difficulty in obtaining a reasonable response rate is the most serious problem with questionnaires. In fact a response rate of 20 per cent is quite good for a postal questionnaire. The seriousness of this is not so much the lack of information but rather the possibility that non-response may be indicative of a certain attitude. This may lead to biased results from the questionnaires that are returned.

The major advantage of the personal interview is that it is much more likely to produce a high response rate. It seems that people are much less willing to decline an interview than they are to refuse to fill in a questionnaire. Furthermore, the interviewer is in a position to help the respondent if he or she requires additional information.

The main weakness in interviewing is that it is costly, not only due to the expense of the interviewer's wages and travel allowances, but also the cost of training the individual interviewers. A further possible weakness is interviewer bias. It is essential that the interviewer asks the questions in a neutral manner and does not load them so that the respondent feels compelled to answer them in a certain way.

Although the postal questionnaire and the personal interview are the two main methods of collecting survey information, there is an increasing use of the telephone as a medium for data collection. Telephone methods are very quick but many people do not possess a telephone. A further disadvantage of the telephone is that respondents may refuse to give information to a stranger over the telephone which could cause problems with non-response. This type of data collection is primarily used in connection with the selling of a product or service.

(b) Questionnaire design

Before considering the design of actual questionnaire forms it is worth while looking at some important peripheral issues relating to postal questionnaires. First, there should be a covering letter with the questionnaire describing the reasons for the survey and assuring the respondents of anonymity. In addition, a stamped addressed envelope is essential and the inclusion of some payment in anticipation of response. This payment need not be in the form of money, but may be a cheap item such as a pen, or entry into a competition with more worthwhile prizes. All of these points are designed to encourage as high a response rate as possible.

As far as the postal questionnaire itself is concerned, it should be laid out as clearly as possible with capital letters and bold type in order to emphasize key words and instructions. In addition, the questions should be as simple to answer as possible and it should look as if great care has been taken to reduce the number of questions to a minimum.

When wording the questions the following points should be borne in mind:

1. The language should be clear and concise and able to be understood by all respondents; for example we should use the word 'stop' rather than 'cease' or 'tell' rather than 'inform'.
2. The questionnaire should avoid leading the respondent to a particular answer; for example, 'Don't you think that ...?'
3. Do not rely too much on the memory of the respondent. 'How much did you spend on food last week?' should produce a reasonably accurate answer. However, 'How much did you spend in an equivalent week last year?' will undoubtedly produce a worthless answer.
4. The use of precoded questions is a great help to the respondent; for example:

How many employees are on your payroll? Tick appropriate box.
less than 100   100–500   more than 500

    ☐   ☐   ☐

Precoded questions also make the necessary analysis easier.

6.4 PUBLISHED SOURCES OF STATISTICS

In the modern age, data is collected on a massive scale, not only by the Government but also by market research firms and international organizations such as the European Economic Community and the United Nations. By far the most important source of such statistical information in the United Kingdom is the Central Statistical Office, which is responsible for the publication of data which has been collected by a number of government departments. The main publications of the Central Statistical Office are:

1. *Annual Abstract of Statistics.* This publication is the main source of official data and contains a large amount of useful and interesting information concerning the United Kingdom. It covers such diverse topics as population, education, weather, transport and communications, and finance.
2. *Monthly Digest of Statistics.* This is a monthly version of the *Annual Abstract* and provides up-to-date information on such topics as prices, wages, population, and employment.
3. *Financial Statistics.* This is a monthly publication which brings together the important monetary statistics of the United Kingdom. It tabulates a wide range of financial information relating to central government, local authorities, public corporations, banks, building societies, and insurance companies. In addition, there is information concerning mortgage rates, interest rates, and foreign exchange rates. There is also a section dealing with overseas finance.
4. *Economic Trends.* This is another monthly publication which includes graphs and numerical statistics on the main economic indicators such as prices, wages and earnings, interest rates, national income, GDP, and consumers' expenditure, as well as changes in the money supply.
5. *National Income and Expenditure Survey.* This annual publication is known as the 'Blue Book'. It contains information on gross national product, gross national income, and gross national expenditure.

Two other government publications are:

1. *Employment Gazette* – a monthly publication giving information on employment, unemployment, and prices.
2. *British Business* – a weekly publication by the Department of Trade and Industry giving information about production, exports and imports of various industries.

In addition to these government publications there are newspapers and journals which provide important financial data. *The Financial Times*, for example, includes daily information on interest rates, foreign exchange rates, and stock prices. Other interesting journals are *The Economist, The Banker,* and *The Journal of the Institute of Bankers.*

TEST EXERCISES

6.1 (a) Sampling methods are frequently used for the collection of data. Explain the terms simple random sampling, stratified random sampling and sampling frame.
    (b) Suggest a suitable sampling frame for each of the following in which statistical data will be collected:
        (i) an investigation into the reactions of workers in a large factory to new proposals for shift working.
        (ii) a survey of students at a college about the relevance and quality of the teaching for their professional examinations;
        (iii) an enquiry into the use of home computers by schoolchildren in a large city.
    (c) Explain briefly, with reasons, the type of sampling method you would recommend in each of the three situations given above.

(CIMA Stage 1: May 1986)

6.2 Read the following statements about the use of stratified random sampling, cluster sampling and simple random sampling in the checking of invoices for errors. Decide which of the statements are true.
(a) Stratified random sampling is likely to provide, in general, more representative samples than cluster sampling.
(b) Simple random sampling is likely to provide, in general, the most representative samples.
(c) Cluster sampling is more prone to bias than simple random sampling.

(CIMA Stage 1: May 1990)

6.3 Which of the following is/are required for an accountant to select a stratified random sample of invoices?
(a) Each invoice must be given an equal chance of being picked.
(b) A record of all invoices is necessary.
(c) The number of invoices in each stratum must be known.

(CIMA Stage 1: Nov. 1989)

6.4. In auditing it is often sufficient to investigate only a sample of the accounts of a company. Describe the advantages of taking a random sample as opposed to a judgement sample.

(ACCA Stage 2: June 1991)

DESCRIBING STATISTICAL DATA

7.1 EXPLORATORY DATA ANALYSIS

One of the most basic tasks involved in statistical work is to take a set of data and process it so as to make its main features clear. There are various aspects to this, both graphical and numerical.

Exploratory Data Analysis (EDA) is an approach developed by John Tukey in the 1960s for this purpose. It allows us to take a set of raw data (i.e. numbers) and obtain certain drawings and simple calculations from it in order to arrive at a feel for what the data set is saying before attempting to proceed, possibly, to more sophisticated types of analysis. The practicality of this approach to data has been greatly facilitated by the development of computer packages which permit the very rapid execution of the drawing and calculation required, even for large data sets. We shall, therefore, in this chapter be making some use of the MINITAB computer package since the philosophy of EDA depends on being able to do the exploration quickly and easily and restriction to manual execution of the processes would largely conceal their power. MINITAB is certainly not the only package which could be used for this purpose, but it is one which is very widely available and easy to use.

Table 7.1

	1977	1978	1979	1980	1981	1982	1983	1984	1985	1986
J	84	71	74	70	42	46	83	61	57	76
F	71	72	91	60	55	51	74	75	79	56
M	64	65	40	89	57	67	71	61	66	61
A	73	77	94	73	58	63	69	63	69	84
M	54	73	96	77	53	62	82	88	69	69
J	80	79	79	85	60	47	77	63	70	68
J	53	68	115	69	57	85	90	78	71	76
A	76	47	73	52	55	54	67	85	86	59
S	64	97	86	60	72	57	88	61	59	80
O	73	70	64	26	89	70	91	80	83	72
N	61	89	84	54	61	71	92	70	65	80
D	62	62	72	51	68	67	97	56	56	74

Consider the monthly figures shown in Table 7.1 (taken from Table 11.6 of the *Monthly Digest of Statistics*) showing the quantities in thousands of cubic metres of hardwood delivered to Great Britain during the 10-year period from January 1977 to December 1986.

A set of 120 numbers presented in this form makes little useful impression on the average reader.

A first diagram which we can obtain in the EDA approach is the *dotplot*. This shows each of the numbers as a dot in the appropriate position above a horizontal number line. This gives a useful general impression of the data but would be very laborious to construct manually. The MINITAB command which produces the dotplot shown in Fig. 7.1 is

DOTPLOT C1

the data having been entered into column C1 for the MINITAB worksheet.

The DOTPLOT command has subcommands which control the calibration of the horizontal line. Our purpose, however, is only to demonstrate the basic power of MINITAB in data analysis, and we shall therefore restrict ourselves to just the basic forms of the commands. For more detail about the MINITAB commands and their respective subcommands the reader is referred to the on-screen help facilities and to excellent manuals and handbooks produced by Minitab Inc.

Another very useful tool offered by EDA is the *stem-and-leaf display* (often abbreviated to 'stemplot'). This sets out all the numbers in the set in a column showing the first digit as a 'stem' and then the subsequent digits as 'leaves'. The basic form of the MINITAB command

STEM-AND-LEAF C1

for the hardwood data above produces the display shown in Fig. 7.2.

Use of the basic command has produced what is technically a 'stretched' stemplot in that each stem digit is given two rows for displaying its leaves. This command also has subcommands, in this case allowing the increment between the stems to be specified and to say how outliers are to be treated. The stemlength here could be changed to give a 'normal' stemplot or even a 'squeezed' stemplot.

Use of the basic command here has identified the outliers 26 and 115 and caused them to be listed separately so that they can be investigated. The display shows that there are two figures in the range 40 to 44, namely 40 and 42, and that three figures lie in this range or 'beyond', these being 40, 42 and the outlying 26. Then three lie in the range 45–49, namely 46, 47 and another 47, giving six in this range or beyond. The line with the parentheses contains the middle value, or the middle two values for a case like this where the total number of values is even. The figure in the parentheses shows the number of values in this line.

MTB > DOTPLOT C1

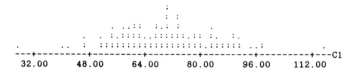

MTB >

Figure 7.1 A dotplot produced by MINITAB.

```
STEM-AND-LEAF DISPLAY OF C1
LEAF DIGIT UNIT =   1.0000
1 2 REPRESENTS 12.


         LO  26,

    3     4* 02
    6     4. 677
   14     5* 11233444
   26     5. 556667777899
   44     6* 000111111222333444
   58     6. 55677788899999
  (22)    7* 0000011111222233333444
   40     7. 56667778999
   29     8* 0000233444
   19     8. 5556688999
    9     9* 01124
    4     9. 677

         HI  115,
```

Figure 7.2 A stem and leaf display produced by MINITAB.

Exercise 7.1.1 Measurement was made of the times taken by 60 employees in a factory to carry out a standard procedure. The times found, in minutes, were as follows:

16	18	21	31	25	15	10	16	14	17
12	20	28	22	19	19	35	32	28	16
21	26	19	30	19	27	20	30	25	20
18	17	33	29	26	18	17	25	21	19
15	26	10	20	16	19	14	20	17	22
28	30	19	31	32	14	27	21	32	29

(a) Construct a dotplot for this set of data.
(b) Construct a stem-and-leaf display using a stemlength of five as in the example above.
(c) If you have MINITAB available, use the DOTPLOT and STEM-AND-LEAF commands for this data set.

7.2 FREQUENCY TABLES

An important merit of the stemplot as a means of presentation is that no information contained in the original data is sacrificed. All the numbers are there, arranged in a visually effective form. If, therefore, the appropriate computing facility is available, then the stemplot is to be recommended. If, however, such a facility is not available, then recourse to more traditional and less efficient methods becomes necessary. These methods are based on the (information destructive) process of converting the set of numbers into the form of a *grouped frequency table*. This involves dividing the range covered by the data into *classes* and counting the numbers of data values which fall into each class. These numbers are the *class frequencies*. The values for the data in Sec. 7.1 on hardwood deliveries to Great Britain range from 26 to 115 and there are obviously many different ways in which that range could be divided up into classes. Consider the set of classes shown in Table 7.2.

Table 7.2

Class
25–34
35–44
45–54
55–64
65–74
75–84
85–94
95–104
105–114
115–124

When the classes are set up in this way the values on the left, namely 25, 35, 45, etc., are called the *lower limits* of the classes and the numbers on the right, namely 34, 44, 54, etc., are called the *upper limits*. The value midway between the upper limit of one class and the lower limit of the next is the *class boundary* between the two classes. Thus 34.5 is the upper class boundary of the first class shown and the lower class boundary of the second class. The value midway between the upper and lower class limits of the same class is sometimes called the *class mark* of that class.

There is no firm rule about how many classes should be used but it is usual to arrange for at least 5 and not more than 15. Less than 5 would lead to inadequate discrimination, while more than 15 would be too many to take in easily and so would rob the frequency table of the main reason for its existence.

The difference between the upper and lower class boundaries of a class is referred to as either the *class width* or *class length* of the class. If it can be conveniently arranged for all classes to have the same class width, as has been done in Table 7.2, then later work is simplified, but for some data it is impractical to have all class widths the same.

Having set up the classes we must now count the number of data items falling into each one. The usual way to do this is to have a column next to the class column which we head 'tally marks'. For each item in turn in the original data we *cross it out* and enter a mark in the tally marks column. It is a good idea to record the tally marks using a five-bar gate method so that we can add them up easily at the end. The number of tally marks recorded against a class is the class frequency for that class. For the hardwood example see Table 7.3. This is a grouped frequency table for the data given.

Table 7.3

Class	Tally marks	Frequency
25–34	1	1
35–44	11	2
45–54	⊥⊩⊩ ⊥⊩⊩ 1	11
55–64	⊥⊩⊩ ⊥⊩⊩ ⊥⊩⊩ ⊥⊩⊩ ⊥⊩⊩ ⊥⊩⊩	30
65–74	⊥⊩⊩ ⊥⊩⊩ ⊥⊩⊩ ⊥⊩⊩ ⊥⊩⊩ ⊥⊩⊩ ⊥⊩⊩ 1	36
75–84	⊥⊩⊩ ⊥⊩⊩ ⊥⊩⊩ ⊥⊩⊩ 1	21
85–94	⊥⊩⊩ ⊥⊩⊩ ⊥⊩⊩	15
95–105	111	3
105–114		0
115–124	1	1

A *cumulative frequency table* is obtained by a simple rearrangement of the classes of an ordinary grouped frequency table. For the example we have been considering the classes are 25–34, 35–44, 45–54, etc., so the class boundaries are 34.5, 44.5, 54.5, etc. To obtain a cumulative frequency table we consider as ranges of values: less than 34.5, less than 44.5, less than 54.5, etc. The number of data values less than 34.5 will be the number in the class 25–34, the number less than 44.5 will be the sum of those in the classes 25–34 and 35–44, and so on.

Thus the frequencies for the *cumulative* frequency table are obtained by *accumulating* those of the ordinary frequency table. For this example Table 7.4 is the cumulative frequency table.

Table 7.4

Range	Frequency
Less than 34.5	1
Less than 44.5	3
Less than 54.5	14
Less than 64.5	44
Less than 74.5	80
Less than 84.5	101
Less than 94.5	116
Less than 104.5	119
Less than 114.5	119
Less than 124.5	120

Strictly, this is a 'less than' cumulative frequency table. A different sort of cumulative frequency table, called an 'or more' cumulative table, can be obtained by accumulating upwards from the bottom of the ordinary frequency table. This latter is far less common and the term 'cumulative frequency table' can be used without ambiguity to describe the 'less than' type of table. It is sometimes of interest to form a *relative frequency table*, and indeed this idea is taken up in Chapter 14. Such a table is formed by converting the frequencies in the ordinary frequency table, sometimes called *raw frequencies*, into relative frequencies by dividing each of them by the total frequency. Dividing each of the frequencies in the frequency table for the hardwood example by 120 gives the relative frequency table shown in Table 7.5.

Table 7.5

Class	Relative frequency
25–34	0.0083
35–44	0.0167
45–54	0.0917
55–64	0.2500
65–74	0.3000
75–84	0.1750
85–94	0.1250
95–104	0.0250
105–114	0.0000
115–124	0.0083

Relative frequencies facilitate easier comparison of tables when the total frequencies involved are different.

A cumulative relative frequency table could be obtained either by accumulating the relative frequencies or by expressing the cumulative raw frequencies as proportions of the total frequency. For the hardwood example the cumulative relative 'less than' table is shown in Table 7.6.

Table 7.6

Range	Relative frequency
Less than 34.5	0.0083
Less than 44.5	0.0250
Less than 54.5	0.1167
Less than 64.5	0.3667
Less than 74.5	0.6667
Less than 84.5	0.8417
Less than 94.5	0.9667
Less than 104.5	0.9917
Less than 114.5	0.9917
Less than 124.5	1.0000

Exercise 7.2.1 Measurement was made of the times taken by 60 employees in a factory to carry out a standard procedure. The times found, in minutes, were as follows:

16	18	21	31	25	15	10	16	14	17
12	20	28	22	19	19	35	32	28	16
21	26	19	30	19	27	20	30	25	20
18	17	33	29	26	18	17	25	21	19
15	26	10	20	16	19	14	20	17	22
28	30	19	31	32	14	27	21	32	29

(a) Group the data into five classes.
(b) Obtain a cumulative frequency table for the data.
(c) Obtain a relative frequency table.
(d) Obtain a cumulative relative frequency table.

7.3 GRAPHICAL PRESENTATION OF FREQUENCY TABLES

In Sec. 7.1 we looked at graphical presentations of sets of numbers in the form of dotplots and stem-and-leaf displays produced by MINITAB. Having arrived at grouped frequency tables as in Sec. 7.2 there are several diagrams which can be drawn, based on these, to improve further our appreciation of what a set of data is saying.

Histograms

A histogram is a block diagram having one block for each class into which the data values are divided.

The proper way to think about a histogram is that the width of a block is proportional to the class width of the class it represents and the area of the block is proportional to the class frequency. Hence the height of a block is proportional to class frequency divided by class width, which can be referred to as the 'frequency density' of the class. If, however, all the classes have the same class width then the definition given above reduces to saying that all blocks must have the same (arbitrary) width and heights proportional to the class frequencies.

If a frequency table has an open-ended class at one or both ends, the usual procedure is to assign its block a width equal to that for the class which is its immediate neighbour. For the hardwood data presented in Sec. 7.1 we have the histogram in Fig. 7.3 based on the frequency table formed in Sec. 7.2. A diagram like this gives an instant impression of what the data set is like.

In particular, it makes clear whether the data set has a symmetrical shape or is *skewed*. If the histogram has a long tail stretching away to the right, the data is said to be *positively skewed*. If there is long tail stretching away to the left, the data set is *negatively skewed*. Positively skewed data sets are fairly common in business and accounting. They would, for example, often be associated with distributions of incomes or of service times in an organization. Negatively skewed data sets are less common. An example of one woud be the distribution of the ages of hearing aid users.

It is worth mentioning here that MINITAB has a command called HISTOGRAM which produces output of the type shown in Fig. 7.4.

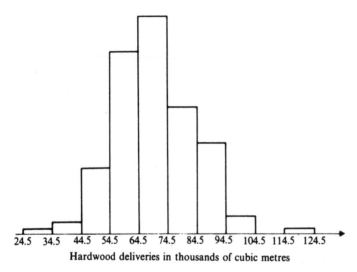

Hardwood deliveries in thousands of cubic metres

Figure 7.3 A histogram.

```
MTB > HISTOGRAM C1

Histogram of C1    N = 120

Midpoint    Count
      30        1  *
      40        2  **
      50       11  ***********
      60       30  ******************************
      70       36  ************************************
      80       21  *********************
      90       15  ***************
     100        3  ***
     110        0
     120        1  *

MTB >
```

Figure 7.4 A histogram as produced by MINITAB.

This output, for the hardwood data, was produced by the command

HISTOGRAM C1

the data being in column C1 of the MINITAB worksheet.

The command produces a frequency table very similar to the one arrived at in Sec. 7.2. Note, however, that the 'MIDDLE OF INTERVAL' is a rounded figure, the true class marks being 29.5, 39.5, 49.5, etc. There is a facility for specifying the class widths but all classes are required to have the same width, so the question of different block widths does not arise and hence the strings of stars are acceptable representations of the blocks.

It is actually very unusual for histograms other than in computer output to be drawn with horizontal rather than vertical blocks. In order to make clear the effect of differing class widths, suppose the last four classes in Table 7.3 had been merged together in view of the small frequencies in the last three. We should then have had the results shown in Table 7.7.

Table 7.7

Class	Frequency	Frequency density = frequency/class width
25–34	1	0.1
35–44	2	0.2
45–54	11	1.1
55–64	30	3.0
65–74	36	3.6
75–84	21	2.1
85–124	19	0.475

The point to note is that the frequency of 19 for the final class has to be divided by 40 whereas all the other frequencies are divided by 10. The resulting histogram is shown as Fig. 7.5.

Note that a histogram of correct shape could have been obtained by drawing blocks for the first six classes with heights proportional to the class frequencies, and then drawing the block for the last class with height scaled down by a factor of 4 since this class has width four times that of all the others.

Frequency polygons

A frequency polygon is in the most general case drawn by plotting for each class 'frequency divided by class width' against class mark. In the case of an open-ended class at either end the class mark is decided by treating the end class as if it had the same class width as its immediate neighbour. The 'polygon' is completed by joining the last point to the horizontal axis at a distance equal to the class width of the end class.

Note that in all cases the points plotted to obtain a frequency polygon are the mid-points of the tops of the blocks of the corresponding histogram.

For a case where all class widths are equal, drawing a frequency polygon amounts to plotting class frequency against class mark for each class and then joining the end points to the axis at one further class width distance. The frequency polygon for the original version of the hardwood data frequency table (Table 7.3) is shown in Fig. 7.6.

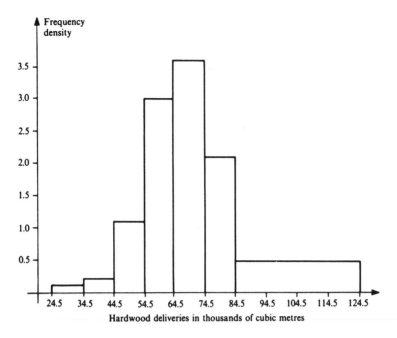

Figure 7.5 A histogram based on a table with unequal class widths.

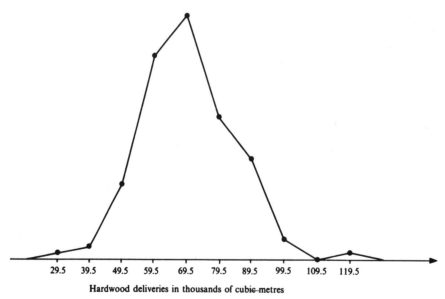

Figure 7.6 A frequency polygon.

Ogives

These diagrams, sometimes called cumulative frequency graphs, are not particularly useful in giving an immediate impression of a set of data but are valuable in further stages of describing the data, as will be seen in Chapter 8.

An ogive is constructed from a cumulative frequency table by plotting the cumulative frequencies against the corresponding class boundaries and joining the resulting points by

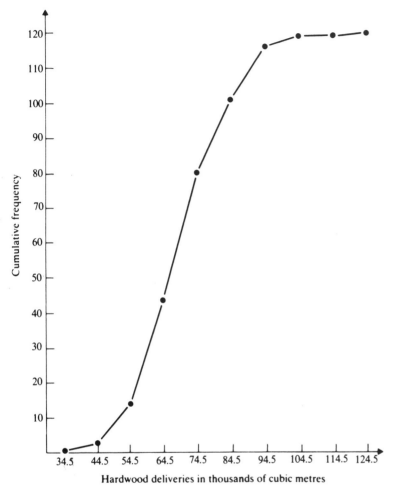

Figure 7.7 An Ogive.

straight lines. Differing class widths have no effect on this diagram. The ogive for the hardwood data cumulative frequency table (Table 7.4) formed in Sec. 7.2 is shown in Fig. 7.7.

Exercise 7.3.1 An incomes survey on a sample of 50 people led to the following table of results for weekly incomes:

Weekly income (£)	Number of people
100 and less than 110	4
110 and less than 120	12
120 and less than 140	14
140 and less than 160	8
160 and less than 190	9
190 and less than 220	3

(a) Draw a histogram from this frequency table.

(b) Draw a frequency polygon from the table.

(c) Form a cumulative frequency table and use it to draw an ogive.

Note In this question the classes have been specified by their class boundaries (see Sec. 7.1) rather than by their class limits. This is another commonly used method for specifying classes in a frequency table, particularly when the variable concerned, like money here, is effectively a continuous variable rather than one restricted to whole number values. Thus, for example, £120 and less than £140 means everything between £120 and £139.99.

7.4 OTHER METHODS OF GRAPHICAL REPRESENTATION

Lorenz curves

The Lorenz curve is a device for demonstrating the evenness or otherwise of the distribution of a property in a sample. We shall explain the construction and interpretation of such a diagram by means of an example.

Example 7.4.1 The table below refers to tax paid by people in various income groups in a sample of 2000. Construct a Lorenz curve from the data and comment upon it.

Annual gross income (£)	Number of people	Total tax paid (£)
Less than 6000	140	60 000
6000 and less than 8000	520	200 000
8000 and less than 10 000	620	660 000
10 000 and less than 14 000	440	700 000
14 000 and less than 20 000	240	740 000
20 000 and less than 32 000	40	680 000

ANSWER The first step is to draw up cumulative frequency tables for the two sets of figures, in this case the number of people and the amount of tax paid. We have

Annual gross income (£)	People	Tax paid (£)
Less than 6000	140	60 000
Less than 8000	660	260 000
Less than 10 000	1280	920 000
Less than 14 000	1720	1 620 000
Less than 20 000	1960	2 360 000
Less than 32 000	2000	3 040 000

The next step is then to convert these into relative cumulative frequency tables by dividing through each column by the column total. For this example we obtain:

Annual gross income (£)	Proportion of people	Proportion of tax
Less than 6000	0.07	0.0197
Less than 8000	0.33	0.0855
Less than 10 000	0.64	0.3026
Less than 14 000	0.86	0.5329
Less than 20 000	0.98	0.7763
Less than 32 000	1.00	1.0000

Finally the Lorenz curve is drawn by plotting these two sets of relative cumulative frequencies against each other and joining the resulting points by a smooth curve. The Lorenz curve for this example is shown as Fig. 7.8.

If all people paid the same amount of tax, then the Lorenz curve would have been a straight line joining the points (0, 0) and (1, 1). Hence this line is called the *line of equal distribution*. The amount by which the plotted Lorenz curve differs from the line of equal distribution is a measure of the amount by which the two distributions differ. Hence the area between the line and the curve is called the area of inequality.

In this example the size of the area reflects the fact that the people with higher incomes pay more tax than those with low incomes. This would obviously be the case even if tax paid were directly proportional to gross income for all people, but the area of inequality is larger than would be the case under that condition because the principle of progressive taxation dictates that those with higher incomes actually pay a higher *proportion* of their incomes in tax.

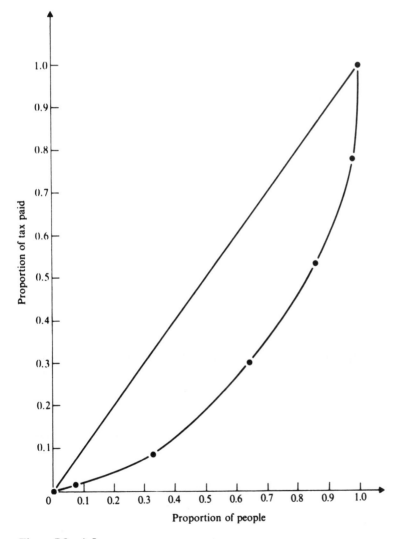

Figure 7.8 A Lorenz curve.

Exercise 7.4.1 The training manager of an accounting firm has introduced a new training programme. The first year the new programme was run was in 1983. The table below gives results for one exam for the years 1983 and 1986.

Marks (%)	Number of students 1983	1986
0 and less than 20	2	0
20 and less than 30	5	5
30 and less than 40	10	10
40 and less than 50	20	20
50 and less than 60	30	45
60 and less than 70	10	30
70+	3	10

Draw a Lorenz curve which compares the results for the two years.

(ACCA Level 1: Dec. 1989)

Time series graphs, semi-log graphs and Z charts

Time series as such will be considered in Chapter 10, but at this point we shall look at what a time series is and at some simple diagrams used to represent this kind of data.

A time series is a set of data values relating to a sequence of points in time. These points are almost always equally spaced, e.g. each month, each quarter, or each year. The great majority of published statistics appear in the form of time series. For instance the Index of Retail Prices is published each month. A time series graph is a graph with time on the horizontal axis and the values of the variable concerned on the vertical axis. Figure 7.9 is an example of a time series graph, obtained by plotting the value of the Index of Retail Prices for each of the 12 months of 1991.

A semi-log graph is a variation on this theme where instead of plotting the values of the variable on the vertical axis we plot the logs of those values. Time is plotted on the horizontal axis just as before. Figure 7.10 shows the 1991 Index of Retail Prices figures plotted on a semi-log graph by looking up their logarithms and plotting these on the vertical axis. This is one possible way of plotting a semi-log graph. Another is to use special semi-log paper which is paper laid out so that distances on the vertical axis are actually the logarithms of the figures printed.

In a semi-log graph equal vertical distances represent equal *proportional* changes. Thus sections of graph having equal slopes represent equal proportional changes in the values of the variable concerned.

Because only proportional changes are of interest, time series measured in different units can be compared on the same semi-log graph. Also semi-log graphs are useful in comparison situations where one of the variables being compared covers a great range of values. In such a case use of an ordinary graph would require using such a small scale on the vertical axis that significant changes in the other variables would be obscured.

A limitation of semi-log graphs is that variables having any zero or negative values cannot be plotted on them.

A Z chart is a device used to compare the progress of a time series during a particular year with the trend of the series over a longer time span. Such a diagram consists of three parts:

1. a simple time series graph for the variable during the year concerned;
2. a cumulative graph of the variable through the year;

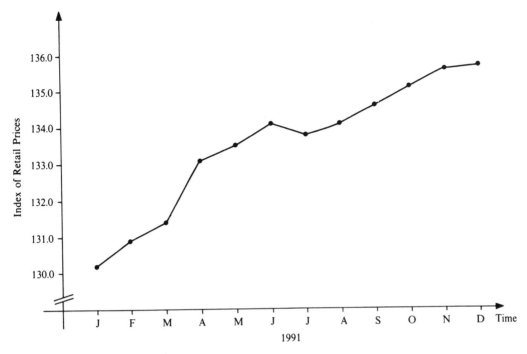

Figure 7.9 A time series graph.

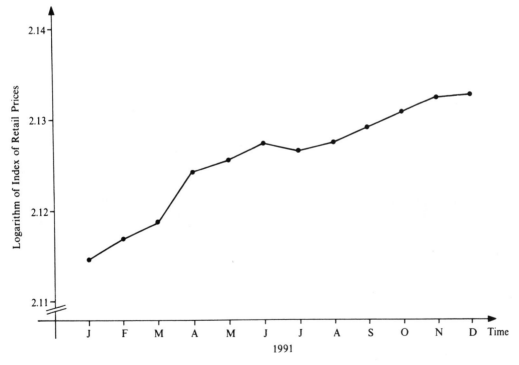

Figure 7.10 A semi-logarithmic graph.

3. a graph showing the sum of the values of the variable for the full year ending in each of the periods of the year.

The name of the diagram arises from the fact that the three parts together form a shape similar to a letter Z.

Example 7.4.2 As a matter of routine a firm collects its monthly sales data. The sales manager displays the data using a Z chart. The following data relates to two years' sales in thousands of pounds.

	1988	1989
Jan.	102	106
Feb.	105	108
March	107	113
April	135	145
May	125	133
June	124	130
July	127	128
Aug.	133	142
Sep.	129	135
Oct.	125	130
Nov.	110	125
Dec.	115	128

Display the sales data as a Z chart.

(ACCA Level 1: June 1990)

ANSWER We shall construct the Z chart for the period January 1989 to December 1989. For this purpose we need a table showing the three sets of figures described in the text above for the three parts of the chart. The table is as follows:

		Data values (a)	Cumulative total (b)	Total for year ending at stated month (c)
1989	Jan.	106	106	1441
	Feb.	108	214	1444
	March	113	327	1450
	April	145	472	1460
	May	133	605	1468
	Jun	130	735	1474
	July	128	863	1475
	Aug.	142	1005	1484
	Sep.	135	1140	1490
	Oct.	130	1270	1495
	Nov.	125	1395	1510
	Dec.	128	1523	1523

The Z chart is as shown in Fig. 7.11.

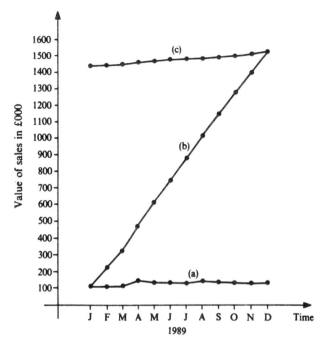

Figure 7.11 A Z chart.

Exercise 7.4.2 UK trade figures (£ hundred million)

	Visible trade items				Invisibles
	Oil (fob)		Non-oil (fob)		
	Exports	Imports	Exports	Imports	Invisible balance
1980	61	58	410	400	14
1981	91	60	416	414	34
1982	107	60	447	474	27
1983	125	55	482	567	53
1984	148	79	554	675	71
1985	161	80	619	731	63
1986	82	41	645	779	93
1987	84	43	710	860	55
1988	60	32	748	984	59
1989	59	44	866	1112	40

(*Source: Economic Trends*, June 1990, Table A5)

(a) Find the balance of trade (visibles) for oil and non-oil (separately), and the balance of payments (visibles and invisibles) for each year from 1980 to 1989, presenting your answers in *one* clear summary table.

(b) Draw a suitable graph to highlight to the layperson the main features of the United Kingdom's trading position shown by the data.

(c) State briefly *four* findings from (a) and (b).

(CIMA Stage 1: May 1991)

The LOTUS 1-2-3 spreadsheet provides good facilities for producing the line graphs considered in this subsection on time series graphs. The numbers to be plotted need to be set out in rows or columns of a spreadsheet, the graphs menu entered and the line graph option chosen. Time should then be selected as the X variable, which goes on the horizontal axis by highlighting in the spreadsheet the row or column of numbers representing the times. Then the times series values, or their logarithms, can be selected as the A values. In the case of a Z chart the cumulative values can be selected as the B values and the year-end totals as the C values. There are good facilities for labelling and giving titles to the graphs. The reader with access to LOTUS 1-2-3 is encouraged to use it to produce the graphs in Example 7.4.2 and Exercise 7.4.2. The reader is referred to the book *Quantitative Analysis for Economics and Business Using LOTUS 1-2-3* by Guy Judge, listed in the bibliography, for examples of graphs of this kind arising in business and economics problems being produced on this spreadsheet.

Bar charts and pie charts

A variety of different diagrams go under the general heading of bar charts. The feature they have in common is that lines, or 'bars', have lengths representing the frequency or other 'value' of some feature. Bar charts are usually employed when the features being considered are of a qualitative nature. For data divided up into quantitative intervals a histogram would be more appropriate.

A pie chart is a circle divided up into sectors having areas representing the frequencies or other values of the features of interest. We shall use the following data to illustrate various different kinds of bar chart and also the pie chart.

Example data Shown below are the numbers of votes obtained and the numbers of seats gained by parties in the general election of 9 April 1992:

Party	Votes recorded	Seats gained
Conservative	14 231 884	336
Labour	11 619 306	271
Liberal Democrat	6 083 661	20
SNP	629 787	3
Plaid Cymru	154 622	4
Others	425 814	17

(*Source: Independent*, 11 April 1992)

One kind of bar chart we could draw to represent the numbers of seats gained is shown in Fig. 7.12.

In this diagram the length of the bar drawn for each group has length proportional to the value of the number of seats gained by the party concerned. The bars could equally well be drawn horizontally.

Another type of bar chart that could be drawn consists of a single bar, either vertical or horizontal, divided into sections whose lengths represent the values of the features being considered. The horizontal version of this kind of bar chart for the numbers of seats would be as shown in Fig. 7.13. This is a *component bar chart*.

Generally speaking, a component bar chart is not so good for representing a single set of data as a bar chart using separate bars. It can be useful when comparing different sets of data, and we shall see this kind of diagram again below.

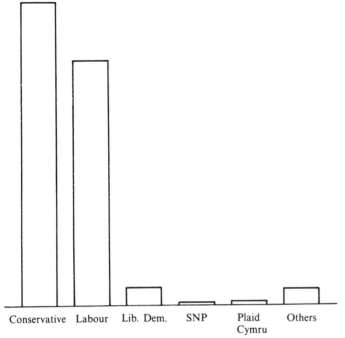

Figure 7.12 A bar chart.

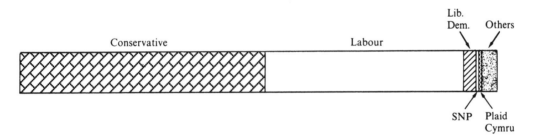

Figure 7.13 A component bar chart.

For a single set of data, use of percentages will not affect the bar chart since the frequencies or values will remain in the same proportions to each other. However, for comparison purposes the use of percentage frequencies or values rather than raw values can be helpful. This is particularly so if the totals of the frequencies or values in the different sets are substantially different, as they are here.

Thus to compare proportions of votes obtained with proportions of seats gained we shall use percentage bar charts.

In order to draw percentage bar charts we need a table showing for each party its number of votes as a percentage of total votes cast and its number of seats as a percentage of total seats.

If using bar charts with separate bars, it would be possible to draw two separated diagrams of the type shown in Fig. 7.12. However, such diagrams are not very easy to compare, and it is better to draw a single bar chart, either vertical or horizontal, with the bars drawn together in pairs. The vertical version of this diagram using the percentage values found above is as shown in Fig. 7.14. This is a *compound bar chart*.

	% of votes	% of seats
Conservative	42.9	51.6
Labour	35.0	41.6
Liberal Democrat	18.4	3.1
SNP	1.9	0.5
Plaid Cymru	0.5	0.6
Others	1.3	2.6
	100	100

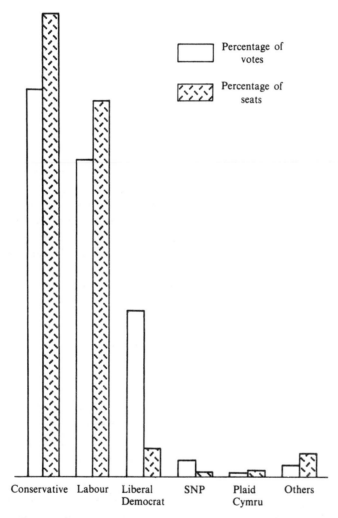

Figure 7.14 A compound bar chart.

Alternatively, we could draw component bar charts with the bars side by side. In the horizontal case this would be as shown in Fig. 7.15.

The usefulness of percentages for comparison purposes is particularly marked when component bar charts are used. Use of raw values would mean two bars of different overall lengths, making the lengths of individual sections difficult to compare. These bar charts highlight the

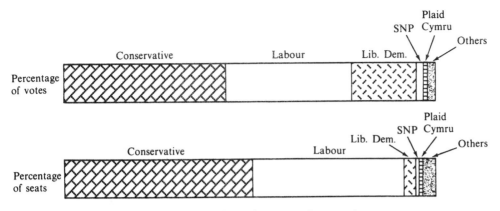

Figure 7.15 Percentage component bar charts for comparing two data sets.

difficulty caused to a small nationally organized party by the 'first past the post' system. The percentage of seats gained by the Liberal Democrats is seen to be significantly smaller than its percentage of votes. Plaid Cymru and the 'others', who are actually the parties holding the seats in Northern Ireland, suffer less because their votes are concentrated in relatively few constituencies.

A pie chart will effectively always be based on percentage values, unless a deliberate effort is made to make the area of the pie represent the total value by using a radius proportional to the square root of that value to draw the circle. The method of construction of a pie chart, having calculated the percentage values, is to divide up the 360 degree angle at the centre of the circle into these percentage parts using a protractor, and then divide up the circle into sectors by drawing lines radiating out from the centre at these angles. The resulting sectors will then have areas representing the percentage values as required.

For this example, using the percentage values found above for votes and seats, we obtain the following:

	Angle at pie chart centre for votes obtained	Angle at pie chart centre for seats gained
Conservative	154	186
Labour	126	150
Liberal Democrat	66	11
SNP	7	2
Plaid Cymru	2	2
Others	5	9

Hence the pie charts are as in Fig. 7.16 where they are shown together for comparison purposes.

Pie charts are very commonly used to display percentage values. Many bar charts and pie charts as well as time series graphs of simple and semi-log types appear in official statistical publications such as *Economic Trends* and *Social Trends*. Local authorities commonly send out with their bills leaflets which show, by means of pie charts, the proportions of council expenditure on various services and charities often use these presentations in their literature to show how they use the donations received.

The drawing of pie charts is a little more difficult than the drawing of bar charts, requiring the use of protractor and compass. However, there are many software packages available,

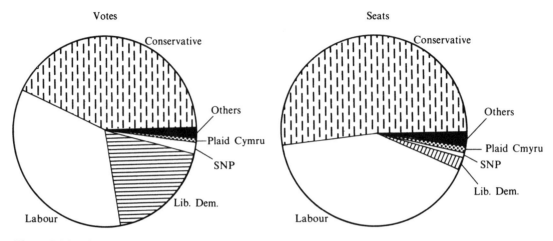

Figure 7.16 Pie charts.

particularly on microcomputers, which produce graphs, bar charts and pie charts as a matter of course. In particular, the LOTUS 1-2-3 spreadsheet has very good facilities for producing bar charts and pie charts. The reader is again referred to the book by Judge (see bibliography) for examples of such diagrams produced using LOTUS 1-2-3.

Exercise 7.4.3 Draw a pair of component bar charts based on the following data taken from *Social Trends* (1990), page 99. It shows percentages of expenditure in various standard categories as found in the 1987 *Family Expenditure Survey* for high and low income families.

Category	High income (%)	Low income (%)
Food	16.4	26.0
Housing	14.7	16.7
Alcoholic drink	4.9	3.6
Tobacco	1.4	4.5
Fuel and light	3.8	12.3
Durable household goods	7.1	5.6
Clothing and footwear	7.6	5.6
Transport and vehicles	16.9	7.0
Miscellaneous goods and services	27.1	18.8

Comment on differences in the expenditure patterns for the two groups.

Pictograms

A pictogram is a form of graphical presentation where repetitions of a picture are used to represent frequencies or other values of a feature. As an example, consider the following data, derived from the 1992 *Annual Abstract of Statistics*, which shows the numbers of people (in thousands) in various spheres of local government employment in Scotland in the third quarter of 1991.

Type of employment	Construction	Housing	Fire service	Health
Thousands employed	13.1	7.3	5.2	2.5

A possible pictogram for this set of data would be as shown in Fig. 7.17.

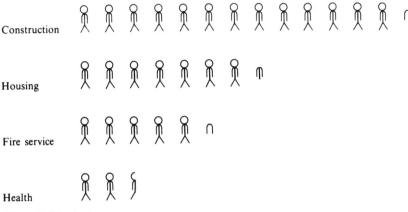

Construction

Housing

Fire service

Health

Figure 7.17 A pictogram.

The pictogram is a fairly commonly used device and gives a good visual impression of a set of data. However, it is not suitable for purposes where full accuracy in representation of the data is necessary.

TEST EXERCISES

7.1 The table shows the salaries (in thousands of pounds) of the employees of a company.

Salary (£'000s)	Number of employees
5 and less than 10	35
10 and less than 15	75
15 and less than 20	96
20 and less than 25	42
25 and less than 35	52

(a) Draw a histogram to represent this set of data.
(b) Draw a frequency polygon for the data.
(c) Form a cumulative frequency table and use it to construct an ogive.

7.2 Draw a pie chart based on the following data taken from *Social Trends* (1990). It shows percentages of household savings held in various ways as found in the *General Household Survey* for 1987.

Form in which savings held	Percentage
Building Society account	53
Interest bearing bank account	22
Post Office savings account	10
Other	15

7.3 (a)   The following table shows the salary, in pounds, of various grades of computing employee in four regions of a country.

Job title	Salary in pounds (£)			
	North	South	East	West
Manager	17 000	18 000	21 000	23 000
Project leader	15 000	19 000	17 000	17 000
Analyst	14 000	14 000	16 000	14 000

Using a suitable form of bar chart display this information graphically.

(b)   A survey produced the following data on the number of terminals on 315 company sites.

Number of terminals	Number of sites
1–4	100
5–10	90
11–20	60
21–50	45
51–100	20
Total	315

Draw a histogram of the above data.

(c)   Explain briefly the difference between a bar chart and a histogram.

(ACCA Level 1: June 1989)

7.4   The number of invoices being processed through a sales ledger, grouped by value, is shown below.

Value of invoice		Number of invoices
(£) At least	(£) Less than	
0	500	20
500	1 000	40
1 000	2 000	80
2 000	4 000	150
4 000	5 000	60
5 000	6 000	30
6 000	7 000	20
7 000 and over		0
Total number		400

Draw a histogram to represent these data.

(CIMA Stage 1: May 1990)

7.5 The senior partner in your firm has asked you to explain the use of Lorenz curves using the following data obtained from the taxation authorities.

Lower level of income before tax (£)	No. of incomes (000s)	Total income before tax (£m)	Total income after tax (£m)
2 000	2 711	11 450	10 850
4 000	4 230	21 050	18 480
6 000	3 550	24 700	20 700
8 000	3 010	27 000	22 200
10 000	6 000	86 000	65 600
20 000	1 285	34 500	25 620
50 000	87	5 650	3 460
100 000	17	2 810	1 430

Answer the following questions for the senior partner using the above data where necessary.

(a) What is a Lorenz curve used for?
(b) How does a Lorenz curve differ from an ogive?
(c) Construct Lorenz curves which compare total income before and after tax.
(d) What is the effect of the taxation policy on the distribution of income?

(ACCA Level 1: Dec. 1991)

8

SUMMARY STATISTICS

8.1 INTRODUCTION

So far in trying to present a set of data in an easy-to-appreciate form we have looked at the grouping of data into frequency tables and at various diagrams. In this chapter we consider the extraction of one or two figures from the body of data in such a way as to obtain a summary of what the data set as a whole is saying.

First we consider extracting one single number to tell us where the 'centre' of the data is. Such a number is referred to as a measure of *central tendency* or of *location* or, more loosely, as an 'average'. (This last is rather a vague term and is best avoided in statistical work.)

Secondly, we consider finding a number to tell us how spread out the data values are. Such a number is called a measure of *variation*. The best known and most commonly used of such measures is the standard deviation. We consider this along with the mean deviation, the coefficient of variation, the range and the quartile deviation.

There are three main measures of central tendency, called the *mean*, the *median*, and the *mode*, and we shall consider each of these in turn first in connection with sets of numbers (ungrouped data) and then in connection with data in frequency table form (grouped data).

8.2 THE MEAN

The full title of this measure of central tendency is the 'arithmetic mean'. This distinguishes it from other, seldom used, measures called the geometric mean and the harmonic mean. However, it can be referred to unambiguously as the mean.

(a) Ungrouped data

To find the mean of a set of numbers we add them all together and divide by the number of items concerned. For example, the mean of the numbers 3, 5, 2, 9, and 11 is

$$\frac{3+5+2+9+11}{5} = \frac{30}{5} = 6$$

To get a feel for what this means imagine five people having in their pockets £3, £5, £2, £9, and £11, respectively. If they put this money into a pool and each took out an equal share they would receive £6 each as the total pool of £30 would be shared between the five of them.

When the word 'average' is used in any publication or media announcement it can be assumed that the mean is intended. Before leaving the mean for ungrouped data it is necessary to learn the mathematical shorthand connected with it. What we have to do is

1. add all the numbers together;
2. divide by the number of items.

In the above example we had five numbers 3, 5, 2, 9, 11. Suppose more generally we had n numbers $x_1, x_2, x_3, \ldots, x_n$. The shorthand for 'add all the x-values together' is Σx (read as sigma x). For example,

$$x_1 = 1, x_2 = 3, x_3 = 7, x_4 = 4, x_5 = 1, x_6 = 8$$
$$\Sigma x = 1 + 3 + 7 + 4 + 1 + 8 = 24$$

Having added all the x-values together we must divide the sum by the number of items in order to obtain the mean, $24/6 = 4$.

The symbol $\bar{x}$ (read x bar) is commonly used to represent the mean. So the mathematical shorthand for the statement above defining the mean of ungrouped data is

$$\bar{x} = \frac{\Sigma x}{n}$$

Exercise 8.2.1 Find the mean of the numbers 4, 2, 8, 7, 4, 5.

(b) Grouped data

The mean of a set of data in the form of a grouped frequency table is in principle found by approximating all the items in a class by the class mark of that class and then finding the mean as for ungrouped data.

Consider the set of data shown in Table 8.1 which relates to the values of 40 invoices issued by a firm on a particular day. We shall be returning to this set of data throughout the chapter to illustrate various summary statistics.

Table 8.1

Invoice value (£)	Frequency, f ($=$ number of invoices)
2 and under 6	1
6 and under 10	6
10 and under 14	6
14 and under 18	10
18 and under 22	8
22 and under 30	9

In order to find the mean, all items in the first class are approximated by the class mark 4, all those in the second class by 8, and so on.

Thus the mean is found by adding one 4, six 8s, etc. and dividing the sum by the total number of invoices, which is $1 + 6 + 6 + 10 + 8 + 9 = 40$.

So the mean is

$$\frac{1\times4+6\times8+6\times12+10\times16+8\times20+9\times26}{1+6+6+10+8+9}=\frac{678}{40}=16.95$$

The mean invoice value is £16.95.

More generally, if the class marks for a grouped frequency table are denoted by x and the frequencies by f, then the mean is calculated as

$$\bar{x}=\frac{\Sigma xf}{\Sigma f}$$

It is common practice to set out the calculation in the form of a table. Thus for the example here we would have Table 8.2.

Table 8.2

Invoice value (£)	Class mark (x)	Frequency (f)	xf
2 and under 6	4	1	4
6 and under 10	8	6	48
10 and under 14	12	6	72
14 and under 18	16	10	160
18 and under 22	20	8	160
22 and under 30	26	9	234
		40	678

Then $\bar{x}=\Sigma xf/\Sigma f=678/40=16.95$

Exercise 8.2.2 The senior partner in your firm has been looking at the market for training courses and has obtained the following data on the cost of one-day courses.

Cost of course (£)	Number of courses
25 and less than 75	2
75 and less than 125	2
125 and less than 175	28
175 and less than 225	19
225 and less than 275	17
275 and less than 325	18
325 and less than 425	7
425 +	7

Find the mean cost of the courses.

(ACCA Level 1: Dec. 1990)

(Note that the open ended final class would normally be treated as if it had the same class width as its neighbour, i.e. £100.)

8.3 THE MEDIAN

(a) Ungrouped data

To find the median of a set of numbers we arrange them in ascending order of size and pick out the one in the middle. The value of this middle number is the median of the set.

For example, 4, 9, 1, 6, 7 have median 6 because arranged in order they are 1, 4, 6, 7, 9 and 6 is the one in the middle.

As a further example consider 1, 3, 4, 7, 7, 8, 8, 10, 11. These have median 7 because they are already in ascending order and the one in the middle is 7. It does not matter that there is another 7 in the set as well.

Both the above examples have involved odd numbers of items. If the number of items is even, the definition given at the beginning has to be slightly modified. In this situation we again arrange the values in ascending order, we pick out the *two* in the middle and the median is then found as the mean of these two.

For example, 9, 7, 5, 2, 12, 14 have median 8 because these in ascending order are 2, 5, 7, 9, 12, 14; the two in the middle are 7 and 9: these have mean 8.

As a further example consider 3, 4, 7, 7, 8, 10, 11, 12. These have median 7.5 because the two in the middle are 7 and 8 and these two numbers have mean 7.5.

In all the examples so far the number of items has been small enough for the data set to be arranged in order either mentally or on paper.

Suppose now, however, that the median of a relatively large data set is required. Procedures for finding such a median are demonstrated using the following example:

83	80	91	81	88	82	87	97	83	99
75	85	72	92	84	90	87	78	93	98
86	80	93	86	88	83	82	101	89	82
85	95	80	89	84	92	76	81	103	94

If computing facilities are not available we can do the following. First strike out the largest number in the set (i.e. 103); then strike out the smallest number in the set (i.e. 72); next strike out the second largest number in the set (i.e. 101); next strike out the second smallest number in the set (i.e. 75). Continue in this way, striking out alternately the largest remaining value and the smallest remaining value until only one number (or two numbers if the total number of items is even) is left. This gives the median.

For the example above the last two figures left when we carry out this procedure are both 86. So the median of the set of 40 numbers is $(86+86)/2=86$.

If, however, a computer package such as MINITAB is available, there are much simpler ways of proceeding. One way, having set the data into column C1 in MINITAB, would be to arrange the values in order in another column using a command such as

ORDER C1 C2

and then PRINT C2 and pick out the 20th and 21st values.

Another way would be to obtain a stem and leaf plot of C1, as described in Chapter 7, and then pick out the two middle values.

Most directly of all, we could give the command

MEDIAN C1

and have the median displayed instantly.

Exercise 8.3.1. Find the median of the following set of numbers:

8	35	45	50	60	68	13	37	46	52	61	70
26	40	47	55	65	71	29	41	48	58	67	75	33

(b) Grouped data

As in the case of ungrouped data, the median is the value in the middle. So we have to look for the number such that half the items are below it and half above.

Thus for finding the median of a set of grouped data it is necessary to use a cumulative frequency table or the corresponding ogive. We shall consider first finding the median from an ogive and then see how this method extends to calculation of the median from a cumulative frequency table.

Consider again the data shown in Table 8.1 relating to the values of 40 invoices issued by a firm on a particular day. The first step is to form a cumulative frequency table (Table 8.3).

Table 8.3

Range of invoice values (£)	Number of invoices, $F(=$ cum. freq.)
Under 6	1
Under 10	7
Under 14	13
Under 18	23
Under 22	31
Under 30	40

From this table we can draw an ogive as shown in Fig. 8.1.

The total frequency is 40 and to obtain the median we divide this by 2, giving 20. We then draw a line at the 40 level on the cumulative frequency axis as far as the ogive. By dropping from the ogive to the horizontal axis we obtain the median. The diagram illustrates this method

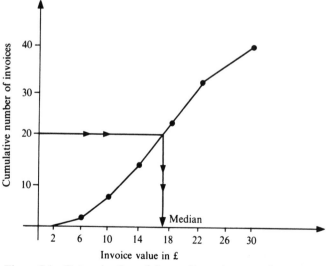

Figure 8.1 Determination of the median using an ogive.

for obtaining the median, but if it is to be used in practice the ogive needs to be drawn to a large scale on graph paper in order to obtain reasonable accuracy.

To see how a median for grouped data can be *calculated*, consider again Fig. 8.1. Since the half-way frequency of 20 is between the frequencies 13 and 23 in the cumulative table, the median must lie between the class boundaries 14 and 18 which correspond to those two cumulative frequencies. The class '14 and under 18' is called the *median class*. How far into this class we need to go to reach the median is found as that proportion of the class width equal to the proportion of the class frequency that 20 is above 13.

Thus we calculate

$$\text{median} = £14 + \frac{(20-13)}{10} \times £4$$

which leads to a value of £14 + £2.80.

That is to say, the median invoice value is £16.80.

Exercise 8.3.2 For the set of data given in Exercise 8.2.2 find the median of the costs of the training courses considered by the senior partner. Obtain your answer:

(a) by drawing the ogive and carrying out the appropriate construction;
(b) by calculation.

8.4 THE MODE

(a) Ungrouped data

The mode of a set of numbers is that number which occurs more often in the set than any other.

Suppose Diane has 2 children, Hilary has 3, Janice has 2, Gillian has 4, Brenda has 2, and Linda has 1. The most commonly occurring value is 2 so this is the modal number of children.

Exercise 8.4.1 What is the mode of the following set of numbers?

$$10, \quad 19, \quad 14, \quad 27, \quad 16, \quad 19, \quad 14, \quad 19$$

(b) Grouped data

The mode of a set of grouped data can be found either graphically or by calculation. The first step in both cases is to find the *modal class*.

For data where all classes have the same class width this is the class with the largest frequency, while if class widths differ we need the class for which

$$\text{frequency density} = \text{frequency/class width}$$

is largest.

Consider again the data on invoice values used in Secs. 8.2 and 8.3.

From Table 8.1 we can obtain Table 8.4 for the purpose of drawing the histogram. The frequency density figure for each class has been obtained by dividing its frequency by its class width.

Table 8.4

Invoice value (£)	Frequency, f	Frequency density
2 and under 6	1	0.250
6 and under 10	6	1.500
10 and under 14	6	1.500
14 and under 18	10	2.500
18 and under 22	8	2.000
22 and under 30	9	1.125

The graphical method involves drawing a histogram and making the construction shown in Fig. 8.2 on the block corresponding to the modal class. (From the definition given above of the modal class we see that it will *always* correspond to the *tallest* block of the histogram.)

If this method is used in practice to find the mode, the histogram must be drawn accurately on graph paper. The construction can be expressed by means of a formula as follows:
Let

L be the lower class boundary of the modal class
U be the upper class boundary of the modal class
H_m be the height of the tallest histogram block
H_{m-} be the height of the block before the tallest one
H_{m+} be the height of the block following the tallest one

Then the mode is given by the formula:

$$\text{Mode} = L + \frac{H_m - H_{m-}}{(H_m - H_{m-}) + (H_m - H_{m+})} \times (U - L)$$

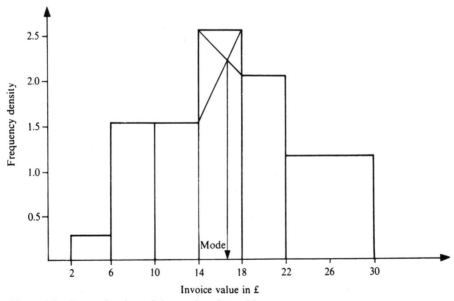

Figure 8.2 Determination of the mode using a histogram.

For the invoice values we have $L=14$, $U=18$, $H_{m-}=6$, $H_m=10$, and $H_{m+}=8$. So the formula tells us that the modal invoice value was:

$$14+\frac{10-6}{(10-6)+(10-8)}\times(18-14)$$

$$=14+[4\times4]/[4+2]=14+16/6=14+2.67=16.67.$$

In this case where the neighbour on the left of the modal class is taller than the one on the right the mode is smaller than the class mark of the modal class, while in cases where the neighbour on the right is taller the mode will be larger than the class mark of the modal class.

Exercise 8.4.2 For the set of data given in Exercise 8.2.2 find the mode of the costs of the training courses considered by the senior partner. Obtain your answer:

(a) by drawing the histogram and carrying out the appropriate construction;
(b) by calculation.

8.5 COMPARISON OF THE MEASURES OF LOCATION

The chief merit of the mean is that it has a body of mathematical theory behind it which makes it more useful in further statistical work than the median or the mode. (We shall look at this use of the mean in Chapters 15 and 16.) Also the mean makes arithmetical use of every item in the data set.

For some sets of data the mean is a value not very close to the centre of the main body of the data. Thus it is not a plausible measure of central tendency in such circumstances. It can happen when there are just a few values a long way from the rest. All values are included in the calculation of the mean and the mean can therefore be drawn towards a few 'freak' values.

Consider the following set of values, which may be the weekly wages (in £'s) of six workers in the maintenance department of a small company:

$$90, \quad 92, \quad 94, \quad 95, \quad 99, \quad 130$$

The mean is 100, but it is an unsatisfactory measure of central tendency because five of the values are less than it. Extreme values are not uncommon in economic data, and so the median is often a more suitable measure for such data than is the mean. The median is not affected by freak values in the data because its value is determined by the middle items only. A further advantage of the median is that it requires, for ungrouped data, no calculation beyond (possibly) finding the mean of two numbers. The great disadvantage of the median is that the mathematical theory concerning it is of a quite sophisticated nature and it cannot be as readily used in further statistical work as can the mean.

The mode has intuitive appeal as a measure of central tendency in that it is the most typical value in a set. The value it takes will, for ungrouped data, be one which actually occurs in the set and will be plausible as the centre of the data. Also the mode for ungrouped data requires no calculation.

A further merit of the mode is that it can be be used for data which is not even numerical. We considered earlier an example involving the numbers of children that Diane, Hilary, Brenda, Linda, Gillian, and Janice had. We might equally well have sought the mode for some other feature of these people, such as the colour of their hair. Suppose Hilary, Brenda, and Linda have blonde hair while Diane and Gillian have dark brown hair, and Janice has ginger hair. We could say that the modal hair colour is blonde. It would make no sense to talk about a mean colour or a median colour. In some situations where numbers are used they are little more than descriptions and the mode would, therefore, again be the most appropriate summary measure. An example of such a situation would be in respect of shoe sizes.

To see the greatest problem involved with the mode for ungrouped data, suppose we had to find the mode of the numbers

$$5, \quad 8, \quad 7, \quad 14, \quad 8, \quad 7, \quad 3$$

Both 7 and 8 have a claim to be the mode since they each occur twice and no other number occurs more than once. This data is *bimodal*. More generally, there could be several modes, and the data would then be described as *multimodal*.

With grouped data it is not so likely that two histogram blocks will be equally the tallest, so making it impossible to identify a single mode. What may happen, however, is that the tallest block and another block could be of quite similar heights, making the choice of the tallest—which gives the modal class—a fairly close one. Just a few extra items in another class could have meant a substantially different mode being found, suggesting some instability in this measure. The mode shares with the median the disadvantage of lacking straightforward mathematical properties.

Exercise 8.5.1 An incomes survey on a sample of 50 people led to the following table of results for weekly incomes.

Weekly income (£)	Number of people
100 and less than 110	4
110 and less than 120	12
120 and less than 140	14
140 and less than 160	8
160 and less than 190	9
190 and less than 220	3

(a) Find the mean, the median, and the mode.
(b) Compare the mean, the median, and the mode in terms of their usefulness as measures of location for this set of data.
  (Note, and be sure you are clear why, that the modal class for this set of data is the class '£110 and less than £120'.)

8.6 DISPERSION MEASURES BASED ON THE MEAN

In this section we consider measures of dispersion or spread in a set of data which is based on the deviations of individual data values from the mean. We shall consider first ungrouped data and then grouped data.

(a) Ungrouped data

If we have n numbers $x_1, x_2, x_3, \ldots, x_n$ with mean $\bar{x}$ then we are concerned with the differences

$$x_1 - \bar{x}, x_2 - \bar{x}, x_3 - \bar{x}, \ldots, x_n - \bar{x}$$

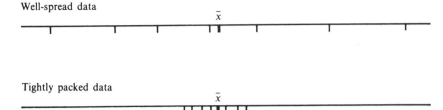

Figure 8.3   Deviations of individual values from the mean in different data sets.

If the data values are tightly packed, all these differences will be small, while if the data values are well spread some of the differences will be large. The two cases are represented in Fig. 8.3.

Thus it would seem sensible to use the 'average' of these differences in some sense as a measure of dispersion. It is no use just taking the mean of the differences because for *any* set of data the positive and negative differences will cancel out, giving result zero.

One way to proceed is just to ignore all negative signs among the deviations and find the mean 'absolute' value. The absolute value of an item is indicated by enclosing it between two vertical lines. So the *mean deviation* is

$$MD = \frac{|x_1 - \bar{x}| + |x_2 - \bar{x}| + |x_3 - \bar{x}| + \cdots + |x_n - \bar{x}|}{n}$$

Using the sigma notation we have

$$MD = \frac{\Sigma |x - \bar{x}|}{n}$$

Example 8.6.1   Find the mean deviation of 3, 5, 2, 9, 11.

ANSWER   The mean is $\bar{x} = 6$ so the differences are

$$3-6, \ 5-6, \ 2-6, \ 9-6, \ 11-6$$

i.e.

$$-3, \ -1, \ -4, \ 3, \ 5$$

(Note in passing that the sum of these values is indeed zero.) Hence the absolute differences are

$$|3-6| = 3, \ |5-6| = 1, \ |2-6| = 4, \ |9-6| = 3, \ |11-6| = 5$$

So the mean deviation is

$$MD = \frac{3+1+4+3+5}{5} = \frac{16}{5} = 3.2$$

Exercise 8.6.1   Find the mean deviation of 4, 2, 8, 7, 4, 5.

The mean deviation is a relatively easy measure to calculate. Like the mean itself, its calculation is based on every value in the data, which in some ways is good, but it does make the measure subject to distortion by freak extreme values. However, the main problem, which makes the mean deviation less popular than it would otherwise be, is that the absolute value function is quite a difficult one to handle mathematically and so there is a lack of simple ways of using it in more advanced statistical work.

In order to obtain a measure which is more immediately useful in this way the deviations of the individual data values from the mean are usually averaged in a way which is arithmetically less easy than the mean deviation method but is mathematically much more amenable.

This leads us to the *standard deviation*. To obtain this measure the deviations of the individual data values from the mean $\bar{x}$ are averaged in the following way:

1. Square all the differences. This removes all minus signs. We have

$$(x_1-\bar{x})^2, (x_2-\bar{x})^2, (x_3-\bar{x})^2, ..., (x_n-\bar{x})^2$$

2. Find the mean of the squared differences. This is

$$\frac{(x_1-\bar{x})^2+(x_2-\bar{x})^2+(x_3-\bar{x})^2+\cdots+(x_n-\bar{x})^2}{n}$$

This is itself a measure of dispersion and is called the *variance*. A problem with the variance is that its units are the square of the units of the data.

3. Take the square root of the result of step 2. This gives the standard deviation

$$s=\sqrt{\frac{(x_1-\bar{x})^2+(x_2-\bar{x})^2+(x_3-\bar{x})^2+\cdots+(x_n-\bar{x})^2}{n}}$$

which has the same units as the original data values.

Using the sigma notation we have:

$$s=\sqrt{\frac{\Sigma(x-\bar{x})^2}{n}}$$

Example 8.6.2 Find the standard deviation of 3, 5, 2, 9, and 11.

ANSWER The mean of these numbers is 6 so the differences from the mean are: $-3, -1, -4, 3, 5$. Hence we see that

$$s=\sqrt{\frac{(-3)^2+(-1)^2+(-4)^2+3^2+5^2}{5}}=\sqrt{\frac{9+1+16+9+25}{5}}$$

$$=\sqrt{(60/5)}=\sqrt{12}=3.46.$$

Exercise 8.6.2 Find the standard deviation of 4, 2, 8, 7, 4, and 5.

For calculation purposes the above formula for s is not very good because it involves working out all the individual differences from the mean. Hence it is more usual to employ the following formula, obtained by simple algebra from the formula above.

$$s=\sqrt{(\Sigma x^2/n)-(\Sigma x/n)^2}$$

Example 8.6.3 Use the calculation formula to find the standard deviation of 3, 5, 2, 9, and 11.

ANSWER $n=5$, $\Sigma x=3+5+2+9+11=30$

$$\Sigma x^2=9+25+4+81+121=240$$

Hence

$$s=\sqrt{(240/5)-(30/5)^2}=\sqrt{48-36}=\sqrt{12}=3.46.$$

Exercise 8.6.3 Use the calculation formula to find the standard deviation of 4, 2, 8, 7, 4, and 5.

The standard deviation is in practice a very important measure of dispersion because of its mathematical properties, which allow valuable results to be readily deduced. The mean and standard deviation together provide a powerful summary of a set of data. However, freak extreme values will distort the standard deviation as well as the mean.

There is an important result due to Chebyshev which says that for *any* set of data, the proportion of values lying within k standard deviations of the mean is at least $1 - (1/k)^2$. Hence, for example, at least 75 per cent of all values lie within two standard deviations of the mean. This is a conservative result and usually the proportions will in fact be higher. A commonly used rule of thumb is that almost all values in a data set can be reckoned likely to lie within three standard deviations either side of the mean (i.e. within a total range of six standard deviations.) The Chebyshev result says that at least 89 per cent will lie in this range.

For data conforming to a normal distribution (see Chapter 14) we shall see the use of the mean and standard deviation in calculating confidence intervals and performing significance tests in Chapters 15 and 16, respectively.

Another measure of dispersion related to the mean is the *coefficient of variation*. This does not directly measure dispersion like the mean deviation and the standard deviation, but is a measure of relative variation, i.e. it measures the dispersion relative to the actual size of the data values concerned. The coefficient of variation is based on the mean and standard deviation and is calculated as

$$CV = (s/\bar{x}) \times 100$$

It is the standard deviation as a percentage of the mean. There are two kinds of situation where this is a useful thing to calculate.

First, it is useful if we have two data sets where the figures are of differing overall size and we want to say which is the 'more variable'. For instance, a standard deviation of £5 per week on a mean weekly income of £150 would be fairly unimportant, whereas a standard deviation of £5 per week on a mean weekly income of £20 would be a serious variation.

Second, if we want to compare the variations in data sets measured in different units, the coefficient of variation is independent of units since mean and standard deviation are in the same units, which therefore cancel out when we calculate the percentage.

Suppose, for example, we wanted to compare the day-to-day variabilities in mileage and petrol consumption for a travelling sales person. If the mileages per day had a mean of 200 miles with a standard deviation of 15 miles, while the petrol consumption had a daily mean of 25 litres with a standard deviation of 3 litres, the standard deviations would not be directly comparable. However, the respective coefficients of variation of 7.5 per cent and 12 per cent are comparable and indicate a greater variability in petrol consumption than in mileage.

(b) Grouped data

The mean deviation and the standard deviation for grouped data are defined by extension of the ungrouped definitions in the same way as we have seen the grouped mean defined by extension of the ungrouped mean. That is to say, we behave as if every member of a class were equal to the class mark of that class and then proceed as for the ungrouped case. Consider again the data on invoice values (Table 8.1). The mean invoice value was seen in Sec. 8.2 to be £16.95. The mean deviation and standard deviation calculations are based on regarding Table 8.1 as meaning that we have one invoice value of £4, six invoice values of £8, six invoice values of £12, etc. Thus we emerge with formulae

$$MD = \frac{\Sigma |x - \bar{x}| f}{\Sigma f} \text{ and } s = \sqrt{\frac{\Sigma (x - \bar{x})^2 f}{\Sigma f}}$$

by the same process as we saw the grouped mean formula emerge in Sec. 8.2.

It is again usual to set out the calculation in tabular form. For the mean deviation we have Table 8.5.

Table 8.5

Invoice values (£)		x	$|x - \bar{x}|$	f	$|x - \bar{x}| f$
2 and under 6		4	12.95	1	12.95
6 and under 10		8	8.95	6	53.70
10 and under 14		12	4.95	6	29.70
14 and under 18		16	0.95	10	9.50
18 and under 22		20	3.05	8	24.40
22 and under 30		26	9..05	9	81.45
Total				40	211.70

Thus the mean deviation is 211.70/40 = £5.29.

A very similar table could be used to find the standard deviation, the only difference being that the $|x - \bar{x}|$ figures would have to be replaced by their squares and the final ratio needs to be square rooted.

However, it is more usual to calculate a grouped standard deviation by using an extension of the ungrouped standard deviation formula, which comes out as:

$$s = \sqrt{(\Sigma x^2 f / \Sigma f) - (\Sigma x f / \Sigma f)^2}$$

Setting this out in the form of a table, we obtain Table 8.6 for the invoice values data.

Table 8.6

Invoice values (£)	x	x^2	f	xf	$x^2 f$
2 and under 6	4	16	1	4	64
6 and under 10	8	64	6	48	384
10 and under 14	12	144	6	72	864
14 and under 18	16	256	10	160	2 560
18 and under 22	20	400	8	160	3 200
22 and under 30	26	676	9	234	6 084
Total			40	678	13 156

$$s = \sqrt{(13\,156/40) - (678/40)^2} = \sqrt{328.9 - 287.3025}$$
$$= \sqrt{41.5975} = £6.45$$

Note that this form of the table does not require advance knowledge of the mean and can be used to find the mean and standard deviation in the same operation. Note also that the column of x^2 values could be omitted as the $x^2 f$ values can be obtained by multiplying together the figures in the x column and the xf column.

Exercise 8.6.4 The senior partner in your firm has been looking at the market for training courses and has obtained the following data on the cost of one-day courses.

Cost of course (£)	Number of courses
25 and less than 75	2
75 and less than 125	2
125 and less than 175	28
175 and less than 225	19
225 and less than 275	17
275 and less than 325	18
325 and less than 425	7
425+	7

Find the variance and standard deviation of the cost of the courses.

(ACCA Level 1: Dec. 1990)

8.7 OTHER DISPERSION MEASURES

(a) The range

The simplest possible measure of dispersion in a set of data is the *range*. This is calculated as the difference between the largest value and the smallest value in the set. The calculation is easy but this measure is very susceptible to extreme values in the data. It is hardly applicable at all to grouped data since its value would depend more on how the classes were defined than on the data itself. Also for ungrouped data it is not usually of any value in more advanced analysis of the data.

An important exception to this last point is in small sample quality control. Here use is made of small random samples of constant size (typically four or five items) which are drawn from a population and have some dimension measured. The ranges in values of the dimension in the samples can be used in drawing control charts, since for samples of this size the range is related in a simple way to the sample standard deviation. See Chapter 18 for discussion of control charts.

(b) The quartile deviation

Because of the sensitivity of the range to extreme values or definition of classes, a variation on the idea which is generally more useful is the *semi-interquartile range* or *quartile deviation*. To obtain this measure the smallest quarter and the largest quarter of the data values are removed from consideration and the range of the remainder considered. It is closely related to the median in that as the median is the figure which has half the data values below it and half above, so the quartiles are the quarter points of the data. The first quartile, denoted $Q1$, has 25 per cent of the data below it and 75 per cent above, and the third quartile, denoted $Q3$, has 75 per cent below it and 25 per cent above.

Having found $Q1$ and $Q3$, the quartile deviation is calculated as

$$QD = \frac{Q3 - Q1}{2}$$

For ungrouped data, $Q1$ and $Q3$ can be found by the same methods, manual and computerized, as those described for finding the median in Sec. 8.3 above.

However, the quartile deviation is more usually employed for grouped data, where the quartiles are again found just as the median was in Sec. 8.3. That is to say, by drawing lines at the 25 per cent and 75 per cent cumulative frequency levels to the ogive and dropping to the horizontal axis, or by means of equivalent calculations. (Note also in passing that these methods could be used to find any other *percentiles*, corresponding to general percentage levels, or *deciles*, corresponding to levels which are multiples of 10 per cent.)

Consider again the data on invoice values which we have been using throughout the chapter. The cumulative frequency table for this set of data was seen as Table 8.3 and the ogive drawn from this table was Fig. 8.1. The ogive is shown again here as Fig. 8.4 and the constructions needed for $Q1$ and $Q3$ are indicated.

The total frequency is 40 and to obtain $Q1$ we divide this by 4, giving 10. We then draw a line at the 10 level on the cumulative frequency axis as far as the ogive. By dropping from the ogive to the horizontal axis we obtain $Q1$.

Similarly, 75 per cent of 40 is 30 so we obtain $Q3$ by drawing a line across at the 30 level on the cumulative frequency axis and dropping to the horizontal axis.

To *calculate* $Q1$ we note that 10 is between 7 and 13 and hence the value of $Q1$ is between 10 and 14. By the same reasoning as was used to calculate the median in Sec. 8.3 we see that

$$Q1 = 10 + \frac{(10-7)}{6} \times 4$$

Hence $Q1 = 10 + 12/6 = 10 + 2 = 12$.
Similarly,

$$Q3 = 18 + \frac{(30-23)}{8} \times 4$$

Hence $Q3 = 18 + 28/8 = 18 + 3.5 = 21.50$.

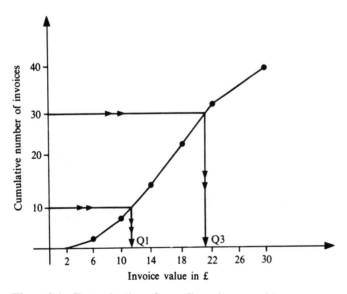

Figure 8.4 Determination of quartiles using an ogive.

So the quartile deviation is

$$QD = \frac{Q3 - Q1}{2} = \frac{21.50 - 12}{2} = \frac{9.5}{2} = 4.75$$

Thus the dispersion in values from one invoice to another, as measured by the quartile deviation, is £4.75.

The quartile deviation, like the mean deviation and the range, cannot be readily used in more advanced statistical analyses.

Exercise 8.7.1 As part of the investigation into the market for fast personal computer systems the information technology director has found the following data on the price of machines. The data collectors had already processed the data into groups.

Price (£) greater than or equal to	less than	frequency
500	1000	4
1000	1500	6
1500	2000	8
2000	2500	13
2500	3000	4
3000	3500	6
3500	4500	4
4500	5500	5

(a) Draw a histogram of the data.
(b) Calculate the mean and standard deviation of the data to three significant figures.
(c) Draw a percentage less than ogive of the data.
(d) What is the median and semi-interquartile range of the data to three significant figures?
(e) How would it be more satisfactory if data was collected by the organization and then classified into groups? What are the two statistical terms which describe the different data sets?

(ACCA Level 1: June 1991)

8.8 A NOTE ON CALCULATORS AND COMPUTERS

It is common for modern electronic calculators to include a facility for automatic calculation of the mean and standard deviation of a set of numbers as well as for finding the sum and sum of squares of the numbers. Hence it is unlikely that, other than possibly for the purpose of answering examination questions, the reader will ever really *need* to carry out such calculations manually. It is nevertheless useful to understand how these formulae arise in order to appreciate the meaning of what the calculator produces.

It is less usual (though no longer so very uncommon) for calculators to include automatic calculation of mean and standard deviation for grouped data. However, the ungrouped data facility could be used for this purpose by inputting the class marks of the classes a number of times equal to their frequencies in the table. Calculators have also made much easier the process of finding the mean and standard deviation using the tabulation approach described above, and eliminated for all practical purposes the need for 'tricks' to ease the arithmetical labour. Computer packages also can very readily produce, even for large data sets, the sort of summary statistics described in this chapter. These are all based on the idea of an ungrouped set of numbers and there is even a school of thought which suggests that because of this widely available facility consideration of grouped data calculations is no longer necessary at all. However, data from published sources is often in grouped form and knowledge of how to handle grouped data would therefore still seem to be relevant.

To illustrate the sort of thing that a statistical computer package can do in this area we consider some commands available in the MINITAB package applied to the following set of 120 numbers.

84	71	74	70	42	46	83	61	57	76
71	72	91	60	55	51	74	75	79	56
64	65	40	89	57	67	71	61	66	61
73	77	94	73	58	63	69	63	69	84
54	73	96	77	53	62	82	88	69	69
80	79	79	85	60	47	77	63	70	68
53	68	115	69	57	85	90	78	71	76
76	47	73	52	55	54	67	85	86	59
64	97	86	60	72	57	88	61	59	80
73	70	64	26	89	70	91	80	83	72
61	89	84	54	61	71	92	70	65	80
62	62	72	51	68	67	97	56	56	74

With this data set held in column C1 use of the command

DESCRIBE C1

results in the output shown in Fig. 8.5.

This shows most of the statistics we have seen in this chapter. The statistic TMEAN is referred to in the MINITAB manual as the 'trimmed mean', calculated after removing the largest and smallest 5 per cent of the data values. This removes any possible effect of freak extremes and therefore gives a more helpful descriptive measure but one without the desirable mathematical properties of the ordinary mean.

Another MINITAB command worth considering at this point is

BOXPLOT C1

which results in the output shown in Fig. 8.6.

This is called a 'box-and-whisker' plot. It is based on a five-figure summary of the data consisting of the median, the first and third quartiles, the minimum value and the maximum value. The ends of the box (letters I) show the first and third quartiles and the +sign inside the box is the median. [There is also a scale showing the interval represented by each tick (−sign)

```
MTB > DESCRIBE C1

                 C1
N               120
MEAN           69.9
MEDIAN         70.0
TMEAN          69.9
STDEV          13.8
SEMEAN          1.3
MAX           115.0
MIN            26.0
Q3             79.0
Q1             61.0
```

Figure 8.5 Output produced by the DESCRIBE comands in MINITAB.

MTB > BOXPLOT C1

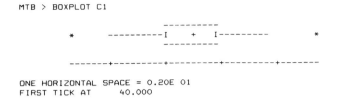

```
ONE HORIZONTAL SPACE = 0.20E 01
FIRST TICK AT     40.000
```

Figure 8.6 A box and whisker plot produced by MINITAB.

and a statement of the value where the first tick appears.] This diagram shows very clearly the lengths of the four quarters of the data and hence permits an appreciation of the extent of its *skewness* (see Sec. 7.3). In this case the +sign being near the centre of the box and the whiskers being of similar length indicate fairly symmetrical data.

If the +sign were towards the left of the box and/or the right-hand whisker were longer than the left-hand one, this would indicate positively skewed data. We could in such a case transform the data by a device such as taking the log or square root of all the values and then replot the diagram to see if the new distribution were more symmetrical. This is a useful thing to do because symmetrical data sets are more readily dealt with by routine statistical analyses than are skewed ones. Different sets of data can be readily compared by printing several box-and-whisker plots one underneath the other.

Grouped data calculations for mean, mean deviation, and standard deviation as given in Tables 8.2, 8.5, and 8.6, respectively, can also be conveniently set out using the columns of a spreadsheet such as LOTUS 1-2-3. Having input the x and f values, a formula involving cell addresses can be used to obtain the top values in columns such as xf or x^2f and these formulae can then be copied down the columns. The built in @SUM function can then be used to obtain column sums and further formulae involving cell addresses used to complete the calculation of mean, mean deviation, standard deviation, or whatever.

TEST EXERCISES

8.1 A sample of the transfer times of data from an intelligent terminal, in microseconds, is as follows:

Time (microseconds)	Frequency
10 and less than 20	6
20 and less than 30	12
30 and less than 35	9
35 and less than 40	12
40 and less than 45	9
45 and less than 55	9
55 and less than 65	3

(a) Express each frequency as a percentage of the total frequency and tabulate this data against each class.
(b) Using the percentages found in (a) draw a histogram of the data.
(c) Find the mean and standard deviation of the data.
(d) Draw an ogive of the data.
(e) Using your ogive (or otherwise) find the median and semi-interquartile range of the data.
(f) Which measures of location and dispersion are most appropriate to this data and why?

(ACCA Level 1: June 1988)

8.2 A company is investigating the cost of absenteeism within its production department. Computer records revealed the following data:

Days absent last year	Number of people
0	94
1–5	203
6–10	105
11–20	68
21–30	15
31–40	10
41+	5
Total	500

(*Source*: Internal company records)

(a) Draw an ogive (cumulative 'less than' frequency) of these data on graph paper and use it to estimate the values of the median, quartile deviation and highest decile. (Do *not* calculate them.)
(b) Explain the meaning of your estimated statistics.
(c) If each day's absence costs the company £150, find the cost of absenteeism in the production department last year.

(CIMA Stage 1: Nov. 1990)

8.3 A firm employs 2100 weekly paid full-time workers. The latest weekly earnings figures available for these workers are given in the following table:

Weekly earnings (£)	Number of workers
0 and under 60	330
60 and under 120	435
120 and under 180	600
180 and under 240	420
240 and under 300	315

(a) Find the mean, the median, and the mode for this set of data.
(b) Say why you believe the mean, median, and mode have such similar values for this particular set of data.
(c) Calculate the mean deviation, the standard deviation, and the quartile deviation for this set of data.
(d) Compare the three measures you have calculated in answer to part (c) as measures of dispersion for this set of data.

8.4 The management of a farm is analysing the output of its herd of cows which produced 115,263 gallons of milk in the last 12 months.

Gallons of milk	Number of cows
Less than 800	1
800–999	3
1000–1199	11
1200–1399	22
1400–1599	24
1600–1799	15
1800–1999	4
2000 and over	1
Total	81

(*Source*: Statlab Research, internal data)

Calculate the arithmetic mean and standard deviation output of milk per cow for this farm.

(CIMA Stage 1: May 1988)

8.5 As part of a marketing exercise your firm collected the following data on the population of a small town:

Age	No. of persons
0 and less than 5	39
5 and less than 15	91
15 and less than 30	122
30 and less than 45	99
45 and less than 65	130
65 and less than 75	50
75 and over	28

(a) Find the mean age of the population.
(b) Find the standard deviation of the population's age.
(c) Display the data using a histogram.
(d) Draw a percentage less than ogive of the data.
(e) What is the median age of the population?

(ACCA Level 1: June 1990)

REGRESSION AND CORRELATION

9.1 THE SINGLE VARIABLE LINEAR REGRESSION MODEL

Regression and correlation are concerned with *relationships* between variables. Viewed at a very basic level, regression can be regarded as a method for finding from a set of data the best relationship *of a specified kind* between the variables concerned, while correlation measures how well that best relationship fits the data. Establishing a relationship of this kind is a useful thing to do because it enables us either to predict the value of one variable from a knowledge of the other, or to seek to exercise control over one variable through setting values for the other.

The principles of a single variable linear regression will be explained using an example.

Example 9.1.1 A company is introducing a job evaluation scheme in which all jobs are graded into points (where points vary according to skill, danger, responsibility, etc.). Pay scales are then drawn up according to the number of points awarded and to other factors, e.g. experience and local conditions. To date, the company has applied this scheme to 10 jobs:

Type of job	A	B	C	D	E	F	G	H	I	J
Points (x)	50	250	70	190	100	120	150	280	160	230
Weekly pay, £ (y)	100	305	125	250	150	160	200	325	210	275

$\Sigma x = 1600 \quad \Sigma x^2 = 309\,800 \quad \Sigma y = 2100 \quad \Sigma y^2 = 494\,600$

(a) Draw a scatter diagram of weekly pay against points.
(b) Find the appropriate least squares regression line linking pay to points, plot this line on the graph and interpret the answer.
(c) Estimate the weekly pay for a job graded at 200 points and assess the likely reliability of the answer.

(CIMA Stage 1: Nov. 1990)

ANSWER

(a) This problem is an example of what is referred to in the section title as single variable regression because we are looking to explain the pay (y) in terms of just one variable, the points score (x). (If the explanation is to be in terms of more than one variable we have *multiple regression*.) The natural first step in looking for a relationship when there is just a single explanatory variable is to plot a graph having the variable we want to explain on the vertical axis and the explanatory variable on the horizontal axis. (However, not every question on single variable regression asks for such a graph.) It is this kind of graph which is called a *scatter diagram*, and the scatter diagram required for this example is shown in Fig. 9.1.

(b) Finding the best relationship between y and x then amounts to finding the curve, of specified type, which passes 'closest' to the data points, in some sense, and then establishing the equation of that curve. The regression technique does not tell us what the best type of curve

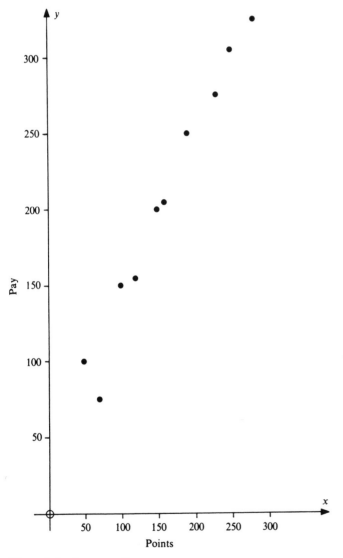

Figure 9.1 A scatter diagram.

is—we must decide that beforehand. From inspection of the scatter diagram here, it would seem that a straight line is a plausible curve to use. This is why the type of regression we are considering is called 'linear' regression. It is the simplest case but one which illustrates most of the principles of regression.

Having decided to use a straight line the regression procedure can be used to find the best straight line.

To see how the straight line which is the regression of y on x is defined see Fig. 9.2. It is the line such that the sum of squares of the vertical deviations of the data points from it is as small as possible. The general equation of such line (see Sec. 2.1) is

$$y = a + bx$$

where a and b are constants. We have to find a and b so as to minimize the sum of squares of the vertical deviations. For this example it means we have to find a and b so as to minimize

$$(a + b \times 50 - 100)^2 + (a + b \times 250 - 305)^2 + (a + b \times 70 - 125)^2 +$$
$$+ (a + b \times 190 - 250)^2 + (a + b \times 100 - 150)^2 + (a + b \times 120 - 160)^2 +$$
$$+ (a + b \times 150 - 200)^2 + (a + b \times 380 - 325)^2 + (a + b \times 160 - 210)^2 +$$
$$+ (a + b \times 230 - 275)^2$$

In general, we need a and b so as to minimize

$$\Sigma(a + bx - y)^2$$

where the summation is over all pairs of data values.

The minimization procedure is an exercise in differential calculus which leads to the following pair of simultaneous equations for a and b:

$$na + b\Sigma x = \Sigma y$$
$$a\Sigma x + b\Sigma x^2 = \Sigma xy$$

where n is the number of pairs of data values.

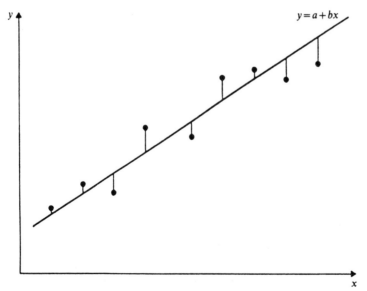

Figure 9.2 Vertical deviations of scatter points from a straight line.

These are called the *normal equations* and they could be used in a particular instance to find a and b by substituting in the values for n, Σx, Σy, Σx^2 and Σxy and then solving. However, it is more usual to find b from a formula obtained by eliminating a between the equations, and then find a using a re-expression of the first equation. Thus we have the formulae:

$$b = \frac{\Sigma xy - (\Sigma x)(\Sigma y)/n}{\Sigma x^2 - (\Sigma x)^2/n}$$

$$a = \frac{\Sigma y - b\Sigma x}{n}$$

The calculations needed are commonly set out in the form of a table and for the example being considered we have:

x	y	x^2	xy
50	100	2 500	5 000
250	305	62 500	76 250
70	125	4 900	8 750
190	250	36 100	47 500
100	150	10 000	15 000
120	160	14 400	19 200
150	200	22 500	30 000
280	325	78 400	91 000
160	210	25 600	33 600
230	275	52 900	63 250
1 600	2 100	309 800	389 550

$$b = \frac{389\,550 - 1600 \times 2100/10}{309\,800 - 1600 \times 1600/10} = \frac{389\,550 - 336\,000}{309\,800 - 256\,000} = \frac{53\,550}{53\,800} = 0.995\,35$$

and

$$a = (2100 - 0.99\,535 \times 1600)/10 = (2100 - 1592.56)/10 = 507.44/10$$
$$= 50.744$$

The equation of the regression line of y on x is

$$y = 50.744 + 0.995\,35x$$

Because of the way it is defined, the line we have calculated is commonly referred to as the *least squares* regression line. This equation is the required best relationship of linear form between the explanatory variable x and the explained variable y.

The regression line can be drawn by choosing any two convenient values of x, calculating the corresponding values of y, plotting the resulting two points and joining them with an extended line. This is done for the example here in Fig. 9.3 using $x=0$ and $x=250$ as the two chosen x values.

It will be agreed by inspection of Fig. 9.3 that the line which the least squares method has produced is a reasonable one and the sort of thing we should have expected if we tried to fit a line 'by eye'. That is to say, by sliding a ruler around and drawing the line we felt intuitively to be closest to the points. The advantages of proceeding by the least squares

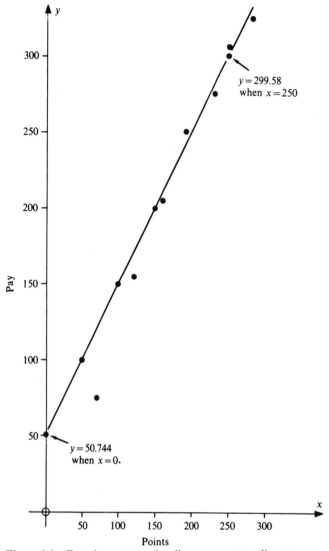

Figure 9.3 Drawing a regression line on a scatter diagram.

method are that it is objective (everybody given the same set of data will come up with the same line) and the *a* and *b* obtained in this way have desirable statistical properties which help us when we come to use the line for making forecasts.

(c) Having found the regression of *y* on *x* we can use it to forecast the value of *y* for a given value of *x*. (Note that this equation should not be used to predict *x* for a given value of *y*—i.e. to predict in this case what number of points would correspond to a specified pay level. If that kind of forecast is required, the regression of *x* on *y* must be calculated and used.) The forecast can be made graphically by reading off from the graph the *y* value corresponding to the given *x* value or by substituting the given *x* value into the regression equation and calculating the value of *y*.

Here we are asked to forecast pay when *x* = 200.

We find

$$y = 50.744 + 0.995\ 35 \times 200 = 50.744 + 199.07 = 249.814$$

To the accuracy of the original data, the forecast pay level is £250 per week. (This is the y value obtained by reading off at $x = 200$ in Fig. 9.3.)

The operation carried out here is, strictly, an *interpolation* since it predicts y for a value of x inside the range of x values in the original data. This is a basically 'respectable' procedure and will always lead to meaningful predictions so long as the regression line is a reasonable fit to the data. Thus we can say that our answer in this case is likely to be reliable. If appropriate distributional assumptions hold for the data we can calculate *confidence limits* for the estimates of a and b. Using the confidence limits for a and b we can find such limits for the predictions for y.

In other circumstances we might want to predict the value of y for an x value outside the range of the original data. A prediction of this kind is called an *extrapolation*. Implicit in doing this is the assumption that the relationship established for the given data holds for the extended range of x values. The further we are from the mean of the original x values when making the prediction, the wider this interval will be for a given level of confidence. Despite these hazards associated with extrapolation, it is something which has to be done in some circumstances, such as in time series forecasting (see Chapter 10) where the whole purpose is to forecast for a time point which has not yet occurred. What is important is to bear in mind the dangers and also not attempt to forecast too far into the future. The confidence limits for an interpolation will always be tighter than for an extrapolation for a given level of confidence.

Exercise 9.1.1 Prior to privatization, the most recent annual sales and profit data (£ million) for distribution companies within the Central Electricity Generating Board (England and Wales) were as follows:

Distribution company	Sales (£m)	Profit (£m)
Norweb	1129	32.1
Manweb	808	26.6
Midland	1181	38.4
South Wales	551	10.3
South West	687	30.0
Southern	1134	65.4
Seeboard	912	27.2
LEB	1050	39.9
Eastern	1497	58.9
East Midlands	1165	52.1
Yorkshire	1140	49.3
North East	740	31.9

(*Source: The Times*, 16 April 1990)

$\Sigma(\text{Sales}) = 11\,994$; $\Sigma(\text{Profit}) = 462.1$; $\Sigma(xy) = 498\,912.2$; $\Sigma(\text{Sales})^2 = 12\,763\,470$; $\Sigma(\text{Profit})^2 = 20\,459.35$.

(a) Find the regression equation of profit on sales, plot it on a scatter diagram, and predict profit for a similar company with sales of £1000 million.
(b) Interpret your analysis.

(CIMA Stage 1: Nov. 1991)

9.2 CORRELATION

Correlation can be regarded as a method for measuring how well the best relationship of a specified kind fits a set of data. When the best relationship is defined, as in the least squares method, as the one which minimizes the sum of squares of the vertical deviations, it would seem reasonable to measure how good that best relationship is by looking at the size of that sum of squares when it has been minimized. Consider Fig. 9.4. The two regression lines have the same equation but the sum of squares of the vertical deviations of the data points about the line in case (a) where the fit is good is much smaller than the sum of squares of the vertical deviations of the data points about the line in case (b) where the fit is poorer. The *correlation coefficient r* is based on the sum of squares of the vertical deviations from the best line expressed as a proportion of the total variation in the y values measured as the sum of squares about their mean. Thus it is based on

$$\frac{\Sigma(a+bx-y)^2}{\Sigma(y-\bar{y})^2}$$

where a and b are obtained using the least squares formulae given in Sec. 9.1. If the fit is good, we see that this ratio will be close to 0 because the numerator will be small. If the fit is poor, the ratio will be close to 1 because there will be almost as much variation about the best line as about the line $y=\bar{y}$. Note that the ratio can never exceed 1, because if the sum of squares about $y=\bar{y}$ were smaller than the sum of squares about $y=a+bx$, then $y=a+bx$ could not be the best line; $y=\bar{y}$ would be better.

The correlation coefficient r is defined by

$$r^2 = 1 - \frac{\Sigma(a+bx-y)^2}{\Sigma(y-\bar{y})^2}$$

In view of the argument above we see that for a good fit, where the ratio is small, r^2 will be close to 1, while for a poor fit, where the ratio approaches 1, r^2 will be close to 0.

The quantity r^2 is called the *coefficient of determination*. By substituting into the r^2 definition the least squares regression formulae for a and b and working through some algebra, we emerge with the formula generally used for calculation of the correlation coefficient, namely

$$r = \frac{\Sigma xy - (\Sigma x)(\Sigma y)/n}{\sqrt{[\Sigma x^2 - (\Sigma x)^2/n][\Sigma y^2 - (\Sigma y)^2/n]}}$$

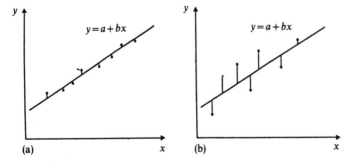

Figure 9.4   (a) positive correlation (b) a less good fit of scatter points to a regression line.

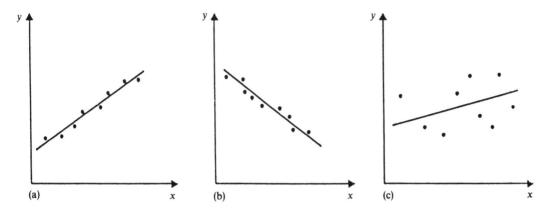

Figure 9.5 (a) a good fit and (b) negative correlation (c) lack of correlation.

If the fit is good and the regression line slopes upwards, r will be close to $+1$.
If the fit is good and the regression line slopes downwards, r will be close to -1.
If the fit is poor, r will be close to 0.
These results are consistent with the points made concerning r^2 above and are illustrated in (a), (b), and (c), respectively, of Fig. 9.5.

As an example of a correlation coefficient calculation consider again the data from Example 9.1.1. We saw that for this data set $n = 10$, $\Sigma x = 1600$, $\Sigma y = 2100$, $\Sigma x^2 = 309\,800$, $\Sigma xy = 389\,550$. In addition to these we need

$$\Sigma y^2 = 100^2 + 305^2 + 125^2 + \cdots + 275^2 = 494\,600$$

(If the correlation coefficient were calculated at the same time as the regression line, a column of y^2 values would be included in the table of calculations. Note also that the numerator of r and part of the denominator are items already calculated when finding the regression coefficient b.) Hence

$$r = \frac{389\,550 - 1600 \times 2100/10}{\sqrt{(309\,800 - 1600 \times 1600/10)(494\,600 - 2100 \times 2100/10)}}$$

$$= \frac{389\,550 - 336\,000}{\sqrt{(309\,800 - 256\,000)(494\,600 - 441\,000)}} = \frac{53\,550}{\sqrt{53\,800 \times 53\,700}} = \frac{53\,550}{53\,600}$$

$$= 0.9972$$

This seems very close to $+1$, indicating a good fit of the line $y = 50.744 + 0.99535x$ to the data points. (The question of testing statistically whether an r value is 'close' to $+1$ or -1 is deferred to Chapter 16.)

Having calculated a correlation coefficient and decided whether it is close to $+1$, to -1, or to 0 there remains a further stage of interpretation. If r is close to zero, does it follow that there is no relationship at all between the variables, i.e. that they are independent?

If the pairs of values can be believed to come from a distribution called the bivariate normal distribution, then this conclusion is valid. However, if we have just taken any old set of pairs of values and carried out the correlation coefficient calculation, then the independence conclusion does not necessarily follow. For what the correlation coefficient measures is how well the best possible straight line fits the data. The fact that r is close to zero, indicating that no straight line fits very well, does not rule out the possibility of some other form of relationship fitting well, and

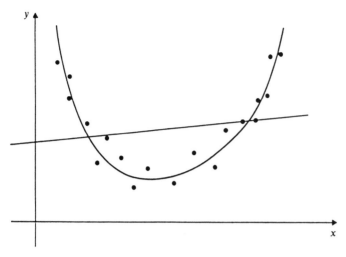

Figure 9.6 x and y lack of correlation as measured by r, but there is a relationship.

hence of the variables not being independent. One possibility is shown in Fig. 9.6 where no straight line will have a small sum of squares of vertical deviations but the parabola fits the data points very well. The straight line is the best possible but the sum of squares about it will be large.

Suppose, on the other hand, that r is found to be close to $+1$ or to -1. Does it follow that changes in the independent variable x are responsible for changes in the dependent variable y, i.e. is there causality?

The answer is that the association need not be, or need not be wholly, causal and the extent of the causality must be decided by examination of each individual situation. Suppose, for example, we were to calculate a correlation coefficient using data on food prices and oil prices. A correlation close to 1 would be found and, while oil prices do affect food prices to some extent through transportation costs, the major part of the relationship would not be causal but a reflection of general inflation in both sets of prices.

Exercise 9.2.1 A cost accountant has derived the following data on the weekly output of standard size boxes from a factory.

Week	Output x (thousands of boxes)	Total cost, y (£'000s)
1	20	60
2	2	25
3	4	26
4	23	66
5	18	49
6	14	48
7	10	35
8	8	18
9	13	40
10	8	33

(a) Calculate the regression equation $y = a + bx$.
(b) Interpret the regression coefficients a and b.
(c) Calculate and interpret the correlation coefficient r.

9.3 ANALYSIS OF VARIANCE AND INTERVAL ESTIMATES

Another method for testing how well a regression model fits a set of data is provided by the technique known as *analysis of variance*. The method uses essentially the same sums of squares as are involved in the correlation coefficient, and the ultimate statistical test is equivalent to that arising from the correlation method. A table format is used, and an analysis of variance table is a part of the standard output given by MINITAB for regression.

We again start with a *total sum of squares*

$$SST = \Sigma(y - \bar{y})^2 = \Sigma y^2 - (\Sigma y)^2/n$$

This is the sum of squares of the y values about their mean. Of this total, the sum of squares of the differences between the mean line and the regression line at the data points can be regarded as being explained by the regression model. Thus we have the *explained sum of squares*

$$SSEx = \Sigma(a + bx - \bar{y})^2$$

and this can be readily manipulated into the form

$$SSEx = b[\Sigma xy - (\Sigma x)(\Sigma y)/n]$$

The *residual sum of squares* can then be found by subtraction as

$$SSU = SST - SSEx$$

The first column of the analysis of variance table contains a statement of the sources of variation and the third column shows these sums of squares. The second column shows the numbers of *degrees of freedom* for the sums of squares. The degrees of freedom for the total sum of squares are the number of *independent* contributions to that sum. This number is $n - 1$. The number of degrees of freedom for the explained sum of squares is the number of explanatory variables in the regression model. Thus for the simple regression model we are considering this number will be 1. Finally the degrees of freedom for the residual can be found by subtraction: $n - 1 - 1 = n - 2$.

In the fourth column of the table the explained sum of squares SSEx and the residual sum of squares SSU are divided by their respective degrees of freedom to give the *mean squares MSEx* and *MSU*.

Then in the fifth column we have the *variance ratio* obtained by dividing out to give $VR = MSEx/MSU$.

Thus we have in Table 9.1 the format for an analysis of variance table for a simple regression.

Table 9.1

Source of variation	Degrees of freedom	Sum of squares	Mean square	Variance ratio
Regression	1	$SSEx$	$MSEx = SSEx/1$	$VR = MSEx/MSU$
Error	$n-2$	SSU	$MSU = SSU/(n-2)$	
Total	$n-1$	SST		

To test the variance ratio manually we have to compare it with the table for the F distribution. The idea of comparing a test statistic with a published table is discussed in Chapter 16. However, MINITAB relieves us of the need to carry out such a procedure by adding a sixth column which shows the probability of a variance ratio as large as the one obtained if the model did not fit the data. Thus if the value of this probability is small (less than 0.05) the model can be taken to have been shown to fit the data.

MINITAB could be used to obtain the regression model for the data in Example 9.1.1 by means of the following lines of input:

MTB>SET C1

DATA>100 305 125 250 150 160 200 325 210 275

DATA>END OF DATA

MTB>SET C2

DATA>50 250 70 190 100 120 150 280 160 230

DATA>END OF DATA

MTB>REGRESSION C1 1 C2

These commands put the y values in column C1 and the x values in column C2. The REGRESSION command then requests regression of the variable in column C1 on the *one* variable in column C2. Figure 9.7 shows part of the output produced by these commands.

This output confirms the regression equation found in our answer to Example 9.1.1. Also in Sec. 9.2 we found the correlation coefficient to be 0.9972. If this value is squared, we obtain 0.994 as the coefficient of determination. This is represented by the statement R-sq $= 99.4$ per cent.

The analysis of variance table is as shown. The variance ratio 1426.89 is so large that to three decimal places the probability of obtaining such a value if there were not a fit would be zero.

Exercise 9.3.1 Obtain the analysis of variance table for the data in Exercise 9.2.1. (Use MINITAB to carry out this task if you have access to the package.)

In the computer output shown in Fig. 9.7 will be noted the statement $s = 6.112$. This number arises as the square root of MSU, in this case 37, and is an estimate of the standard error of the deviations about the regression line. It is important because it features in estimates of the variability in estimates made from the regression equation.

Matters of estimation and confidence intervals are taken up in a more fundamental way in Chapter 15, but we conclude this section by demonstrating the mechanics of the method for obtaining interval estimates from regression models.

Example 9.3.1 The Genesis Driving School Ltd possesses a fleet of cars of the same make and model, each car having approximately equal usage. The assistant chief accountant is currently

```
The regression equation is
C1 = 50.7 + 0.995 C2

Predictor        Coef       Stdev
Constant       50.743       4.638
C2            0.99535     0.02635

s = 6.112       R-sq = 99.4%

Analysis of Variance

SOURCE         DF          SS         MS        F        p
Regression      1       53301      53301  1426.89    0.000
Error           8         299         37
Total           9       53600
```

Figure 9.7 Output produced by the REGRESSION command in MINITAB.

reviewing the company's vehicle replacement policy with the aim of deciding the optimum age at which to replace cars. Over the past 12 months the company has kept a full record of the service and maintenance costs for each of its cars. The following table shows, for a random sample of 12 cars, the age (in years) and the annual costs (in £s) of service and maintenance.

Car	Age (years), x	Cost (£), y
A	1	300
B	4	660
C	3	500
D	4	600
E	5	750
F	2	420
G	2	450
H	1	340
I	3	520
J	5	700
K	4	640
L	2	480

You can use the following summations:

$\Sigma x = 36$ $\Sigma y = 6360$ $\Sigma xy = 21\,250$
$\Sigma x^2 = 130$ $\Sigma y^2 = 3\,593\,000$ $s = 28.564$

(a) Draw a scatter plot of the data and comment on the appropriateness of fitting a straight line relationship.
(b) Using the method of least squares, estimate a relationship of the form $y = a + bx$, where y is the annual cost and x is the age of the car. Interpret your values of a and b in the context of this question.
(c) The cost information concerning one of its cars, aged five years, has been mislaid. Obtain a 95 per cent interval estimate for the cost of this car over the previous 12 months.

(ACCA Level 2: June 1991)

ANSWER
(a) A scatter plot for this set of data is shown in Fig. 9.8.
    It would appear from this diagram that a straight line would be a reasonable relationship to fit to the data.
(b) Calculating b and then a using the formulae set out in Sec. 9.1 leads to the regression equation

$$y = 234.092 + 98.6364x$$

    The interpretation of the coefficients is that £234 is an annual maintenance and service cost which can be expected to apply to every car, even one of age zero. Then on top of this a car can be expected to require a further sum of £99 to be spent on these items for each additional year of age.
(c) If we insert the value $x = 5$ into the regression equation we obtain $y = 234.092 + 98.6364 \times 5 = 234.092 + 493.182 = 727.274$. This is a 'point estimate' of the cost for a five-year-old car. To obtain an interval estimate we need to think first about the standard error of

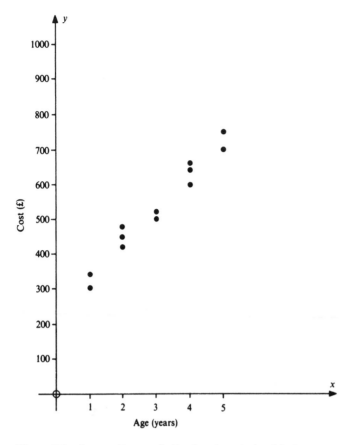

Figure 9.8 Scatter diagram indicating the relationship between age and cost.

this prediction. This is given by

$$s\sqrt{1+\frac{1}{n}+\frac{(5-\bar{x})^2}{\Sigma(x-\bar{x})^2}}=28.564\sqrt{1+\frac{1}{12}+\frac{2^2}{130-36\times36/12}}$$

$$=28.564\sqrt{1.8333+4/22}=28.564\times\sqrt{2.0151}=40.5478$$

To find how many standard errors each side of the point estimate the interval needs to extend we must first note the number of degrees of freedom of MSU, which is $n-2=12-2=10$. This means that we are involved with a t-distribution having 10 degrees of freedom. We are also told that the interval is to be a 95 per cent interval. Since 95 per cent = 100 per cent − 5 per cent we must go to the t-distribution table in Appendix 2 and use the figure in the 10 degrees of freedom row and the 5 per cent column. This figure is 2.23. So the 95 per cent interval estimate is from

$$727.274-2.23\times40.5478$$

to

$$727.274+2.23\times40.5478$$

i.e.
$$637 \text{ to } 818$$

The assistant chief accountant can be 95 per cent confident that the cost for a five-year-old car will be in the range from £637 to £818.

Exercise 9.3.2 In an investigation into the relationship between the number of weekly loan applications and the current mortgage rate, 15 weeks were selected at random from among the 260 weeks of the past five years. The data is shown below.

Week	Mortgage rate %, x	Number of loan applications, y
1	11.0	75
2	13.5	65
3	13.0	62
4	12.0	76
5	15.0	50
6	14.0	58
7	14.5	54
8	13.5	64
9	10.0	87
10	11.0	79
11	10.5	80
12	12.0	72
13	12.5	69
14	13.0	65
15	13.0	61

The output from a least squares regression program (using the model, $y = a + bx$) is given below:

$x = 12.5667$	$SD(x) = 1.4744$
$y = 67.8000$	$SD(y) = 10.3316$
$a = 153.3990$	$SE(a) = 5.7701$
$b = -6.8116$	$SE(b) = 0.4562$
$r = -0.9721$	residual $s^2 = 6.3349$

(a) Explain to a manager, with no statistical training, the meaning of the following terms. In each case use the values displayed by the computer output to illustrate your answer.
   (i) Regression coefficients, slope and intercept.
   (ii) Coefficient of determination.
   (iii) Residual standard deviation.
(b) Using graph paper draw a scatter diagram of the data, and plot the least squares regression line on this diagram.
(c) Calculate a 95 per cent confidence interval for the number of loan applications in a week when the mortgage rate is 14 per cent.

(ACCA Level 2: Dec. 1990)

Note that in view of the power and wide availability of computer packages for carrying out regression tasks it is in practice much more important to be able to interpret the meaning of regression and correlation results produced by a computer, as in this exercise, than to have great facility with the computations.

It will be clear to the reader that a package such as MINITAB offers enormous scope for experimenting with all sorts of sophisticated regression models with no computational effort. It would, for example, be possible to regress on several variables to seek a *multiple regression* model of the form

$$y = a + b_1 x_1 + b_2 x_2 + b_3 x_3 + b_4 x_4$$

by reading values for y, x_1, x_2, x_3, and x_4 into columns C1, C2, C3, C4, and C5 respectively and issuing the regression command

REGRESSION C1 4 C2 – C5

which asks for a regression of the variable in column C1 on the variables in columns C2, C3, C4, and C5.

The output would be of the same basic form as that for simple regression. There are estimates for the five coefficients, an analysis of variance table and a coefficient of *multiple* determination R-sq giving the proportion of variation explained by the multiple regression model. The square root of this is the coefficient of multiple correlation.

Spreadsheets such as LOTUS 1-2-3 lend themselves to regression and correlation work, and the reader is referred to the book by Judge listed in the bibliography for detail on this point. It is also not uncommon for hand calculators to include a facility for the automatic calculation of the coefficients for a simple regression model along with the correlation coefficient.

9.4 REGRESSION AND CORRELATION WITH TRANSFORMATIONS

If a scatter diagram is drawn and a straight line does not appear a likely form of relationship between the variables, it may be that transforming one or both of the variables in some way will lead to a new pair of variables for which a straight line will be a reasonable fit. Examples of transformations which can be usefully tried in such circumstances are logarithms, square roots, squares or negative reciprocals. It is left to the reader's imagination to think of others. With a computer package such as MINITAB the computation of the transformed variables is totally painless. Having put the original variable in column C1, its square root, say, can be put in column C3 by the command

MTB > C3 = SQRT(C1)

In this section we give an example, and leave the reader with an exercise, involving use of logarithmic transformations.

Example 9.4.1 Fast Foods Limited is a major food retailing company which has recently decided to open several new restaurants. In order to assist with the choice of siting these restaurants the management of Fast Foods Limited wished to investigate the effect of income on eating habits. As part of its report a marketing agency produced the following table showing the percentage of annual income spent on food, y, for a given annual family income(£), x.

x	y
5 000	62
7 500	48
10 000	37
12 500	27
20 000	22
25 000	18

(a) Plot on separate scatter diagrams:
  (i) y against x:
  (ii) $\log_{10} y$ against $\log_{10} x$,
  and comment on the relationship between income and percentage of family income spent on food.
(b) Use the method of least squares to fit the relationship

$$y = ax^b$$

to the data. Estimate a and b.
(c) Estimate the percentage of annual income spent on food by a family with an annual income of £18 000.

(ACCA Level 2: Dec. 1987)

ANSWER

(a) (i) Figure 9.9 is the scatter diagram of y against x.
   (ii) The logarithms are set out in the following table:

x	5000	7500	10 000	12 500	15 000	20 000	25 000
$\log_{10} x$	3.6990	3.8751	4.0000	4.0969	4.1761	4.3010	4.4979
y	62	48	37	31	27	22	18
$\log_{10} y$	1.7924	1.6812	1.5682	1.4914	1.4314	1.3424	1.2553

The scatter diagram of $\log_{10} y$ against $\log_{10} x$ is shown as Fig. 9.10.

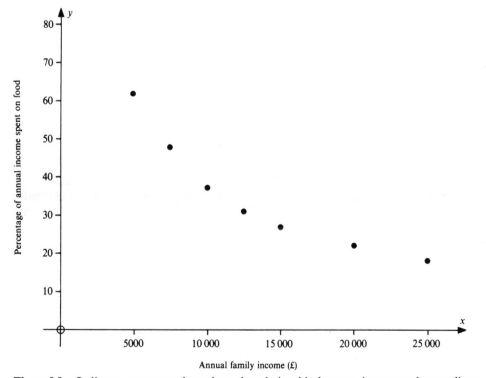

Figure 9.9 Ordinary scatter graph to show the relationship between income and expenditure on food.

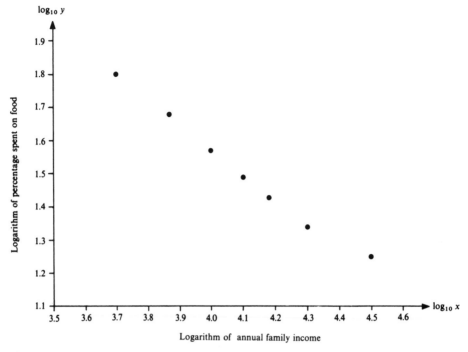

Figure 9.10 Semi-log scatter graph to show the relationship.

Inspection of the two scatter diagrams suggests that the data points following the taking of logarithms are closer to a straight line than the untransformed values. The relationship between income and percentage of income spent on food is an inverse one which is not linear, but if logarithms are taken then the fitting of a linear model is relevant to establishing a meaningful relationship.

(b) If we take logs of both sides in the proposed relationship

$$y = ax^b$$

we obtain

$$\log_{10} y = \log_{10} a + b \log_{10} x$$

So if we carry out the usual regression calculations on the logarithms we shall obtain b and $\log_{10} a$ from the two formulae. Setting $X = \log_{10} x$ and $Y = \log_{10} y$ we have from the figures in the answer to part (a)(ii) above

$$\Sigma X = 28.646 \qquad \Sigma X^2 = 117.6531 \qquad \Sigma Y = 10.5623 \qquad \Sigma XY = 16.1494 \qquad n = 7.$$

Hence

$$b = \frac{42.9254 - (28.646 \times 10.5623/7)}{117.6531 - (28.646 \times 28.646/7)} = \frac{-0.2985}{0.42549} = -0.7015$$

$$\log_{10} a = (10.5623 + 0.7015 \times 28.646)/7 = 4.3796 \text{ so } a = 23\,968$$

Thus the fitted relationship of form $y = ax^b$ is estimated as

$$y = 23\,968 \, x^{-0.7015}$$

(c) The estimated percentage of annual income spent on food by a family with an annual income of £18 000 is

$$23\,968 \times 18\,000^{-0.7015} = 23\,968 \times 0.001034966 = 24.8 \text{ per cent}$$

Exercise 9.4.1 Venus Tableware Limited is an important tableware producer in the country of Blueland. In this country the amount of imports and exports of ceramic tableware is insignificant when compared to local production and so it can reasonably be concluded that total Blueland production in any one year is essentially equal to total sales. The following table shows the total Blueland production, the Venus Tableware sales, and the consequent market share that Venus Tableware commanded within Blueland for the eight-year period 1980–87.

Year	Total Blueland production ('000 tonnes)	Venus Tableware sales ('000 tonnes)	Venue Tableware market share (%)
1980	744	113	15.2
1981	773	108	14.0
1982	828	131	15.8
1983	900	144	16.0
1984	936	146	15.6
1985	977	157	16.1
1986	1007	163	16.2
1987	1066	175	16.4

(a) Plot on a scatter diagram the logarithm of total Blueland production against the year. Interpret your scatter diagram.
(b) Express the total Blueland production time series in the form

$$y = ab^x$$

where $y =$ total Blueland production (in '000 tonnes)

$$x = \text{year} - 1980.$$

Estimate a and b and interpret your value of b.
(c) Use the model fitted in part (b) to predict the total Blueland production for the years 1988, 1989, and 1990.
(d) The chief accountant of Venus Tableware wishes to use the total Blueland production time series to forecast company sales. As Venus Tableware had increased its market share from 15.2 to 16.4 per cent, he felt it might be wise to produce two sets of forecasts:
   (i) a pessimistic forecast, assuming that the market share remains at 16.4 per cent;
   (ii) an optimistic forecast where the company's market share increases by 0.2 per cent over each of the next three years to reach 17.0 per cent by 1990.
   Obtain a set of optimistic and pessimistic forecasts for Venus Tableware annual sales for each of the next three years.
(e) Outline the main shortcomings of regression based forecasting techniques.

(ACCA Level 2: June 1988)

(*Notes* 1. When time is the explanatory variable, as in this question, it is usual to 'code' it in some way to make the numbers easier to use. In this case 1980 is subtracted from the years to give x values 0, 1, 2, 3, 4, 5, 6, and 7.
2. Taking logarithms in the model suggested in part (b) in this case gives $\log_{10} y = \log_{10} a + x \log_{10} b$ so only the y variable is logged. The regression formulae give $\log_{10} b$ and $\log_{10} a$.)

9.5 RANK CORRELATION

Sometimes we need to measure the strength of linear relationship between variables using data which can be trusted only to the extent of its rank ordering. That is to say, if one data value is, say, larger than another then that fact can be believed, but no use can be made of the claimed difference in magnitudes of the two items. This situation might arise through inaccuracies of measurement but more commonly it is as a result of the kind of variables involved. It occurs commonly in marketing research situations where the subject of a survey might be given, say, five sweets and asked to rank them in order or assign them marks. In the former case the resulting data will clearly be in ranked form, but in the latter also the data can be trusted only to the extent of rank ordering. The difference in acceptability between a sweet assigned 8 marks and one assigned 6 marks cannot be meaningfully accepted to be the same as the difference in acceptability between a sweet assigned 5 marks and one assigned 3 marks.

If we have data of this type the strength of linear association can be measured by, if necessary, converting the two sets of figures into ranks and then, in principle, calculating the ordinary correlation coefficient using the ranks. The coefficient obtained in this way is called *Spearman's coefficient of rank correlation* and is commonly denoted by the symbol r'.

Example 9.5.1 At the end of a financial year the chief accountant of each of 10 engineering companies was asked to compute six accounting ratios (A, B, C, D, E, and F) to describe his or her company's performance. The accounting ratios D, E, and F for the 10 companies were as follows:

Company	Ratio D	Ratio E	Ratio F
1	1.30	1.30	1.45
2	1.45	1.20	1.20
3	1.30	1.25	1.30
4	0.95	0.80	0.75
5	1.80	1.75	1.90
6	1.50	1.60	1.65
7	1.05	1.35	1.50
8	1.30	1.05	0.90
9	0.90	0.95	0.85
10	0.90	1.10	1.00

(a) Calculate Spearman's rank correlation between:
  (i) ratio D and ratio E,
  (ii) ratio E and ratio F,
  and hence complete the following Spearman's rank correlation matrix.

	A	B	C	D	E	F
A	1.0	−0.7	0.8	−0.8	−0.9	−0.7
B	−0.7	1.0	−0.8	0.9	0.8	0.7
C	0.8	−0.8	1.0	−0.8	−0.7	−0.6
D	−0.8	0.9	−0.8			
E	−0.9	0.8	−0.7			
F	−0.7	0.7	−0.6			

(b) Use the correlation matrix described in part (a) to divide the six accounting ratios into two distinct groups. Explain your reasoning.

(ACCA Level 2: Dec. 1988)

ANSWER

(a) Although the rank correlation coefficient is based on the ordinary correlation coefficient formula, it is not necessary to calculate it using this formula. Since the x values are the numbers 1 to n in some order and the y values are also the numbers 1 to n in some (in general different) order the formula can be simplified by algebraic manipulation into the following form

$$r = 1 - \frac{6\Sigma d^2}{n(n^2 - 1)}$$

where the d's are the differences in the corresponding pairs of ranks. This is the form invariably used for calculation of Spearman's coefficient.

For (i) we have:

Ratio D rank:	6	8	6	3	10	9	4	6	1.5	1.5
Ratio E rank:	7	5	6	1	10	9	8	3	2	4
d:	-1	3	0	2	0	0	-4	3	-0.5	-2.5
d^2:	1	9	0	4	0	0	16	0	0.25	6.25

Note that in ranking the figures for ratio D the smallest number has been ranked 1 and the largest has been ranked 10. It would have been equally acceptable to rank in the reverse order. The only requirement is that the same rule is used consistently for all variables in the problem.

Note also that in the case of ratio D there are ties in the ranking. That is to say companies 9 and 10 both have ratios equal to 0.9 and companies 1, 3, and 8 all have ratios of 1.30. This situation is dealt with by giving each item in a tied set the mean of the ranks they would have had if they had been slightly different. Thus companies 9 and 10 both have ranks equal to the mean of 1 and 2, which is 1.5, and companies 1, 3, and 8 all receive the mean of 5, 6, and 7, which is 6. From the last row in the table above we see that $\Sigma d^2 = 45.5$.

Hence

$$r' = 1 - \frac{6 \times 45.5}{10 \times (100 - 1)} = 1 - \frac{273}{990} = 0.724$$

For (ii) we have:

Ratio E rank:	7	5	6	1	10	9	8	3	2	4
Ratio F rank:	7	5	6	1	10	9	8	3	2	4

Since the two sets of ranks are identical it is clear without calculation that $\Sigma d^2 = 0$ and hence that $r' = 1$.

So the given Spearman's rank correlation matrix can be completed:

	A	B	C	D	E	F
A	1.0	−0.7	0.8	−0.8	−0.9	−0.7
B	−0.7	1.0	−0.8	0.9	0.8	0.7
C	0.8	−0.8	1.0	−0.8	−0.7	−0.6
D	−0.8	0.9	−0.8	1.0	0.7	0.7
E	−0.9	0.8	−0.7	0.7	1.0	1.0
F	−0.7	0.7	−0.6	0.7	1.0	1.0

(b) The two groups into which the ratios can be divided are seen to be {A, C} and {B, D, E, F}. This is the case because all the ratios within each of these groups have a positive rank correlation with all the others in the same group, but a negative rank correlation with all those in the other group.

Since Spearman's coefficient is calculated on exactly the same principles as the ordinary correlation coefficient, the same general ideas apply to its interpretation as applied to the correlation coefficient in Sec. 9.2.

Note, however, that it would be possible for two variables to have rank correlation equal to 1 while the ordinary correlation coefficient is less than 1. This would arise if, for example, variable y were the square of variable x. Suppose we had:

x:	1	2	3	4	5	6	7	8
y:	1	4	9	16	25	36	49	64

The correlation coefficient would not be 1 because these pairs of values do not lie on a straight line. However, the rank correlation coefficient would be 1 because the ranks of the y values would be the same as those of the x values.

It is *not* possible for two variables to have ordinary correlation equal to 1 and rank correlation less than 1, because the fact that the pairs of values lie on a straight line would imply equal rank orderings and therefore a Spearman's coefficient of 1.

Exercise 9.5.1 Two management accountants rank the credit worthiness of seven companies as follows:

Company	H	I	J	K	L	M	N
MA1	Second	Fourth	Sixth	First	Fifth	Third	Seventh
MA2	Fourth	Third	Fifth	Second	Sixth	First	Seventh

Spearman's coefficient of rank correlation

$$R(\text{rank}) = 1 - [6\Sigma d^2 / n(n^2 - 1)]$$

will be closest to

(A) −0.79; (B) −0.14; (C) zero; (D) 0.21; (E) 0.79.

(CIMA Stage 1: May 1990)

TEST EXERCISES

9.1 It is believed that the price of a house in a certain city may be related to its distance from the centre of the city. These distances (in miles) can easily be obtained from a map and are given below for the 12 houses in the sample.

House	A	B	C	D	E	F	G	H	I	J	K	L
Price (£000)	63	75	59	75	100	108	100	90	70	96	84	100
Distance	5.5	5.7	5.2	4.9	3.3	2.1	2.2	3.1	4.2	3.1	3.5	2.8

(a) Plot the data in a scatter diagram and comment on its main features.
(b) Using least squares, find the regression equation of house price on distance from the city centre.
(c) The overall average distance from the city centre is 4.5 miles. Use this information to estimate the population mean house price.

(ACCA Level 2: Dec. 1991)

9.2 CB plc produces a wide range of electronic components including its best selling item, the laser switch. The company is preparing the budgets for 1989 and knows that the key element in the master budget is the contribution expected from the laser switch. The records for this component for the past four years are summarized below, with the costs and revenues adjusted to 1989 values.

Sales	(units)	1985 150 000 (£)	1986 180 000 (£)	1987 200 000 (£)	1988 230 000 (£)
Sales revenue		292 820	346 060	363 000	448 800
Variable costs		131 080	161 706	178 604	201 160
Contribution		161 740	184 354	184 396	247 640

It has been estimated that sales in 1989 will be 260 000 units.

(a) As a starting point for forecasting 1989 contribution, project the trend using linear regression.
(b) Calculate the 95 per cent confidence interval of the individual forecast for 1989 if the standard error of the forecast is £14 500 and the appropriate t value is 4.303, and interpret the value calculated.
(c) Comment on the advantages of using linear regression for forecasting and the limitations of the technique.

(CIMA Stage 3: May 1989)

9.3 Your company is planning a takeover of a small UK chain of multiple stores whose main competitors are cooperatives. As part of the preliminary work you have been asked to investigate relationships between turnover, number of stores, and region. Data for nine regions on the number of stores and turnover (£ million) of multiples and cooperatives in 1985 is given below:

Multiples									
Region	A	B	C	D	E	F	G	H	I
Stores (x)	952	253	360	484	593	639	498	371	416
Turnover (y)	3657	819	1250	1302	1861	1635	1452	717	1179

Cooperatives									
Region	A	B	C	D	E	F	G	H	I
Stores (x)	379	322	210	366	575	451	489	257	550
Turnover (y)	260	236	194	308	445	427	286	130	335

(*Source: Market Research Society Yearbook*, 1986 amended)

The least squares regressions of turnover on stores have been calculated via MINITAB (a computer program). They are as follows:

$$y = -508.50 + 4.04x, \ r = 0.95 \text{ (multiples)}$$
$$y = \ \ \ 22.73 + 0.67x, \ r = 0.83 \text{ (cooperatives)}$$

(a) On the same graph plot scatter diagrams of y against x, including the regression lines, and interpret your results.
(b) For a region with 500 stores of each type, predict the turnover for multiples and for cooperatives, and comment on the likely accuracy of these predictions.
(c) By any method you consider appropriate, compare turnover per store between multiples and cooperatives.

(CIMA Stage 1: May 1987)

9.4 A management accountant is analysing the data relating to retail sales on behalf of marketing colleagues. The marketing staff believe that the most important influence upon sales is local advertising undertaken by the retail store. The company also advertises by using regional television areas. The company owns more than 100 retail outlets, and the data below relates to a sample of 10 representative outlets.

Outlet number	Monthly sales (£'000s) y	Local advertising by the retail store (£'000s per month) x_1	Regional advertising by the company (£'000s per month) x_2
1	220	6	4
2	230	8	6
3	240	12	10
4	340	12	16
5	420	2	18
6	460	8	20
7	520	16	26
8	600	15	30
9	720	14	36
10	800	20	46

The data has been partly analysed and the intermediate results are available below.

$$\Sigma y = 4550 \quad \Sigma y^2 = 2\,451\,300 \quad \Sigma x_1 y = \ \ 59\,040$$
$$\Sigma x_1 = 113 \quad \Sigma x_1^2 = \ \ \ 1\,533 \quad \Sigma x_2 y = 121\,100$$
$$\Sigma x_2 = 212 \quad \Sigma x_2^2 = \ \ \ 6\,120 \quad \Sigma x_1 x_2 = \ \ 2\,780$$

(a) Examine closely, using coefficients of determination, the assertion that the level of sales varies more with movements in the level of local advertising than with changes in the level of regional company advertising.
(b) Further analysis of the raw data reveals a coefficient of multiple correlation of 0.99 and hence a coefficient of multiple determination of 0.98. Using the least squares multiple regression equation, a sales forecast for an outlet in the same area as outlet 8 in the original data has been prepared for a planned level of £12 000 of local advertising. This produces a sales forecast of £597 333 for the next month. Interpret the above information for the marketing manager to explain the value and limitations of regression analysis in sales forecasting. What other factors should be taken into account when preparing a sales forecast?

(CIMA Stage 3: May 1988)

9.5 An operative using a new process produced the following numbers of items in the first, second, third, fourth, and fifth hours, respectively: 20, 40, 50, 55, 55.

(a) Plot a scatter graph of items per hour, y, against the hour concerned, x.
(b) Calculate the regression equation of y on x and the correlation coefficient between y and x.
(c) Find the logarithms of the values 1, 2, 3, 4, and 5 of the time variable and call the resulting new variable z. Calculate the regression equation of y on z and the correlation coefficient between y and z.
(d) Comment on your answers to parts (b) and (c) with reference to your graph drawn in answer to part (a).

TIME SERIES

10.1 A TIME SERIES AND ITS COMPONENTS

As mentioned in Chapter 7, a time series is a series of values for a variable relating to a sequence of points in time.

Usually, and certainly in all cases we shall consider, the time points are equally spaced. Well-known examples of time series are the monthly trade figures, monthly unemployment figures, and the annual profit figures for a company.

We saw in Chapter 7 how a simple graph of a time series could be plotted by having time on the horizontal axis and the variable of interest on the vertical axis, plotting the values of the variable against their times of occurrence and joining the resulting points together. Figure 10.1 shows a general graph of this type based on quarterly data and covering several years. This graph is intended to illustrate the different kinds of variation which can exist in a time series.

The nearly straight line through the middle of the graph shows the overall direction of movement of the variable with time. In the example shown there is a general upward movement. This type of variation is called the *trend* (or sometimes the 'long-term trend' or 'secular trend'). The trend maintains the same general direction for a long time.

The gently curving line which moves from side to side of the trend line represents *cyclical variation* in the time series. This is an approximately periodic variation in the data values, and the period, in as much as it can be discerned, will be of several years' duration. The amplitude of the cycles may also vary from one part of the time series to another. This is the kind of variation involved in 'business cycles'.

The variation highlighted by the lines joining the plotted points together is the *seasonal variation*. This is the variation from one part of the year to another. Seasonal variation is usually regular in its period and its amplitude and we shall see later how this regularity is exploited in its analysis. In the example shown, we have larger values in the second and third quarters of the year (Q2 and Q3) than in the first and fourth quarters (Q1 and Q4). Hence this example could represent ice-cream sales or travel statistics. The opposite general seasonal pattern could be expected for unemployment figures.

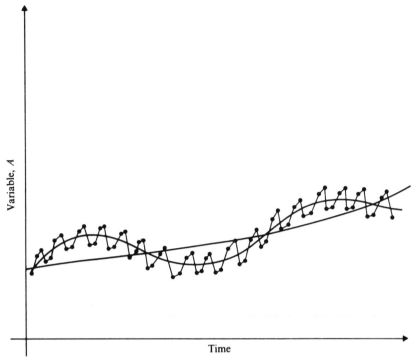

Figure 10.1 A general time series graph.

A fourth kind of variation, which cannot be effectively represented on the graph, is called *residual variation*. This, as its name implies, is the variation which is left over in the observed data when the trend, and the cyclical and seasonal variations have been accounted for. Residual variation is associated with random one-off occurrences such as strikes or natural disasters, with sampling errors that occur in data collection, or with rounding errors in processing and presentation of the data.

10.2 ESTIMATION OF THE COMPONENTS

Having seen the four components of a time series, we turn now to the matter of analysing an observed series into its component parts. There are basically two reasons why this is a useful thing to do. First, it enables us seasonally to adjust past data by removing the seasonal effect. This is done, for instance, to trade and unemployment figures which are published in seasonally adjusted form as well as in their raw state, and is of value in enabling users to discern more readily the underlying pattern in the figures, without the distortion caused by seasonality. Second, it enables forecasts of future values to be made by extrapolating the trend into the future and then combining the appropriate adjustments. A further but less common use of the analysis is in assessing the effects of one-off occurrences by eliminating all the regular variations present at a particular time point to reveal the residual variation at that point.

(a) Time series models

In order to analyse our time series into components we must have a *model* for its structure. That is to say we must specify how we believe the components are combining together to give the observed time series values.

The standard notation is to denote the observed values by A, the trend by T, the cyclical variation by C, the seasonal variation by S, and the residual variation by R.

There are two particularly common models employed. The first is the additive model, where the observed value A is regarded as the sum of the components, i.e.

$$A = T + C + S + R$$

The second is the multiplicative model, where the observed value is regarded as the product of the components, i.e.

$$A = T \times C \times S \times R$$

The additive model has limitations in that it assumes the magnitude of different types of variation to be independent of each other. It assumes, for instance, that the same seasonal quantity is added at the same period each year. However, if a time series is reasonably long with a steep trend or a marked cyclical effect it is usually found that the seasonal fluctuations are larger in magnitude where the trend is larger or at the top of a cycle than they are where the trend is smaller or at the bottom of a cycle. The multiplicative model takes this into account rather better by always multiplying by the same seasonal factor at the same time each year. Thus if trend and cycle values are larger, something larger is multiplied by the constant factor.

In this chapter our attention will be restricted to *short* time series, so the cyclical variation C will not manifest itself. Thus the models to which we can restrict our attention are the reduced additive model:

$$A = T + S + R$$

and the reduced multiplicative model:

$$A = T \times S \times R$$

The exposition in subsection (b) below is given in terms of the reduced additive model, and there follows Example 10.2.1 which uses this model. However, the ideas can be readily extended to the reduced multiplicative model. It is necessary simply to replace all subtractions in the manipulations by divisions and all additions by multiplications. Example 10.3.2 carries out a full analysis using the reduced multiplicative model.

(b) Approach to the analysis

The first step in analysing a time series is to find the trend T. There are numerous methods of varying levels of sophistication for doing this. Two very rough ones which are sometimes used are to plot the points on a graph and draw the best line by eye; and the 'method of semi-averages' which involves finding the mean of the earlier half of the data and plotting it against the mid-point of the time period to which it applies, doing the same for the later half and then joining the two points together to give a trend line. The main methods used, and the ones we shall use in the examples here, are regression, as described in Chapter 9, and the *method of moving averages*, which will be explained below.

Having found the trend T we can perform the second step in the analysis by going to the model $A = T + S + R$.

The A values are known, being the original data, and so are the T values, which have just been calculated. Hence by subtracting the known T values from the corresponding known A values we can obtain values for $S + R$, since subtraction in the model gives:

$$A - T = S + R$$

The third step is now to average the $S+R$ values over the corresponding time points. Thus if we were dealing with monthly data we should first average all January $S+R$ values, then average all February $S+R$ values, then average all March $S+R$ values, and so on. The reasoning behind this is that the residual variation R is a random effect and so by taking averages in this way we can hope that such random effects will be removed, leaving us with seasonal terms S for the various parts of the year. Either the mean or the median could reasonably be used in this averaging process. The median has points to commend it here because it is not affected by extreme values. Thus if in a particular February, say, there was a major strike affecting the figures, it would be better to leave that February out when finding the average of the February $S+R$ effects. The median would do this while the mean would spread the effect of the strike over all terms in the calculation. However, for the sake of consistency we shall in all of the examples here use the mean to average our $S+R$ values in accordance with more usual practice. The fourth step depends on the purpose of the analysis. If the residual variation for a particular time points were of interest it could be found by a further subtraction giving

$$A - T - S = R$$

If the purpose of the analysis were seasonal adjustment of past data, the procedure would be to subtract the appropriate S values from the original A values giving the seasonally adjusted series

$$A - S$$

If the purpose were the forecasting of future values, the fourth step would involve extrapolating the trend into the future and then adding on the appropriate seasonal term, i.e. forecast future values of the variable using

$$A = T + S$$

The residual variation is by its nature unpredictable and cannot be taken into account when making such forecasts.

In what follows we shall see examples of both seasonal adjustment and forecasting problems.

(c) Mechanics of the analysis

In order to demonstrate in detail the method of analysis we shall work through an example using the method of moving averages to find the trend. The example will be used to explain the method of moving averages and comparison will be made with the use of regression as a way of finding the trend.

Example 10.2.1 The number of daily visitors to a hotel, aggregated by quarter, is shown below for the last three years.

Year	Quarter 1	Quarter 2	Quarter 3	Quarter 4
1986	—	—	—	88
1987	90	120	200	28
1988	22	60	164	16
1989	10	80	192	—

The following additive model is assumed to apply:

$$\text{series} = \text{trend} + \text{seasonal variation} + \text{residual (irregular)}$$

(a) Find the centred moving average trend.
(b) Find the average seasonal variation for each quarter.

(CIMA Stage 1: Nov. 1989)

ANSWER The calculations needed for answering this question are set out in Fig. 10.2 in what is a standard layout for dealing with problems of this sort. The steps taken are described in what follows.

The first stage is to obtain a four-quarterly moving average from the data. The point of this is that it is an average over every complete year in the data, i.e. over complete sets of seasons. If the data was monthly, the natural moving average would be a 12-monthly moving average. Using a moving average over complete years in the data there will be no net seasonal effects present in the resulting figures.

In essence taking a four-quarterly moving average involves calculating the mean of every set of four successive values in the data set. The column headed 'A' in Fig. 10.2 contains the given performance figures and the next column headed 'four-quarterly total' is the first step towards

		A	Four-quarterly total	Two-step total	T	$A-T=S+R$	$A-S$
1986	Q4	88					138
1987	Q1	90					143
			498				
	Q2	120		936	117	3	119
			438				
	Q3	200		808	101	99	98
			370				
	Q4	28		680	85	-57	78
			310				
1988	Q1	22		584	73	-51	75
			274				
	Q2	60		536	67	-7	59
			262				
	Q3	164		512	64	100	56
			250				
	Q4	16		520	65	-49	66
			270				
1989	Q1	10		568	71	-61	63
	Q2	80	298				
	Q3	192					

	1987	1988	1989	Means	Corrected means	S
Q1	—	-51	-61	-56	-53.125	-53
Q2	3	-7	—	-2	0.875	1
Q3	99	100	—	99.5	102.375	102
Q4	-57	-49	—	-53	-50.125	-50
				$\overline{-11.5}$		
				$-11.5/4 = -2.875$		

Figure 10.2 Analysis and seasonal adjustment of a quarterly time series.

finding the four-quarterly moving average. It shows the sum of each successive group of four data items. The first four figures, from Q4 of 1986 to Q3 of 1987, add up to 498; the second group of four figures, from Q1 of 1987 to Q4 of 1987, add up to 438; and so on. These sums were written at the mid-points of the time periods to which they apply.

Because in this case we have (as is commonly the case) the year divided into an even number of time points, the totals appear *between* time points. Hence we cannot just divide the totals by four to obtain the required moving average trend values T as we need these actually on the time points where the A values are. So in cases like this where we have an *even* number of time points in each year we must next calculate a column of two-step moving totals by taking the sum of each successive pair of values in the first moving total column. This gives the column headed 'two-step total'. The values in this column are on the time points as required and the trend values T can be calculated by dividing each one by the number of data items which contributed to it. In this example involving quarterly data this means dividing by 8. If the data had been monthly, we should have needed to divide by 24.

The method of moving averages is thus seen to be quite a simple method to operate, and certainly it is the standard method to use in dealing with questions of this type. We can, however, see certain problems that it raises which would not have occurred if the (more involved) method of regression had been used. First, we do not have a trend value T for every time point. We have no T values for Q4 of 1986, Q1 of 1987 or for Q2 and Q3 of 1989. This means less information on which to base our $S + R$ averages at the next stage. Second, we do not obtain an actual equation for the trend. This is not particularly important in situations where the objective is to do seasonal adjustments but causes difficulty if the intention is to extend the trend into the future for forecasting purposes. As we shall see in Sec. 10.3, we are reduced to crude approximation or to a graphical approach. The method of moving averages can in practice be used for a preliminary analysis to see whether a linear trend is present, and could then be used for the analysis proper if the trend were found to be definitely not linear.

Having found the T values the next step is to subtract the T value from the A value at every time point for which this is possible. This results in the set of values shown in the column headed '$A - T = S + R$'.

In order to find the averages of the $S + R$ values it is usual to rewrite them in a second table as shown in the lower part of Fig. 10.2. The columns are labelled by the years and the rows by the 'seasons', so that the averages required are along the rows. The results are shown in the column headed 'Means'. An adjustment is needed before the S values can be regarded as having been found. By definition, the seasonal effects are variations between one part of the year and another. Hence there can be no net seasonal effect over all the seasons combined and for the additive model this means that the sum of the seasonal effects must be zero. If, as in this case, the sum of the averages is not zero, it must be adjusted to zero by subtracting the mean of the averages from each individual average. This gives the column headed 'Corrected means'. In the calculations for this example the working has been to three decimal places, and it is necessary to work to reasonable accuracy if we are not to run the risk of error in the final answer. However, in stating the final values for the seasonal effects there is no justification for claiming greater accuracy than the original data. Hence the values have been rounded in the final column headed 'S'.

A final column (not asked for in the question) has been added to the upper table in Fig. 10.2 to illustrate seasonal adjustment. The figures in this column, headed '$A - S$' have been obtained by subtracting the appropriate S terms from the original values A.

Exercise 10.2.1 The table below shows the numbers of units sold of a company's product quarter by quarter over a period of three-and-a-half years.

	Q1	Q2	Q3	Q4
1987	100	125	127	102
1988	104	128	130	107
1989	110	131	133	107
1990	109	132		

(a) Use the method of moving averages to find a set of trend values.
(b) Use the additive model to obtain a seasonal term for each quarter.
(c) Make some suggestions as to what the company's product might be.
(d) Obtain a set of seasonally adjusted values for the period covered by the data.
(e) Find the residual term for the first quarter of 1989.

10.3 FORECASTING

The basic analysis of our time series model

$$A = T + S + R$$

is the same here as in Sec. 10.2. The difference comes in the fact that we now want to use the results of the analysis to predict future values of the variable A.

When the analysis is to be used for this purpose it is helpful to use regression to find the trend as it gives an equation which can be extrapolated to give future trend values. So the first example we shall consider in this section uses the regression method, as explained in Sec. 9.2, to obtain the trend.

Example 10.3.1 Shown below are the quarterly output figures for a certain firm during the period 1984–87. Fit a straight line trend to this data using regression and use the additive model for a time series to predict output for each of the four quarters of 1988.

1984				1985				1986				1987			
Q1	Q2	Q3	Q4	Q1	Q2	Q3	Q4	Q1	Q2	Q3	Q4	Q1	Q2	Q3	Q4
20	12	10	18	23	14	13	22	28	18	17	26	30	21	20	28

ANSWER Consider Fig. 10.3. The dots are obtained by plotting the given values and these are joined by the solid black lines in the usual way for a time series graph.

The straight black line is the least squares regression line for the data, obtained as shown below using the formulae for a and b. The predicted values for 1988 are obtained by applying the appropriate seasonal adjustments to the values on the regression line when it is extrapolated into 1988. These predicted values are shown joined by broken lines.

The bulk of the analysis is shown in Fig. 10.4. The first two columns of this table show the times and output figures as given. In order to find the trend we seek to fit to this data a straight line having equation

$$p = a + bt$$

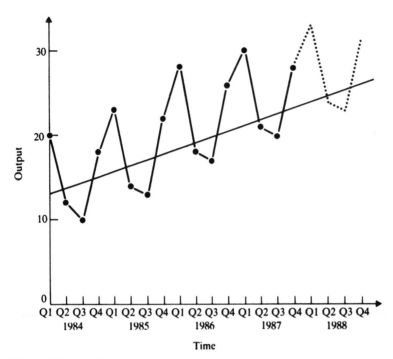

Figure 10.3   A time series graph and its projection to future time points.

		Output, p	Time, t	pt	t	T	$p - T = S + R$
1984	Q1	20	−15	−300	225	14.375	5.625
	Q2	12	−13	−156	169	15.125	−3.125
	Q3	10	−11	−110	121	15.875	−5.875
	Q4	18	−9	−162	81	16.625	1.375
1985	Q1	23	−7	−161	49	17.375	5.625
	Q2	14	−5	−70	25	18.125	−4.125
	Q3	13	−3	−39	9	18.875	−5.875
	Q4	22	−1	−22	1	19.625	2.375
1986	Q1	28	1	28	1	20.375	7.625
	Q2	18	3	54	9	21.125	−3.125
	Q3	17	5	85	25	21.875	−4.875
	Q4	26	7	182	49	22.625	3.375
1987	Q1	30	9	270	81	23.375	6.625
	Q2	21	11	231	121	24.125	−3.125
	Q3	20	13	260	169	24.875	−4.875
	Q4	28	15	420	225	25.625	2.375
		320	0	510	1360		

	1984	1985	1986	1987	Means
Q1	5.625	5.625	7.625	6.625	6.375
Q2	−3.125	−4.125	−3.125	−3.125	−3.375
Q3	−5.875	−5.875	−4.875	−4.875	−5.375
Q4	1.375	2.375	3.375	2.375	2.375
					Sum = 0

Figure 10.4   Analysis of a time series using linear regression to find the trend.

where p represents the output and t is the time. The first requirement is that the time should be in numerical form. The most efficient way to do this for calculation purposes is to take time zero as being at the end of 1985 and the unit of time as half of a three-month period. Hence the column of t values shown.

We can then use the formulae for a and b from Chapter 9, which in this example will take the form:

$$b = \frac{\Sigma pt - (\Sigma p)(\Sigma t)/n}{\Sigma t^2 - (\Sigma t)^2/n} \qquad a = \frac{\Sigma p - b\Sigma t}{n}$$

Thus we have

$$b = (510 - 0)/(1360 - 0) = 510/1360 = 0.375$$
$$a = (320 - 0)/16 \qquad = 320/16 \quad = 20$$

So the equation of the regression line is $p = 20 + 0.375t$.

Having obtained this trend line, we can now find the column of trend values, headed 'T' in the table, by substituting in turn the values $t = -15$, $t = -13$, $t = -11, \ldots, t = 13$, $t = 15$ in the expression $20 + 0.375t$. (For example, $20 - 0.375 \times 15 = 14.375$ which is the first value in the column.) At this point we use the model $p = T + S + R$ to say that $p - T = S + R$ and hence, by subtracting the T values which we have established from the given p values, we obtain a column of $S + R$ values.

The final column is then employed in the usual way as shown in the lower table of Fig. 10.4 to establish an S value for each season by taking the mean $S + R$ value over corresponding seasons. (Since the sum of the means here is zero, no correction is needed.) Hence we have the four seasonal figures shown and the output for the four quarters of 1988 can now be predicted.

For Q1 we have

$$t = 17 \text{ so } T = 20 + 0.375 \times 17 = 20 + 6.375 = 26.375$$

So the forecast is

$$26.375 + 6.375 = 32.75$$

which we round to 33. For Q2 we have

$$t = 19 \text{ so } T = 20 + 0.375 \times 19 = 20 + 7.125 = 27.125$$

So the forecast is

$$27.125 - 3.375 = 23.75$$

which we round to 24. For Q3 we have

$$t = 21 \text{ so } T = 20 + 0.375 \times 21 = 20 + 7.875 = 27.875$$

So the forecast is

$$27.875 - 5.375 = 22.50$$

which we round to 23. For Q4 we have

$$t = 23 \text{ so } T = 20 + 0.375 \times 23 = 20 + 8.625 = 28.625$$

So the forecast is

$$28.625 + 2.375 = 31$$

Next we consider a forecasting example where the trend is found by the method of moving averages. This example also demonstrates use of the multiplicative model

$$A = T \times S \times R$$

Example 10.3.2 The daily output (in units) from a factory is as shown in the following table for a four-week period.

	Monday	Tuesday	Wednesday	Thursday	Friday
Week 1	360	400	480	600	660
Week 2	350	430	490	580	680
Week 3	380	440	490	590	690
Week 4	390	450	400	600	690

(a) Use the method of moving averages to find a set of trend values.
(b) Display on a graph the actual data with the trend values.
(c) Use the multiplicative model to find, to two decimal places, the daily variation pertaining to each day of the week.
(d) Forecast the output for Monday and for Tuesday of week 5.

ANSWER

(a) The steps involved in finding the trend in this example are extremely similar to those explained in Sec. 10.2. The bulk of the calculations for the problem are shown in Fig. 10.5 and the trend values are shown boxed in the upper table there.
   The example shows that the ideas we have been considering apply not just to a year divided into quarters or months or whatever, but can apply equally well to weekly data divided into days. Since the division is into an *odd* number of days, the figures in the first moving total column are on the time points, and there is no need for a two-step moving total to bring them to the time points.
(b) Figure 10.6 shows the actual data and the trend values on a graph.
(c) After the T values have been found we turn to the model

$$A = T \times S \times R$$

The next step is to divide both sides by T to obtain

$$A/T = S \times R$$

This leads to the column of values at the top right of Fig. 10.5. Following the same approach as used for the additive model earlier, we now average the $S \times R$ values over corresponding time points. This is done in the table in the lower part of Fig. 10.5. In the additive model the mean of the seasonal terms was required to be zero in order for there to be no net seasonal addition over the whole year, but in the multiplicative model it is necessary for the mean of the seasonal terms to be 1 in order for there to be no net seasonal multiplier over the whole year. In this case the mean of the seasonal terms is seen to be 1.002. The procedure for correction is to divide each of the terms by this figure to leave a set whose mean is 1. The resulting set of average daily variations is shown boxed in the lower part of Fig. 10.5.

		A	Five-step total	T	A/T = S × R
Week 1	Mon	360			
	Tue	400			
	Wed	480	2500	500	0.960
	Thur	600	2490	498	1.205
	Fri	660	2520	504	1.310
Week 2	Mon	350	2530	506	0.692
	Tue	430	2510	502	0.857
	Wed	490	2530	506	0.968
	Thur	580	2560	512	1.133
	Fri	680	2570	514	1.323
Week 3	Mon	380	2570	514	0.739
	Tue	440	2580	516	0.853
	Wed	490	2590	518	0.946
	Thur	590	2600	520	1.135
	Fri	690	2610	522	1.322
Week 4	Mon	390	2620	524	0.744
	Tue	450	2630	526	0.856
	Wed	500	2630	526	0.951
	Thur	600			
	Fri	690			

Week 1	Week 2	Week 3	Week 4	Means	Corrected means	Average Daily variation
	0.692	0.739	0.744	0.725	0.723	0.72
	0.857	0.853	0.856	0.855	0.853	0.85
0.960	0.968	0.946	0.951	0.956	0.954	0.95
1.205	1.133	1.135		1.157	1.155	1.16
1.310	1.323	1.322		1.318	1.315	1.32
				5.012		
		5.0118/5 = 1.002				

Figure 10.5 Analysis of a time series using a five-step moving average and the multiplicative model.

(d) The next question is that of how to proceed to extrapolate the trend in order to multiply by the average daily variation terms and make the required forecasts. One possibility is to extend by eye the curve through the trend points shown in Fig. 10.6 and read off the values at the time points concerned. This curve and the author's extension of it (with which the reader is entitled to disagree) is included in Fig. 10.6.

Reading off the T values for the first two days of week 5 we obtain 217 for Monday and 218 for Tuesday. Hence the required forecast for Monday is $217 - 5 = 212$ and the forecast for Tuesday is $218 + 0 = 218$.

In cases where the growth (or decline) in trend values from one time point to another is fairly regular, an alternative to drawing a trend value graph is to calculate the average change in trend per quarter and add on to the latest trend value this average change multiplied by the number of quarters forward for which we want to forecast. This is a very rough and ready method and in graphical terms it amounts to joining the first and last points by a straight line and extending that line. The result it gives in this case is not too disastrous as

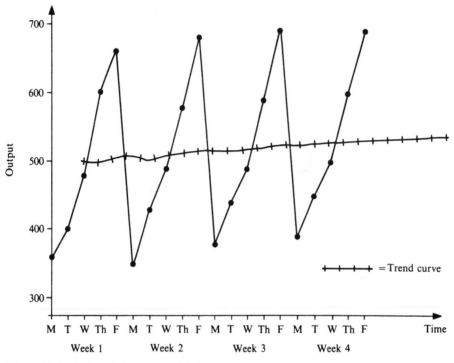

Figure 10.6 A time series graph with five-step moving average trend.

joining first and last points happens to give an extension not massively different from the extended trend on the graph.

The trend increases from 500 on the Wednesday of week 1 to 526 on the Wednesday of week 4, which is a change of 26 over 15 days. Hence the average increase per day is $26/15 = 1.733$. On this basis the predicted trend value for the Monday of week 5 is $526 + 3 \times 1.733 = 526 + 5.2 = 531.2$. So the forecast is $531.2 \times 0.72 = 382.46$ which we round to 382.

The predicted trend value for the Tuesday of week 5 is $526 + 4 \times 1.733 = 526 + 6.932 = 532.932$. So the forecast is $532.932 \times 0.85 = 453$.

Use of spreadsheets

Note that the calculations involved in time series analysis lend themselves to operations on a spreadsheet such as LOTUS 1-2-3. In fact Figs 10.2 and 10.5 were set up on spreadsheets and all the computations were done using spreadsheet formulae. In view of the substantial quantity of calculation involved in time series problems it is well worth the time to set things up in this way. As pointed out in Chapter 7, LOTUS 1-2-3 also produces good quality time series graphs. Readers interested in pursuing this point are referred to Chapter 4 of *Quantitative Analysis for Economics and Business Using LOTUS 1-2-3* by Guy Judge (see bibliography).

Exercise 10.3.1 The quarterly sales of a product are monitored by a multiplicative series model. The trend in sales is described by $Y = 100 + 5X$ where Y denotes sales volume and X denotes the quarterly time period.

The trend in sales for the most recent quarter (first quarter 1991, when $X = 20$) was 200 units. The average seasonal variations for the product are as follows:

Quarter	First	Second	Third	Fourth
Seasonal effect (%)	0	−20	+40	−20

The price of a unit was £1000 during the first quarter of 1991. This price is revised every quarter to allow for inflation, which is running at 2 per cent a quarter.

(Note that the seasonal variations given in this question mean seasonal factors of 1.0, 0.8, 1.4, and 0.8 in the sense explained.)

(a) Produce sales volume forecasts for the three remaining quarters of 1991, both actual and deseasonalized.
(b) Produce forecasts for (actual) sales revenue for the three remaining quarters of 1991, stating any assumptions.
(c) Explain briefly, in terms suitable for a management report, how the product has been performing to date.

(CIMA Stage 1: May 1991)

TEST EXERCISES

10.1 The table below shows the numbers of disputes taking place in a certain industry during the period 1986–91.

	Q1	Q2	Q3	Q4
1986	15	16	21	16
1987	14	13	19	15
1988	9	9	17	11
1989	6	6	12	8
1990	5	6	10	6
1991	6	6	9	7

(a) Use the method of moving averages to find a set of trend values.
(b) Use the additive model to obtain a seasonal term for each quarter.
(c) Adjust the time series for seasonal variations.

10.2
(a) Why is data adjusted for seasonal variation?
(b) The quarterly sales (units) of brand X for the last two years are given below.

Quarter	1	2	3	4
1987	45	66	79	40
1988	64	99	105	60
1989	90			

Past experience has shown that the average seasonal variations for this product field are as follows:

Q1	Q2	Q3	Q4
−10%	+20%	+30%	−40%

A multiplicative model is assumed to apply (sales = trend × seasonal × random).
(i) Seasonally adjust the sales of brand X.
(ii) Plot both the original sales and seasonally adjusted sales on the same time series graph.
(iii) Summarize the meaning of your results.

(CIMA Stage 1: May 1989)

(Note that the seasonal variations given in this question mean seasonal factors of 0.9, 1.2, 1.3, and 0.6 in the sense explained in the chapter).

10.3 The table below shows the sales figures in thousands of pounds for a particular product over a time span of four years.

	Jan., Feb., March, April	May, June, July, Aug.	Sep., Oct., Nov., Dec.
1988	28	16	30
1989	34	23	31
1990	34.5	21	28
1991	35	25	34

(a) Use the method of moving averages to find a set of trend values.
(b) Use the additive model to obtain a seasonal term for each period.
(c) Forecast the sales for each of the three periods in 1990.

10.4 A company's trend in sales, Y, is described by the equation $Y = 500 + 9X$, where X denotes the quarter of the year. The next period to require a sales forecast is the third quarter of the year and is denoted by $X = 20$. Past experience suggests the average quarterly variation in sales is as follows:

Q1	Q2	Q3	Q4
+30%	−20%	−25%	+15%

Using a multiplicative model (sales = trend × seasonal × random), the sales forecast for the next quarter, when $X = 20$, is

(A) 510;   (B) 544;   (C) 635;   (D) 725;   (E) 850.

(CIMA Stage 1: May 1990)

(The seasonal variations given must first be converted into seasonal factors. See note on Test Exercise 10.2 above.)

10.5 The sales (in units) for an item whose sales show a marked seasonal pattern are given in the table below.

	Q1	Q2	Q3	Q4
1989	325	382	350	363
1990	393	452	430	421
1991	471	530	500	510

(a) Use regression to find a set of trend values.
(b) Use the additive model to obtain a seasonal term for each quarter.
(c) Use your answers to parts (a) and (b) to make forecasts of the sales figures for the four quarters of 1992.

INDEX NUMBERS

11.1 CONSTRUCTION OF INDEX NUMBERS

An index number is used to show the way in which a variable we are interested in, often price, is changing with time. It does this by expressing the price at the time of interest (called the given time) as a percentage of the price at some other fixed time (called the base time). The construction of various different types of index number will be demonstrated in this section by reference to the data given below.

Example data

A survey of four companies which make similar products produced the data shown in Table 11.1 on the price (*P*) of the products and the quantity (*Q*) sold in three separate years.

Table 11.1

Year	1		2		3	
	P	*Q*	*P*	*Q*	*P*	*Q*
Company A	2	6	3	7	3	10
Company B	4	2	4	7	5	8
Company C	4	12	6	3	5	9
Company D	8	9	7	14	9	4

(Data from ACCA Level 1: June 1988)

As a very simple example, suppose we wanted to calculate a price index for the company A product using year 1 as base year and year 2 as given year. This index would be $(3/2) \times 100 = 150$ per cent. The price at the given time is 50 per cent up on what it was at the base time for this company's product.

Note in passing that the ratio

$$\text{Given time price/Base time price} = 3/2 = 1.5$$

(not expressed as a percentage) is called the *price relative* for the company A product using year 1 as base year and year 2 as given year. We shall have cause to look again later at price relatives.

Note also that the value of an index number at base time must always be 100 since it is

$$\text{(Base time price/Base time price)} \times 100 = 1 \times 100 = 100$$

Hence in published statistics it is usual to declare the base date by means of a statement like

$$\text{'13 January } 1987 = 100\text{'}$$

The above example is an extremely simple one involving just one item. In practice we are concerned with combining together the price changes in several items to produce an overall index. This is the idea in the Index of Retail Prices where price changes in a wide variety of items (see Sec. 11.2) are combined together to produce what is commonly regarded as a 'cost of living' index. In the context of the example being considered here we shall combine together the changes in prices for the products of the four different companies to obtain an overall price index.

Index numbers giving all items equal weight

As a first step let us ignore the quantities sold of the different products and think about ways in which prices might be combined to produce an index.

1. The simple aggregative index Suppose we want to express the price in year 2 as a percentage of the price in year 1. One way to approach this would be to look at

$$\text{company A price} + \text{company B price} + \text{company C price} + \text{company D price}$$

comparing this in year 2 with its value in year 1. This gives

$$[(3+4+6+7)/(2+4+4+8)] \times 100$$
$$= (20/18) \times 100 = 111.11 \text{ per cent}$$

This is called a simple aggregative index because it compares one aggregate of prices with another.

In general, if base year prices are denoted by P_0 and given year prices by P_n, the simple aggregative index is

$$(\Sigma P_n / \Sigma P_0) \times 100$$

2. The simple mean of price relatives Suppose again that we want to calculate a price index using year 1 as base year and year 2 as given year using prices alone. Another way we might proceed would be to calculate a separate index for each of the products and then take the mean of these indices. This can be achieved by calculating the price relative for the product of each company, finding the mean of the price relatives and finally multiplying the result by 100. For this example we have:

$$\{[(3/2) + (4/4) + (6/4) + (7/8)]/4\} \times 100$$
$$= \{[1.500 + 1.000 + 1.500 + 0.875]/4\} \times 100 = (4.875/4) \times 100 = 121.875 \text{ per cent}$$

In general, if base time prices are denoted by P_0 and given time prices by P_n, then the simple mean of price relatives is

$$\{[\Sigma(P_n/P_0)]/k\} \times 100$$

where k is the number of items.

Exercise 11.1.1 Calculate:

(a) the simple aggregative index;
(b) the simple mean of price relatives using year 1 as base year and year 3 as given year.

Index numbers giving all items equal weight are of little use in practice because some items are more important than others and so should be given more weight in determining the value of the index. The simple aggregative index has a further particular disadvantage in that its value is affected by the units for which the prices of different items are included. For example, an index combining meat and milk prices will have one value if we use pounds of meat and pints of milk but a wholly different value if we use tons of meat and gallons of milk.

However, the index numbers we have been considering so far are worth looking at because those used in practice are extensions of these, giving different weights to different items—namely weighted aggregative indices and weighted means of price relatives.

Index numbers giving different weights to different items

1. Weighted aggregative indices The number of items which are paid for, produced, consumed, or whatever, can be regarded as a measure of how important that item is in determining the overall level of price change. So in weighted aggregative indices the prices of the different items are weighted by the quantities relating to some point in time. There are several different types of weighted aggregative index corresponding to quantities from different time points being used as weights.

(a) *The Laspeyres index.* Here the quantities relating to the base time are used as weights. Thus for our example data the Laspeyres price index using year 1 as base year and year 2 as given year is

$$\left(\frac{3 \times 6 + 4 \times 2 + 6 \times 12 + 7 \times 9}{2 \times 6 + 4 \times 2 + 4 \times 12 + 8 \times 9}\right) \times 100$$

$$= (161/140) \times 100 = 115.00 \text{ per cent}$$

In general, denoting base time prices by P_0, base time quantities by Q_0, and given time prices by P_n we see that the formula for the Laspeyres index is

$$(\Sigma P_n Q_0 / \Sigma P_0 Q_0) \times 100$$

Exercise 11.1.2 Calculate the Laspeyres price index using year 1 as base year and year 3 as given year.

(b) *The Paasche index.* Here the quantities relating to the given time are used as weights. So for our example data the Paasche price index using year 1 as base year and year 2 as given year is

$$\left(\frac{3 \times 7 + 4 \times 7 + 6 \times 3 + 7 \times 14}{2 \times 7 + 4 \times 7 + 4 \times 3 + 8 \times 14}\right) \times 100$$

$$= (165/166) \times 100 = 99.40 \text{ per cent}$$

In general, denoting base time prices by P_0, given time prices by P_n, and given time quantities by Q_n we see that the formula for the Paasche index is

$$(\Sigma P_n Q_n / \Sigma P_0 Q_n) \times 100$$

Exercise 11.1.3 Calculate the Paasche price index using year 1 as base year and year 3 as given year.

(c) *The typical year index.* This is also a weighted aggregative index in that it is of the form

$$(\Sigma w P_n / \Sigma w P_0) \times 100$$

where the *w*'s are weights. The weights this time are the quantities relating to a time which is neither the base time nor the given time. To illustrate this we calculate for our example data the price index for year 1 as base year and year 3 as given year with year 2 quantities as the weights. This gives

$$\left(\frac{3 \times 7 + 5 \times 7 + 5 \times 3 + 9 \times 14}{2 \times 7 + 4 \times 7 + 4 \times 3 + 8 \times 14}\right) \times 100$$

$$= (197/166) \times 100 = 118.67 \text{ per cent}$$

If base year prices are denoted by P_0, given year prices by P_n, and quantities for the 'other' year, known as the *typical year*, by Q_t, then the general formula for the typical year index is

$$(\Sigma P_n Q_t / \Sigma P_0 Q_t) \times 100$$

Exercise 11.1.4 Calculate the typical year price index using year 2 as base year and year 3 as given year with year 1 quantities as weights.

Quantity indices and the value index All the index numbers considered so far have been price indices. They have compared the price of a combination of items from the four companies at one time with the price of the same combination of items at another time. In some situations, however, such as the Index of Industrial Production, it is required to compare the quantity produced at one time with the quantity produced at another time. A simple aggregative quantity index would be obtained by simply comparing the sum of the quantities for the given year with the sum of quantities for the base year. i.e.

Simple aggregative quantity index $= (\Sigma Q_n / \Sigma Q_0) \times 100$

A simple mean of relatives would be found by calculating the quantity relative Q_n / Q_0 for each item and then obtaining the mean of these.

Simple mean of quantity relatives $= \{[\Sigma(Q_n / Q_0)]/k\} \times 100$

where *k* is the number of items.

The importance of an item in determining a quantity index can be measured by the price of that item, e.g. a given increase in number of Rovers produced would be more important than an identical increase in the number of Minis.

Thus a weighted aggregative quantity index is calculated by using the prices at some specified point in time to weight the quanities in both numerator and denominator. For example,

the Laspeyres quantity index is $(\Sigma Q_n P_0 / \Sigma Q_0 P_0) \times 100$

and

the Paasche quantity index is $(\Sigma Q_n P_n / \Sigma Q_0 P_n) \times 100$

The value index is something having the same general form as a weighted aggregative index in that it has a sum of products of price × quantity in the numerator and another sum of price × quantity products in the denominator. However, it is neither a price index nor a quantity index; it measures the change in total value of sales, production, wage bill, or whatever, as a result of changes in both price and quantity.

$$\text{Value index} = (\Sigma P_n Q_n / \Sigma P_0 Q_0) \times 100$$

Calculating the value index for our example data taking year 1 as base year and year 2 as given year, the numerator shows the total value of items sold in year 2 and the denominator the total value of items sold in year 1.

$$\left(\frac{3 \times 7 + 4 \times 7 + 6 \times 3 + 7 \times 14}{2 \times 6 + 4 \times 2 + 4 \times 12 + 8 \times 9} \right) \times 100$$

$$= (165/140) \times 100 = 117.86 \text{ per cent}$$

Exercise 11.1.5 Calculate the value index using year 1 as base year and year 3 as given year.

Comments on the different types of weighted aggregative index The Laspeyres is the most commonly used of the weighted aggregative indices. The Index of Industrial Production is essentially a Laspeyres quantity index. It is good from a practical administrative point of view because once the weights have been found they are fixed until it is decided to move to a new base date. The other side of this coin is that if the pattern of demand, production, or whatever, is subject to serious change then the weighting system could become out of touch with the current pattern. It is argued that in times of inflation Laspeyres will tend to overstate the inflation rate since no account is taken of the effect on the cost of living of reduction in demand for items whose prices have risen particularly rapidly. A further merit of this type of index is that every value in a published Laspeyres series is referring to the same basket of goods.

The Paasche index has the merit of using an up-to-date basket of goods and so is talking about the change in price of what is *now* actually being bought, produced, or whatever. This is especially useful if the pattern is subject to marked changes, though there may be some understatement of inflation because of reduction in demand for some items whose prices have risen rapidly. A major practical problem with the Paasche index is that of how to get the up-to-date weights; the amount of data collection may be very expensive or difficult, perhaps impossibly so. Hence the Paasche index is not very commonly used. Each time a Paasche index is calculated the reference is to a different basket of goods, so successive values in a Paasche series are not directly comparable.

The 'typical year index' is useful where we have good data available on quantities for some particular year as a result, for example, of its having been a census of production year, while some other year is desirable as base year, perhaps for reasons of compatibility with other indices. The basket of goods is fixed so this index avoids the need for extensive data collection and gives series of figures which are comparable with each other. The weights will not be as up to date as those in the Paasche index, but will not be as out of date as those in the Laspeyres index if the weighting year is later than the base year. Furthermore, being a compromise year relieves the effect on the index of changes in demand between base year and given year resulting from alteration in prices. If the weighting year is earlier than the base year, these 'Laspeyres problems' will be intensified rather than diminished.

2. Weighted means of relatives This is an extension of the simple mean of price relatives idea, where instead of just taking a straight mean of the relatives we add them together with a different weight multiplying each one and then divide out by the sum of the weights. Thus the general form for the weighted mean of price relatives is:

$$[\Sigma(P_n/P_0)w/\Sigma w] \times 100$$

where the w's are weights. The usual weighting here is not by quantities as in the weighted aggregative indices but by *values* (i.e. price $\times$ quantity) relating to some point in time. Once again weightings from all sorts of different times can be used (though they are not given people's names in this case) and the same sort of comments about the relative merits of these different times apply as in the weighted aggregative case. Weighted means of relatives as a whole are very important in practice, the great majority of indices published in the United Kingdom being of this type. We shall think about why this is so later.

(a) *Weighting by base time values.* Here the weights are $w = P_0Q_0$. For the example data this index using year 1 as base year and year 2 as given year is

$$\left(\frac{(3/2) \times 2 \times 6 + (4/4) \times 4 \times 2 + (6/4) \times 4 \times 12 + (7/8) \times 8 \times 9}{(2 \times 6) + (4 \times 2) + (4 \times 12) + (8 \times 9)}\right) \times 100$$

This reduces to $(161/140) \times 100 = 115.00$ per cent, which is the same value as we obtained for Laspeyres, and this is hardly surprising if we think about the formula:

$$[\Sigma(P_n/P_0)(P_0Q_0)/\Sigma(P_0Q_0)] \times 100 = (\Sigma P_nQ_0/\Sigma P_0Q_0) \times 100$$

which is the Laspeyres index.

Exercise 11.1.6 Find the base weighted mean of price relatives using year 1 as base year and year 3 as given year.

(b) *Weighting by given time values.* Here the weights are $w = P_nQ_n$. For the example data this index using year 1 as base year and year 2 as given year is

$$\left(\frac{(3/2) \times 3 \times 7 + (4/4) \times 4 \times 7 + (6/4) \times 6 \times 3 + (7/8) \times 7 \times 14}{(3 \times 7) + (4 \times 7) + (6 \times 3) + (7 \times 14)}\right) \times 100$$

This reduces to $(172.25/165) \times 100 = 104.39$ per cent.

Exercise 11.1.7 Calculate the given time weighted mean of price relatives using year 1 as base year and year 3 as given year.

(c) *Weighting by 'typical' time values.* Here the weights are $w = P_tQ_t$, referring to a year which is neither base year nor given year. Again this is appropriate if the weights available for some particular year are good, but some other year is wanted as the base year. This is the method used for the Index of Wholesale Prices.

For the example data using year 1 as base year and year 3 as given year with year 2 values as weights this index is

$$\left(\frac{(3/2) \times 3 \times 7 + (5/4) \times 4 \times 7 + (5/4) \times 6 \times 3 + (9/8) \times 7 \times 14}{(3 \times 7) + (4 \times 7) + (6 \times 3) + (7 \times 14)}\right) \times 100$$

This reduces to $(199.25/165) \times 100 = 120.76$ per cent.

Exercise 11.1.8 Calculate the weighted mean of price relatives using year 2 as base year and year 3 as given year with year 1 values as weights.

Of the two broad types of index number giving different weights to different items, weighted aggregative indices are the easier to calculate. Also the units problem referred to earlier in relation to the simple aggregative index is overcome in the weighted aggregative index because the weights are generally numbers of units.

Weighted means of price relatives are more difficult to calculate but are more commonly used. Their chief merit is that they allow separate indices for sub-groups of items to be combined together using their weights to give an overall index. In particular, this kind of index is used for the Index of Retail Prices considered in the next section.

Exercise 11.1.9 The hourly wage rates of part-time workers in a company together with the hours worked per week are given below. The data is shown for three consecutive years.

Worker	Year 1		Year 2		Year 3	
	rate (£)	hours	rate (£)	hours	rate (£)	hours
A	3	4	2	7	4	10
B	4	6	5	8	6	12
C	5	9	8	9	7	14

(a) Using year 1 as a base construct a Laspeyres index for the hourly wage rate.
(b) Using year 1 as a base construct a Paasche index for the hourly wage rate.
(c) Contrast the results for the Laspeyres index and for the Paasche index.
(d) What advantages does a Laspeyres index have over a Paasche index?
(e) Why is a weighted index of price relatives to be preferred to a Laspeyres or Paasche index in measuring changes in retail prices?

(ACCA Level 1: Dec. 1988)

Aids to calculation

1. Tabular format The calculations in this section have for purposes of explanation been set out as large fractions. However, it is usually more efficient to set out these calculations in a table format, and we give below the calculations of the Laspeyres and Paasche price indices with year 1 as base year and year 2 as given year using this format. All the other index number calculations can be cast into the same form and we leave it as an exercise for the reader to do this.

	P_0	Q_0	P_n	Q_n	P_0Q_0	P_nQ_0	P_nQ_n	P_0Q_n
Company A	2	6	3	7	12	18	21	14
Company B	4	2	4	7	8	8	28	28
Company C	4	12	6	3	48	72	18	12
Company D	8	9	7	14	72	63	98	112
Total					140	161	165	166

Laspeyres price index $= (161/140) \times 100 = 115.00$ per cent
Paasche price index $ = (165/166) \times 100 = 99.40$ per cent

2. Spreadsheets When considered in the tabular format shown above, index number calculations lend themselves readily to being calculated on a spreadsheet such as LOTUS 1-2-3. The figures for prices and quantities can be entered into columns in the spreadsheet and then formulae using cell addresses, suitably copied down the columns, can be used to obtain columns containing all the relevant products of pairs of numbers. The @SUM function can then be used to obtain the column totals and further formulae using cell addresses will give the required index values. For examples of the use of LOTUS 1-2-3 for index number calculations of this kind see Chapter 3 of *Quantitative Analysis for Economics and Business Using LOTUS 1-2-3* by Guy Judge (see bibliography).

11.2 INDEX OF RETAIL PRICES

This is probably the best known of all UK official statistics and has general acceptability to both sides of industry and to people of most political persuasions as an indicator of domestic price inflation. Objections are sometimes raised that it does not properly represent the inflation experienced by some sections of the community and because it omits certain items which some people feel should be included, such as the capital element of mortgage repayments, insurance and pension contributions, and income tax. However, through its being administered by the Retail Prices Index Advisory Committee (which includes members from the TUC, the CBI, and trade and consumer groups as well as civil servants) responsible to the Secretary of State for Employment, the Index of Retail Prices is generally accepted as a fair attempt to give an overall measure of price inflation. The index is accepted by both sides in wage negotiations, it has been used for certain government-backed savings schemes, many pensions, particularly in the public sector, are linked to it, and certain sub-indices are used for annual updating of insurance cover. Some of these uses will be covered in Sec. 11.3. Because the Index of Retail Prices is so important we shall in this section look at how it is constructed.

In essence it is a weighted mean of price relatives with its base date at 13 January 1987.

It is not possible to include every imaginable product and service in the index and indeed it would not materially improve the index if this could be done. What is needed is a representative selection of products and services, and in all 350 are used. These 350 items can be classified into 95 sections, which can in turn be classed into 11 groups. The first step is to obtain a price relative for each of the 350 items using the Tuesday nearest the middle of the month for which the index is to be quoted as the given time, and the Tuesday nearest the middle of the immediately preceding January as base time. This requires obtaining on the Tuesday nearest the middle of each month 150 000 separate price quotations. Some of these can be obtained centrally but discovering most of the shop prices involves Department of Employment staff from unemployment benefit offices visiting a set sample of shops all over the country to record prices actually being charged.

Having obtained the 350 price relatives, a weighted mean is calculated within each of the 95 section indices. The weights used for this purpose are the proportions, expressed as parts in 1000 of expenditure on each of the 350 items as found by the *Family Expenditure Survey* for the year ended the previous June. Hence during each year a different set of weights is being used, and this helps keep the index up to date in its weighting pattern.

Having found the 95 section indices, these can in turn be combined together using their total section weights to give the 11 group indices. Here we see the advantage of using a weighted mean of relatives. This process of combining sub-indices would not have been possible if a weighted aggregative method had been used to obtain the 95 section indices.

Combining the 11 group indices together using their weights then gives the overall index for the month of interest as given time and the preceding January as base time. We have a *link-based* series of index numbers. For publication purposes reference must be made back to January 1987 as base date. This involves multiplying the index as calculated above by all January-to-January indices back to January 1987. Thus, for example, the published index for July 1989 was obtained as follows:

(Calculated index with July 1989 given and January 1989 as base)

× (index for January 1989 given and January 1988 as base)

× (index for January 1988 as given and January 1987 as base)

Note that the product of the last two terms in the above is what would be published as the index for January 1989. The advantage of this procedure over relating the original relatives directly to January 1987 before calculating the weighted mean is that it allows the proportional change in price in any particular period to be weighted by an up-to-date basket of goods.

Separate quarterly indices are published for one-person and two-person pensioner households, but although the weighting pattern differs considerably from that of the general index (in whose calculation such households are omitted if at least three-quarters of the income is from National Insurance sources) the actual index differs very little from the general index. This is an encouragement to believe in the general index as a reasonable average inflation measure.

The Index of Retail Prices is published each month under its 11 main group headings: food, alcoholic drink, tobacco, housing, fuel and light, durable household goods, clothing and footwear, transport and vehicles, services, meals bought and consumed outside the home, and miscellaneous goods. Some of these groups are broken down for publication purposes into sub-groups. For example, the transport and vehicles group is broken down into two sub-groups: motoring and cycling, fares.

For each group and sub-group included there is shown both its own index and its weighting in the overall index as parts in 1000.

As an example of how a sub-group index is made up from sections and their representative items, consider the motoring and cycling sub-group of the transport and vehicles group shown in Table 11.2.

Table 11.2 Motoring and cycling sub-group

Section	Items
Purchase of vehicles	Specified models of second-hand cars and motor scooters
Maintenance of vehicles	Charges for specified jobs
	Car and motor cycle tyres
Petrol and oil	Petrol
	Engine oil
Motor licences	Annual car licence
	Annual motor cycle licence
Motor insurance	Third party insurance rates for specified cars and motor cycles

First news of the Index of Retail Prices comes in a press release from the Department of Employment usually on the Friday four-and-a-half weeks after the Tuesday on which the prices were collected. Initial publication of the index broken down into groups, sub-groups and sections is in the monthly *Employment Gazette*. It is subsequently repeated in various summary statistical publications including the *Monthly Digest of Statistics*, *Economic Trends* and the *Annual Abstract of Statistics*.

Exercise 11.2.1

(a) Explain the principles and methods involved in the compilation and construction of the UK General Index of Retail Prices under the following headings:
  (i) base year;
  (ii) weights;
  (iii) items included;
  (iv) data collection;
  (v) calculation.
(b) Give *two* specific business applications of the index.

(CIMA Stage 1: Nov. 1988)

11.3 INTERPRETATION AND USE OF INDEX NUMBERS

(a) Points changes and percentage changes

Consider the selection of values for the Index of Retail Prices in Table 11.3.

Table 11.3

October	1986	388.4	(15 Jan. 1974 = 100)
January	1987	394.4	(15 Jan. 1974 = 100)
October	1987	102.9	(13 Jan. 1987 = 100)
July	1989	115.5	(13 Jan. 1987 = 100)

The increase from October 1987 to July 1989 was 12.6 *points*. We must be careful not to refer to this as 12.6 per cent. The percentage change is

$$(12.6/102.9) \times 100 = 12.2 \text{ per cent}$$

It is the year-on-year percentage changes which are generally of interest, and these are the figures quoted most widely in the media each month.

(b) Comparison of index values using different base dates

Consider again the set of figures shown in Table 11.3 and suppose now that we want to compare the value of the index at October 1987 with its value at October 1986. Direct comparison is clearly impossible since these figures relate to different base dates. The procedure is to 'convert' the October 1986 figure to January 1987 as base date by dividing by the figure for January 1987 using January 1974 as base date, a procedure known as *splicing*. Thus we obtain $(388.4/394.4) \times 100 = 98.5$. This can now be compared with the figure of 102.9 for October 1987, showing an increase of 4.4 points or $(4.4/98.5) \times 100 = 4.5$ per cent.

(c) Index numbers as deflators

In times of inflation index numbers can be used to produce comparisons in real terms rather than in monetary terms, i.e. they can be used to 'deflate' the effects of inflation.

The procedure is simply to divide each of the figures to be compared by the value of the appropriate index for the time point to which the figure relates.

In annual pay negotiations, representatives of the labour side seek in general to obtain a percentage increase on current rates for those they represent which is larger than the percentage increase during the year just ended in the Index of Retail Prices. This is necessary in order for there to be a *real* increase in rates or 'improvement in standard of living'.

(d) Index linking in insurance

Most insurance companies encourage their clients to reduce the risk of being under-insured on house and contents policies by having the cover adjusted each year using appropriate index numbers. This involves multiplying the cover at renewal date by the proportional change in the appropriate index over the year just ended. For buildings, the index used is one of construction costs, while for private house contents it is common to use the 'durable household goods' group index from the Index of Retail Prices.

Exercise 11.3.1 The senior partner in your firm wishes to compare real wages for the years 1979 to 1989. The actual wage rates, in pounds, for these years are given below. A Laspeyres price index, covering food and transport for 1979 to 1984 with 1979 = 100 already exists and is given below. Further data has been collected to allow a Laspeyres index for 1984 to 1989 with 1984 = 100 to be constructed.

Year	Price index 1979 = 100	Money wage (£)	Food Price	Food Quantity	Transport Price	Transport Quantity
1979	100	98				
1980	105	105				
1981	107	110				
1982	111	117				
1983	115	121				
1984	117	125	21.1	15	2.9	47
1985		129	21.5	16	3.0	51
1986		133	22.0	18	3.3	52
1987		136	22.5	18	3.4	54
1888		140	22.8	20	3.6	56
1989		152	23.0	21	3.8	59

(a) Construct a Laspeyres price index for the years 1984 to 1989 using 1984 = 100 and rounding the figures to the nearest whole number.
(b) Construct a price index for 1979 to 1989 with 1984 = 100 and round this index to the nearest whole number.
(c) Construct a series for real wages for 1979 to 1989.
(d) On the same graph show the price index, the actual wages, and the real wages for 1979 to 1989, using 1984 = 100.

(ACCA Level 1: Dec. 1990)

TEST EXERCISES

11.1 A company sells two sorts of freezers—'upright' and 'chest'. In total, it sold the same number of freezers in 1991 as in 1990. In 1990, it sold twice as many 'uprights' as 'chests', but sold equal numbers of 'uprights' and chests' in 1991. Upright freezers sold for £300 and 'chests' for £200 throughout the period. An index number for revenue for 1991, based on 1990 = 100, is closest to
(A) 50; (B) 63; (C) 88; (D) 94; (E) 100.

(CIMA Stage 1: Nov. 1991)

11.2 A village grocer's records show that he sold the following quantities of basic foods at the stated prices in January 1991 and January 1992.

	January 1991		January 1992	
	Price	Quantity	Price	Quantity
Milk	25p per pint	6000 pints	30p per pint	6250 pints
Sugar	44p per kilo	2300 kilos	59p per kilo	2600 kilos
Tea	150p per lb	1600 lbs	165p per lb	1800 lbs
Bread	350p per loaf	4200 loaves	40p per loaf	4300 loaves

(a) Explain why a simple aggregative index would be particularly unsuitable for this data.
(b) Calculate a simple mean of price relatives index using January 1991 as base time and January 1992 as given time.
(c) Explain why simple (or unweighted) index numbers are little used in practice.
(d) Calculate a weighted mean of price relatives index using January 1991 as base time and January 1992 as given time with base time quantities as weights.
(e) What can you say about the index calculated in answer to part (d)?

11.3 For a certain product, data is available on last quarter's sales, by value, and on the current quarter's prices and sales volume. Which one of the following index number types can be calculated, using the last quarter as base?

(a) Laspeyres price index.
(b) Laspeyres quantity (volume) index.
(c) Paasche price index.
(d) Paasche quantity (volume) index.
(e) Sales value index.

(CIMA Stage 1: Nov. 1990)

11.4 A company wishes to measure the change in its performance using an index calculated from the data given below on numbers of items sold and their prices in 1990 and 1991.

Item	1990 Price (£)	Number	1991 Price (£)	Number
A	2.50	90	2.70	200
B	3.80	150	4.00	160
C	4.10	180	4.50	120

Calculate:

(a) the value index;
(b) the Laspeyres quantity index;
(c) the Paasche quantity index;
(d) the weighted mean of quantity relatives using 1991 weights.

(In all these calculations 1990 should be used as base year and 1991 as given year.)
  Explain the meaning of the results obtained.

11.5 In the UK Index of Retail Prices for December 1986 (January 1974 = 100) the approximate index for beer was 500 and that for cheese was 400. Consider the following statements about December 1986:

(a) The price of beer was lower than the price of cheese.
(b) The price of beer was higher than the price of cheese.
(c) The change in the price of beer was 20 per cent greater than the change in the price of cheese since January 1974.

Which is true?
(A) (a) only;   (B) (b) only;   (C) (c) only;   (D) (b) and (c) only;   (E) none of the above is necessarily true.

(CIMA Stage 1: May 1988)

$$12$$

PROBABILITY

12.1 INTRODUCTION

As a preliminary to considering probability we shall look at some very basic ideas concerning sets.

The term *set* can be applied to any collection of objects, and the individual objects are called the *members* or *elements* of the set. In general, the objects in the population being considered will have several characteristics, and classification by different characteristics will cause different divisions into sets.

Suppose, for example, that of the 200 people working for a firm 150 are male and 50 female while 40 are graduates and 160 are non-graduates. Suppose also that 10 of the females are graduates. We could consider the set of all male workers and the set of all female workers. This would be a different division into sets to that which we would obtain by considering the set of graduates and the set of non-graduates.

The sort of questions to which basic set theory addresses itself are those of deciding how many objects belong to all of several specified sets or of deciding how many objects belong to at least one of several specified sets. Thus in this case we might ask:

1. How many workers are both females and graduates?
2. How many workers are female or graduates or both?

To see how set theory deals with such questions we need to introduce some notation. Sets are usually denoted by capital letters.

Denote the set of females by F and the set of graduates by G. The numbers in those sets are denoted by $|F|$ and $|G|$ so we have $|F| = 50$ and $|G| = 40$.

Question 1 asks for the number belonging to both F and G. This set is called the *intersection* of F and G and is denoted $F \cap G$. We are actually told in the given information that $|F \cap G| = 10$. Question 2 asks for the number belonging to F or to G or to both. This is called the *union* of F and G and is denoted by the expression $F \cup G$.

Consider Fig. 12.1. This is called a *Venn diagram* and the areas of the shapes represent notionally the numbers of members of the respective sets. By inspection of the diagram we see

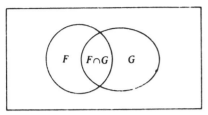

Figure 12.1   Venn diagram showing two sets and their intersection.

that if we find $|F|+|G|$ we do not quite have $|F\cup G|$ because the area in the overlap has been counted twice. Thus we must subtract it once. This gives the important rule:

$$|F\cup G|=|F|+|G|-|F\cap G|$$

So in this example we have $|F\cup G|=50+40-10=80$, i.e. 80 of the workers are females or graduates or both.

One further set theory idea which is necessary for the study of probability is that of the *complement* of a set. The complement of a set consists of all those members of the population which do *not* belong to the set. So in this example the complement of the set F, which is denoted by the symbol $\bar{F}$ is the set of all male workers

$$|\bar{F}|=200-50=150$$

Using these very simple ideas about sets we can now turn to considering probability as such. We shall use the definition which considers probability in terms of long run frequencies. This definition says that if an experiment is repeated infinitely many times, then the probability of a given event is the proportion of the repetitions which result in that event occurring.

In principle this definition allows probabilities to be associated only with experiments which can be repeated infinitely many times. In practice, however, it can be applied in most situations to which one would want to apply probability. The definition has its origins and its most obvious applications in gambling situations such as tossing coins, rolling dice, spinning roulette wheels or drawing cards from packs. A few references will be made to coin and dice experiments to illustrate some of the most basic ideas, but our main concern will be with examples relevant to accounting and business studies.

Suppose we have a perfectly fair coin, i.e. one whose weight is absolutely evenly distributed. If such a coin were tossed infinitely many times, half the tosses would result in a head. Hence for this coin the probability of a head is 0.5.

At this point it is necessary to introduce a shorthand notation for probability statements. The above statement that 'the probability of a head is 0.5' is written

$$P(\text{head})=0.5$$

Next suppose we consider a fair die and imagine this being rolled infinitely many times. One-third of the rolls will result in either a 3 or a 6 so we can say that the probability of a score divisible by 3 is $1/3$.

$$P(\text{score divisible by 3})=1/3$$

Note at this point that it follows from our definition that the total probability associated with any experiment is 1 since every repetition (i.e. proportion 1 of repetitions) must result in something happening.

For simple cases like the two considered so far, where all outcomes on each repetition of the experiment are equally likely, the probability definition we are using reduces to the statement that the probability of an event can be calculated as the *relative frequency*:

$$\frac{\text{Number of outcomes favourable to the event}}{\text{Total possible number of outcomes}}$$

(In fact, this simple derivative of the basic definition is surprisingly often of use and will be seen to be relevant to many of the problems considered in the remainder of this book.)

In the coin example there are two possible outcomes: head and tail. Hence

$$P(\text{head}) = 1/2 = 0.5$$

In the die example there are six possible outcomes 1, 2, 3, 4, 5, and 6. Of the six outcomes two are favourable to the event 'score divisible by 3'. Hence

$$P(\text{score divisible by 3}) = 2/6 = 1/3$$

At this point let us look at how set theory ideas can help us in dealing with probabilities. We are concerned in probability with the set whose elements are all the possible outcomes of the experiment being considered, and we are interested in that particular subset of outcomes favourable to the event whose probability we want to know. Thus it is helpful to have a set diagram representing all the possible outcomes of the experiment and showing those subsets in whose probabilities we are interested.

For the coin example, we have the situation shown in Fig. 12.2. There are two possible outcomes, each with probability 0.5.

For the die example, we have the situation shown in Fig. 12.3. There are six possible outcomes. Of these the two outcomes 3 and 6 are favourable to the event 'score divisible by 3'.

Using Venn diagrams in this way is helpful to us in looking at probabilities of combinations of events and at conditional probabilities, as we shall see in later sections.

Example 12.1.1 The table below shows the numbers of claims made in the last year by the 10 000 motorists insured with a particular insurance company.

Figure 12.2 Possible outcomes, and their probabilities, when a coin is tossed.

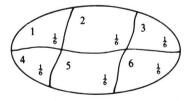

Figure 12.3 Possible outcomes, and their probabilities, when a die is rolled.

Number of claims	Insurance group			
	I	II	III	IV
0	950	2850	2150	850
1	250	950	750	450
2 or more	50	350	250	150

(a) What is the probability that a motorist selected at random:
   (i) made no claim last year?
   (ii) belongs to a low insurance group (I or II) and made at least one claim last year?
   (iii) belongs to a high insurance group (III or IV) *and* made fewer than two claims last year?
(b) Given that a motorist belongs to insurance group IV, what is the probability that he made no claim last year?

ANSWER These questions can be approached using the relative frequency method for calculating probabilities.

(a) (i) The number of motorists making no claims was

$$950 + 2850 + 2150 + 850 = 6800$$

and the total number of motorists was 10 000. Hence P(no claim) $= 6800/10\ 000 = 0.68$.
   (ii) Number in low groups making at least one claim was

$$250 + 950 + 50 + 350 = 1600$$

Hence P(low group and at least one claim) $= 1600/10\ 000 = 0.16$.
   (iii) Number in high group making less than two claims was

$$2150 + 850 + 750 + 150 = 3900$$

Hence P(high group and at least two claims) $= 3900/10\ 000 = 0.39$.
(b) Number of motorists in group IV was $850 + 450 + 150 = 1450$. Of these, the number making no claim was 850. Hence P(group IV motorist makes no claim) $= 850/1450 = 0.586$.

Exercise 12.1.1 The following table shows the absence records of 1000 employees in a certain company during a year. The employees are divided into three categories according to method of payment.

	Days absent		
	0	1–3	4 or more
Hourly paid	60	120	220
Weekly paid	100	110	90
Monthly paid	150	80	70

(a) Calculate the probability of an employee chosen at random being hourly paid.
(b) Calculate the probability of an employee chosen at random having a record of no absences in the year.
(c) Calculate the probability of an employee chosen at random being hourly paid *and* having a record of no absences.

(d) Calculate the probability of an employee known to be hourly paid having a record of no absences.

12.2 THE ADDITION RULE

Events are said to be *mutually exclusive* if the fact that one of them occurs means that none of the others can then possibly occur.

If a coin is tossed once, the events 'head' and 'tail' are mutually exclusive.

If a die is rolled once, the events 'five' and 'six' are mutually exclusive. However, the events 'even score' and 'score divisible by three' are not mutually exclusive because if the roll resulted in a 6 both those events would occur together.

Events being mutually exclusive means that no pair of them has an outcome in common. In terms of a Venn diagram the situation is as shown in Fig. 12.4.

If events are mutually exclusive, the probability that one of them will occur (and, by definition, it is not possible for more than one of them to occur) is the sum of their individual probabilities. In terms of the diagram this is represented by the fact that the probability of the union of two non-overlapping events is the sum of their individual probabilities. Thus if A and B are mutually exclusive events, we have the *addition rule for mutually exclusive events*:

$$P(A \cup B) = P(A) + P(B)$$

This extends immediately to any number of events.

Example 12.2.1 A fair die is rolled once. What is the probability of a five or an even score?

ANSWER

$$
\begin{aligned}
P(\text{five} \cup \text{even score}) &= P(\text{five}) + P(\text{even score}) \\
&= 1/6 + 1/2 = 2/3
\end{aligned}
$$

For the case where events are not mutually exclusive consider Fig. 12.5 and suppose once again we want to know $P(A \cup B)$, the probability of occurrence of either A or B.

In this case we have the possibility that A and B will both occur at the same time. If we add together the probabilities of all the outcomes in A with the probabilities of all the outcomes in B, we shall have included twice over the probabilities of the outcomes common to both A and B. Hence the probability of the simultaneous occurrence of A and B must be subtracted out.

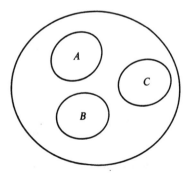

Figure 12.4 Mutually exclusive events.

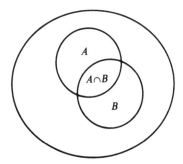

Figure 12.5 Diagram illustrating the addition rule for probabilities.

This gives the generalized *addition rule*:

$$P(A \cup B) = P(A) + P(B) - P(A \cap B) \tag{12.1}$$

Example 12.2.2 A fair die is rolled once. What is the probability of an even score or a score divisible by 3?

ANSWER

$$P(\text{even score} \cup \text{score divisible by 3})$$
$$= P(\text{even score}) + P(\text{score divisible by 3}) - P(6)$$
$$= 1/2 + 1/3 - 1/6$$
$$= 2/3$$

Exercise 12.2.1 Use the reasoning employed in obtaining expression (12.1) above to derive a general expression for $P(A \cup B \cup C)$.

12.3 THE MULTIPLICATION RULE

Events are said to be *independent* if the fact that one of them occurs has no effect on the probability of any of the others occurring.

As an example of independent events suppose we toss a coin and roll a die. What happens to the coin will be in no way related to what happens to the die so the events 'head on coin' and '6 on die' will be independent events.

If events are independent, the probability that all of them will occur is the product of their individual probabilities

$$P(A \cap B) = P(A)P(B)$$

For the example suggested above this rule says:

$$P(\text{head on coin} \cap 6 \text{ on die}) = P(\text{head on coin}) \times P(6 \text{ on die})$$
$$= \qquad 1/2 \times 1/6 = 1/12$$

For this simple example the result can be checked from first principles. The experiment has 12 possible outcomes which are equally likely:

$$\text{H1} \quad \text{H2} \quad \text{H3} \quad \text{H4} \quad \text{H5} \quad \text{H6} \quad \text{T1} \quad \text{T2} \quad \text{T3} \quad \text{T4} \quad \text{T5} \quad \text{T6}$$

Hence the probability of the particular outcome *H6* is 1/12.

In general this multiplication rule for independent events is an extremely useful result, particularly when used in combination with the addition rule of Sec. 12.2.

Example 12.3.1 A production process involves three stages. At the first stage an item is equally likely to be dealt with by one of five machines A, B, C, D, and E.

At the second stage there are three machines F, G, and H. Of these F and G each deal with 30 per cent of items, while H, which is a newer and faster machine, deals with 40 per cent.

At the third stage there are four machines I, J, K, and L. These deal with 10, 20, 30, and 40 per cent, of items, respectively.

(a) Find the probability that an item chosen at random has been processed by machines A, F, and I.
(b) Find the probability that an item chosen at random has been processed by either B or C at the first stage, by either G or H at the second stage, and by either J or K at the third stage.
(c) Find the probability that an item chosen at random has been dealt with by one of C, D, or E at the first stage and then by one of J, K, and L at the third stage.

ANSWER
(a) $P(A) = 0.2$; $P(F) = 0.3$; $P(I) = 0.1$.
Hence $P(A$ and F and $I) = 0.2 \times 0.3 \times 0.1 = 0.006$.
(b) $P(B \cup C) = 0.2 + 0.2 = 0.4$; $P(G \cup H) = 0.3 + 0.4 = 0.7$; $P(J \cup K) = 0.2 + 0.3 = 0.5$
Hence $P(B \cup C$ and $G \cup H$ and $J \cup K) = 0.4 \times 0.7 \times 0.5 = 0.14$.
(c) In this part what happens at stage 2 is irrelevant and contributes just a factor of 1 to the probability product.
$P(C \cup D \cup E) = 0.2 + 0.2 + 0.2 = 0.6$
$P(J \cup K \cup L) = 0.2 + 0.3 + 0.4 = 0.9$
Hence $P(C \cup D \cup E$ and $J \cup K \cup L) = 0.6 \times 0.9 = 0.54$.

Exercise 12.3.1 A computer monitor is made up from four sub-assemblies: a chassis, an electronics board, a screen, and a panel of switches. Quality control investigations reveal that 1 per cent of chassis sub-assemblies are defective, 5 per cent of electronics boards, 10 per cent of screens, and 5 per cent of the panels of switches.

(a) Find the probability that a computer monitor contains no defective sub-assemblies.
(b) Find the probability that a computer monitor contains one defective sub-assembly.

12.4 CONDITIONAL PROBABILITIES AND BAYES' THEOREM

Independence and mutual exclusiveness can be thought of as opposites. If events are independent, the occurrence of one has no effect at all on the probabilities of the others occurring. If events are mutually exclusive, the occurrence of one has a very dramatic effect on the probabilities of the others occurring: it reduces those probabilities to zero. In this section we consider the in-between situation where the occurrence of one event does have some effect on the probability of the occurrence of another without making that probability zero. This is the realm of *conditional probability*. We are looking at the probability of an event A, say, given that another event B (called the *conditioning* event) has occurred.

The standard notation for this probability is $P(A|B)$ (read as 'probability of A given B'). In order to understand how this kind of probability is defined, see Fig. 12.6. We know that event B has occurred and, given this fact, we want to know the probability of occurrence of event A.

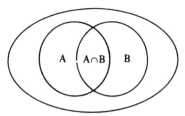

Figure 12.6 Diagram illustrating the definition of conditional probability.

Because B has occurred, the only outcomes that can have occurred are those in set B. Hence the only way A can occur is if we have an outcome which is in both A and B, i.e. an outcome in $A \cap B$. The chance of this happening is the chance of an $A \cap B$ outcome as a proportion of all the possible B outcomes which might have occurred. Hence the conditional probability of A given B is defined as

$$P(A|B) = P(A \cap B)/P(B)$$

Example 12.4.1 An accountant is given three identical-looking, unlabelled floppy disks, each containing two programs. One disk contains two perfect programs, one disk contains two faulty programs, and one disk contains one perfect and one faulty program. After selecting a disk at random the accountant randomly selects one of the two programs. If the program selected is perfect, the probability the *other* program on this disk is *also* perfect is

(A) 1/4;   (B) 1/3;   (C) 1/2;   (D) 2/3;   (E) none of these.

(CIMA Stage 1: May 1989)

Answer From the definition of conditional probability we have

$$P(\text{two perfect programs} \mid \text{one perfect}) = \frac{P(\text{both perfect})}{P(\text{one perfect})} = \frac{1/3}{2/3} = \frac{1}{2}$$

The answer is C.

Example 12.4.2

(a) Two cards are drawn from a standard pack. What is the probability that both are aces?
(b) Three cards are drawn from a standard pack. What is the probability that all three are aces?

Answer
(a) This question involves conditional probability because the probability of the second card being an ace depends on whether the first one was.

The definition says that $P(\text{second ace} \mid \text{first ace}) = \dfrac{P(\text{both aces})}{P(\text{first ace})}$

Hence $P(\text{both aces}) = P(\text{first ace}) \times P(\text{second ace} \mid \text{first ace})$
$$= (4/52) \qquad \times (3/51)$$
$$= 1/221 = 0.0045$$

(b) This is an extension to part (a) where the product of two probabilities has to become a product of three.

$P(\text{all 3 aces}) = P(\text{first ace}) \times P(\text{second ace} \mid \text{first ace}) \times$
$$P(\text{third ace} \mid \text{first two both aces})$$

$$= (4/52) \times (3/51) \times (2/50)$$
$$= 1/5525 = 0.000\,181$$

The following exercise requires a further extension.

Exercise 12.4.1 In a promotion for cigarettes, a leaflet pictures a roulette wheel with 37 numbers, 7 of which are randomly arranged winning numbers. The purchaser is allowed to scratch off 7 of the 37 numbers in the hope of winning a prize. It is therefore possible to select 0, 1, 2, 3, 4, 5, 6, or 7 winning numbers on each leaflet.

(a) What is the probability of a purchase not winning a prize?
(b) If there are 1 million purchases during the promotion, what are the chances of the 'super prize' (the super prize is when all seven selections are winners) being won?

(CIMA Stage 1: May 1991)

Bayes' theorem is a result which follows from the definition of conditional probability and allows us to express a conditional probability in terms of the reverse conditional probability. This is often a useful thing to do.

We have seen the definition

$$P(A|B) = P(A \cap B)/P(B) \tag{12.2}$$

Interchanging the letters gives

$$P(B|A) = P(B \cap A)/P(A) \tag{12.3}$$

From (12.3) it follows that

$$P(B \cap A) = P(B|A) \times P(A) \tag{12.4}$$

But $P(A \cap B)$ is the same thing as $P(B \cap A)$ so we can substitute in (12.2) to obtain

$$P(A|B) = \frac{P(B|A)P(A)}{P(B)} \tag{12.5}$$

This is a rudimentary form of Bayes' theorem.

The way Bayes' theorem is normally stated is to regard A as one of a number of events of interest which are mutually exclusive and which between them include all the outcomes. Commonly there will be just two events: A and $\bar{A}$.

In order that the theorem may be stated in a fairly general form, suppose there are four such events: A, X, Y, Z. This situation is shown in Fig. 12.7.

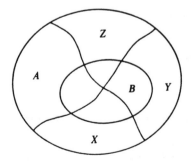

Figure 12.7 A, X, Y and Z are mutually exclusive events which exhaust the sample space.

We can if we wish partition B into four parts as

$$B = (B \cap A) \cup (B \cap X) \cup (B \cap Y) \cup (B \cap Z)$$

The four parts are mutually exclusive so the addition rule says:

$$P(B) = P(B \cap A) + P(B \cap X) + P(B \cap Y) + P(B \cap Z)$$

The terms on the right-hand side can then be rewritten using (12.4) to give

$$P(B) = P(B|A)P(A) + P(B|X)P(X) + P(B|Y)P(Y) + P(B|Z)P(Z)$$

Substituting this in the denominator on the right-hand side of (12.5) then gives Bayes' theorem in the form:

$$P(A|B) = \frac{P(B|A)P(A)}{P(B|A)P(A) + P(B|X)P(X) + P(B|Y)P(Y) + P(B|Z)P(Z)}$$

This can be readily extended to a partitioning of B into any number of parts.

In the commonly used case where the partitioning is into just A and $\bar{A}$ this reduces to

$$P(A|B) = \frac{P(B|A)P(A)}{P(B|A)P(A) + P(B|\bar{A})P(\bar{A})}$$

Example 12.4.3 To select trainee accountants a firm uses a two-stage selection process. If successful at the first stage the applicant passes to the second stage which is an interview with the head of the accounting department. It has been suggested that an intelligence test be used to supplement the first stage interview. In order to look at the effectiveness of the test it will initially be used to supplement the first stage interview.

The probability of failing the test is 0.8. The probability of someone being appointed having passed the test is 0.3. The probability of someone being appointed having failed the test is 0.1.

(a) What is the probability of a candidate being appointed?
(b) If a candidate is not appointed, what is the probability that he or she passed the test?
(c) If, on average, 15 per cent of applicants are called for first interview, what is the overall probability of an applicant being appointed?

(ACCA Level 1: Dec. 1988)

ANSWER

(a)
$$P(\text{appointed}) = P(\text{appointed}|\text{pass test}) \times P(\text{pass test})$$
$$+ P(\text{appointed}|\text{fail test}) \times P(\text{fail test})$$
$$= 0.3 \times 0.2 + 0.1 \times 0.8$$
$$= 0.06 + 0.08 = 0.14$$

(b)
$$P(\text{pass}|\text{not appointed}) = \frac{P(\text{not appointed}|\text{pass}) \times P(\text{pass})}{P(\text{not appointed})}$$

by Bayes' theorem.

Hence

$$P(\text{pass test}|\text{not appointed}) = \frac{0.7 \times 0.2}{1 - 0.14} = \frac{0.14}{0.86} = 0.1628$$

(c) Overall probability of appointment is $0.15 \times 0.14 = 0.021$.

Exercise 12.4.2 An electronic assembly consists of two parts A and B.

$$P(A \text{ fails}) = 0.2$$
$$P(B \text{ fails} | A \text{ fails}) = 0.75$$
$$P(B \text{ fails} | A \text{ does not fail}) = 0.15$$

Find:

(a) $P(A \text{ fails} | B \text{ fails})$;
(b) $P(A \text{ fails} | B \text{ does not fail})$.

TEST EXERCISES

12.1 There are two events, X and Y. P denotes probability and X' means 'not X'.

$$P(X) = 0.4 \quad P(Y) = 0.5 \quad P(X \text{ and } Y) = 0.1$$

Therefore, $P(X' \text{ and } Y)$ equals

(A) 0.1; (B) 0.2; (C) 0.3; (D) 0.4; (E) 1.0.

(CIMA Stage 1: Nov. 1990)

12.2 X and Y are two mutually exclusive events. X' signifies 'not X' and Y' signifies 'not Y'. $P(X) = 0.6$. $P(X'$ and $Y') = 0.1$. $P(X \text{ or } Y)$ equals

(A) 0.18; (B) 0.50; (C) 0.72; (D) 0.9; (E) none of the preceding options.

12.3 Erewhon has a total population of 50 000 people made up of two tribes, the Ogodesi, of whom there are 20 000, and the Dabsedi, of whom there are 30 000. The Ogodesi always tell the truth while the Dabsedi can be reckoned to tell the truth randomly with probability 0.25 and to lie with probability 0.75. Having been forced to crash land in Erewhon, an airman comes across a native in the middle of the day. If the native, in response to a question, agrees it is daytime, use Bayes' theorem to find the probability that he is an Ogodesi and hence a person on whom the airman can rely.

12.4 A production process has four stages. Out of every 100 items setting out on the process the following numbers can be reckoned to be rejected at each of the stages:

Stage	Number rejected per initial 100
1	12
2	5
3	3
4	1

(a) What is the probability that an item going into stage 1 will eventually emerge as a completed unit of production?
(b) What is the probability that a unit will get as far as entering stage 3?
(c) What is the probability that an item entering stage 3 will be rejected at that stage?
(d) How many units should be started at stage 1 if 1000 completed units of production are required?

12.5 In a certain firm spells of absence from work are classified in terms of duration (three days or less/more than three days) and whether or not a medical certificate is produced. In one department the probability that a spell of absence lasts more than three days is 0.4 and the probability that a medical certificate will be produced if it does last more than three days is 0.75. However, if the duration of the absence is three days or less, the probability of a certificate being produced is only 0.1.

Given that a medical certificate is produced for a particular absence, use Bayes' theorem to find the probability that the spell of absence lasted more than three days.

DECISION ANALYSIS

13.1 STRUCTURING DECISIONS INVOLVING UNCERTAINTY

Business decision making is a highly complex matter involving the collection and adroit utilization of a diversity of information, both qualitative and quantitative. Proficiency in this field requires much experience of the business situation and it is certainly beyond the scope of this book to equip anybody to become an effective decision maker. The more modest task we have set ourselves is to furnish the reader with a useful way of thinking about what is involved in a decision-making problem, and with some widely used techniques which people have found in practice to be useful aids in solving such problems, particularly in the financial area.

The structure of a decision-making problem can be helpfully considered under four headings.

(a) The objectives

The decision maker must first be clear as to what he or she wants to achieve as the result of decisions made. In the financial situation this will commonly be maximization of profit. However, this is by no means the only objective a decision maker might have. Other examples would be maximization of revenue or maximization of market share. Such objectives could well conflict with each other in that, for instance, the longer-term benefits of a larger market share might well warrant accepting less than maximum possible profit in the short term. Resolving conflicts of this kind to arrive at a clear objective is a major aspect of the decision-making art.

(b) The strategies

Having formulated the objective, the next element to be considered is the set of courses of action which might be followed in pursuit of its achievement. These possible courses of action we shall refer to as the strategies available. The strategies might be a set of possible investment decisions, the decisions to launch or not to launch a new product, or the decisions to introduce or not to introduce a new payments system for production workers. It is important that thought is given to identifying possible strategies available in a particular situation before trying to make a decision as to which one to adopt.

(c) The uncertainties

Most of the difficulty would be removed from decision making if the decision maker knew what conditions were going to prevail for the working out of his chosen strategy. The decision on whether or not to invest in new equipment would be eased if one knew what sort of economic climate was in prospect. It is to help people facing such a decision that the current proliferation of economic forecasts is produced. A pricing decision on a new product would be eased if the intentions of competitors were known. The different conditions which might prevail are called *states of nature*. The word *risk* is used in a particular sense in this context. A situation is one of risk, as opposed to just general uncertainty, if it is possible to ascribe probabilities to the various states of nature that could prevail. Estimates of these probabilities can be arrived at by means of, for example, market research surveys or analysis of past sales records.

(d) The utilities

In order to assess the effectiveness or *utility* of different strategies in meeting the objectives under the uncertainties about the states of nature, we must have some measure of what a strategy can achieve. In the accounting context this measure will almost certainly be a monetary one and all the examples in this book will evaluate strategies in monetary terms. Money is a convenient measure here, as in accounting generally, because it is objective and easily quantifiable. However, there are situations where the objective may not be a monetary one but concerned rather with, for example, customer satisfaction or the health of employees. In such cases the utility of a strategy in achieving the objective would need to be measured in non-monetary terms. Even if the utility is monetary it is not self-evident how a figure expressing how much utility a strategy has is to be arrived at. The different criteria considered in later sections of this chapter for making choices between strategies reflect different possible ways of measuring utility.

13.2 EXPECTED VALUES

A commonly used way of measuring the utility of a strategy, and the one with which we shall be mainly concerned, is by means of its expected monetary value or EMV. As a prelude to discussing this measure and the way it is used in decision-making problems, we shall look briefly at the basic idea of expected value, which is important in its own right as it appears in other contexts besides the decision-making one.

Consider an experiment with each of whose outcomes is associated a particular value of some variable. A simple example of such an experiment would be the rolling of a fair die, the variable being the number of spots on the face which appears uppermost. (A variable of this kind whose value depends on the outcome of a probability experiment is called a *random variable*.) There are six possible outcomes and the associated numbers of spots are 1, 2, 3, 4, 5, and 6. A question we might ask is the following. If this die were rolled a very large number of times, what is the mean number of spots we should obtain per roll? This is what is meant by the *expected* number of spots that will result when the die is rolled.

Now if the die were rolled infinitely many times, the proportions of rolls which would result in 1, 2, 3, 4, 5, or 6 are all 1/6. Also by the long-run frequency definition of probability, these proportions are the probabilities of these values. So the mean score over infinitely many rolls will be:

$$(1/6) \times 1 + (1/6) \times 2 + (1/6) \times 3 + (1/6) \times 4 + (1/6) \times 5 + (1/6) \times 6 = 3.5$$

The expected number of spots on the uppermost face when the die is rolled is 3.5. It does not matter that this is not a possible score on any single roll. It is the mean of the scores that would be achieved over a large number of rolls.

In general, the expected value of a random variable is defined by

$$\text{Expected value} = \sum_{\text{All possible outcomes}} (\text{Probability of outcome}) \times (\text{Value})$$

which is usually abbreviated to

$$\text{Expected value} = \sum pV$$

It is the mean of the values the random variable will take over many repetitions of the experiment.

Example 13.2.1 A retail shop has space to display one of two different products, coded A and B. The demand for each product can take one of three levels, high, medium, or low. The shop manager has assessed the probabilities of each level of demand and the corresponding profit. The details are given below.

	Level of demand	Probability	Profit
Product A	High	0.2	£2
	Medium	0.5	£1.50
The profit for low demand is £0.75			
Product B	High	0.3	£1.50
	Low	0.1	£0.50
The profit for medium demand is £1.00			

Using the criterion of maximum expected profit, what product should the shop display?

(ACCA Level 1: June 1989)

ANSWER Since total probability must be 1, the probability of low demand for product A is $1 - 0.2 - 0.5 = 0.3$.
Hence expected profit from A is

$$£(0.2 \times 2.00 + 0.5 \times 1.50 + 0.3 \times 0.75) = £(0.4 + 0.75 + .225)$$
$$= £1.375$$

Probability of medium demand for B is $1 - 0.3 - 0.1 = 0.6$. Hence expected profit from B is

$$£(0.3 \times 1.5 + 0.6 \times 1.00 + 0.1 \times 0.50) = £(0.45 + 0.60 + 0.05)$$
$$= £1.10$$

Since product A leads to higher expected profit, this is the one which should be displayed.

Exercise 13.2.1 In a forthcoming sales promotion each pack of cigarettes is to contain a leaflet with eight 'scratch off' square patches, randomly arranged. The purchaser will scratch off one patch to reveal the value of a small prize. The value of the eight patches on the leaflet is to be as follows:

Value of prize	£0.20	£0.50	£1.00
Number of patches	5	2	1

The company has to decide on the number of packs in which to put leaflets, given a budget of £75 000. Find the 'average cost' of a leaflet, and deduce the number of leaflets you would use and why.

(CIMA Stage 1: May 1991)

The decision rule which involves choosing the strategy giving the highest expected monetary value, is called the *Bayes decision rule*. The solution to a Bayes decision rule problem involving a single decision is often conveniently set out in the form of a table known as a *pay off table*. The pay off table method is illustrated in Example 13.2.2 below and can then be used in answering Exercise 13.2.2.

Example 13.2.2 Classic Cars Limited is a car rental firm which has 15 cars for hiring purposes. Each day 10 of these cars are rented to regular customers and the daily demand for the remaining cars may be assumed to have a Poisson distribution with mean 4.

(a) Determine the probabilities that 10, 11, 12, 13, 14, and 15 cars are used on any one day. Hence calculate the expected number of cars rented each day.
(b) The daily holding cost to the firm of possessing a car is considered to be £6 whether or not it is used, while maintenance costs for each car total £2 for each day the car is used. If the daily hiring charge is £20, find the firm's expected daily profit.
(c) Determine whether it would be advisable for the firm to change its number of cars from 15 to either 14 or 16, assuming that the daily demand does not alter.
(d) For what range of values of the daily holding cost would the situation of possessing 15 cars be optimal?

(ACCA Level 2: June 1988)

ANSWER

(a) These probabilities are the probabilities of 0, 1, 2, 3, 4, or 5 of the four 'spare' cars being used. They are found using a Poisson probability distribution with mean 4.
   As explained in Chapter 14 below, they can be found either by use of the Poisson formula or by using a published table of Poisson probabilities. Probabilities relevant to various parts of what follows are shown below and it is left as an exercise for the reader to verify these after having studied Chapter 14.

$$P(0)=0.0183, \ P(1)=0.0733, \ P(2)=0.1465, \ P(3)=0.1954,$$

$$P(4)=0.1954, \ P(5)=0.1563, \ P(6)=0.1042,$$

$$P(5 \text{ or more})=1-(0.0183+0.0733+0.1465+0.1954+0.1954)$$

$$=1-0.628=0.3711$$

$$P(6 \text{ or more})=0.3711-0.1563=0.2148$$

For part (a) the probabilities $P(5)$ and $P(6)$ are not relevant since 15 cars will be used if 5 *or more* of the 'spare' cars are demanded. Hence the required probabilities for numbers of cars used are:

$$P(10)=0.0183, \ P(11)=0.0733, \ P(12)=0.1465, \ P(13)=0.1954,$$
$$P(14)=0.1954, \ P(15)=0.3711.$$

The expected number rented is

$$10 \times 0.0183 + 11 \times 0.0733 + 12 \times 0.1465 + 13 \times 0.1954 + 14 \times 0.1954 + 15 \times 0.3711 = 13.59.$$

(b) The daily contribution from a car which is hired out is £20 − £2 = £18. The fixed cost per day of holding 15 cars is 15 × £6 = £90. Hence with the expected number out per day being 13.59, the expected daily profit is 13.59 × £18 − £90 = £154.62.

(c) It is this part of the answer which can be set out in the form of a pay off table. This is as follows:

| Demand | Probability, p | Number of cars held | | | | | |
| | | 14 | | 15 | | 16 | |
		Profit, £V	pV	Profit, £V	pV	Profit, £V	pV
10	0.0183	96	1.76	90	1.65	84	1.54
11	0.0733	114	8.36	108	7.92	102	7.48
12	0.1465	132	19.34	126	18.46	120	17.58
13	0.1954	150	29.31	144	28.14	138	26.97
14	0.1954	168	32.83	162	31.66	156	30.48
15	0.1563	168	26.26	180	28.13	174	27.20
16 or more	0.2148	168	36.09	180	38.66	192	41.24
			153.95		154.62		152.49

The profit figure in each case is calculated by finding £18 times the number of cars supplied and then subtracting £6 times the number of cars held.

It is seen from this table that on the expected value criterion it is *not* advisable for the firm to change its number of cars to either 14 or 16.

(d) The expected daily contribution from 14 cars is

$$£153.95 + 14 \times £6 = £153.95 + £84 = £237.95$$

The expected daily contribution from 15 cars is

$$£154.62 + 15 \times £6 = £154.62 + £90 = £244.62$$

So the difference in contributions is £244.62 − £237.95 = £6.67. Thus as long as the daily cost of holding a car is less than £6.67 it is worth having 15 cars rather than 14.

The expected daily contribution from 16 cars is

$$£152.49 + 16 \times £6 = £152.49 + £96 = £248.49$$

So daily contribution for 16 cars exceeds that for 15 by £248.49 − £244.62 = £3.87. Thus it is not worth holding a sixteenth car unless the daily cost of holding a car falls below £3.87.

The range of daily holding costs for which having 15 cars remains optimal is the range from £3.87 to £6.67.

Exercise 13.2.2 A football club has an opportunity to get its programmes printed at a reduced rate if it agrees with its printers to purchase a fixed number of programmes for every game for the next three seasons. Records show that, in round figures, the number of programmes sold per game is in the following proportions:

Number of programmes	Proportion of games %
2000	15
2500	20
3000	25
3500	25
4000	15

The variation from game to game is in reality predictable to a certain extent depending on the reputed attractiveness of the opposition. Under the special offer, the club can buy the programmes at 45p per copy, as against a normal cost of 50p per copy. Programmes are sold at £1.00 each, and unsold programmes are worth 2p each to a paper recycling firm.

Calculate the expected profit per game to the club under each of the policies of buying 2000, 2500, 3000, 3500 and 4000 programmes per game if it accepts the special offer. Hence show that the best policy under the special offer conditions is to buy 3000 programmes per game, and state the expected profit per game on this arrangement.

13.3 DECISION TREE ANALYSIS

Decision tree analysis is a decision-making method using the Bayes decision rule which is useful when a sequence of decisions has to be made, rather than just a single decision as in Sec. 13.2.

The following example will be used to illustrate the notation and basic layout of a tree diagram as well as the use of such a diagram to solve a decision-making problem.

Example 13.3.1 The Brownhill Manufacturing Company is considering the production of a new consumer item with a five-year product lifetime. In order to manufacture this item it would be necessary to build a new plant. After having considered several alternative strategies, management is left with the following three possibilities.

1. Build a large plant at an estimated cost of £600 000. This strategy faces two types of market conditions: high demand with a probability of 0.7 or low demand with a probability of 0.3. If the demand is high, the company can expect to receive an annual cash flow of £250 000 for each of the next five years. If the demand is low the cash flow would consist of a loss of £50 000 each year because of large fixed costs and inefficiencies.
2. Build a small plant at an estimated cost of £350 000. This strategy also faces two types of market conditions: high demand with a probability of 0.7 or low demand with a probability of 0.3. The annual cash flow over the five-year period for the small plant is £25 000 if the demand is low and £150 000 if the demand is high.
3. Do not build a plant initially. This strategy consists of leaving the decision for one year while more information is collected. The resulting information can be positive or negative, with estimated probabilities 0.8 and 0.2, respectively. At the end of this time management may

decide to build either a large plant or a small plant at the same costs as at present providing the information is positive. If the resulting information is negative, management would decide to build no plant at all. Given positive information the probabilities of high and low demand change to 0.9 and 0.1, respectively, regardless of which plant is built. The annual cash flows for the remaining four-year period for each type of plant are the same as those given in strategies 1 and 2. All costs are given in present value terms and should not be discounted.

(a) Draw a decision tree to represent the alternative courses of action open to the company.
(b) Determine the expected return for each possible course of action and hence decide the best course of action for the management of Brownhill Manufacturing Company.
(c) A building firm offers a discount to Brownhill if the company agrees to have a large plant built immediately. What percentage discount is necessary to change the best course of action?

(ACCA Level 2: Dec. 1989)

ANSWER

(a) The decision tree for this problem is shown in Fig. 13.1. In such a diagram each decision to be made is represented by a square. For purposes of illustration one such square in Fig. 13.1 is labelled 'Decision point'. Emanating from the decision point we have one line for each strategy that might be adopted. The uncertainties in a decision tree are represented by circles. In Fig. 13.1 one of these circles is labelled 'Expected value point'. Emanating from each expected value point we have one line for each state of nature which might prevail, and marked on that line is the probability of the corresponding state of nature.

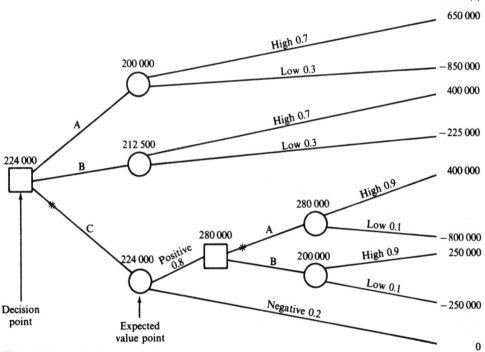

Figure 13.1 A decision tree diagram.

The diagram is drawn from left to right, taking account of every decision and uncertainty and showing the relationships between them. Eventually all the decisions and uncertainties will be accounted for and on the right-hand side of the diagram we shall have lines with nothing on the end. At the end of each line we write the value of the outcome corresponding to the succession of decisions and states of nature which led to the point concerned.

(b) Solving the problem now involves working through the diagram from right to left. Against each expected value point we note the expected value obtained using the probabilities on the lines emanating from that point and the values at the ends of those lines. Thus for the four circles whose emanating lines finish on the right-hand side of the diagram we have

$$0.9 \times 400\,000 + 0.1 \times (-800\,000) = 280\,000$$
$$0.9 \times 250\,000 + 0.1 \times (-250\,000) = 200\,000$$
$$0.7 \times 650\,000 + 0.3 \times (-850\,000) = 200\,000$$
$$0.7 \times 400\,000 + 0.3 \times (-225\,000) = 212\,500$$

Against each decision point we note the best expected value that can be obtained at the end of a line emanating from that decision point and we put an asterisk on the appropriate line. Thus for the decision point towards the bottom of Fig. 13.1 we have the value 280 000 as this is the larger of the numbers at the ends of lines emanating from that point.

We can then calculate the expected value at the (marked) expected value point at the bottom of the diagram as

$$0.8 \times 280\,000 + 0.2 \times 0 = 224\,000$$

Finally we can go to the initial decision point. The largest number at the end of a line emanating from here is 224 000. So the best sequence of decisions is to begin by seeking further information. If this is positive then build a large plant. The expected profit from this best procedure is £224 000.

(c) The expected profit from building a new plant immediately is inferior to this by £24 000. So to make this worth while it would be necessary for the cost of building the new plant immediately to be reduced by £24 000.

Thus the percentage discount required is

$$\frac{£24\,000}{£600\,000} \times 100 = 4 \text{ per cent.}$$

Exercise 13.3.1 Gordon Electronics is considering the launch of a new range of lighting equipment which will have a project horizon of five years. If the new range is introduced without further market research, it is thought that demand will be either high (with probability 0.7) or low (with probability 0.3). However, it is possible to commission a market research survey which will produce either a good forecast (with probability 0.6) or a bad forecast. It has been decided that if the survey yields a good forecast, there will be increased marketing effort which will yield an increased annual contribution. In this case the probability of a high demand is 0.9. However, if the survey produces a bad forecast, it has been decided that the company will not introduce the new range but continue with the old range of products.

The accounts department of Gordon Electronics has produced the following financial information.

1. Annual contribution (£) if the new range of equipment is introduced and no market survey is commissioned:

Year	1	2	3	4	5
High demand	20 000	40 000	50 000	30 000	10 000
Low demand	10 000	15 000	20 000	10 000	5 000

2. Increased annual contribution if the survey provides a good forecast:

High demand	£10 000 pa
Low demand	£ 5 000 pa

The survey cost is £10 000.

3. Annual contribution (t) if the new range of equipment is not introduced and the old range of products is continued:

Year	1	2	3	4	5
	20 000	20 000	15 000	10 000	5 000

The company's cost of capital is 15 per cent pa
Assume that all income occurs at the year end.

Present value factors (at 15%)	1	2	3	4	5
	0.8696	0.7561	0.6575	0.5718	0.4972

(a) Draw a decision tree to represent the various courses of action open to the company.
(b) Calculate the present value of contributions for each possible action/outcome combination.
(c) Calculate the expected present value for each of the following three situations:
  (i) launching the new range without a market research survey;
  (ii) not introducing the new range of equipment;
  (iii) carrying out a market research survey and taking appropriate action.
(d) Recommend a course of action to the company.
(e) If the probability that the market survey produces a good forecast changes from 0.6 to 0.5, would this alter your recommendation?

(ACCA Level 2: Dec. 1990)

13.4 PERFECT INFORMATION AND FURTHER DECISION-MAKING CRITERIA

If the decision maker knew what state of nature was going to prevail, he or she would simply choose the strategy giving the best return for that state of nature. Thus *perfect information* about the state of nature would remove all uncertainty, and the decision maker's problems would be solved. Unfortunately this is not possible, but perfect information is none the less a useful thing to think about, because uncertainty about the state of nature can usually be *reduced* at a price by market research or some other appropriate method of investigation. By finding out how much better off the decision maker would be if he or she had perfect information it is possible to set an upper limit on what it is worth paying to seek real information.

The value of perfect information is calculated by finding the expected return that would be achieved with perfect information and subtracting from it the expected return from the strategy which is best in the absence of perfect information.

Example 13.4.1 A petrol station sells sandwiches as a side line. It buys in these sandwiches from a bakery and sells them at 80p. Experience suggests that, in round figures, the numbers of sandwiches demanded are 80, 100, or 120 with probabilities 0.3, 0.5, and 0.2 respectively. Unsold sandwiches are of no value. If the same number of sandwiches is bought each day, the cost to the petrol station owner is 45p each, while if he states his requirement on a daily basis he has to pay 47p each.

(a) Find the number of sandwiches which should be bought each day if the petrol station owner wants to buy at 45p each, and state the expected daily profit in this case.
(b) What is the maximum amount it would be worth paying for perfect information about the daily demand for sandwiches?

ANSWER
(a) This part can be answered exactly as in Sec. 13.2 by means of a table as follows:

| | | Sandwiches bought for sale | | | | | |
| | | 80 | | 100 | | 120 | |
Sandwiches demanded	Probability p	Profit V	pV	Profit V	pV	Profit V	pV
80	0.3	28	8.4	19	5.7	10	3.0
100	0.5	28	14.0	35	17.5	26	13.0
120	0.2	28	5.5	35	7.0	42	8.4
			£27.9		£30.2		£24.4

The best policy is to buy 100 sandwiches per day.
This leads to an expected daily profit of £30.20 per day.

(b) If the petrol station owner had perfect information about the number of sandwiches that would be demanded each day, he could buy just enough to meet demand, and avoid any waste. The expected profit in this situation would be:

$$0.3 \times (0.8 - 0.47) \times 80 + 0.5 \times (0.8 - 0.47) \times 100 + 0.2 \times (0.8 - 0.47) \times 120$$
$$= 7.92 + 16.5 + 7.92$$
$$= £32.34$$

Thus the increase in daily profit as a result of having perfect information is seen to be £32.34 − £30.20 = £2.14.

So £2.14 is the maximum amount it could be worth paying for perfect information about the daily demand for sandwiches.

Exercise 13.4.1 Consider again the situation described in Exercise 13.2.2. Find the value of perfect information about the number of programmes which will be demanded for each individual football match.

The Bayes decision rule using expected monetary value which has been used in the preceding sections is concerned with the mean return that a strategy will give if used in a large number of repetitions of the situation being considered. This is a reasonable approach, and the Bayes rule is the most commonly used criterion for choosing between strategies. Its weakness, however, is that in a particular instance it may lead to a disastrous decision. For a large organization the occasional disaster will not matter unduly, and consistent use of the Bayes decision rule can be expected to lead to enough better-than-expected results to cancel out the worse-than-expected ones. For a small operator, however, one very bad decision could spell doom and so he would prefer a procedure which he knows will guard him against disaster even if the expected gain from it is less than under the Bayes rule. This is the thinking behind the simple decision criterion known as the *maximin* principle.

To illustrate this principle consider again the table of returns drawn up in answer to part of Example 13.4.1 above, but with the probabilities, p, and the pV values omitted.

	Sandwiches bought for sale		
	80	100	120
Sandwiches	Profit	Profit	Profit
demanded	V	V	V
80	28	19	10
100	28	35	26
120	28	35	42

The *smallest* daily profits that can occur if 80, 100, or 120 sandwiches, respectively, are bought in are £28, £19, and £10. The maximin principle would therefore advocate a policy of buying 80 sandwiches per day because this *maximizes* the return if the state of nature is such as to *minimize* profit under the chosen strategy. The maximin principle is a pessimistic approach to decision making in that it considers the case of nature doing its worst in the light of the decision taken. In general we see that the maximin principle operates by finding the minimum value in each column and then choosing the column having the largest minimum level.

The opposite approach to that in the maximin rule is reflected in the *maximax* rule. Here the decision maker is seen as an optimistic (or desperate) person whose attention is on the *best* outcome that might occur as a result of his or her strategy. This may be because he or she believes in nature's benevolence or it may be that only the best outcome is of any real use and therefore is prepared to take a gamble in the hope of achieving it. For the example here the maximum daily returns to be achieved from buying 80, 100, or 120 sandwiches are respectively £28, £35, and £42. So the maximax principle suggests buying 120 sandwiches because this maximizes the return obtained if nature behaves in such a way as to maximize profit under the chosen strategy. Operating the maximax principle amounts to finding the largest return in the whole table and then choosing the strategy corresponding to the column in which that largest value lies.

It will be noted that the maximin and maximax criteria make no use of the probabilities of occurrence of the different states of nature. Hence they are criteria which can be employed in cases of genuine uncertainty as opposed to risk, where such probabilities are not known. However, there will usually be some information available concerning the probabilities of occurrence of the various states of nature, even though it may be very rough, and it is an argument against these criteria that they waste such information.

Exercise 13.4.2 Consider the table drawn up in answer to Example 13.2.2. Use it to find the strategy which the car hire company should adopt on the basis of:

(a) the maximin criterion;
(b) the maximax criterion.

TEST EXERCISES

13.1 Each week a small hardware shop purchases for £40 per unit a perishable product which it then tries to sell for £70 per item. Every item that is sold incurs a selling cost of £5. At the end of each week any items that are not sold are returned to the manufacturer who refunds £25 for each item returned. From past experience customer demand each week can be described by the following probability distribution.

Customer demand	1	2	3	4	5
Probability	0.05	0.2	0.4	0.25	0.1

(a) Determine the contribution to profit for each combination of weekly purchase quantity and customer demand.
(b) One decision criterion is based on the method of expectation.
   (i) Determine the number of products the store manager should order each week using the criterion of expected value of weekly contribution.
   (ii) Given this order size and with all other data unchanged, obtain the minimum selling price that the store can set without sustaining an expected loss.
(c) An alternative decision criterion is the maximin decision criterion. Determine the optimum weekly order size using this criterion.
(d) In the context of this question outline briefly the limitations of the two decision criteria used.
(e) The store manager is considering two proposals for increasing sales of the product:
   (i) Advertising in a local newspaper at a weekly cost of £10, which would change the probabilities of customer demand to 0.0, 0.1, 0.2, 0.5, and 0.2, respectively.
   (ii) Cutting the price of the product to £60, which would alter the probabilities to 0.0, 0.0, 0.1, 0.3, and 0.6 respectively. Would either of these proposals be worth while (based on the criterion of expected contribution)? Make a recommendation to the store manager.

(ACCA Level 2: Dec. 1991)

13.2 Each week a company sells ladies' fashion clothes direct to the public by advertising in the Saturday press. One garment only is advertised each week. On each occasion the company has to decide in advance how many garments to buy from a (contracted) designer. Agency fees and newspaper charges total £1400 for each weekly advertisement.

The next garment to be advertised will cost £79 and will sell at £199. Any unsold items are passed on to the trade for about one-half of their cost, i.e. a loss of £40 per garment in this case. The recent sales of comparable garments, all priced in the region of £200, have been as follows:

Number of garments sold	Number of occasions
1–19	0
20–39	8
40–59	20
60–79	8
80–99	4
100 and over	0
Total	40

(a) Form a probability distribution of sales from the frequency table above. (You may assume mid-points are 10, 30, 50, etc.)
(b) Draw up a profit table for each sales–production combination.

(c) Apply the probabilities to the profit table and hence recommend a product policy to maximize profit.
(d) Comment on the current policy of buying in 50 garments for each week.

(CIMA Stage 1: Nov. 1988)

13.3 A company has to decide which advertising method to use in marketing a product in the next period. Advertising method A, which is currently used, costs £10 000 per week and is expected only to maintain sales. From past experience of using advertising method A, the likelihood of weekly sales in the next period (with A) has been estimated as shown:

Unit weekly sales	Probability of weekly sales if A used
0–200	0
200–400	0.3
400–600	0.4
600–800	0.2
800–1000	0.1

Advertising method B would cost £37 000 per week and sales would be expected to be 50 per cent higher than with A. Advertising method C would cost £60 000 per week and sales would be expected to be 100 per cent higher than with A.
The current contribution, taking A into account, is £100 per unit sold.
You are required to use a simple decision tree with expected values, to recommend the best action to take and to comment on the answer.

(CIMA Stage 1: Nov. 1990)

13.4 The Venus Department Store operates a customer loan facility. If one of its new customers requests a loan then Venus either refuses it, gives it a high loan limit, or gives it a low loan limit. From a number of years' past experience the probability that a new customer makes a full repayment of a loan is known to be 0.95, while the probability of non-repayment is 0.05 (these probabilities being independent of the size of loan limit). The average profit, (or loss) in £, per customer made by Venus is given by the following table.

	Loan limit	
	High	Low
Full repayment	50	20
Non-repayment	−200	−30

(a) In the past the company has used a selection criterion that is totally arbitrary (i.e. it is not influenced by the customer's ability to repay). Represent the information in a decision tree. What recommendation would you make to the management of Venus if a new customer requests a loan?
(b) Venus can apply to an agency to evaluate the credit rating of a customer. This agency would provide a rating for the customer as either a good risk or a bad risk, this credit rating being independent of the size of the loan being considered. Analysis of the last 1000 customer ratings by this agency revealed the following information.

Agency credit rating	Type of customer		Total
	Full repayment	Non-repayment	
Good customer	790	10	800
Bad risk	160	40	200
Total	950	50	1000

Determine the value of this credit rating to Venus.
(c) The Venus management believes that this first agency is not very good at selecting the non-payers. It considers contacting a second agency which guarantees perfect information concerning the credit rating of the customers.
   Explain the meaning of the term 'perfect information' in the context of this question.
   Calculate the value of this perfect information.

(ACCA Level 2: June 1991)

13.5 A software company has just won a contract worth £80 000 if it delivers a successful product on time, but only £40 000 if this is late. It faces the problem now of whether to produce the work in-house or to sub-contract it. To sub-contract the work would cost £50 000, but the local sub-contractor is so fast and reliable as to make it certain that successful software is produced on time.

If the work is produced in-house the cost would be only £20 000 but, based on past experience, would have only 90 per cent chance of being successful. In the event of the software *not* being successful, there would still be the options of either a 'late rejection' of the contract (at a further cost of £10 000) or of 'late sub-contracting' the work on the same terms as before. With this late start the local sub-contractor is estimated to have only a 50/50 chance of producing the work on time or of producing it late. In this case the sub-contractor still has to be paid £50 000, regardless of whether he meets the deadline or not.

(a) Draw a decision tree for the software company, using squares for decision points and circles for outcome (chance) points, including all relevant data on the diagram.

(b) Calculate expected values as appropriate and recommend a course of action to the software company with reasons.

(CIMA Stage 1: May 1990)

PROBABILITY DISTRIBUTIONS

14.1 THE BINOMIAL DISTRIBUTION

Discrete probability distributions

All the probability examples considered in Chapter 12 involved, in a general way, discrete distributions of probability. For the experiments and other situations considered there, each had a set of distinct possible outcomes and with each such outcome was associated a probability.

Looking at the matter a little more technically, it is the values of a random variable resulting from an experiment which follow a probability distribution. So a simple example to demonstrate the idea of a discrete probability distribution would be the score obtained on a single roll of a fair die. This variable can take six distinct values 1, 2, 3, 4, 5, or 6 and the probability associated with each of these values is 1/6.

Usually, however, the expression 'discrete probability distribution' is used in a more restricted sense. It is used to refer to the set of probabilities associated with the distinct random variable values resulting from a particular type of experiment. For example, the binomial distribution considered in this section is an instance of a discrete probability distribution in this sense. The values of a random variable associated with an experiment satisfying certain general conditions follow this distribution. Hence by studying this discrete probability distribution we can make statements about the probabilities associated with all experiments satisfying these general conditions. The Poisson distribution considered in Sec. 14.2 does the same thing for experiments satisfying a different set of general conditions.

A wide range of practical situations lead to random variables which follow the binomial and Poisson distributions, and the examples and exercises presented in this section and the next attempt to reflect this diversity of application.

Permutations and combinations

In order to deal with binomial probabilities we need to be able to think about the number of ways in which objects can be selected from larger sets or can be arranged among themselves. In discussing *permutations* (or *selections* as they are sometimes called) we are thinking of a situation where all orderings of the objects being considered are in some way different from each other, i.e. they are distinguishable. Suppose we have n such objects and want to know in how many different ways we can select a set consisting of r objects. This is the number of permutations of r from n and is denoted $_nP_r$.

The first object can be chosen in n ways. That object is no longer available when we come to make the second choice. Hence there are $(n-1)$ ways in which the second object can be chosen. So the number of different pairs which can appear as the first two objects is

$$n \times (n-1)$$

Two objects being now unavailable, the third object can be chosen in $(n-2)$ ways. So the number of different sets of three objects which can appear as the first three in our set is

$$n \times (n-1) \times (n-2)$$

Continuing with the same reasoning until r objects have been chosen we see that the number of different possible sets of r objects is

$$_nP_r = n \times (n-1) \times (n-2) \times (n-3) \times \cdots \times [n-(r-1)]$$

This can be written more tidily if we introduce *factorial* notation.

The symbol $n!$ is read as 'n factorial' and means n multiplied successively by every integer smaller than itself down to 1. For example,

$$4! = 4 \times 3 \times 2 \times 1 = 24$$
$$5! = 5 \times 4 \times 3 \times 2 \times 1 = 120$$

In general

$$n! = n \times (n-1) \times (n-2) \times (n-3) \times \cdots \times 3 \times 2 \times 1$$

Note also the special convention $0! = 1$ which is not covered by this general definition. The $0!$ convention is important in calculating binomial and Poisson probabilities.

Using the factorial notation, the expression obtained above for numbers of permutations can be written as

$$_nP_r = \frac{n!}{(n-r)!}$$

Example 14.1.1 In the course of a specified working period an auditor can hope to complete work on four sets of accounts of a particular size. If she is presented with eight such sets of accounts, how many different sequences of four might be dealt with in the first period?

ANSWER $\qquad$ This is $\dfrac{8!}{4!} = \dfrac{8 \times 7 \times 6 \times 5 \times 4 \times 3 \times 2 \times 1}{4 \times 3 \times 2 \times 1}$

$$= 8 \times 7 \times 6 \times 5 = 1680$$

Exercise 14.1.1 A candidate must attempt six questions from nine in an examination. How many different sequences of six might appear in his script?

In discussing *combinations* (or *arrangements* as they are sometimes called) we are thinking of a situation where different orderings of the same set of objects are indistinguishable. Combinations are usually of more interest than permutations.

In the context of Example 14.1.1 we should have been concerned with combinations rather than permutations if the question had been how many different *sets* of accounts might be dealt with in the first period rather than how many different *sequences*. Suppose we call the accounts *ABCDEFGH*. In asking about sequences of four the sequences

$$
\begin{array}{cccc}
B & D & F & G \\
D & B & G & F \\
B & F & G & D \\
D & G & B & F \\
F & B & D & G
\end{array}
$$

would each be a separate contribution to the total of 1680 which we found. However, these, along with various others, would count as only one set of four accounts that might have been dealt with. Similarly, every other set of four accounts would generate a number of sequences equal to the number of ways these four could be arranged among themselves. So in order to find the number of different sets that might have been dealt with we need to divide the total number of sequences by the number of sequences generated by each set. The number of ways four items can be arranged among themselves, by the reasoning used above in introducing permutations, is $4 \times 3 \times 2 \times 1 = 4! = 24$.

So the number of different sets of four accounts which might have been dealt with is $1680/24 = 70$.

In general the number of ways of choosing r items from n if the same set in different orders is to count only once will be found by dividing the number of selections $_nP_r$ by $r!$, the number of ways each set of r items can be rearranged among themselves. This is called the number of combinations of r items among n items and is denoted $_nC_r$. We see that

$$
_nC_r = \frac{n!}{r!(n-r)!}
$$

Example 14.1.2 Ten recruits to a firm are to be distributed between two departments. In how many ways can this be done if department X is to receive six of them and department Y is to receive four?

ANSWER We are looking here at the number of ways of arranging for six among the ten to be department X recruits.

Thus the answer is

$$
\frac{10!}{6!4!} = \frac{10 \times 9 \times 8 \times 7}{4 \times 3 \times 2 \times 1} = 210
$$

Exercise 14.1.2 A firm decides to conduct a survey involving the gathering of information from six of its twelve largest customers. In how many ways can a random sample of six be chosen from the group of twelve?

Pascal's triangle

For cases where the total number n of items is small Pascal's triangle provides an alternative method for finding numbers of combinations. It is very simple in that it involves no arithmetic beyond addition of pairs of numbers. It is not to be recommended if the total number n of items exceeds 10, unless several $_nC_r$ figures for the same value of n are required.

The easiest way to write Pascal's triangle from the point of view of interpretation is as follows:

$$
\begin{array}{ccccccccccccc}
 & & & & & & 1 & & 1 & & & & \\
 & & & & & 1 & & 2 & & 1 & & & \\
 & & & & 1 & & 3 & & 3 & & 1 & & \\
 & & & 1 & & 4 & & 6 & & 4 & & 1 & \\
 & & 1 & & 5 & & 10 & & 10 & & 5 & & 1 \\
 & 1 & & 6 & & 15 & & 20 & & 15 & & 6 & & 1 \\
1 & & 7 & & 21 & & 35 & & 35 & & 21 & & 7 & & 1
\end{array}
$$

etc.

Each row of the triangle is obtained from the preceding row by adding together pairs of adjacent numbers and writing the sum between them on the line beneath. You might like to generate the next two lines to confirm your understanding of this. The next line is 1, 8, 28, 56, 70, 56, 28, 8, 1.

In order to find $_nC_r$ we go to the nth row of the triangle as drawn and pick out the number which has r numbers on its left.

The binomial distribution: an example and the general case

We begin by considering the instance of a door-to-door salesman of encyclopaedias who reckons from past experience that if he can gain entrance to a house he has probability 0.4 of making a sale there. We look at the probability that he will sell exactly three encyclopaedias if he gains admission to five houses. The probability of a sale is 0.4 so the probability of no sale is $1-0.4=0.6$. In order for there to be exactly three sales at the five houses there must be three sales and two no sales.

Suppose initially that the sales are at the first three houses. Then

$$P(\text{sale} \cap \text{sale} \cap \text{sale} \cap \text{no sale} \cap \text{no sale})$$
$$= P(\text{sale}) \times P(\text{sale}) \times P(\text{sale}) \times P(\text{no sale}) \times P(\text{no sale})$$
$$= 0.4 \times 0.4 \times 0.4 \times 0.6 \times 0.6 = (0.4)^3 \times (0.6)^2$$

Next suppose the sales are at the second, third, and fifth houses.

$$P(\text{no sale} \cap \text{sale} \cap \text{sale} \cap \text{no sale} \cap \text{sale})$$
$$= P(\text{no sale}) \times P(\text{sale}) \times P(\text{sale}) \times P(\text{no sale}) \times P(\text{sale})$$
$$= 0.6 \times 0.4 \times 0.4 \times 0.6 \times 0.4 = (0.4)^3 \times (0.6)^2$$

Similarly, every other combination of three sales and two no sales has probability $(0.4)^3 \times (0.6)^2$. These combinations are mutually exclusive. Hence the required probability of exactly three sales is found by adding together these contributions of $(0.4)^3 \times (0.6)^2$ for all the separate combinations. So

$$P(\text{exactly 3 sales}) = (0.4)^3 \times (0.6)^2 \times (\text{Number of combinations of 3 sales and 2 no sales})$$

This number of combinations can be found from Pascal's triangle or by calculating 5!/3!2! and is seen to be 10.

Hence

$$P(\text{exactly 3 sales}) = (0.4)^3 \times (0.6)^2 \times 10$$
$$= 0.064 \times 0.36 \times 10 = 0.23$$

In general the conditions which must be met by an experiment in order for the binomial distribution to apply to it are the following:

1. There must be a fixed number of trials—call this number n.
2. Each trial must have *two* possible outcomes—*succeed* and *fail*.
3. The success probability must be the same on every trial—p.

The last condition implies that the trials are independent. We note that these conditions were met in the example just considered. The salesman was assumed to gain entry to a stated number of houses, namely five, so condition 1 was satisfied. Each of the entries had two possible outcomes, namely sale or no sale, so condition 2 was satisfied. The probability of a sale resulting from any entry was the same, namely 0.4, and so condition 3 was satisfied.

When conditions 1, 2, and 3 are met, the number of successes obtained in the n trials is said to follow a binomial distribution and the probabilities of specified numbers of successes are given by

$$P(r \text{ successes}) = {}_nC_r p^r (1-p)^{n-r}$$

where r can take each of the values $0, 1, 2, \ldots, n$. In our example above n was 5, p was 0.4, and r was 3.

Published tables allow binomial probabilities to be looked up for various combinations of n and p values but only a limited number of such combinations can be included without the table becoming very large. Hence if binomial probabilities are required it is often necessary to calculate them using the formula given above. A common area of application of the binomial distribution is in quality control sampling for defectives and the next example is of this nature.

Example 14.1.3 A sampling scheme involves taking a sample of ten items from each batch produced and rejecting the batch if more than two defectives are found. If in fact 5 per cent of all items are defective, what is the probability that a batch will be rejected?

ANSWER In order for a batch to be rejected it must contain 3, 4, 5, 6, 7, 8, 9, or 10 defectives, so direct calculation of the rejection probability would involve finding the probabilities of these various numbers defective and adding them together. This would, however, be a laborious process and a much better approach would be to find the probabilities of 0, 1, and 2 defectives, add these together and subtract the result from the total probability which is always 1.

We have here a binomial situation with $n=10$ and $p=0.05$, so

$$P(2 \text{ defectives}) = \frac{10!}{2!8!}(0.05)^2(0.95)^8 = \frac{10 \times 9}{2 \times 1} \times 0.0025 \times 0.6634 = 0.0746$$

$$P(1 \text{ defective}) = \frac{10!}{1!9!}(0.05)^1(0.95)^9 = 10 \times 0.05 \times 0.6302 = 0.3151$$

$P(0 \text{ defectives})$ does not really need the full majesty of the binomial formula for its calculation as we are simply looking at the probability of 10 independent events each with probability 0.95.

However, if we remember the convention that $0!=1$, this case does fit the general binomial pattern.

$$P(0 \text{ defectives}) = \frac{10!}{0!10!}(0.05)^0(0.95)^{10} = 1 \times 1 \times 0.5987 = 0.5987$$

Hence

$$P(0) + P(1) + P(2) = P(2 \text{ or fewer defectives})$$
$$= 0.0746 + 0.3151 + 0.5987 = 0.9884$$

So

$$P(\text{batch rejected}) = P(\text{more than 2 defectives}) = 1 - 0.9884 = 0.0116$$

Just 1.16 per cent of batches can be expected to be rejected by this sampling scheme.

Exercise 14.1.3 A batch of items is believed to contain 20 per cent defectives. A sample of six items is taken at random from the batch. Use the binomial distribution to find the probability that the sample contains:

(a) one defective;
(b) two or more defectives.

Mean and standard deviation of the binomial distribution

The mean of a distribution is defined to be the expected value of the random variable to which it relates, i.e. it is the mean value the random variable could be expected to have over a large number of repetitions of the experiment. In the case of the binomial distribution this means considering many sets of n trials and asking for the mean number of successes per set of n trials. The door-to-door salesman considered in our earlier example had a probability 0.4 of a sale on each entry so in a set of five entries he could on average expect to make $5 \times 0.4 = 2$ sales. In general, the mean for a binomial distribution relating to n trials with probability p of success on each is calculated as np. In accordance with the general expected value formula considered in Chapter 13 the basis of this calculation is using

$$\sum_{r=0}^{n} r \times {}_nC_r p^r (1-p)^{n-r}$$

This sum comes out as np. The standard deviation of a distribution is a measure of the variation in value of the random variable from one repetition of the experiment to another. It is calculated on the same principle as the standard deviation of a set of data in as much as we find the expected value of $(\text{variable} - \text{mean})^2$ and then take the square root of the result. For a binomial distribution relating to n trials with probability p of success on each this means finding

$$\sqrt{\sum_{r=0}^{n} (r-np)^2 \times {}_nC_r p^r (1-p)^{n-r}}$$

and this works out as

$$\text{standard deviation} = \sqrt{np(1-p)}$$

For the door-to-door salesman where $n = 5$ and $p = 0.4$ this says

$$\text{standard deviation} = \sqrt{5 \times 0.4 \times 0.6} = \sqrt{1.2} = 1.095$$

This is a measure of the variation in the number of sales that the salesman can expect from one set of five entries to another.

The same results apply to the mean and standard deviation of a distribution as were noted in Chapter 8 in the context of data. That is to say, we can use the (conservative) Chebyshev result that a range of k standard deviations either side of the mean can be expected to contain a proportion of at least

$$1 - (1/k)^2$$

of the distribution. Thus at least 75 per cent of repetitions of the experiment will result in a random variable value within two standard deviations of the mean and at least 89 per cent of repetitions will result in a value within three standard deviations of the mean. [The reader should confirm these percentages by substituting $k = 2$ and $k = 3$, respectively, in the expression $1 - (1/k)^2$.]

Example 14.1.4 Ten per cent of the matches produced by a certain company are defective. It sells the matches in boxes of 500. Within what symmetrical range about the mean can the company expect 89 per cent of the boxes to have their number of defectives?

ANSWER $n = 500$ and $p = 0.1$, so the mean number of defectives per box is $np = 500 \times 0.1 = 50$. The standard deviation is

$$\sqrt{np(1-p)} = \sqrt{500 \times 0.1 \times 0.9} = \sqrt{45} = 6.7$$

So 89 per cent at least of boxes can be expected to have a number of defective matches in the range

$$50 - 3 \times 6.7 \text{ to } 50 + 3 \times 6.7, \quad \text{i.e. } 50 - 20.1 \text{ to } 50 + 20.1$$

At least 89 per cent of boxes will contain a number of defectives somewhere in the range 30–70.

Exercise 14.1.4 A firm takes on recruits for training in cohorts of 100. The drop-out rate on the training course is 50 per cent. Between what limits can the number of successful recruits produced by at least 75 per cent of cohorts be expected to lie?

14.2 THE POISSON DISTRIBUTION

In considering the binomial distribution we were concerned with experiments having a fixed number of trials, n, and were interested in how many of those trials resulted in a success. Hence a random variable following a binomial distribution could take any of the values $0, 1, 2, 3, 4, \ldots, n$.

In considering the Poisson distribution we are concerned with the number of occurrences in an interval (possibly of time or distance or volume) of a phenomenon which could in principle occur any number of times in that interval. Examples would be the number of telephone calls arising at an exchange in a particular minute, the number of errors on a page of printing, or the number of red cells in a 1 ml sample of blood. These random variables can take values $0, 1, 2, 3, 4, \ldots$. So the Poisson distribution is again a discrete distribution, but there is no upper limit on what value the random variable can take. The condition which must be met in order for the Poisson distribution to be relevant is that the occurrences of the phenomenon must be *completely at random*. The mathematical expression of this condition and the derivation of the probability formula from it involves ideas beyond the scope of this book. Hence we shall not attempt to derive the formula, as we did in the binomial case, but merely state it and then go on to see its use. The Poisson probability formula is

$$P(r \text{ occurrences}) = \frac{m^r e^{-m}}{r!}$$

where m is the mean number of occurrences to be expected in an interval of the length being considered. In this expression e is just a number $(2.71828\ldots)$ and quantities of the form e^{-m} can be found using tables or from most modern calculators.

Example 14.2.1 Printing errors in the work produced by a particular firm occur randomly at an average rate of 0.6 per page. What is the probability that a seven-page pamphlet prepared by the firm contains more than three errors?

ANSWER The mean number of errors per page is 0.6. So in a seven-page pamphlet the mean number of errors is $7 \times 0.6 = 4.2$.

$$P(0 \text{ errors}) = \frac{4.2^0}{0!} e^{-4.2} = \frac{1}{1} e^{-4.2} = 0.015$$

$$P(1 \text{ error}) = \frac{4.2^1}{1!} e^{-4.2} = \frac{4.2}{1} \times 0.015 = 0.063$$

$$P(2 \text{ errors}) = \frac{4.2^2}{2!} e^{-4.2} = \frac{17.64}{2} \times 0.015 = 0.132$$

$$P(3 \text{ errors}) = \frac{4.2^3}{3!} e^{-4.2} = \frac{74.088}{6} \times 0.015 = 0.185$$

Hence

$P(\text{pamphlet contains more than 3 errors}) = 1 - (0.015 + 0.063 + 0.132 + 0.185) = 1 - 0.395 = 0.605$

Published tables allow Poisson probabilities to be looked up for various values of m. Since there is only one parameter, these tables can be produced for a wide range of values and so are of considerable practical importance. They afford the usual way of finding Poisson probabilities.

Exercise 14.2.1 Ships arrive randomly at a port at an average rate of two per day and a maximum of three ships per day can be handled. At a fixed daily cost of £2000 facilities can be extended so as to increase this maximum to four ships per day. If the profit to be made from a ship is £10 000, is this extension of facilities worth while?

Mean and standard deviation of the Poisson distribution

These measures have the same significance as for the binomial distribution and are calculated on the same principles. We have met the mean m already in the Poisson probability formula. If infinitely many intervals of the length we are concerned with are considered, the mean number of occurrences of the phenomenon per interval would be m.

The standard deviation measures the variation from one interval to another in the number of occurrences of the phenomenon. For a Poisson distribution with mean m the standard deviation is $\sqrt{m}$. The same general results apply to the mean and standard deviation of the Poisson distribution as we have seen applying to sets of data and to the binomial distribution.

14.3 THE POISSON APPROXIMATION TO THE BINOMIAL DISTRIBUTION

If we have a binomial experiment (i.e. n trials, two outcomes, and the same probability of success on each trial) where the number of trials is large compared with the number of successes that could reasonably occur, the situation is like a Poisson one. The upper limit n on the number of successes is so large compared with what is likely to occur that it may as well be infinite.

Thus if we have a binomial situation where the success probability p is less than 0.1, then the binomial probabilities can be approximated using the Poisson distribution with mean $m=np$. This condition is seen to be appropriate because it says that the mean number of successes per set of n trials is less than one-tenth of the possible number of successes, n. This is a useful approximation to make because Poisson probability tables are so much more comprehensive than binomial probability tables.

Example 14.3.1 Of the components produced by a certain firm 1.6 per cent are faulty. What is the probability that a box of 50 components contains two or more defectives?

ANSWER This is really a binomial problem. Each box is a set of $n=50$ trials, and each trial has two outcomes in that a component can be either faulty or not faulty.

The probability of a success (i.e. a faulty component) is $p=0.016$. The binomial calculation is

$$P(2 \text{ or more defectives})=1-[P(0 \text{ defectives})+P(1 \text{ defective})]$$

$$=1-\left[(1-0.016)^{50}+\frac{50!}{1!49!}(0.016)(1-0.016)^{49}\right]$$

$$=1-(0.984^{50}+50\times0.016\times0.984^{49})$$

$$=1-(0.446+0.363)=1-0.809=0.191.$$

The Poisson approximation involves using the Poisson distribution with mean $m=np=50\times0.016=0.8$. Then

$$P(2 \text{ or more defectives})=1-[P(0 \text{ defectives})+P(1 \text{ defective})]$$

$$=1-\left[\frac{0.8^0 e^{-0.8}}{0!}+\frac{0.8 e^{-0.8}}{1!}\right]$$

$$=1-(0.449+0.359)=1-0.808=0.192$$

The two results are very similar, showing the approximation to be good for this case, where p is very small.

Exercise 14.3.1 The proportion of articles produced by a company which are defective is 0.5 per cent. They are sold in boxes of 100 and the company guarantees to replace any box containing more than two defectives. The cost of this replacement is £2. The company is considering introducing a new inspection scheme which will cost 5p per box but eliminate all defectives. Use the Poisson approximation to the binomial distribution to decide whether this inspection scheme is worth while.

14.4 CONTINUOUS PROBABILITY DISTRIBUTIONS

All the probability distributions considered so far have been discrete probability distributions, as described in Sec. 14.1, in that they concern variables (number of successes, number of occurrences) which can take only certain distinct values. Often we are concerned with variables which can take any values, at least within a certain range, and in order to deal with such variables as these we need the idea of a continuous probability distribution. In dealing with continuously distributed variables we cannot talk about the probability of the variable taking any single nominated value as we could for discrete distributions. For example, we cannot ask for the probability that a person chosen at random will have weight 71.325 kg or that a metal rod produced by a certain machine will have length 2.7183 m. Such probabilities of individual values for continuously distributed variables must always be zero. What we are required to consider is whether the variable will take a value in a specified *range*. Thus, for example, we can ask for the probability that a person will weigh between 68.7 and 69.4 kg or for the probability that a rod will have length between 3.74 and 3.78 m. Consider Table 14.1 which shows the values of the invoices issued by a firm on a particular day.

Table 14.1

£	£	£	£	£	£	£	£	£	£
17.35	6.80	9.05	14.80	24.70	23.45	29.90	9.95	15.90	22.40
16.45	11.50	17.55	18.60	9.40	13.35	26.60	6.65	10.25	19.00
23.95	18.45	12.70	19.05	15.15	18.30	15.16	12.80	23.40	5.55
8.75	18.80	20.45	15.80	22.50	19.10	14.55	11.15	16.35	26.60

Using the methods explained in Chapter 7 these figures can be grouped into frequency tables of various kinds and diagrams can be drawn that are based on the tables. A relative frquency table is shown in Table 14.2 giving the proportions of invoice values in different classes.

Table 14.2

Class	Relative frequency
£2 and under £6	0.025
£6 and under £10	0.150
£10 and under £14	0.150
£14 and under £18	0.250
£18 and under £22	0.200
£22 and under £26	0.150
£26 and under £30	0.075

A histogram and frequency polygon could be drawn based on Table 14.2 as shown in Fig. 14.1. The area of each block of the histogram represents the relative frequency of values in the class concerned and the total area of the histogram is the total relative frequency which is 1. This is the same as the total area of the polygon.

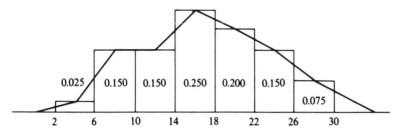

Figure 14.1   Histogram and frequency polygon based on relative frequencies.

Next imagine we had a much larger set of the same type so that a finer division of the range, into £2 intervals, could be justified. Suppose that Table 14.3 was the relative frequency table obtained.

Table 14.3

Class	Relative frequency
£4 and under £6	0.025
£6 and under £8	0.080
£8 and under £10	0.070
£10 and under £12	0.050
£12 and under £14	0.100
£14 and under £16	0.130
£16 and under £18	0.120
£18 and under £20	0.110
£20 and under £22	0.090
£22 and under £24	0.080
£24 and under £26	0.070
£26 and under £28	0.050
£28 and under £30	0.025

The histogram and frequency polygon for this relative frequency table are shown in Fig. 14.2. Again the area of each block of the histogram represents the relative frequency of values in the class, and the total area of the histogram, which is the same as the area under the frequency polygon, is 1, the total relative frequency.

Next imagine taking this process to its limit where we have the whole population and are able to divide the range into infinitely small sections. In this situation the relative frequency polygon will become a smooth curve and the area under it between any two values will

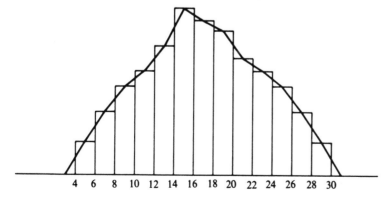

Figure 14.2   Histogram and frequency polygon when narrower classes are used.

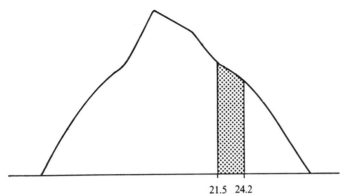

21.5 24.2

Figure 14.3 The limiting case – a probability density function (p.d.f.) curve.

represent the probability of the variable assuming a value in that range. This is shown for the limiting case of our example in Fig. 14.3. The shaded area is the probability of a value between £21.50 and £24.20.

Every continuously distributed variable has associated with it a curve of this kind, which is called a probability density function (p.d.f.) curve. Handling probabilities for continuously distributed variables is a matter of dealing with areas under p.d.f. curves, and we shall see examples of these operations in the following sections.

14.5 THE NORMAL DISTRIBUTION

This is the best known and most widely used of all continuous probability distributions. One reason for this is that many distributions of such variables as lengths, weights, and times follow, at least approximately, normal distributions. A second major reason for the importance of the normal distribution follows from a mathematical result called the Central Limit Theorem. This theorem says in essence that if we add together a large enough number of independent random variables which are identically distributed in *any* way then the sum will be approximately normal. This has considerable practical implications in sampling where it tells us that if we take large enough samples of a variable distributed in any way, then the sample means will be approximately normally distributed. We shall see the importance of this in subsequent chapters. The p.d.f. curve for a normal distribution has the characterisic 'bell shape' shown in Fig. 14.4.

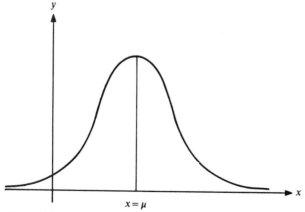

Figure 14.4 The normal distribution p.d.f. curve.

The bell is completely determined for any particular normal distribution if we know the mean, μ and the standard deviation, σ, of that distribution.

The value of the mean tells us where the centre of the bell is and the value of the standard deviation tells us how spread out it is. Thus a small standard deviation means that we have a tall, thin bell while a large standard deviation means a short, fat bell. Note that the total area under every bell must be 1 since we are talking about a p.d.f. curve and hence the total area beneath it represents the total probability.

The mathematical equation of the normal distribution p.d.f. curve is quite a complex one involving the mean and the standard deviation. Direct calculation of areas from this equation would require use of a computer or at least a very sophisticated electronic calculator. Fortunately, such direct calculation is made unnecessary by the following important fact:

The area under a normal p.d.f. curve beyond a specified number of standard deviations from the mean is always the same, regardless of the particular mean and standard deviation values.

Thus normal distribution problems can be solved by calculating the number of standard deviations by which a value of interest differs from the mean and then looking up in a table the area under the p.d.f. curve beyond that number of standard deviations from the mean. Such a table appears in Appendix 2.

Example 14.5.1 The mean life of a certain type of electric light bulb is 1400 hours, with a standard deviation of 300 hours.

(a) If the manufacturer guarantees a life of 100 hours, what percentage of bulbs can he expect to have returned?
(b) At what length of life should the guarantee be set in order for 95 per cent of bulbs to be found satisfactory?

ANSWER

(a) The p.d.f. curve for this example is shown in Fig. 14.5. The number of standard deviations between 1000 and 1400 is

$$\frac{1400 - 1000}{300} = 1.33$$

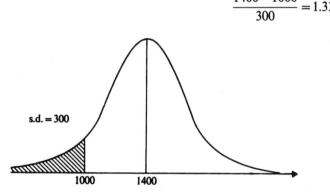

Figure 14.5 The shaded area represents the probability of a value below 1000 hours.

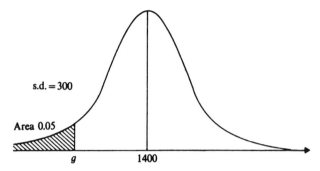

Figure 14.6 The shaded area represents a probability of 0.05.

Referring to the table of tail areas of the normal distribution, we see that the area under the curve beyond 1.33 standard deviations from the mean is 0.0918.

Thus the percentage of bulbs the manufacturer can expect to have returned is 9.18 per cent.

(b) To answer this part of the question we need to use the normal distribution table in reverse since we know that a tail area of $1-0.95=0.05$ is required, and we have to find the value which cuts off this area.

The diagram for this part is shown in Fig. 14.6, the unknown guarantee figure being denoted by g. Looking up the area 0.05 to the best accuracy possible in the normal distribution table, we estimate that the figure having area 0.05 beyond it lies about half-way between 1.64 and 1.65 standard deviations from the mean, i.e. at 1.645 standard deviations from the mean.

Using this estimate, we see that the guarantee needs to be set at $g = 1400 - 1.645 \times 300 = 1400 - 493.5 = 906.5$ hours.

Exercise 14.5.1 The weights of a large number of packs of soap powder are normally distributed with mean 35 grams and standard deviation 5 grams.

(a) What is the probability that a pack drawn at random weighs more than 30 grams?
(b) Above what weight can we expect to find the heaviest 2 per cent of packs?

14.6 APPROXIMATIONS INVOLVING THE NORMAL DISTRIBUTION

The normal approximation to the binomial distribution

Suppose we have a binomial experiment, as described in Sec. 14.1, where the number of trials, n, is large and the success probability, p, on each trial is close to 0.5 so that the distribution is approximately symmetric. Then the binomial probabilities of specified numbers of successes in the n trials can be approximated using the normal distribution with the same mean and standard deviation as the appropriate binomial distribution.

The sort of values needed for n and p in order for this approximation to be a reasonable one can be conveniently described by saying we must have p in the range

$$0.1 \leqslant p \leqslant 0.9$$

and also both $np > 5$ and $n(1-p) > 5$.

Thus the closer p is to 0.5, the less stringent is the requirement on the size of n for a reasonable approximation.

The normal approximation to the binomial distribution is a useful one to make because the normal distribution table can be applied to any normal distribution problem whatever while the binomial table needs to be a very restricted one. Hence solution of problems using the binomial distribution is likely to require full calculation of binomial probabilities. This can be very tedious.

In approximating a binomial distribution by a normal distribution a difficulty arises which did not occur when we approximated a binomial distribution by a Poisson distribution in Sec. 14.3. This stems from the fact that the binomial is a discrete distribution while the normal is continuous. Hence when considering a binomial experiment we want to talk about the probability of three successes or four successes, say, in the n trials, but the normal, being a continuous distribution, does not allow us to talk about the probabilities of individual values like this. Rather we must talk about the probabilities of specified *ranges* of values. The remedy is to regard the area under the normal curve between $m - 0.5$ and $m + 0.5$ (for any whole number m) as 'belonging to' the particular m. Thus if we want to know the probability of three successes we find the area under the normal curve between 2.5 and 3.5.

Similarly, $P(3$ or more successes) is found by calculating the area under the normal curve above 2.5 (since the probability of 3 is to be included) while P (more than 3 successes) is found by calculating the area under the normal curve above 3.5 (since 3 is *not* to be included).

The addition or subtraction of 0.5, as appropriate, in cases such as these is referred to as the *continuity correction* necessary because a discrete distribution is being approximated by a continuous one.

Example 14.6.1 A fair coin is tossed 100 times. Use the normal approximation to the binomial distribution to find the probability that the number of heads obtained is more than 45 but less than 60.

ANSWER Mean $= np = 100 \times 0.5 = 50$.

$$\text{Standard deviation} = \sqrt{np(1-p)} = \sqrt{100 \times 0.5 \times 0.5} = \sqrt{25} = 5$$

So number of standard deviations below $45.5 = (50 - 45.5)/5 = 4.5/5 = 0.9$. Hence the normal tail area below 45.5 is 0.1841.

The number of standard deviations above $59.5 = (59.5 - 50)/5 = 9.5/5 = 1.9$. Hence the tail area above 59.5 is 0.0287.

So the probability of a number of heads which is more than 45 and less than 60 is

$$1 - (0.1841 + 0.0287) = 1 - 0.2128 = 0.7872$$

Exercise 14.6.1 A production process yields 10 per cent defective items. If 200 items are selected randomly from the process, use the normal approximation to the binomial distribution to find the probability of more than 25 defectives.

The normal approximation to the Poisson distribution

If we have a Poisson distribution where the mean number m of occurrences in an interval of the length being considered is large, then the Poisson probabilities can be approximated using a normal distribution with mean m and standard deviation $\sqrt{m}$. The approximation works adequately if $m > 30$, and a continuity correction is again needed since we are once more approximating a discrete distribution by a continuous distribution.

Example 14.6.2 The number of accidents occurring on average each year in a factory is 36. They occur completely at random. Use the normal approximation to the Poisson distribution to find the probability that in 1987 there were more than 40 accidents.

ANSWER $m = 36$ and $\sqrt{m} = 6$, so we need a normal distribution with mean 36 and standard deviation 6.

The number of standard deviations by which 40.5 exceeds 36 is $(40.5 - 36)/6 = 4.5/6 = 0.75$ so the tail area above 40.5 is 0.2266.

Hence the probability of more than 40 accidents in 1987 is 0.2266.

Exercise 14.6.2 A certain switchboard receives on average 144 calls per hour in a random process. Find the probability that in a particular hour the number of calls received is more than 135 but less than 155.

TEST EXERCISES

14.1 A committee of three accountants and two lawyers is to be formed from a group of seven accountants and five lawyers. The number of possible different selections is
(A) 45; (B) 175; (C) 210; (D) 350; (E) 792.

(CIMA Stage 1: May 1991)

14.2 Razor blades of a certain kind are sold in packets of five. The following table shows the distribution of 100 packets according to the number of faulty blades they contained.

Number of faulty blades	0	1	2	3	4	5
Number of packets	80	17	2	1	0	0

Calculate the mean number of faulty blades per packet and, assuming a binomial distribution, the proportion of all blades produced which are faulty.

Use your result to calculate the probabilities of 0, 1, 2, 3, 4, or 5 faulty blades in a packet and hence find the numbers of packets out of the total of 100 which could be expected to contain these respective numbers of faulty blades.

14.3 Each newly recruited person in a certain organization receives a period of training and subsequently takes an examination to qualify for skilled work. Assuming a probability of 0.8 that a recruit will pass the examination, find the probability that out of a group of ten recruits at least seven will qualify for skilled work.

14.4 The number of minor accidents in a factory on any day follows a Poisson distribution with a mean of 1.5 accidents. The probability of there being *at least one* accident tomorrow is closest to
(A) 0.22; (B) 0.30; (C) 0.33; (D) 0.66; (E) 0.78.

(CIMA Stage 1: Nov. 1991)

14.5 Past experience shows that the number of accidents in a certain factory each week follows a Poisson distribution. If the probability of there being no accidents in a week is 1 per cent, the average (mean) number of accidents in a week is closest to
(A) 0.3679; (B) 0.9048; (C) 2.3; (D) 4; (E) 4.6.

(CIMA Stage 1: Nov. 1991)

14.6 Monthly demand for a product is approximately normally distributed with a mean of 10 000 units and a standard deviation of 2000 units. The probability of monthly demand being less than 6000 units is
(A) 0.0013; (B) 0.0228; (C) 0.0475; (D) 0.2257; (E) 0.4772.

(CIMA Stage 1: Nov. 1989)

14.7 Many workers in a factory carry out a routine task for which the time is planned to be 90 minutes. Last week it was found that the time actually taken was normally distributed with a mean of 85.8 minutes and a standard deviation of 5 minutes. The percentage of these routine tasks completed within the allocated time is closest to
(A) 70;   (B) 80;   (C) 84;   (D) 88;   (E) 95.

(CIMA Stage 1: May 1990)

14.8 For a group of 1800 employees of a manufacturing company, IQ is approximately normally distributed with mean 110 and standard deviation 12. It is known from experience that for a particular job only persons with IQs of at least 95 are intelligent enough to do it, but that those with IQs greater than 120 soon become bored and unhappy with it. On the basis of IQ alone, how many of the 1800 employees would you expect to be suitable for the work?

ESTIMATION

15.1 SAMPLING DISTRIBUTION OF THE MEAN

These are many situations where it is impracticable to examine all of the values in a population. Consequently it may be more sensible to take a sample from a population and then make some inferential statement about this underlying population. Inevitably some error is caused by the fact that not all of the population values are observed; but, with care, this error may only be small. In Chapter 6 we described many methods of taking samples from an underlying population; in this and subsequent chapters we assume that the sample is selected randomly; that is, each member of the population has an equal chance of being in the sample.

Let us suppose that a sample of n observations $x_1, x_2, x_3, ..., x_n$ is taken from a given population. The sample mean is, say, $\bar{x}_1 = (x_1 + x_2 + \cdots + x_n)/n = (\Sigma x)/n$. Suppose we take further samples from the same population and calculate the mean of each of these samples, in such a way that $\bar{x}_2$ is the mean of sample 2, $\bar{x}_3$ is the mean of sample 3, and so on. We see that the sample mean has a distribution which is referred to as the sampling distribution of the mean.

Suppose that the population has mean μ and variance σ^2, and a random sample $x_1, x_2, x_3, ..., x_n$ is taken from this population. As we have selected our sample randomly the n values can be considered to be independent random variables, such that their mean is μ and their variance σ^2. Hence

$$\text{mean of } \bar{x} = \frac{\text{mean}(x_1) + \text{mean}(x_2) + \cdots + \text{mean}(x_n)}{n}$$

$$= \frac{\mu + \mu + \cdots + \mu}{n} = \frac{n\mu}{n} = \mu$$

and

$$\text{variance of } \bar{x} = \frac{\text{var}(x_1) + \text{var}(x_2) + \cdots + \text{var}(x_n)}{n^2}$$

since all x values are independent of each other. Hence

$$\text{var}(\bar{x}) = \frac{(\sigma^2 + \sigma^2 + \cdots + \sigma^2)}{n^2} = \frac{n\sigma^2}{n^2} = \frac{\sigma^2}{n}$$

We conclude that the sampling distribution of the mean of n observations, taken from a population with mean μ and variance σ^2, has mean μ and variance σ^2/n. The standard deviation of the sample means, $\sigma/\sqrt{n}$, is often called the standard error of the mean. If a population, in addition to having μ and σ^2 as its mean and variance, is normal, then the sampling distribution of the mean is also normal (with mean μ and variance σ^2/n). We see from these results that the larger the value of n, the smaller is the variance of the sample mean, and hence the closer we would expect $\bar{x}$ to be to μ. Figure 15.1 illustrates this point.

This theory can be developed to find the mean and variance of the sum of n independent random variables $x_1, x_2, \ldots, x_n$, that come from a distribution with mean μ and variance σ^2.

$$\text{mean } (\Sigma x) = n\mu$$
$$\text{variance } (\Sigma x) = n\sigma^2$$
$$\text{standard deviation } (\Sigma x) = \sigma\sqrt{n}$$

Furthermore it can be shown that if $x_1, x_2, \ldots, x_n$ are independent random variables from a normal distribution (with mean μ, standard deviation σ) then Σx also comes from a normal distribution (with mean $n\mu$, standard deviation $\sigma\sqrt{n}$).

Example 15.1.1 The Crispy Cookie Company produces a range of pre-packed biscuits which are sold in 500 g packets. A biscuit is produced by baking a measured quantity of the appropriate mixture, and then a specified number of biscuits is placed into each packet. Because the baking process cannot be completely controlled, there is an unavoidable variation in the weights of biscuits produced. Each packet is therefore automatically weighed, and any packets weighing less than the required 500 g are returned for reprocessing. Whenever a packet is rejected in this way, it is estimated to cost £0.1.

The company is about to start selling a new type of biscuit which has an average weight of 40 g and a standard deviation of 6 g. At full production, the weekly output of this biscuit will be 500 000 packets and the cost per packet (in £) is given by

$$0.05 + 0.01n$$

where n is the number of biscuits in each packet.

(a) If 13 biscuits are put into each packet, what will be the mean and standard deviation of the weight of a packet?

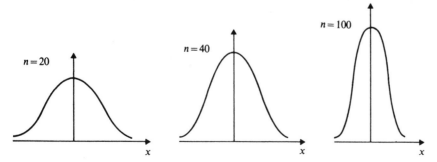

Figure 15.1 Sampling distributions of sample mean for different values of n.

(b) Explain briefly why the weight of a packet of biscuits will be approximately normally distributed. What is the probability that a packet of 13 biscuits will be rejected as underweight?
(c) Determine the minimum cost number of biscuits per packet by calculating the average weekly production cost for packet sizes of 13, 14, and 15 biscuits.

(ACCA Level 2: June 1987)

ANSWER

(a) If there are 13 biscuits in a packet, the weight of the packet is given by

$$\Sigma x = x_1 + x_2 + \cdots + x_{13}$$

where x_i is the weight of the ith biscuit in the packet.

$$\text{mean } (\Sigma x) = n\mu = 13(40) = 520 \text{ g}$$

$$\text{standard deviation } (\Sigma x) = \sigma\sqrt{n} = 6\sqrt{13} = 21.6 \text{ g}$$

(b) It is reasonable to suppose that the weights of the individual biscuits are approximately normal, and hence the sum of these weights can be assumed to be normal. The probability of an underweight packet is

$$P(\Sigma x < 500) = P\left(z < \frac{500 - 520}{21.6}\right) = P(z < -0.92)$$

From the normal tables, the probability of a z score of less than -0.92 is 0.179; i.e. 17.9 per cent of packets will be rejected as underweight.
(c) The expected weekly cost is made up of a rejection cost and a production cost. For a packet of 13 biscuits,

$$\text{rejection cost} = 500\,000 \times 0.179 \times 0.1 = £8950$$

$$\text{production cost} = 500\,000 \times (0.5 + 0.01 \times 13) = 90\,000$$

giving a total cost of £98 950.
    For a packet of 14 biscuits,

$$P(\text{underweight packet}) = P\left(z < \frac{500 - (14 \times 40)}{6\sqrt{14}}\right) = P(z < -2.67) = 0.004$$

so

$$\text{rejection cost} = 500\,000 \times 0.004 \times 0.1 = £200$$

$$\text{production cost} = 500\,000 \times (0.05 + 0.01 \times 14) = £95\,000$$

giving a total cost of £95 200.
    For a packet of 15 biscuits, the production cost alone will be

$$500\,000 \times (0.05 + 0.01 \times 15) = £100\,000$$

and so 14 is the optimum number of biscuits per packet.

In this example we made the assumption that the weights of the individual biscuits were normal. Although this is probably a sensible assumption, it was not essential to make this assumption. In fact, if we take large random samples of a variable distributed in any way, then the sample means (and totals) are approximately normally distributed. We now present this statement more formally as the Central Limit Theorem.

The Central Limit Theorem

If several samples of size n are taken from a population with mean μ and variance σ^2, then, if n is large, the distribution of the sample mean, $\bar{x}$, is approximately normal, with mean μ and variance σ^2/n, and this approximation improves as n increases.

What do we mean by large n in this theorem? This is not easy to answer as it depends on the closeness of the population distribution to the normal distribution. Usually n greater than 30 is a sufficient restriction, but a smaller value of n may be appropriate if the underlying population already has similarities to the normal distribution.

Note that there is no reference to the underlying distribution of the population values in the Central Limit Theorem. It emphasizes that the normal distribution is a most important probability distribution. In particular, many inferential statistical techniques involve the use of the normal distribution through the Central Limit Theorem.

Example 15.1.2 The lifetimes of a particular car battery are known to come from a distribution with mean 30 months and standard deviation of 9 months. Calculate the sampling distribution of the mean of a random sample of 36 such car batteries. Also derive the probability that the sample mean of these 36 car batteries is greater than 32 months.

ANSWER Here we are not told the underlying distribution of the lifetime of a car battery. However, it matters very little because of the Central Limit Theorem. In fact, it is likely that the distribution of the lifetimes is approximately normal, so $n = 36$ is certainly large enough to state that $\bar{x}$ would have a normal distribution with mean $= 30$ and standard error $= 1.5 (= 9/\sqrt{36})$. As $(32 - 30)/1.5 = 1.33$, we see from the standard normal tables that the required probability is 0.09.

Sampling distribution of proportions

In finance it is often necessary to consider qualitative data; for example, to calculate the proportion of invoices over £25, or to discover how many expense claims are incorrect. Suppose we have a population containing a proportion, π, of items that possess an attribute of interest (e.g. defective). If many samples of size n are taken and for each sample we calculate the sample proportion, p, of defectives present, then in a similar way to that of the sample means we may use the Central Limit Theorem to make the following statement:

When n is large and π is not near to zero or one, then p is approximately normal with mean π and variance $(1 - \pi)/n$.

Again the restrictions on n and π are not very specific. A rule of thumb is that both $n\pi$ and $n(1 - \pi)$ are greater than 5.

Example 15.1.3 When patients suffering from a disease are given certain treament the probability of a cure is 0.8. If this treatment is given to a random sample of 64 patients suffering from the disease, determine:

(a) the mean and standard deviation of the patients cured;
(b) the probability that less than 50 patients are cured?

ANSWER

(a) In this example we know that $\pi = 0.8$ and $n = 64$. Hence the sample proportion has mean $\pi = 0.8$ and standard deviation

$$\sqrt{\pi(1-\pi)/n} = \sqrt{(0.8 \times 0.2)/64} = 0.05$$

(b) This part of the question is simply an application of the normal approximation to the binomial as described in Sec. 14.6. Since

$$\frac{49.5 - (64 \times 0.8)}{\sqrt{(64 \times 0.8 \times 0.2)}} = \frac{-1.7}{3.2} = -0.53$$

we require the area under the normal curve more than 0.53 standard deviations below the mean. The area is 0.298.

Before we delve more deeply into estimation we briefly consider the standard normal curve again as tabulated in Appendix 2. By observation of these tables we can see that exactly 95 per cent of the area under a normal curve lies within 1.96 standard deviations of the mean. In a similar way we can show that 90 per cent of the area lies within 1.645 standard deviations and 99 per cent lies within 2.58 standard deviations of the mean. These results are illustrated in Fig. 15.2. These values (1.96, 1.645, 2.58) will figure prominently in the next two chapters and should be learnt now. It will save much needless effort later on.

Exercise 15.1.1 The weight of cereal in a standard packet is normally distributed with a mean of 502 g and a standard deviation of 3.75 g. Random samples of 16 packets are selected.

(a) Calculate the mean and standard deviation of the mean weight of cereal per packet in a random sample of 16 packets.
(b) Estimate the probability that a sample will yield a mean of less than 500 g.

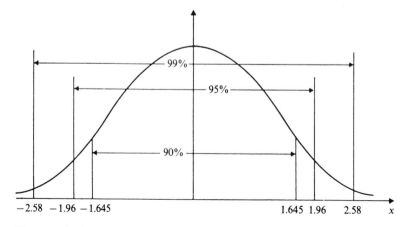

Figure 15.2 Important percentiles of the standard normal distribution.

15.2 ESTIMATION OF POPULATION PARAMETERS

When we use the data of a sample to tell us something about the population from which the sample was taken, the only thing we can be sure of is that we do not have all the truth about the population. Thus it is necessary to proceed in some scientific manner so that we can have a high degree of confidence that the truth lies within specified limits. In this section we want to try to decide on numerical values for the parameter(s) of the population of interest, on the basis of the sample data at our disposal.

Point estimation

A point estimate is a number obtained from computations on the observed sample data, which serves as an approximation to the population parameter of interest. There are a number of desirable properties that point estimators should possess, which make one estimator better than any others. The usual estimators are:

1. If μ is the unknown population mean, then the sample mean, $\bar{x} = (\Sigma x)/n$ is a suitable estimate; that is, $\hat{\mu} = \bar{x}$.
2. If π is the unknown population proportion, then the sample proportion, p, is the most suitable estimate.
3. If σ^2 is the unknown population variance, then the most suitable estimate is represented by $\hat{\sigma}^2 = \Sigma(x_i - \bar{x})^2/(n-1)$. This result may seem surprising to readers, however, the more obvious value $s^2 = \Sigma(x_i - \bar{x})^2/n$ always tends to underestimate the population variance, σ^2, and is therefore biased. This is not the case with $\hat{\sigma}^2$. In the same way $\hat{\sigma}$ is the most suitable estimate of the unknown population standard deviation, σ. Note that when n, the sample size, is large there is little difference between the computed values of $\hat{\sigma}$ and s. In general, the expression 'sample standard deviation' is used to mean s.

Example 15.2.1 Martin Electronic Controls Limited is a small manufacturer of electronic components, specializing in industrial control equipment. Prior to an external audit, the chief accountant of this company decided to undertake a preliminary spotcheck and sampled 18 sales items from the previous month in order to have some general idea as to their overall value. The values, in £, of these sales items are given in the following table.

82	30	98	116	80	150	200	88	70
90	160	100	86	76	90	140	76	68

(Note that, using the usual terminology, $\Sigma x = 1800$ and $\Sigma x^2 = 207\,200$.)
   Construct point estimates for

(a) population mean;
(b) population proportion of sales items valued at more than £120;
(c) population standard deviation.

(ACCA Level 2: Dec. 1987)

ANSWER

(a) Our estimate for the population mean is

$$\hat{\mu} = \bar{x} = \frac{1800}{18} = 100, \text{ i.e. £100}$$

(b) As there are 4 out of 18 sales items valued at more than £120 then the point estimate of the population proportion is $\hat{\pi}=p=4/18=0.22$.

(c) Our estimate of the population standard deviation is

$$\hat{\sigma} = \sqrt{\frac{(\Sigma x^2 - n\bar{x}^2)}{n-1}} = \sqrt{\frac{1}{17}(207\ 200 - 1800 \times 100)}$$

$$= £40$$

Interval estimation

An interval estimate is an interval determined by two numbers obtained from computations on the observed sample values, and is expected to contain the unknown true value of the parameter in its interior. Consider the following example:

Example 15.2.2 An accountant wishes to investigate the collection times for debts owing. He has found from experience that the collection times are approximately normally distributed with a standard deviation of 10 days. If the collection times are too large then the company may have the threat of liquidation, so it is important to have an accurate estimate of the mean collection time. To do this he takes a sample of 25 invoices from last year's trading and finds a mean of $\bar{x}=44$ days. How accurate is $\bar{x}$ as a point estimate of the population mean, μ?

ANSWER We know that the probability of 0.95 that a normally distributed variable will take some value within 1.96 standard deviations of its mean; and since we know that $\bar{x}$ has a normal distribution with mean μ and standard deviation $\sigma/\sqrt{n}$, it follows that

$$P\left(-1.96 < \frac{\bar{x}-\mu}{\sigma/\sqrt{n}} < +1.96\right) = 0.95$$

and hence

$$P\left(-1.96\frac{\sigma}{\sqrt{n}} < \bar{x}-\mu < +1.96\frac{\sigma}{\sqrt{n}}\right) = 0.95$$

In our example, $\sigma=10$ and $n=25$ so $\sigma/\sqrt{n}=2$. Therefore

$$P(-3.92 < \bar{x}-\mu < +3.92) = 0.95$$

The accountant feels quite confident that the sample mean $\bar{x}=44$ differs from the population value μ, by less than 3.92 days. The magnitude of the difference is called the error of the estimate and can only be expressed in terms of probability since μ is unknown.

What is a 95 per cent confidence interval for μ based on the original sample of 25? We see that

$$P(\mu - 3.92 < \bar{x} < \mu + 3.92) = 0.95$$

or

$$P(\bar{x} - 3.92 < \mu < \bar{x} + 3.92) = 0.95$$

We call the interval $(\bar{x} - 3.92, \bar{x} + 3.92)$ or (40.08, 47.92) the 95 per cent *confidence interval* for μ, and the end points of the interval are called the confidence limits for μ.

For a general situation it follows that if our population is approximately normally distributed then

$$P\left(\bar{x} - 1.96\frac{\sigma}{\sqrt{n}} < \mu < \bar{x} + 1.96\frac{\sigma}{\sqrt{n}}\right) = 0.95$$

so that our general 95 per cent confidence interval takes the form

$$\left(\bar{x} - 1.96\frac{\sigma}{\sqrt{n}}, \quad \bar{x} + 1.96\frac{\sigma}{\sqrt{n}}\right)$$

This statement tells us that in the long run of repeatedly taking random samples of size n from the population, 95 per cent of the time our confidence interval will bracket μ.

In this section we have dealt only with normally distributed populations. However, the Central Limit Theorem makes this restriction unnecessary when the sample size is large.

Example 15.2.3 The average time in days required to deliver orders by an electrical company is to be estimated. A sample of 60 orders is selected randomly from recent trading. The sample mean is 5.9 days and $\hat{\sigma}$, the sample estimate of the population standard deviation, is 1.7 days. Compute a 95 per cent interval estimate of the delivery times.

ANSWER A 95 per cent confidence interval for μ takes the form

$$\bar{x} - 1.96\frac{\sigma}{\sqrt{n}} \quad \text{to} \quad \bar{x} + 1.96\frac{\sigma}{\sqrt{n}}$$

as we have seen. However, the population standard deviation, σ, is not known. Fortunately, when n is large, not too much error is incurred by using its unbiased estimate, $\hat{\sigma}$, as a substitute. Therefore we use

$$\bar{x} - 1.96\frac{\hat{\sigma}}{\sqrt{n}} \quad \text{to} \quad \bar{x} + 1.96\frac{\hat{\sigma}}{\sqrt{n}}$$

As we shall see in Sec. 15.3 we are unable to use this approximation when n is small (less than 30). In the above example our confidence interval is

$$5.9 - 1.96 \times \frac{1.7}{\sqrt{60}} \quad \text{to} \quad 5.9 + 1.96 \times \frac{1.7}{\sqrt{60}}$$

i.e.

$$5.47 \quad \text{to} \quad 6.33 \text{ days}$$

It may be that a 95 per cent confidence interval is not suitable for the situation in question; for example, a 99 per cent confidence interval (of the form $\bar{x} \pm 2.58\sigma/\sqrt{n}$) or a 90 per cent confidence interval (of the form $\bar{x} \pm 1.645\sigma/\sqrt{n}$) may be preferred. We see that the interval widens as we increase the level of confidence. Conversely we can shorten the confidence interval by reducing the degree of confidence.

Example 15.2.4 During an audit, a random sample of 50 invoices was observed from a large population. The sample mean value was calculated to be £52.40 and the standard deviation £5.60.

Estimate the standard error of the mean, and compute a 90 per cent confidence interval for the true population mean.

ANSWER The standard error of the mean is estimated by $\hat{\sigma}/\sqrt{n}$. We are not given the value of $\hat{\sigma}$, but the value of s. However,

$$\frac{\hat{\sigma}}{\sqrt{n}} = \frac{s}{\sqrt{n-1}}$$

$$\frac{\hat{\sigma}}{\sqrt{n}} = \frac{5.60}{7} = 0.80$$

This measure can now be used to give an interval estimate for the population mean. Here we calculate a 90 per cent confidence interval to be

$$52.40 - (1.645 \times 0.80) \quad \text{to} \quad 52.40 + (1.645 \times 0.80)$$

i.e.

$$£51.08 \quad \text{to} \quad £53.72$$

Suppose we are not satisfied with the accuracy of this estimate. How large an additional sample should we take so that we can be reasonably sure, with a probability of 0.90 say, that the estimate will not be in error by more than £1?

As the sample size increases, so the standard error decreases. Since 90 per cent of the central area of the normal curve corresponds to 1.645 standard deviations on both sides of μ, it follows that n must satisfy the equation

$$1.645 \frac{\hat{\sigma}}{\sqrt{n}} = 1$$

Thus

$$n = (1.645\hat{\sigma})^2 = (1.645 \times 0.80 \times \sqrt{50})^2$$
$$= 86.6$$

i.e. an additional sample of 87 is required.

In a similar manner to the population mean we often wish to compute an interval estimate for the population proportion, π. By using the result of Sec. 15.1 that the sample proportion, p, has a normal distribution with mean π and standard deviation $\sqrt{\pi(1-\pi)/n}$, provided n is reasonably large and π is not near 0 or 1, then we would expect a 95 per cent confidence interval to be

$$p - 1.96 \sqrt{\frac{\pi(1-\pi)}{n}} \quad \text{to} \quad p + 1.96 \sqrt{\frac{\pi(1-\pi)}{n}}$$

Unfortunately, this interval also depends on π, which is, of course, unknown. However, if we approximate π by p, an approximate 95 per cent confidence interval for π is

$$p - 1.96 \sqrt{\frac{p(1-p)}{n}} \quad \text{to} \quad p + 1.96 \sqrt{\frac{p(1-p)}{n}}$$

Example 15.2.5 From a large population of accounts, a random sample of 200 was taken. From these it was noticed that 18 possessed some irregularity. Obtain a 95 per cent confidence interval for the true proportion of defectives among the accounts.

ANSWER The sample proportion, $p = 18/200 = 0.09$. Thus, our estimate for the standard error of a proportion is

$$\sqrt{\frac{0.09 \times 0.91}{200}} = 0.0202$$

A 95 per cent confidence interval for π is

$$0.09 - (1.96 \times 0.0202) \quad \text{to} \quad 0.09 + (1.96 \times 0.0202)$$

i.e.

$$0.050 \quad \text{to} \quad 0.130$$

We are 95 per cent confident that the true proportion of defective accounts lies between 0.05 and 0.13.

Exercise 15.2.1 From a random sample of 400 qualified accountants, the mean annual salary was found to be £12 000 and the standard deviation £3000. Calculate the standard error of the mean and compute a 99 per cent confidence interval for the mean salary of all qualified accountants.

Exercise 15.2.2 In a random sample of 250 persons applying to a finance company for a loan, 40 were refused. Compute a 95 per cent confidence interval for the correct proportion who do not receive a loan.

15.3 SMALL SAMPLE ESTIMATION

Previously, given a sample of size n, we have used the result that $(\bar{x} - \mu)/(\sigma/\sqrt{n})$ has a standard normal distribution in order to obtain confidence limits for the population mean, μ. As we have already seen σ is often not known and we then need to estimate it by its unbiased estimator, $\hat{\sigma}$. This gives good results for large samples but exaggeratedly narrow confidence intervals when n in small. To avoid the error involved in replacing σ by $\hat{\sigma}$ when we have a small sample size, a new distribution called Student's t-distribution is introduced.

W. S. Gosset (a statistician to Guinness Brewery writing under the name 'Student') investigated the problem of determining the exact distribution of the variable

$$\frac{\bar{x} - \mu}{\hat{\sigma}/\sqrt{\pi}}$$

in samples from a normal distribution. The t-distribution (as tabulated in Appendix 2) is exact when the underlying population is normal and a close approximation otherwise. Furthermore, the t-distribution is similar to that of the standard normal distribution, being symmetrical but more spread out, as illustrated in Fig. 15.3.

Tables give values of the t-distribution corresponding to what is called the number of 'degrees of freedom', denoted by v, and various probabilities. In this case $v = n - 1$; that is, one less than the sample size, corresponding to use the divisor $n - 1$ rather than n in defining the sample

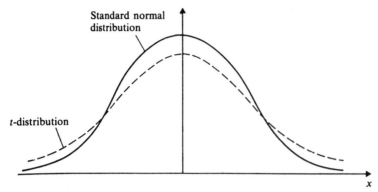

Figure 15.3 Comparison of t-distribution with standard normal distribution.

standard deviation. We know that for the standard normal distribution 95 per cent of the population lies between ± 1.96. The corresponding points for the t-distribution are given in Table 15.1.

Table 15.1

v	t-value
3	3.18
10	2.23
30	2.04
∞	1.96

For an infinite number of degrees of freedom the t-distribution is identical to the standard normal distribution. For our purposes if n is greater than 30 it is reasonable to use the standard normal distribution. We illustrate its use by means of two examples.

Example 15.3.1 You are required to assess the total value of 900 sales items in a company's ledger. Due to lack of available time you do not check every item in the ledger, but take a random sample of 2 per cent of the items. The values of the 18 selected accounts are:

£	£	£	£	£	£
45	58	49	70	38	80
38	15	50	40	45	75
35	43	100	44	41	34

(a) Estimate the mean and standard deviation of the population.
(b) Give a point estimate of the total of all 900 items.
(c) Provide 95 per cent confidence limits for the total value of all 900 accounts.

ANSWER

(a) The unbiased estimates of μ and σ are

$$\hat{\mu} = \bar{x} = \frac{\Sigma x}{n} = \frac{900}{18} = £50$$

and

$$\hat{\sigma} = \sqrt{\frac{1}{n-1}(\Sigma x_i^2 - n\bar{x}^2)} = \sqrt{\frac{1}{17}(51\,800 - 45\,000)} = £20$$

(b) A point estimate for total value $= 900 \times 50 = £45\,000$.

(c) A 95 per cent confidence interval for μ takes the form

$$\bar{x} \pm t\frac{\hat{\sigma}}{\sqrt{n}}$$

where t is the relevant value of the t-distribution with $18 - 1 = 17$ degrees of freedom. From Appendix 2 we find that the required t-value is 2.11. Thus the 95 per cent confidence interval for μ is

$$50 - \frac{2.11 \times 20}{\sqrt{18}} \quad \text{to} \quad 50 + \frac{2.11 \times 20}{\sqrt{18}}$$

or

$$£40.05 \quad \text{to} \quad £59.95$$

We can now obtain a 95 per cent confidence interval for the total value of the population by merely multiplying each limit by the number of values in the population, 900. Here $40.05 \times 900 = £36\,045$ and $59.95 \times 900 = £53\,955$. Therefore the confidence limits for the total value are £36 045 and £53 955.

Exercise 15.3.1 A sample of size 16 from a normal population yielded the sample values $\bar{x} = 14.5$, $s = 5$. Find 95 per cent confidence limits for μ, the population mean.

TEST EXERCISES

15.1 During an internal audit, an accountant had to sample a very large batch of invoices for value and for errors. A simple random sample of 200 invoices revealed a mean value of £90 with a standard deviation of £40.

(a) Find the standard error of the mean.
(b) Find 99 per cent confidence limits for the mean value of the whole batch.
(c) Explain briefly why it is not possible to find 100 per cent confidence limits for the mean value of the batch from a sample.
(d) Find 95 per cent confidence limits for the error rate of the whole batch if 20 invoices showed errors.
(e) Find the sizes of samples required in (b) and (d) in order to double the accuracy of your answers.

(CIMA Stage 1: Nov. 1989)

15.2 A simple random sample of 50 invoices reveals that the mean value is £105 with a standard deviation of £25. Determine 90 per cent confidence limits for the whole (large) batch of invoices.

(CIMA Stage 1: Nov. 1989)

15.3
(a) Outline the central limit theorem and comment briefly on its application to inferential statistics.
(b) Taurus Components Ltd, a manufacturer of electrical parts and accessories, is currently examining the cost of assembling one of its major products. From considerable past experience it has been established that the mean labour time to assemble this component is 90 minutes. However the chief works engineer is convinced that the assembly procedures could be improved. Consequently he has developed a new assembly method, and has randomly

assigned operators to carry out a trial run. After allowing these operators to get used to the new procedures, he timed the assembly of a sample of 10 components. The results (in minutes) are shown below:

$$79 \quad 74 \quad 112 \quad 95 \quad 83 \quad 96 \quad 77 \quad 84 \quad 70 \quad 90$$

(i) Calculate unbiased estimates of the mean and standard deviation for the assembly time of the product using the new assembly method.

(ACCA Level 2: June 1989)

15.4 The weekly wage amounts, in £, of 25 employees who have an overtime payment are given in the following table.

70	166	140	150	126
151	133	200	145	170
200	118	132	149	130
125	165	167	240	120
210	137	140	136	130

(You may use the summations $\Sigma x = 3750$, $\Sigma x^2 = 591\,900$)

Determine the unbiased point estimates of the mean and standard deviation for this population.

(ACCA Level 2: June 1991)

HYPOTHESIS TESTING

16.1 BASIC CONCEPTS

In the preceding chapter we dealt with one aspect of inferential statistics, namely the problem of estimating unknown population parameters from sample data. In this chapter we consider a related problem of deciding whether or not a particular belief about a population is supported by our sample values.

When we use sample data to test a hypothesis, we realize that the observations will not fit the hypothesis perfectly, even if the hypothesis is true. So it is necessary to observe how close the sample observations are to the hypothesis and decide whether the difference could reasonably be attributed to chance or whether it is due to the falsity of the hypothesis. As in the previous chapter we can never know the truth; all we can do is make decisions in some scientific manner so that we have a reasonable chance of reaching the correct conclusions.

In order to illustrate the ideas of hypothesis testing, consider the following example:

Example 16.1.1 In a market survey concerned with home loans, a random sample of 262 people who had taken out a first mortgage during the last year was interviewed. As a result of the interview it was discovered that 49 of these people obtained their mortgage from a bank. A view which has recently been expressed is that the banks are currently providing as many as 30 per cent of all loans for first mortgages. Does your sample evidence support or contradict this view?

ANSWER We begin by setting up a *null hypothesis*, H_0, namely that the true proportion of first mortgages that are provided by the banks is 0.3 (or 30 per cent). We also need an *alternative hypothesis*, H_1, so that if the null hypothesis is rejected, we will accept the hypothesis, H_1. In this example

$$H_0: \pi = 0.3, \quad H_1: \pi \neq 0.3$$

where π is the true proportion of first mortgages that are provided by the banks.

We want a small probability of rejecting H_0 (and thus accepting H_1) if H_0 is true. The probability of this happening is called the *level of significance* of the hypothesis test. In this example there is no stipulated level of significance and so we shall use the commonly used value

5 per cent (or 0.05). Thus if we find that the sample proportion from the market survey is so different from 0.3 as to have no more than a 5 per cent chance of occurring then we can justifiably reject H_0. Any such sample proportion is considered to be significantly different from 0.3, the term *significant* being used in a technical statistical sense as meaning 'unlikely to be due to chance'. Sample proportion values far enough away from 0.3 to cause us to reject H_0 make up a set of values called the *critical region* of the test.

In Chapter 15 we have seen that if sample sizes are reasonably large then the sample proportions are distributed normally with mean π and standard deviation $\sqrt{\pi(1-\pi)/n}$. In this example p is normally distributed with mean $\pi=0.3$ and standard deviation $\sqrt{0.3 \times 0.7/262}=0.0283$. We can then determine the critical region specifically, in the following way:

$$P\left(-1.96 \leqslant \frac{p-\pi}{\sqrt{\pi(1-\pi)/n}} \leqslant +1.96\right)=0.95$$

from normal tables. If we assume that $H_0 : \pi=0.3$ is true, then

$$P\left(-1.96 \leqslant \frac{p-0.3}{0.0283} \leqslant +1.96\right)=0.95$$

$$P[0.3-1.96(0.0283) \leqslant p \leqslant 0.3+1.96(0.0283)]=0.95$$

$$P(0.245 \leqslant p \leqslant 0.355)=0.95$$

Thus, if H_0 is true, there is just a 5 per cent probability that the sample proportion will turn out to be either below 0.245 or above 0.355. Hence the critical region of the test is

$$p \leqslant 0.245, \quad p \geqslant 0.355$$

If p falls in these regions we reject H_0 (see Fig. 16.1). We now see that the actual sample proportion is

$$p=\frac{49}{262}=0.187 \text{ (using continuity correction } p=49.5/262=0.189)$$

We therefore reject the null hypothesis and conclude that there is sufficient sample evidence to contradict the view that 30 per cent of first mortgages are provided by the bank. The sample proportion of 18.7 per cent is far too low to support the view.

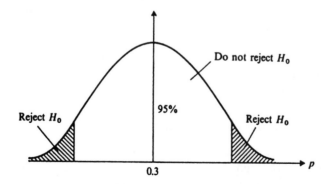

Figure 16.1 Rejection regions for H_0.

We now leave this example and consider the general structure of hypothesis tests. All tests considered in this chapter are carried out using the following procedure comprising six steps.

Step 1 Identify the null and alternative hypotheses of the test. The null hypothesis, H_0, is the hypothesis under test; for example, $H_0: \pi = 0.3$. In testing whether the sample information is consistent with H_0, some alternative hypothesis, H_1, is stated; for example, $H_1: \pi \neq 0.3$. Note that while the procedure can lead to our rejecting H_0, it cannot lead us to accept formally that the null hypothesis is true.

Step 2 Choose the appropriate significance level for the test. The significance level, α, of the test is the probability that we reject H_0 when it is, in fact, true. We have to decide how small this probability has to be before we take this decision. Traditionally, it is set equal to 0.05, 0.01, or 0.001. In the previous example we set $\alpha = 0.05$.

Step 3 Choose a suitable test statistic. From the simple information, some statistic is calculated which is used to test the null hypothesis; for example, the sample proportion p, or a standardized equivalent, $(p - \pi)/\sqrt{\pi(1-\pi)/n}$. Generally speaking, the test statistic is chosen so that as its value gets larger (or smaller), the null hypothesis becomes more and more unlikely, i.e. there is a direct relationship between the value of the test statistic and the truth of the null hypothesis.

Step 4 Determine the critical region. We now have to decide how large (or small) the value of the test statistic must be in order that the null hypothesis is to be rejected if our probability of false rejection is equal to the required significance level. In our example, the critical region was

$$p \leqslant 0.245, \quad p \geqslant 0.355$$

or

$$\frac{p - \pi}{\sqrt{\pi(1-\pi)/n}} \leqslant -1.96, \quad \frac{p - \pi}{\sqrt{\pi(1-\pi)/n}} \geqslant +1.96$$

Step 5 Compute the test statistic from the sample data. For example,

$$p = 0.187 \quad \left(\text{or} \ \frac{p - \pi}{\sqrt{\pi(1-\pi)/n}} = -3.99 \right)$$

Step 6 Decide whether or not to reject H_0. If the computed test statistic lies in the critical region we reject H_0. If, on the other hand, it lies outside this region we conclude that the sample evidence is insufficiently strong to reject H_0.

One- and two-tailed alternatives

In Example 16.1.1 we used hypotheses of the form.

$$H_0: \pi = \pi_0, \quad H_1: \pi \neq \pi_0$$

where $\pi_0 = 0.3$. In many situations the more natural hypotheses might be

$$H_0: \pi = \pi_0, \quad H_1: \pi > \pi_0$$

In other words, we would reject H_0 if the unknown population proportion was significantly greater than π_0. A hypothesis of this form is called a one-tailed alternative. In this case the entire

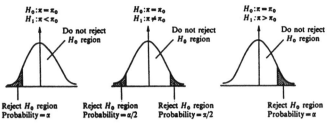

Figure 16.2 Rejection regions for one- and two-tailed alternative hypotheses.

significance probability is at one end of the distribution, as illustrated in Fig. 16.2. An alternative hypothesis of the form

$$H_1: \pi < \pi_0$$

is also a one-tailed alternative, whereas the alternative hypothesis

$$H_1: \pi \neq \pi_0$$

is referred to as a two-tailed alternative. The difference in procedures for the two types of alternative hypothesis will be illustrated in the examples of Sec. 16.2 and 16.3.

Types of error

We have already referred to the error of rejecting H_0 when H_0 is, in fact, true. This error is called the type 1 error and the probability of its occurrence is the significance level, α, of the test. There is, however, a second kind of error, that of accepting H_0 when it is false and the alternative hypothesis is true. This is commonly referred to as the type 2 error and its probability is denoted by β. So our two error probabilities are:

$$\alpha = P(\text{type 1 error}) = P(\text{reject } H_0 | H_0 \text{ true})$$
$$\beta = P(\text{type 2 error}) = P(\text{accept } H_0 | H_0 \text{ false})$$

In general, α is under our control, and ideally we would like it to be close to zero, but unfortunately as we try to decrease α, β increases. So, for a given quantity of information, we have to compromise between the two types of error. What we can do is, for a fixed significance level, to decrease β by increasing the sample size, n. A good test will have a small α and a small β. The quantity $1 - \beta$ is called the *power* of the test and so for a good test we want the power to be close to 1.

16.2 TESTS USING THE NORMAL DISTRIBUTION

We now apply the basic concepts of the previous section to some specific problems that require a test statistic with an underlying normal distribution. Because of the Central Limit Theorem this is true in many circumstances.

Population mean

Let us consider an underlying population which is normal with known variance, σ^2, but unknown mean, μ. We take some sample observations $x_1, x_2, ..., x_n$ and test whether or not μ

equals some specified value, μ_0, say. Our null hypothesis is $H_0: \mu = \mu_0$ with the two-tailed alternative $H_1: \mu \neq \mu_0$. When H_0 is true the test statistic

$$T = \frac{\bar{x} - \mu}{\sigma/\sqrt{n}}$$

has a standard normal distribution. If the significance level is $\alpha = 0.05$, H_0 is rejected if the test statistic lies outside the interval -1.96 to $+1.96$. In other words, we reject H_0 if $\bar{x}$ is more than 1.96 standard errors from μ_0.

If the underlying population is not normal the test statistic is still approximately normal for large values of n. In addition, if σ^2 is not known, then, as in the case of confidence intervals, we can substitute its unbiased estimate, $\hat{\sigma}^2$, provided $n > 30$.

Example 16.2.1 A packaging device is set to fill detergent packets with a mean weight of 16 ounces. The standard deviation is known to be 0.5 ounces. It is important to check the machine periodically because if it is overfilling it increases the cost of materials, whereas if it is underfilling the firm is liable to prosecution. A random sample of 25 filled boxes is weighed, and shows a mean net weight of 16.25 ounces. What conclusion can be drawn at the 0.05 level of significance?

ANSWER As we wish to know whether the filling machine is working correctly or incorrectly a two-tailed test is applied:

$$H_0: \mu = 16 \quad \text{and} \quad H_1: \mu \neq 16$$

The significance level is $\alpha = 0.05$.

As $\sigma = 0.5$ is available, we can use the test statistic $T = (\bar{x} - \mu)/(\sigma/\sqrt{n})$ which has a standard normal distribution providing we assume that the underlying weight distribution is normal or that $n = 25$ is large enough for $\bar{x}$ to be asymptotically normal. Consequently the critical region is $T \geqslant 1.96$ and $T \leqslant -1.96$, which results in the following decision rule:

Accept H_0 if T lies between -1.96 and $+1.96$

Reject H_0 otherwise

When the sample of $n = 25$ yields a sample mean, $\bar{x}$, of 16.25 then

$$T = \frac{16.25 - 16}{0.5/\sqrt{25}} = 2.5$$

Clearly this falls in the critical region and we can therefore conclude that the machine is not working correctly. It seems reasonable to stop packaging and make the necessary adjustments to the filling device.

Note that in the above example the hypothesis test was carried out in the same sequence of stages as described in Sec. 16.1.

Example 16.2.2 A departmental manager believes that the average value of a large population of invoices is £10. The accountant, however, disagrees with him and believes it is some value below this figure. In order to test his belief the accountant takes a random sample of 36 invoices with $\bar{x} = £9.50$, and $\hat{\sigma}^2 = £4.00$. Formulate and perform a test at the 0.05 level of significance.

ANSWER Again we use the sequence of six steps as described in Sec. 16.1

1. As the accountant specifically wishes to show that the mean invoice value is less than £10, we set up a one-tailed test

$$H_0: \mu = 10, \quad H_1: \mu < 10$$

2. $\alpha = 0.05$.
3. Here σ^2 is unknown, but as n is large enough for $\bar{x}$ to be approximately normal we can use the test statistic

$$T = \frac{\bar{x} - \mu}{\hat{\sigma}/\sqrt{n}}$$

   which has a standard normal distribution.
4. The critical region is $T < -1.645$, as illustrated in Fig. 16.3. Clearly if $\bar{x}$ is much smaller than £10 then the value of T will fall in the critical region.

5. $T = \dfrac{9.50 - 10.00}{2/\sqrt{36}} = -1.5.$

6. As the value of T does not fall in the critical region we do not have enough evidence to reject the manager's claim.

Exercise 16.2.1 A paint manufacturer claims that one can of his paint will cover an average 80 square metres with a standard deviation of 10 square metres. A government inspector wants to test the validity of this claim. He takes a sample of 36 cans and finds that the average is 75 square metres. The result is less than stipulated, but is it low enough to reject the claim?

Differences between population means

There are many circumstances in which we have interest in two different populations, not necessarily in the specific values of the population means, but in determining whether or not these values are the same. A typical two-tailed test would have the following hypotheses:

$$H_0: \mu_1 = \mu_2, \quad H_1: \mu_1 \neq \mu_2$$

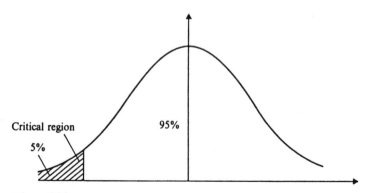

Critical region
5%
95%

Figure 16.3

where the subscripts 1 and 2 refer to populations 1 and 2. In order to test these hypotheses we take independent random samples of size n_1 and n_2, respectively, from the populations. If the difference between the two samples means, $\bar{x}_1$ and $\bar{x}_2$, is large enough then we accept H_1, that the population means are different.

Assuming that the populations are normal with known variances, σ_1^2 and σ_2^2, then from Sec. 14.6 we see that $(\bar{x}_1 - \bar{x}_2)$ has a normal distribution with mean $(\mu_1 - \mu_2)$ and variance $\sigma_1^2/n_1 + \sigma_2^2/n_2$. Thus

$$\frac{(\bar{x}_1 - \bar{x}_2) - (\mu_1 - \mu_2)}{\sqrt{\sigma_1^2/n_1 + \sigma_2^2/n_2}}$$

has a standard normal distribution. When H_0 is true $\mu_1 - \mu_2 = 0$, so the test statistic for testing the difference between means is

$$T = \frac{\bar{x}_1 - \bar{x}_2}{\sqrt{\sigma_1^2/n_1 + \sigma_2^2/n_2}}$$

This test statistic is still suitable if the two populations are not exactly normal, or if the variances are unknown and replaced by $\hat{\sigma}_1^2$ and $\hat{\sigma}_2^2$, provided n_1 and n_2 are both greater than 30.

Example 16.2.3 A study of ages of employees of two industries was undertaken to find out if the age of employees in Industry A was greater than the age of employees in Industry B. Eighty employees from Industry A had a mean age of 38.6 years and a standard deviation of 4.4 years. One hundred employees from Industry B had a mean age of 36.1 years and a standard deviation of 3.8 years. Perform a suitable test (at the 1 per cent level of significance).

ANSWER

1. $H_0: \mu_A = \mu_B$, $\quad H_1: \mu_A > \mu_B$.
2. Let $\alpha = 0.01$.

3. $T = \dfrac{\bar{x}_A - \bar{x}_B}{\sqrt{\hat{\sigma}_A^2/n_A + \hat{\sigma}_B^2/n_B}}$

   which has a standard normal distribution when H_0 is true.
4. The critical region is $T > 2.33$.

5. $T = \dfrac{38.6 - 36.1}{\sqrt{4.4^2/80 + 3.8^2/100}} = 4.02.$

6. T is well into the critical region, so we have a great deal of evidence to support the statement that the mean age of employees in company B is less than the mean age of employees in company A.

Exercise 16.2.2 A dispute exists between workers on two production lines. The workers on production line A claim that they are paid less than those on production line B. The company accountant investigated this claim by examining the pay of 36 workers from each production line. He obtained the following information:

$$n_A = 36 \quad \bar{x}_A = £93 \quad \hat{\sigma}_A = £6$$
$$n_B = 36 \quad \bar{x}_B = £94.50 \quad \hat{\sigma}_B = £7.50$$

Formulate an appropriate test.

Population proportion

As was seen in Example 16.1.1, the normal approximation to the binomial, which was employed to solve estimation problems for a proportion π, can also be used to test hypotheses about π.

Example 16.2.4 A salesman claims that on average he obtains orders from at least 40 per cent of his prospects. For a random sample of 50 prospects he obtains just 15 orders. Can his claim be rejected on the basis of the sample result, at the 5 per cent level of significance.

ANSWER This problem can be considered to be one of testing the hypothesis:

1. $H_0: \pi = 0.4$ and $H_1: \pi < 0.4$.
   This is a one-sided test if we are assuming that the salesman is unlikely to underestimate his selling prowess.
2. The significance level $\alpha = 0.05$ is stipulated.
3. As $n = 50$ is large enough for the normal approximation to be valid, then

$$T = \frac{p - \pi}{\sqrt{\pi(1 - \pi)/n}}$$

   has a standard normal distribution. Here p is the sample proportion and π the value stipulated in the null hypothesis.
4. If $T > -1.645$ then our results are consistent with the null hypothesis. If not, p is sufficiently less than π to make it unlikely that H_0 is correct.
5. In fact

$$T = \frac{(15/50) - 0.4}{\sqrt{0.4 \times 0.6/50}} = -1.44$$

   Note that it is, in fact, more correct to use the continuity correction, giving

$$T = \frac{(15.5/50) - 0.4}{\sqrt{0.4 \times 0.6/50}} = -1.30$$

6. There is insufficient evidence to reject the salesman's claim that he obtains orders from at least 40 per cent of his prospects.

Differences between proportions

This is a problem which occurs frequently in statistical work. For example, we may wish to know if there is any difference in the proportion of smokers and non-smokers who suffer from a certain medical problem; or, if there is any difference between the percentage of male and female teenage drivers involved in fatal car accidents. Problems of this type can be treated as problems of testing the hypothesis $H_0: \pi_1 = \pi_2$ in which π_1 and π_2 are the two population proportions of the attribute of interest. If n_1 and n_2 denote the sample sizes taken and p_1 and p_2 the resulting sample proportions obtained, then the variable $(p_1 - p_2)$ can be approximated by a normal distribution with mean $\pi_1 - \pi_2$ and standard deviation given by

$$\sqrt{\frac{\pi_1(1 - \pi_1)}{n_1} + \frac{\pi_2(1 - \pi_2)}{n_2}}$$

When assuming that the hypothesis $H_0: \pi_1 = \pi_2$ is true, the mean of the distribution of $(p_1 - p_2)$ equals zero. We can also amend the standard deviation by letting $\pi_1 = \pi_2 = \pi$ such that

$$p = \frac{n_1 p_1 + n_2 p_2}{n_1 + n_2} = \frac{\text{number in the two samples with the attribute}}{\text{total number in the two samples}}$$

The test statistic is then

$$z = \frac{p_1 - p_2}{\sqrt{p(1-p)(1/n_1 + 1/n_2)}}$$

If we have a two-tailed alternative, we reject H_0 if z is greater than 1.96 or less than -1.96, when we are testing at the 0.05 level of significance.

Example 16.2.5 Quattro plc has two divisions: Division A and Division B. Each of these divisions manufactures the same goods and the group management wishes to compare the efficiency level of each division as measured by the number of faulty items manufactured.

A random sample is taken in each division as follows:

Division	Sample size	Number of faulty items
A	400	20
B	500	40

You are required to assess whether the evidence suggests there is any significant difference between the level of efficiency in the two divisions.

(CIMA Level 2: May 1991)

ANSWER For Division A, the proportion of faulty items is

$$p_1 = \frac{20}{400} = 0.05$$

Similarly for Division B, this proportion is

$$p_2 = \frac{40}{500} = 0.08$$

Hence

$$p = \frac{20+40}{400+500} = \frac{60}{900} = 0.0667$$

Setting up the null hypothesis (H_0) that there is no difference in the proportion faulty against the alternative (H_1) that there is a difference, we have

$$H_0: \pi_1 = \pi_2$$
$$H_1: \pi_1 \neq \pi_2$$

The difference between the proportions then gives the z statistic

$$z = \frac{0.08 - 0.05}{\sqrt{(60/900)(840/900)(1/400 + 1/500)}} = 1.79$$

From the normal tables we see that $z = 1.79$ is greater than the 10 per cent critical value but not greater than the 5 per cent value 1.96. Hence we might conclude that there is slight (but not significant) evidence of a difference in proportion defective between the two divisions.

Exercise 16.2.3 The Saturnite Marketing Agency has been commissioned to perform a study to determine whether there is a difference in the proportion of men who supervise the household finances in the North compared with the South. Saturnite selected a random sample of 120 households in the North and 150 households in the South. In the northern sample, 77 households stated that the man of the house supervised the family finances while 104 of the southern households responded that way. What should be concluded if the test is performed at the 5 per cent level of significance.

16.3 TESTS USING THE *t*-DISTRIBUTION

As with confidence intervals, we often make use of Student's *t*-distribution in hypothesis testing when we have small sample sizes.

Population mean

If a sample, $x_1, x_2, \ldots, x_n$, is taken from a normal population with mean μ and unknown variance σ^2, then the exact distribution of $(\bar{x} - \mu)/(\hat{\sigma}/\sqrt{n})$ is a *t*-distribution with $v = n - 1$ degrees of freedom. Even if the underlying population is not normal then this result can be taken to be approximately true. We now use this result in a testing situation.

Example 16.3.1 A major oil company is considering the inclusion of an additive in its petrol in order to increase the number of miles per litre obtainable by a certain make of car. Under test at the moment is an additive named Bemax, which is available from a local supplier. To test the performance of the additive an independent agency tests 10 cars with the Bemax additive, all cars being of the same make, type, and size. The results obtained are presented in the table below.

Additive	Miles per litre									
Bemax	10.7	11.3	9.9	10.8	10.1	10.4	11.1	10.2	10.5	10.6

The established mean mileage of 10 miles per litre for the petrol without the additive had been obtained from a very large sample of cars of this type.

(a) Estimate the increase in miles per litre with the additive.
(b) Test whether the increase in miles per litre given by the Bemax additive is significant when compared with the established petrol consumption.

(ACCA Level 2: Dec. 1989)

ANSWER
(a) The estimated mean mileage per litre with the Bemax additive is

$$\bar{x} = \frac{\Sigma x}{10} = \frac{105.6}{10} = 10.56$$

This is an increase of 0.56 miles compared with no additive.

(b) The estimated standard deviation, $\hat{\sigma}$, for the Bemax additive is

$$\hat{\sigma} = \sqrt{\frac{10}{9}\left(\frac{\Sigma x^2}{10} - 10.56^2\right)} = \sqrt{\frac{10}{9}\left(\frac{1116.86}{10} - 10.56^2\right)}$$

$$= 0.438$$

We now test whether the sample values are significantly greater than the established mean mileage of 10 miles per litre.

1. We set up the null hypothesis

$$H_0: \mu = 10$$

against the alternative hypothesis that the Bemax additive increases the overall mileage

$$H_1: \mu > 10$$

2. Assume a significance level of 5 per cent.
3. As the sample size is small and σ is not known the appropriate test statistic is

$$T = \frac{\bar{x} - \mu}{\hat{\sigma}/\sqrt{n}}$$

which has a t-distribution with $\nu = n - 1 = 9$ degrees of freedom if H_0 true.
4. We have a one-tailed test, so the critical region is $T > 1.83$.
5. The calculated value of the test statistic is

$$T = \frac{10.56 - 10}{0.438/\sqrt{10}} = 4.05$$

which is greater than 1.83 and hence falls well into the critical region.
6. We reject H_0 and conclude that there is very strong evidence that the Bemax additive increases mileage per litre.

Matched t-test

A t-test can also be used in the comparison of two populations when there is a natural pairing of sample observations. In many situations the sample information is collected as pairs of values, such as when determining the productivity level of each worker before and after a training programme. These are referred to as paired observations, or matched pairs.

For paired observations, the appropriate test for the difference between the means of the two samples is first to determine the difference between each pair of values, and then test the null hypothesis that the average difference in the population is zero, rather like the one sample test for the population mean described above.

Example 16.3.2 You are currently investigating the replacement of electric typewriters with electronic machines. One argument often put forward for such replacement is that of improved speed as measured in words per minute. Eight typists from the company typing pool are involved in an experiment where they undertake work of a comparable nature on both types of machine. The results are shown in the table below.

Typist	Electric machine (wpm)	Electronic machine (wpm)
1	72	76
2	69	67
3	56	61
4	63	63
5	59	64
6	68	74
7	59	65
8	62	70

You are required to decide whether the evidence from the experiment supports the argument put forward for introducing electronic typewriters.

(CIMA Level 2: Nov. 1988)

ANSWER As there is one observation for the electric machine and the electronic machine for each of the eight typists, we see that the condition for natural pairing of observations exists.

In order to determine whether or not there is any significant difference between the two populations we find the differences between the paired observations, giving us

$$4 \quad -2 \quad 5 \quad 0 \quad 5 \quad 6 \quad 6 \quad 8$$

Now suppose that these differences come from a possible population of differences with mean μ. If $\mu > 0$ then the electronic machine has a higher wpm value than that of the electric machine.

1. $H_0: \mu = 0 \; H_1: \mu > 0$.
2. Set $\alpha = 0.05$.
3. The test statistic

$$T = \frac{\bar{x} - 0}{\hat{\sigma}/\sqrt{n}}$$

has a t-distribution with $v = n - 1 = 7$ degrees of freedom, where $\bar{x}$ and $\hat{\sigma}$ are determined from the sample differences.
4. From the t-tables in Appendix 2 the critical region is $T > 1.89$.
5. Here

$$\bar{x} = \frac{\Sigma x}{n} = \frac{32}{8} = 4$$

and

$$\hat{\sigma} = \sqrt{\frac{1}{n-1}(\Sigma x^2 - n\bar{x}^2)} = \sqrt{\tfrac{1}{7}(206 - 128)} = 3.338$$

Thus

$$T = \frac{4}{3.38/\sqrt{8}} = 3.39$$

The evidence from the experiment is strong enough to reject the null hypothesis and to conclude that increased speed may be obtained from electronic machines.

There are a number of statistical packages available that will carry out a matched t-test from the original raw data. Figure 16.4 shows the output from the MINITAB package when the data of Example 16.3.2 is entered into columns 1 and 2. We would only reject H_0 if the value of P was less than the significance level (0.05).

Independent sample t-test

In Sec. 16.2 we described a procedure for testing the difference between two population means using the normal distribution. This test assumes either that the population variances (σ_1^2 and σ_2^2) are known or that n_1 and n_2 are large (both greater than 30) so that σ_1^2 and σ_2^2 can be estimated by their sample estimates $\hat{\sigma}_1^2$ and $\hat{\sigma}_2^2$, respectively. However, if these circumstances are not satisfied, the test statistic

$$T = \frac{\bar{x}_1 - \bar{x}_2}{\hat{\sigma}\sqrt{(1/n_1)+(1/n_2)}}$$

can be used to test for differences between the means of the two populations. Under $H_0: \mu_1 = \mu_2$, the test statistic has approximately a t-distribution with $n_1 + n_2 - 2$ degrees of freedom providing the additional necessary assumption that the variances of the two populations are equal (i.e. $\sigma_1^2 = \sigma_2^2$) is reasonable. A pooled estimate for the population variance is

$$\hat{\sigma}^2 = \frac{(n_1 - 1)\hat{\sigma}_1^2 + (n_2 - 1)\hat{\sigma}_2^2}{n_1 + n_2 - 2}$$

Example 16.3.3 A major oil company is considering the inclusion of an additive for their petrol in order to increase the number of miles per litre obtainable by a certain type of car. Under test at the moment are two additives, Apex and Bemax, which are available from different suppliers. To test the performance of the two additives an independent agency tests eight cars with the Apex

```
MTB > print c1 c2

ROW    C1     C2

  1    72     76
  2    69     67
  3    56     61
  4    63     63
  5    59     64
  6    68     74
  7    59     64
  8    62     70

MTB > let c3=c2-c1
MTB > ttest [0] c3

TEST OF MU = 0.000 VS MU N.E. 0.000

            N      MEAN     STDEV    SE MEAN         T    P VALUE
C3          8     3.875     3.271      1.156      3.35      0.012
```

Figure 16.4

additive and ten cars with the Bemax additive, all cars being of the same make, type, and size. The results obtained are presented in the table below.

Additive	Miles per litre									
Apex	10.4	10.7	10.2	10.5	9.8	10.0	10.6	10.8		
Bemax	10.7	11.3	9.9	10.8	10.1	10.4	11.1	10.2	10.5	10.6

The established mean mileage of 10 miles per litre for the petrol without either of these additives had been obtained from a very large sample of cars of this type.

Perform a test to discover whether there is a significant difference between the mean petrol consumption given by the two additives.

(ACCA Level 2: December 1989)

ANSWER There are eight observations for the Apex additive and independently ten observations for the Bemax additive. The independent sample t-test is therefore appropriate.

1. $H_0: \mu_1 = \mu_2, \quad H_1: \mu_1 \neq \mu_2$
2. Set $\alpha = 0.05$.

3. $T = \dfrac{\bar{x}_1 - \bar{x}_2}{\hat{\sigma}\sqrt{(1/n_1) + (1/n_2)}}$

   has a t-distribution with $v = n_1 + n_2 - 2 = 16$ degrees of freedom.
4. From t-tables the critical region is $T \langle -2.12, T \rangle + 2.12$.
5. From the question $\bar{x}_1 = 10.375$, $\bar{x}_2 = 10.56$. Also

$$\hat{\sigma}^2 = \frac{7(0.1221) + 9(0.1916)}{16} = 0.1612$$

   is the pooled estimate of the population variance.

$$T = \frac{10.375 - 10.56}{0.401\sqrt{\frac{1}{8} + \frac{1}{10}}} = -0.97$$

   which does not fall in the critical region.
6. We do not reject H_0. There is not enough evidence to conclude that the petrol consumptions for the two additives are different. The sample differences that occur can reasonably be attributed to chance.

The above test is valid providing the underlying observations from the two populations can be assumed to come from a normal distribution and also that the variances for the two additives are equal. In the context of this question it seems reasonable to assume that both of these conditions are satisfied.

As in the case of matched t-tests, there are a number of statistical packages that will carry out an independent sample t-test from the raw data. Figure 16.5 shows the output from the MINITAB package when the data of Example 16.3.3 is entered into columns 1 and 2. Here the P-value is greater than 0.05 so there is not enough evidence to reject H_0.

```
MTB > print c1 c2

 ROW     C1     C2

   1    10.4   10.7
   2    10.7   11.3
   3    10.2    9.9
   4    10.5   10.8
   5     9.8   10.1
   6    10.0   10.4
   7    10.6   11.1
   8    10.8   10.2
   9           10.5
  10           10.6

MTB > twosample c1 c2;
SUBC> pooled.

TWOSAMPLE T FOR C1 VS C2
       N      MEAN      STDEV    SE MEAN
C1    8     10.375     0.349      0.12
C2   10     10.560     0.438      0.14

95 PCT CI FOR MU C1 - MU C2: (-0.59, 0.22)

TTEST MU C1 = MU C2 (VS NE): T= -0.97  P=0.35  DF=  16

POOLED STDEV =       0.401
```

Figure 16.5

Exercise 16.3.1 In an experiment on the reaction times in seconds of two individuals A and B, the following results were obtained.

A	0.41	0.38	0.37	0.42	0.35	0.38
B	0.32	0.36	0.38	0.33	0.38	

Examine the hypothesis that there is no difference between the mean reaction times of A and B.

Correlation

In Chapter 9 we looked at the calculation and use of the sample correlation coefficient, r. Often the values from which we calculate it are a sample of paired values from an underlying population; so r can be used to draw conclusions about the unknown population correlation coefficient, ρ. The most common conclusion we wish to draw is that there is or is not correlation between the two variables. We then have the hypotheses

$$H_0: \rho = 0, \quad H_1: \rho \neq 0$$

If the two samples both come from approximately normal distributions then the test statistic

$$T = \frac{r}{\sqrt{(1 - r^2)/(n - 2)}}$$

has a t-distribution $v = n - 2$ degrees of freedom. The hypotheses can be tested by comparing with a critical value of the t-distribution at a given level of significance.

Example 16.3.4 A management accountant is analysing data relating to retail sales on behalf of marketing colleagues. The marketing staff believe an important influence upon sales is local advertising undertaken by the retail store. The data below relates to a sample of 10 representative outlets.

Outlet number	Monthly sales, y	Local advertising (£000 per month, x)
1	220	6
2	230	8
3	240	12
4	340	12
5	420	2
6	460	8
7	520	16
8	600	15
9	720	14
10	800	20

$$\Sigma y = 4550, \quad \Sigma x = 113, \quad \Sigma y^2 = 2\,451\,300, \quad \Sigma x^2 = 1533, \quad \Sigma xy = 58\,040$$

You are required to calculate the sample product–moment correlation coefficient and test for its significance.

(CIMA Level 2: May 1988)

ANSWER The sample correlation coefficient is

$$r = \frac{\Sigma xy - (\Sigma x)(\Sigma y)/n}{\sqrt{[\Sigma x^2 - (\Sigma x)^2/n][\Sigma y^2 - (\Sigma y)^2/n]}}$$

$$= \frac{58\,040 - (113)(4550)/10}{\sqrt{[1533 - (113)^2/10][245\,1300 - (4550)^2/10]}}$$

$$= 0.671$$

Is it likely that we would get such a value purely by chance? To test rigorously we follow through the procedure described above.

1. $H_0: \rho = 0, \quad H_1: \rho \neq 0$.
2. $\alpha = 0.05$.

3. $T = \dfrac{r\sqrt{n-2}}{\sqrt{1-r^2}}$

   has a t-distribution with $v = 10 - 2 = 8$ degrees of freedom.
4. The critical region is $T > 2.31$ and $T < -2.31$.

5. $T = \dfrac{0.671\sqrt{8}}{\sqrt{1 - (0.671)^2}} = 2.56$

6. Since the computed value of T is greater than 2.31, the null hypothesis of no correlation is rejected.

TEST EXERCISES

16.1 A new wages structure is introduced throughout the large number of factories in the Hoopoint kitchen appliance manufacturing industry. The following values of output per man-hour are obtained from eight randomly selected factories just before and another eight just after its introduction (16 different factories in all).

| | Output per man-hour | |
Old wages structure	New wages structure
54	55
81	56
50	47
40	64
49	26
58	51
63	48
45	53

It is suggested that the change in the wages structure has in fact produced no overall change in output per man-hour. Perform an appropriate t-test to test this hypothesis and report your conclusion. State any assumptions you make.

(ACCA Level 2: Dec. 1990)

16.2 As part of an investment portfolio analysis, two similar companies which operate in the same market are being compared in terms of their earnings per share. The companies' annual results over the last six years have provided the following information:

| | Earnings per share(p) | |
Year	Company A	Company B
1980	14.3	13.8
1981	15.6	14.6
1982	17.2	16.4
1983	16.4	16.8
1984	14.9	15.0
1985	17.6	16.4

The person performing the analysis calculated the mean and standard deviation of each company's results and then computed a t-statistic as follows:

Company	Mean (p)	Standard deviation (p)
A	16.0	1.2977
B	15.5	1.2050

$$t = \frac{16.0 - 15.5}{\sqrt{\dfrac{1.2977^2}{6} + \dfrac{1.2050^2}{6}}} = 0.69 (10 \,\text{df})$$

He then concluded that the result was insignificant on both a one- and two-tailed basis, and consequently decided that the two companies have the same average earnings per share.

(a) Critically evaluate the analysis which has been performed and give three reasons why the procedure used and the conclusion reached are inappropriate and invalid.
(b) Perform an appropriate analysis of the data and state your conclusions.

(ACCA Level 2: June 1986)

16.3 A manufacturer claimed that at least 95 per cent of the equipment he supplied to a factory conformed to specifications. An examination of a sample of 200 pieces of equipment revealed that 18 were faulty. Test his claim at the 1 per cent level of significance.

CHI-SQUARED TESTS

17.1 THE CHI-SQUARED DISTRIBUTION

Many of the tests described in Chapter 16 used data comprising specific measurements, i.e. quantitative data. We now consider tests that compare frequencies of occurrence. These tests are of particular use when we wish to test a theory about qualitative observations (like the type of company, or the quality of a product).

Suppose we have a set of observed frequencies $O_1, O_2, ..., O_n$ and we wish to test some hypothesis about these frequencies. Let us suppose that if our hypothesis was exactly true then we would have expected the frequencies $E_1, E_2, ..., E_n$, the expected frequencies. The test statistic for testing the differences between the observed and expected frequencies is

$$\frac{(O_1 - E_1)^2}{E_1} + \frac{(O_2 - E_2)^2}{E_2} + \cdots + \frac{(O_n - E_n)^2}{E_n}$$

which we can write in shorthand form as

$$\chi^2 = \sum \frac{(O_i - E_i)^2}{E_i}$$

(χ is the Greek letter chi). Now if our hypothesis were true, we should expect the χ^2 statistic to be small because the differences between the corresponding observed and expected frequencies would be small, but if the hypothesis was totally incorrect then some of the differences would be large and hence the χ^2 statistic would be large. We need to specify the critical value such that if the χ^2 statistic lies below it we can believe the hypothesis to be true, but that if the statistic lies above it we can conclude the hypothesis to be false. Such values are provided by the χ^2 tables (see Appendix 2). As with the t-distribution, there are many such distributions, depending on the number of degrees of freedom as illustrated in Fig. 17.1.

We now consider an example.

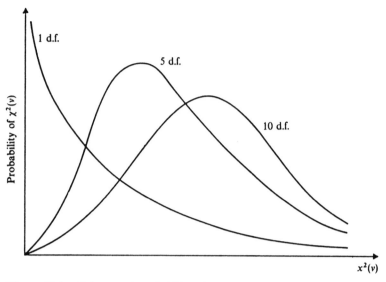

Figure 17.1 Chi-squared probability distributions for $y = 1$, 5 and 10.

Example 17.1.1 Over a period of time Autoquest, a car insurance company, monitored the number of car accidents within a certain region. In particular, the company recorded the day of the week on which accidents occurred. The results are shown in the following table.

Day of week	Mon.	Tues.	Wed.	Thurs.	Fri.	Sat.	Sun.
Number of accidents	46	42	45	46	49	29	23

Investigate the hypothesis that accidents are spread uniformly throughout the week. Interpret your results.

(ACCA Level 2: June 1990)

ANSWER Under the hypothesis that accidents are spread evenly through the week then we would expect an equal number of accidents on each of the seven days. The expected number of accidents in each of these seven days is

$$\frac{1}{7}(46 + 42 + 45 + 46 + 49 + 29 + 23) = 40$$

As we know the sum of the observed frequencies to be 280 then the sum of the expected frequencies has to be the same. Therefore, the expected frequency of the last time interval is determined when the expected frequencies of the first six days are known. Thus the number of degrees of freedom is $v = 7 - 1 = 6$. From the tables, the critical region is

$$\chi^2_{\text{stat}} > 12.6$$

at the 0.05 level of significance.

The actual value of the χ^2 statistic is

$$\chi^2 = \frac{(46-40)^2}{40} + \frac{(42-40)^2}{40} + \frac{(45-40)^2}{40} + \frac{(46-40)^2}{40} + \frac{(49-40)^2}{40} + \frac{(29-40)^2}{40} + \frac{(23-40)^2}{40} = 14.8$$

We therefore conclude accidents are not spread uniformly over the seven days. By comparing the observed and expected frequencies it is seen that there are fewer accidents on Saturday and particularly Sunday as compared with the other days of the week.

At this stage we must point out that a χ^2 test should only be used when all expected frequencies are not less than 5. Although we do not suggest that this requirement is strictly adhered to, it should be pointed out that if this condition is violated, inaccuracies occur in the test. To avoid this difficulty it is often sensible to combine frequencies of adjacent classes.

Exercise 17.1.1 When an accident is reported at a factory, the time of occurrence is recorded on the accident record form. From the most recent forms, the following time pattern was determined.

Time of accident	Number of accidents
Between 9.00 a.m. and 11.00 a.m.	20
Between 11.00 a.m. and 1.00 p.m.	20
Between 1.00 p.m. and 3.00 p.m.	24
Between 3.00 p.m. and 5.00 p.m.	36

Test the hypothesis that accidents are spread evenly through the day using a level of significance of 0.05.

17.2 GOODNESS-OF-FIT TESTS

Goodness-of-fit tests are used to test whether a set of observed frequencies differs significantly from a specified probability distribution; for example, binomial, Poisson, exponential, or normal. The procedure is to calculate, using the observed frequencies, the best estimates of the parameters belonging to the specified probability distribution. We then use these estimates to calculate the expected frequencies for the distribution and compare them with the observed frequencies. Again, no expected frequency should be less than 5.

In goodness-of-fit tests, the number of degrees of freedom of the χ^2 distribution reduces to

$$\boxed{v = \text{number of classes} - 1 - \text{number of estimated parameters}}$$

Example 17.2.1 A tool hire company has six cement mixers for hire but complaints have been received about the non-availability of mixers and the manager is wondering whether to increase the number available.

Fortunately, detailed records have been kept and the following data is available for the last 1000 working days.

Daily demand (Number of mixers)	Number of occasions
0	11
1	35
2	81
3	143
4	176
5	177
6	149
7	108
8	65
9	37
10	18

The manager would like to offer a 95 per cent service level but does not know how many mixers to have available. Having had some statistical training he suspects that the demand data approximates to a Poisson distribution.

Test the hypothesis that the observed data approximates to a Poisson distribution;

(CIMA Level 2: Nov. 1990)

ANSWER The mean demand $= \Sigma fx / \Sigma f$

$$= \frac{(0 \times 11) + (1 \times 35) + (2 \times 81) + (3 \times 143) + (4 \times 176) + (5 \times 177)}{1000}$$

$$+ \frac{(6 \times 149) + (7 \times 108) + (8 \times 65) + (9 \times 37) + (10 \times 18)}{1000}$$

$$= 4.898, \text{ or } 4.9, \text{ say}$$

In Sec. 14.3 we saw that the parameter m, of a general Poisson distribution is the mean of the distribution. Thus

$$P(x \text{ demands}) = \frac{4.9^x e^{-4.9}}{x!} \quad \text{for} \quad x = 0, 1, 2, \dots$$

The expected values, assuming a Poisson distribution, are shown in the following table:

x	$P(x)$	Expected frequency $= 1000\ P(x)$	Observed frequency	$\dfrac{(O-E)^2}{E}$
0	0.0074	7.4	11	1.75
1	0.0365	36.5	35	0.06
2	0.0894	89.4	81	0.79
3	0.1460	146.0	143	0.06
4	0.1789	178.9	176	0.05
5	0.1753	175.3	177	0.02
6	0.1432	143.2	149	0.23
7	0.1002	100.2	108	0.61
8	0.0614	61.4	65	0.21
9	0.0334	33.4	37	0.39
10	0.0164	16.4	18	0.16
$\geqslant 11$	0.0119	11.9	0	11.90
				16.23

Since the number of parameters used in estimating the expected frequencies is 1 (namely the mean, m), the number of degrees of freedom is $12-1-1=10$. The critical value of the χ^2 distribution with ten degrees of freedom is 18.3. Then since $16.23 < 18.3$, we conclude that the Poisson distribution is a good fit to the data.

Exercise 17.2.1 The following table shows the observed number of machine breakdowns per day in the engineering plant during a period of 50 days.

No. of breakdowns per day, x	Observed frequency, f
0	4
1	9
2	15
3	11
4	5
5	4
6	1
7	1

It is believed that the distribution of machine breakdowns per day conforms to a Poisson distribution. Calculate the mean number of breakdowns each day and hence test this belief at the 5 per cent level of significance.

The MINITAB package does not have a command that performs the χ^2 goodness-of-fit test directly, although if there are two columns containing the observed and expected frequencies then the χ^2 statistic can be calculated using the following commands.

$$\text{LET C3}=(\text{C1}-\text{C2})*(\text{C1}-\text{C2})/\text{C2}$$
$$\text{SUM C3}$$

where column 1 contains the observed frequencies and column 2 the expected frequencies.

17.3 CONTINGENCY TABLES

If each member of a sample can be classified according to two criteria of classification, the results can be displayed in a contingency table. Contingency tables are used to examine the independence of the two factors in the sense that knowledge of the cell in which an observation is classified in respect to one factor has no effect on the probability of being in one of the cells of the other factor. Let us consider the following example:

Example 17.3.1 The four production plants of Zeus Company Limited are based at Aybridge, Beedon, Crambourne, and Deepool. A random sample of employees at each of these four plants have been asked to give their views on a productivity-based wage deal that the company is proposing. The table below summarizes these views.

View	Aybridge	Production plant Beedon	Crambourne	Deepool
In favour	80	40	50	60
Against	35	30	40	25

Test the hypothesis that there is no significant difference in views between the production plants. Explain what action might have been taken to reach a clearer decision.

(ACCA Level 2: June 1988)

ANSWER Here we have an example of a contingency table; in fact it is a 2×4 contingency table because there are two rows and four columns; that is, there are two views and four production plants. A general contingency table is referred to as an $r \times c$ contingency table, where r is the number of rows, and c is the number of columns in the contingency table. In the above example we want to find out whether or not there is any evidence of an association between the view on a productivity-based wage deal and the production plant. The hypotheses to be tested are:

H_0: There is no association between view and production plant (i.e. independence exists).

H_1: There is a relationship between the two factors.

Under the null hypotheses that the proportion in favour of the wage deal is independent of the production plant, the probability that an observation falls in the ith row and the jth column, say, is the product of the probability that it falls in the ith row and the probability that it falls in the jth column (see Sec. 12.3). If we consider the top left-hand cell of our example:

$$\text{Expected frequency} = 360 \times \frac{115}{360} \times \frac{230}{360} = \frac{115 \times 230}{360} = 73.47$$

Note that this value is obtained by multiplying the total of the first row and the total of the first column and then dividing by the overall total. In exactly the same way we can show that the following general result applies.

> The expected frequency of any cell is the production of its row total and the column total, divided by the overall total.

Using this general result we obtain the expected frequencies for the above data.

	Aybridge	Beedon	Crambourne	Deepol	Total
In favour	$\frac{115 \times 230}{360} = 73.47$	$\frac{70 \times 230}{360} = 44.72$	$\frac{90 \times 230}{360} = 57.5$	$\frac{85 \times 230}{360} = 54.31$	230
Against	$\frac{115 \times 130}{360} = 41.53$	$\frac{70 \times 130}{360} = 25.28$	$\frac{90 \times 130}{360} = 32.5$	$\frac{85 \times 130}{360} = 30.69$	130
Total	115	70	90	85	360

Again, we have to decide whether or not the expected frequencies, calculated on the assumption that H_0 is true, differ significantly from the observed frequencies. The test statistic is, as before

$$\chi^2 = \sum_{\text{all classes}} \frac{(O - E)^2}{E}$$

and has a χ^2 distribution with $(r - 1)(c - 1)$ degrees of freedom, when H_0 is true. The number of degrees of freedom is obtained from:

Number of classes − number of restrictions (number of independent totals)

$$= rc - [(r-1) + (c-1) + 1]$$
$$= (r-1)(c-1)$$

Returning to the earlier set of data we see that the critical value is 7.84 when the number of degrees of freedom $= (2-1) \times (4-1) = 3$ and using a 0.05 level of significance.

Analysing the discrepancy between the observed and expected frequencies,

$$\Sigma \frac{(O-E)^2}{E} = \frac{(80-73.47)^2}{73.47} + \frac{(40-44.72)^2}{44.72} + \frac{(50-57.5)^2}{57.5} + \frac{(60-54.31)^2}{54.31}$$

$$+ \frac{(35-41.53)^2}{41.53} + \frac{(30-25.28)^2}{25.28} + \frac{(40-32.5)^2}{32.5} + \frac{(25-30.69)^2}{30.69} = 7.34$$

As the observed value of χ^2 statistic is less than the table value (7.84) we do not reject the null hypothesis (at the 5 per cent significance level). The decision is not clear cut, so it may be instructive to take another larger set of random samples of employees which could give a clearer decision.

Example 17.3.2 Over a period of time Autoquest, a car insurance company, monitored the number of car accidents within a certain region. Each accident was classified as slight (minor damage but no personal injuries), or serious (damage to vehicle and personal injury), or fatal (damage to vehicles and loss of life). The size of the car insured by the company was also recorded. The following tables summarize the information collected.

Number of accidents		Size of car		
		Small	Medium	Large
Type of accident	Slight	68	71	51
	Serious	46	26	8
	Fatal	6	3	1

Does this data indicate that the type of accident is associated with the size of the car insured? Provide a full interpretation of your results.

(ACCA Level 2: June 1990)

ANSWER The chi-square tests of association require that the expected frequencies in all cells be at least 5.0. To ensure this, either the rows or columns may have to be combined. Setting up the null hypothesis that there is no association between size of car and type of accident, the expected frequencies would be:

	Small	Medium	Large	Total
Slight	$\frac{120 \times 190}{280} = 81.43$	$\frac{100 \times 190}{280} = 67.86$	$\frac{60 \times 190}{280} = 40.71$	190
Serious	$\frac{120 \times 80}{280} = 34.29$	$\frac{100 \times 80}{280} = 28.57$	$\frac{60 \times 80}{280} = 17.14$	80
Fatal	$\frac{120 \times 10}{280} = 4.29$	$\frac{100 \times 10}{280} = 3.57$	$\frac{60 \times 10}{280} = 2.14$	10
Total	120	100	60	280

It is seen that all three expected frequencies in the bottom row are less than 5. Therefore we need to combine the second and third rows. Combining in this way maintains the relevance of the information as the combined row can be labelled as serious/fatal accidents. The following observed and expected frequencies result from the combinations:

Observed			Expected		
68	71	51	81.43	67.86	40.71
52	29	9	38.58	32.14	19.28

The chi-square statistic is therefore

$$\sum \frac{(0-E)^2}{E} = \frac{(68-81.43)^2}{81.43} + \frac{(71-67.86)^2}{67.86} + \frac{(51-40.71)^2}{40.71} + \frac{(52-38.58)^2}{38.58} + \frac{(29-32.14)^2}{32.14} + \frac{(9-19.28)^2}{19.28}$$

$$= 2.21 \qquad + 0.15 \qquad + 2.60 \qquad + 4.67 \qquad + 0.31 \qquad + 5.48$$

$$= 15.42$$

This value is significant compared with the chi-squared distribution with 2 degrees of freedom. As $15.42 > 5.99$ we reject the null hypothesis; that is, the data contradicts the belief that there is no association between type of accident and size of car so we can be reasonably sure that the data indicates an association between the claims involving personal injury and the size of the car insured. In particular, we see that the largest contribution to the χ^2 statistic occurs for large cars in the serious/fatal category (5.48). By inspection of the observed and expected frequencies, it is seen that a lower proportion of large cars is involved in serious or fatal injuries when compared with the reported claims on medium cars.

The χ^2 distribution is a continuous distribution, whereas the observed frequencies are discrete measurements. This creates slight inaccuracies when the number of degrees of freedom is small and the overall total of observed frequencies is small. A more accurate result is obtained for 2×2 contingency tables if we use Yates' continuity correction (see Sec. 14.6 for the rationale behind the use of a continuity correction). This is achieved by reducing each difference by $\frac{1}{2}$ in absolute value before squaring it, i.e.

$$\chi^2 = \sum \frac{(|0-E|-0.5)^2}{E}$$

Example 17.3.3 Crownhouse Ltd is a market research company specializing in the collection of opinions from the general public. The company is currently undertaking a study into the effects of incentives to increase the returns from its surveys. The objective of the study is to study the effect of a monetary incentive on response rate.

A number of questionnaires were posted to potential respondents, some containing a financial incentive for a prompt response and others without such an incentive. Each potential respondent was classified as either social type X or social type Y according to occupation. A follow-up letter was sent to all respondents who had not returned the questionnaire by a two-week deadline. The data obtained from this study is shown in the table below.

Social type	Financial incentive given?	Returned before deadline	Questionnaire response Returned after follow-up letter	Not returned
X	Yes	37	3	20
	No	25	1	19
Y	Yes	39	2	19
	No	18	2	35

By combining the rows and columns appropriately test the hypothesis that the questionnaire response rate is independent of whether or not a financial incentive is provided.

(ACCA Level 2: Dec. 1991)

ANSWER Very few respondents returned the questionnaire after the follow-up letter, and hence we would expect some of the expected frequencies to be smaller than 5. It is necessary therefore to combine the second column with either the first or third column in order to remove these low expected frequencies. Indeed, as the main aim of the study is to monitor the immediate effect of a financial incentive, it would seem sensible to combine those returned after the deadline with the non-responses as both categories had clearly not been influenced by the enclosed money.

As we wish to investigate the belief that the financial incentive will affect the response rate we combine rows 1 and 3 and also combine rows 2 and 4. The resulting table, after combining rows and columns, is

Financial incentive given?	Questionnaire response	
	Returned before deadline	Not returned before deadline
Yes	76	44
No	43	57

We can set up the null hypothesis that the proportion of the general public that responded by the deadline is independent of whether or not they receive a financial incentive. If this hypothesis is true the expected number of persons in each category is as shown in the table below.

	Returned	Not returned
Yes	64.91	55.09
No	54.09	45.91

Analysing the discrepancy between the observed and expected frequencies using Yates' correction:

$$\chi^2 \text{ statistic} = \sum \frac{(|O-E|-\frac{1}{2})^2}{E} = 10.59^2\left(\frac{1}{64.91} + \frac{1}{55.09} + \frac{1}{54.09} + \frac{1}{45.91}\right) = 8.28$$

If the null hypothesis is true, this value should have approximately a chi-squared distribution with 1 degree of freedom. As the 5 per cent chi-squared value is 3.84, the above result is significant and so the financial incentive did affect the response rate. By considering the observed frequencies we see that 63 per cent of persons given a financial incentive return the questionnaire before the deadline, compared with 43 per cent of persons not given the incentive. Hence a financial incentive does significantly increase the likelihood of response.

Exercise 17.3.1 A company which has a range of profitable products is experiencing serious cash flow problems. The management accountant has decided to analyse the data relating to debtors, for she suspects that those debtors who owe more to the company are the ones who are taking longer to settle. A sample of 400 debts is produced and is analysed under the following headings:

(a) Period outstanding *beyond* the normal credit period:
   1–2 weeks, slow;
   3–4 weeks, very slow;
   5–6 weeks, warning letter;
   7–8 weeks, legal action.
(b) Amount of debt:
   £1000–1999, small;
   £2000–2999, medium;
   £3000–3999, large;
   £4000–4999, substantial.

The clerks in the department have undertaken an examination of the 400 debts, and have produced the table below:

	Slow	Very slow	Warning letter	Legal action
Small	12	15	16	17
Medium	15	17	21	27
Large	17	26	26	41
Substantial	26	32	37	55

Use the chi-square test to substantiate, or refute, the suspicion of the management accountant.

(CIMA Level 2: May 1987)

The χ^2 test for association in a contingency table can be analysed by the MINITAB package using either the CONTINGENCY or CHISQUARE commands. The CONTINGENCY command is used if there are two columns indicating to which row and column each observation belongs. This command forms a contingency table from the columns and calculates the expected frequencies, the value of $(O-E)^2/E$ for each cell and the χ^2 statistic. If the data is already in the form of a table of frequencies (which is the case in this chapter), then the CHISQUARE command operates on the contingency table to produce the same output as the

CONTINGENCY command. So for example, the data shown in Example 17.3.1 would be stored in three columns as:

	C1	C2	C3	C4
	80	40	50	60
	35	30	40	25

and the appropriate command would be

CHISQUARE C1 C4

TEST EXERCISES

17.1 Quattro plc has four divisions—A, B, C, and D. Each division manufactures the same goods and the group management wishes to compare the efficiency level of each division as measured by the number of faulty items manufactured.

A random sample is taken in each division as follows:

Division	Sample size	Number of faulty items
A	400	25
B	500	29
C	450	29
D	500	40

You are required to assess whether the evidence suggests there is any significant difference between the level of efficiency in the four divisions.

17.2 It is suspected that the number of faulty products produced by a manufacturing industry varies depending on which day of the week they were made. In order to test this a random sample of 200 products is taken from the warehouse, and after inspection yields the following results.

Product	Day of manufacture		
	Monday	Tuesday–Thursday	Friday
Perfect	32	94	34
Faulty	3	21	16

Use the χ^2 test to decide if these results indicate that there is a connection between faulty products and when they were made.

17.3 A quality control laboratory tests 120 packs, each containing 10 bolts. Each bolt is tested to destruction and the following distribution of failures found:

Number of failures	0	1	2	3	4	5
Number of packets with this number of failures	50	40	18	6	4	2

Calculate the mean number of defectives per packet and show that if all bolts are assumed equally likely to fail the test then the probability of failure is 0.03.

After suitable regrouping of the data, test at the 5 per cent level whether the observations agree with the appropriate binomial distribution.

ADDITIONAL APPLICATIONS OF SAMPLING

18.1 INTRODUCTION TO STATISTICAL QUALITY CONTROL

When articles are being mass produced on a production line there is inevitably a certain amount of variation in their specifications. However, the process, which has been under control for some time, may develop a fault which alters these specifications. The role of the quality-control inspector is to notice this change as quickly as possible so that the fault can be corrected.

No further knowledge of statistical method is required in this chapter as the principles of Chapters 14–16 are sufficient. In this section we look at three different aspects of quality control. Firstly, we consider the monitoring of the specifications of single articles. Then we extend the theory to sampling groups of articles. Finally, we investigate the situation where manufactured items are classified only as defective (unacceptable) or non-defective (acceptable).

(a) Control charts for observations

In the manufacture of a large number of articles it is expected that the specifications vary slightly. If the distribution of these specifications is known we can calculate the proportion of articles whose dimensions fall within *control limits*. These control limits can be shown visually on a *control chart*, as illustrated in Fig. 18.1. A control chart is designed to help the quality-control inspector to detect whether the observations are values from the same population, or whether the population has changed in some way.

In the control chart of Fig. 18.1 we have drawn warning limits and action limits. *Warning limits* are drawn in such a way that we would expect 95 per cent of the observations to lie within these limits if the process is under control. If a value lies outside these limits then the inspector should immediately take a further observation. Two consecutive observations outside these limits would almost certainly indicate a fault in the process. We would expect nearly all of the observations to lie between the *action limits*. As far as we are concerned we refer to 99.8 per cent of all possible values as the percentage lying within these limits. Then if the process is under

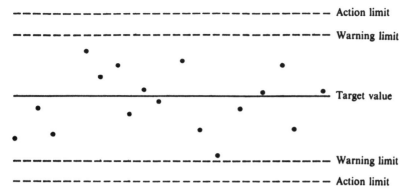

Figure 18.1 Control chart showing warning limits and action limits.

control only 1 in 500 observations falls outside the action limits. Therefore, if a value does fall outside, the process should immediately be stopped.

Let us consider the following example.

Example 18.1.1 A chemical plant shows the following hourly production over a period of 10 hours:

Hour	1	2	3	4	5	6	7	8	9	10
Production	140	131	142	121	134	145	131	148	132	136

The manager of the plant states that this mean production rate is what is expected of him and asks you to calculate from the data the upper and lower control limits that he can use on a control chart that he proposes to set up. These limits are to be adequate to cover a risk level of 1 in 20 in order to warn him (or the plant operator) of possible changes in the process.

Calculate

(a) the mean, variance, and standard deviation of these 10 production figures;

(b) the upper and lower control limits for the chart and show on a control chart the control limits with some specimens of hourly recordings.

ANSWER

(a) Sample mean, $\bar{x} = \dfrac{1}{10}(140 + 131 + \cdots + 136) = 136$

Sample variance, $s^2 = \dfrac{1}{n}\Sigma(x - \bar{x})^2 = 57.2$

Sample standard deviation, $s = 7.56$

(b) Now s is not an unbiased estimator of the population; we require

$$\hat{\sigma} = s\sqrt{\frac{n}{n-1}} = 7.97$$

As the sample size is small, and the value of σ is unknown then our control limits are of the form where t is the relevant value of the t-distribution with $n-1 = 9$ degrees of freedom.

From tables we see that 95 per cent of the distribution lies between -2.26 and $+2.26$. Thus, our warning limits are

$$136 - (2.26 \times 7.97) \text{ to } 136 + (2.26 \times 7.97)$$

i.e.

$$117.99 \text{ to } 154.01$$

So, we conclude that if we produce a value between 118 and 154 units per hour (inclusive), then we can safely believe that the process is under control. If, however, a value lies outside this range then there is a strong possibility that there is a fault in the system.

The control chart is shown in Fig. 18.2. Let us suppose that later in the process we obtain the following production levels:

Hour	50	51	52	53	54	55	56	57	58	59	60	61	62	63
Production	138	142	136	130	117	124	140	148	143	137	130	120	116	112

These production levels are also shown in Fig. 18.2. Although a value falls below the control limit at the 54th hour, it is likely that it is due to the usual chance variation that exists within the process. The process should not be stopped at this stage. However, it should certainly cease after the 63rd hour, as there are two consecutive observations below the lower warning limit.

(b) Control charts for sample means

So far we have considered the situation where only one observation is taken at regular intervals; these charts can be used in a similar way when small samples are taken regularly. This is a

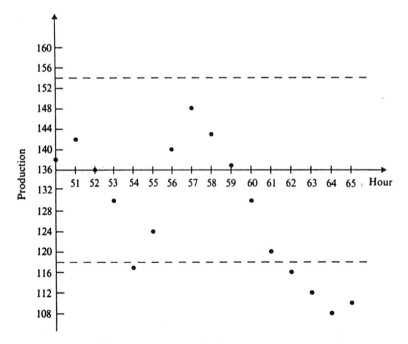

Figure 18.2 Control chart for individual observations given in Example 18.1.1.

particularly useful procedure when we have a manufacturing process making a large number of articles. In this case it is fairly easy to take relatively small samples in spot checks in order to control the overall quality of the goods.

Suppose we take samples of n measurements at regular intervals. If the values come from an approximately normal distribution with population mean μ and population standard deviation σ when the process is under control, then 95 per cent of the time the sample mean will lie between the limits $\mu - 1.96\sigma/\sqrt{n}$ and $\mu + 1.96\sigma/\sqrt{n}$. In exactly the same way 99.8 per cent of the sample means lie within the limits $\mu - 3.09\sigma/\sqrt{n}$ and $\mu + 3.09\sigma/\sqrt{n}$.

Example 18.1.2 Experience has shown that under normal conditions a process produces items of mean diameter 3.00 inches with a standard deviation of 0.01 inch. Find the standard error of the mean of samples of four items and state the limits within which sample means will lie for:

(a) 95 per cent of samples, and
(b) virtually all samples.

Draw up a control chart for the means of samples of four items showing inner and outer limits. Plot the means given in the following table on your chart and comment on the picture revealed.

Means of samples of size 4 taken at 10-minute intervals				
Time (hours)	3.00	3.10	3.20	3.30	3.40
Mean diameter (inches)	3.003	3.004	2.995	3.001	2.992
Time (hours)	3.50	4.00	4.10	4.20	4.30
Mean diameter (inches)	2.996	3.001	3.003	3.006	3.011
Time (hours)	4.40	4.50	5.00	5.10	5.20
Mean diameter (inches)	3.005	2.995	2.997	2.993	2.990
Time (hours)	5.30	5.40	5.50	6.00	6.10
Mean diameter (inches)	2.991	2.992	2.990	2.986	2.984

ANSWER

$$\mu = 3.00,\ \sigma = 0.01,\ n = 4 \text{ so } \frac{\sigma}{\sqrt{n}} = \frac{0.01}{2} = 0.005$$

(a) $\mu - 1.96\dfrac{\sigma}{\sqrt{n}} = 3.00 - 1.96 \times 0.005 = 2.9902$

By symmetry, $\mu + 1.96\dfrac{\sigma}{\sqrt{n}} = 3.0098$.

The warning limits 2.9902 and 3.0098 are drawn in Fig. 18.3.

(b) The action limits are $\mu - 3.09\dfrac{\sigma}{\sqrt{n}}$ and $\mu + 3.09\dfrac{\sigma}{\sqrt{n}}$, namely 2.8455 and 3.1545.

We see that the process can be considered to be under control until 5.10 hours. After this time there are four observations which are all very close to the lower warning limit. These can possibly be overlooked as the difference from μ could have been attributed to chance.

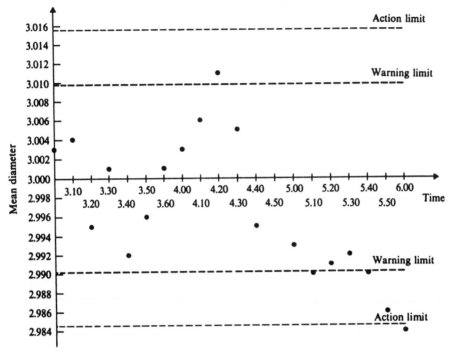

Figure 18.3 Control chart for sample means given Example 18.1.2.

The final two observations confirm the suspicion that a fault has arisen and the process should be stopped immediately.

Often in practice the population standard deviation will not be known. One possibility in this case is to take a large number of items from the process and calculate $\hat{\sigma}$ as an estimate of σ. The factors 1.96 and 3.09 can then be used as in the foregoing examples. If only a relatively small amount of data were available for estimation of σ, the same principle could be used, but t-distribution points would have to replace 1.96 and 3.09. However, what is often done in the small sample context is to calculate the ranges w of a number of small samples and then use the mean, denoted by $\bar{w}$, of these ranges as a measure of variation in the data. As was pointed out in Sec. 8.7, for small samples the range is simply related to the standard deviation and so $\bar{w}$ is simply related to σ. Tables are published giving the factors by which $\bar{w}$ needs to be multiplied to give the warning and action limits for sample sizes n up to 12.

(c) Control chart for defectives

So far we have dealt with control charts being applied to continuous measurements. Now we turn to situations where it is more practical to classify an item as either satisfactory or defective. This is particularly appropriate when we are examining a finished product and deciding if it meets the required standard.

To find out if the process is under control, we take samples at regular intervals, and compute the proportion of defectives within the sample. These proportions are plotted on a control chart for which the warning and action limits are computed from the binomial distribution with parameters n (the sample size) and π (the proportion of defective articles when the process is stable). We have seen in earlier chapters that computations involving the binomial distribution are often tedious when n is large, so we might use the Poisson or normal distributions as an approximation when they are appropriate.

Example 18.1.3

(a) In a large sample taken of production 42 items were rejected out of a total of 1000. It was decided that control samples of 200 would be taken at a given frequency.

Calculate the expected mean and the 95 per cent and 99 per cent levels for the control chart.

(b) The chart, based on figures calculated in answer to (a) above, was brought into use and after a period during which 15 control samples were taken the following rejects were recorded:

Sample reference	Number of rejects
1	8
2	11
3	9
4	6
5	12
6	8
7	13
8	11
9	14
10	15
11	18
12	10
13	8
14	12
15	7

Draw the chart showing the upper action and warning limits and plot on it the above results.

What appears to have happened to cause the sudden change between samples reference 11 and 12?

ANSWER

(a) From the large sample, $p = 0.042$. As $np = 200 \times 0.042 > 5$ we can use the normal approximation to the binomial.

Warning limits for the proportion are

$$p - 1.96 \sqrt{\frac{p(1-p)}{n}} \quad \text{and} \quad p + 1.96 \sqrt{\frac{p(1-p)}{n}}$$

i.e.

$$0.0142 \quad \text{and} \quad 0.0698$$

We conclude that if the process is under control, 95 per cent of the time there will be between 3 and 13 defectives (inclusive) out of the 200 articles in the sample.

Action limits for the proportion are

$$p - 2.58 \sqrt{\frac{p(1-p)}{n}} \quad \text{and} \quad p + 2.58 \sqrt{\frac{p(1-p)}{n}}$$

$$0.0054 \quad \text{and} \quad 0.0786$$

Therefore, if the process is stable, 99 per cent of the time there will be between 2 and 15 defectives (inclusive).

(b) The warning limits and the action limits are illustrated on Fig. 18.4. Note that in this example our action limits are based on the 99 per cent level rather than the 99.8 per cent level that we have previously used. It seems clear that the process was interrupted between samples 11 and 12. A fault was recognized at sample 11. This fault was rectified so that the later results were an improvement.

The theory developed in this section forms the foundation for the important role of quality control, or statistical process control (SPC) within both manufacturing and service industries. The prime aim of SPC is the important problem of keeping a process at a specified stable level, or to identify improvements in the process. In consequence it has received widespread application in industry. Quality control became identified as a discipline by Shewhart in the 1930s; however, in the 1980s it was advantaged by W. E. Deming and others who follow a total-quality philosophy. As a result of this increased awareness many companies have developed improved quality procedures, resulting in a greater usage of control techniques.

18.2 THE ROLE OF SAMPLING IN AUDITING

The main role of an external auditor is to ensure that the accounts of a company are fair and comply with the law. In the early development of auditing it was not unusual for the auditor to make a full examination of all of the financial dealings that many of the larger companies are involved with. Usually, this problem is overcome by checking only a small portion of the

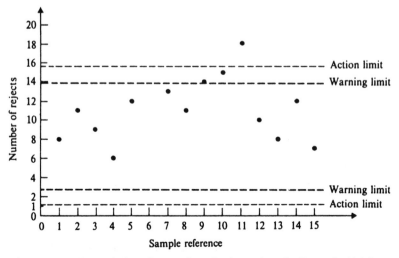

Figure 18.4 Control chart for number of rejects given in Example 18.1.3.

accounts and then using this information to make a generalized statement concerning the entire population of accounts. This, of course, is sampling.

Unlike other areas where sampling has been employed, the use of judgement sampling is widespread in accountancy. Although this has lessened over the last twenty to thirty years, it seems that only the very large accountancy firms make use of statistical sampling methods. The reasons for this are twofold. Firstly, in the early stages of statistical development there was very little research undertaken in the field of finance. Although this is no longer true, much of the recent work is not documented because of its financial value to accountancy firms. The second reason for the lack of statistical sampling methods in accountancy is the poor statistical background of many of the older accountants. This should not be such a problem in the future, as most accountants now meet some statistics in their qualifying period.

The advantages of statistical sampling over judgement sampling are the same as those described briefly in Sec. 6.2 of this book. In effect, it enables an optimum sample size to be calculated for the precision required; or, alternatively, for a given sample size it enables the degree of accuracy to be known. This, of course, is important when an accountancy firm may be liable to prosecution if it is found to be negligent or if it has carried out an inadequate audit. If the firm can show that its audit was carried out with a method which has a recognized scientific basis it is on safer ground than if the method was one that was purely subjective, no matter how experienced the auditor.

In this section we describe five applications of statistical sampling methods of auditing. Each of these techniques is described individually.

(a) Estimation sampling of variables

Here the theory of Chapter 15 is used to estimate the total value of a population of accounts based on a sample of items. Clearly, we can use the result

$$\text{Estimate of value of population} = \frac{\text{population size}}{\text{sample size}} \times \text{value of sample}$$

when the sample is selected randomly. Typical examples in finance include the estimation of:

1. the value of stock;
2. the value of assets;
3. the value of errors;
4. the value of liabilities.

Let us consider an example where we require to calculate the sample size in order to satisfy a given degree of accuracy.

Example 18.2.1 It is known from past experience that the standard deviation of a population of 20 000 entries is $\sigma = £250$. We wish to estimate the value of these 20 000 entries, but as time is short it is decided that only a random sample of the entries can be examined. However, it is essential that the estimate is within one million pounds of the correct value with a degree of confidence of 99 per cent. What is the minimum sample size that can be taken?

ANSWER We require $P[-1\,000\,000 < 20\,000(\bar{x} - \mu) < 1\,000\,000] > 0.99$, i.e.

$$P(-50 < \bar{x} - \mu < 50) > 0.99 \quad \text{where } \frac{\bar{x} - \mu}{\sigma/\sqrt{n}} \text{ has a standard normal distribution}$$

Then

$$2.58\,\frac{\sigma}{\sqrt{n}} < 50$$

$$\sqrt{n} > \frac{2.58 \times 250}{50} = 12.9$$

$$n > 12.9^2 = 166.4$$

The minimum sample size is 167 entries.

(b) Estimation sampling of attributes

Here we wish to estimate the number, or proportion, of the population having a certain quality (or attribute). In auditing, its usual application is in the estimation of the number of errors within a set of accounts. However, other applications may include:

1. the proportion of debts that are currently six months overdue;
2. the number of employees receiving overtime payments in a certain week.

The following result is of use:

Estimate of the number in population with attribute

$$= \frac{\text{population size}}{\text{sample size}} \times \text{number in sample with attribute}$$

Using the theory of Chapter 15 we can obtain approximate confidence limits for our estimate.

Example 18.2.2 An auditor wishes to estimate how many of $N = 50\,000$ invoices from last month's trading contain some minor irregularity. A random sample of $n = 250$ items reveals 10 with errors. Calculate approximate 95 per cent confidence limits for the population.

ANSWER Even though the sample proportion, p, is small, the sample size is sufficiently large to allow the normal approximation to the binomial to be reasonably valid. Hence the 95 per cent confidence limits are

$$N\left(p \pm 1.96\,\sqrt{\frac{p(1-p)}{n}}\right) = \ 50\,000\left(0.04 \pm 1.96\,\sqrt{\frac{0.04 \times 0.96}{250}}\right)$$

$$= 785 \text{ and } 3215$$

(c) Discovery sampling

Discovery sampling is concerned with the examination of a population for a single case of serious error. The type of situations that come under such a heading are:

1. misappropriation of money;
2. fraud;
3. breakdown of internal control.

If such an error is found, sampling is immediately stopped and the error reported.

In discovery sampling the probability of such an error can be considered to be very small. This enables us to make calculations more simply by using the Poisson approximation to the binomial distribution (see Sec. 14.3).

Example 18.2.3 Suppose we have a large population in which the error rate is 0.5 per cent. Find the probability of finding an error if a random sample is taken with size: (a) $n=40$, (b) $n=100$, (c) $n=600$.

ANSWER

(a) $\pi=0.005$, $n=40$. So, using the Poisson approximation, $m=n\pi=0.2$, and

$$P(\text{no error})=P(r=0)=e^{-m}=e^{-0.2}=0.82$$

There is only an 18 per cent chance of finding an error.

(b) $\pi=0.005$, $n=100$, $m=0.5$.

$$P(\text{no error})=e^{-0.5}=0.61$$

There is a 39 per cent chance of finding an error.

(c) $\pi=0.005$, $n=600$, $m=3$.

$$P(\text{no error})=e^{-3}=0.05$$

There is a 95 per cent chance of finding an error.

(d) Acceptance sampling

An internal auditor is employed by a company to monitor its accounting system, and to check that it is functioning as it should. To aid him in this role he may take samples of items at regular intervals to check that the error rate does not rise above a specified level. This is acceptance sampling and is merely an application of quality control to accounting. In acceptance sampling we are only concerned with errors that are not as serious as fraud or deception, for example:

1. wrong date;
2. incorrect addition;
3. not rubber-stamped;
4. not signed by recommended person.

In general, acceptance sampling is not of use to the external auditor who is only concerned with the taking of one sample.

Example 18.2.4 Each week an internal auditor of a large company checks a sample of 500 of the financial transactions to show that the accountancy system is working correctly. A certain number of slight errors is to be expected, in fact inevitable, but the company believe that it is essential to keep the error rate below 2 per cent. How many errors need to occur in the sample before the auditor can be confident that the stipulated error rate has been violated (at the 95 per cent level)?

ANSWER If the error rate was 2 per cent, there is a probability of only 0.05 that he would find more than

$$(500\times0.02)+1.645\sqrt{500\times0.02\times0.98}=15.15$$

errors (by using the normal approximation to the binomial distribution). If the auditor finds 16 or more errors he can be reasonably confident that the error rate has been violated.

(e) Monetary unit sampling

This is a recent method of sampling which is useful for estimating the value of error in the population from a sample of items. By using the result

Estimate of total value of errors in population

$$= \frac{\text{total value of population}}{\text{total value of sample}} \times \text{total value of errors in sample}$$

We see that a more accurate estimate of the total error value is obtained if the sample values are larger rather than small. We could achieve this by stratifying according to some criterion of value and then selecting a high proportion of large sample values. In monetary unit sampling we achieve this by selecting items with probabilities that are proportional to their value. Thus an item valued at £5 is five times more likely to be included than an item valued at £1. Let us consider a very simple example to illustrate the procedure.

Example 18.2.5 We have a population of 15 items. We wish to select a sample of five in such a way that the probability of selection is proportional to their value. The population values are:

£10   £30   £1   £5   £24   £38   £3   £20   £2   £40   £8   £15   £18   £5   £31

ANSWER Initially we calculate a series of cumulative totals; here we have

£10   £40   £41   £46   £70   £108   £111   £131   £133   £173   £181   £196   £214   £219   £250

These values are obtained by adding, cumulatively, the values in the population; for example, $10 + 30 = 40$, $40 + 1 = 41$.

As the overall total is £250 we choose five random numbers (from random number tables) between 001 and 250. Suppose these numbers are

089   140   060   249   195

Let us consider the random number 089.

As the sum of the first five values in the population is less than £89 we include item 6 (with value £38) in our sample. In the same way

140 corresponds to item 10 (value £40)

60 corresponds to item   5 (value £24)

249 corresponds to item 15 (value £31)

195 corresponds to item 12 (value £15)

(A more efficient way of selecting the random numbers might have been to use a systematic sampling approach, i.e. choose a number between 0 and 50, 39 say, and then use the random numbers 39, 89, 139, 189, 239 for selecting the items.)

These are five statistical sampling techniques of use to auditors. The use of statistical sampling is still criticized on two counts by a number of accountants. First, it is thought that the randomization process itself is time consuming and inconvenient. However, much of the necessary financial documentation is now kept on a computer and it is quite easy to program any computer to produce sample data at random. The second criticism is that they believe that the experienced auditor can often produce a more suitable sample than one by random sampling. A statistician would argue that this knowledge and experience should be used to stratify the population, only at the very end is there a need for the randomness to enter the sampling process.

We believe that the development of statistical sampling techniques to finance will continue to increase. It is the duty of all aspiring accountants to familiarize themselves with these methods.

TEST EXERCISES

18.1 A machine is programmed to produce ball bearings which have a mean diameter of 17.50 mm and a standard deviation of 0.06 mm. In order to determine that the machine maintains proper standards a sample of nine ball bearings is taken every hour and the mean diameter is calculated from the sample.

(a) Calculate a 95 per cent confidence limit related to the above standards.
(b) Using the limits calculated in (a) draw a control chart plotting the following sample means:

Sample reference	1	2	3	4	5	6	7	8	9
Mean (mm)	17.47	17.50	17.49	17.52	17.54	17.57	17.51	17.52	17.50

(c) Comment on the results in relation to the limits you have calculated.

18.2 Batches of 100 components were taken at fixed intervals of time from a production line and tested. The following figures are the number of components found to be defective in each of the batches:

4	3	2	0	7	5
2	4	1	3	4	6

(a) Calculate the mean proportion defective.
(b) Draw up a quality control chart for samples 200 of the components such that the inner limit is equal to the mean plus one standard error and the outer limit is equal to the mean plus two standard errors.
(c) Could your chart be used for batches of 50 components? If not, why not?

19

LINEAR PROGRAMMING

19.1 PROBLEM FORMULATION

This chapter looks at a set of optimization models commonly used in business and decision making. These models have a number of features in common. They require the decision maker to identify a desired objective—such as maximization of profit or minimization of costs—and to determine key factors which limit what can and cannot be done in the context of this objective.

The following problems are typical of those which might be investigated by such optimization models.

1. Maximizing profit when there are limits on the number of people employed, available capital, and market demand.
2. Determining the most economic diet which satisfies nutritional requirements.
3. Transporting a product from several origins to a number of destinations so that transport costs are minimal.
4. Assigning production jobs to machines in such a way that production costs are least.

This text concentrates on three such optimization models. Firstly, we look at a general-purpose model known as linear programming. The other two models are more specialized and are known as the transportation model (see Sec. 19.4) and the assignment model (see Sec. 19.5).

Linear programming is a technique that enables managers to make decisions concerning the best use of limited resources. In most businesses there are insufficient resources to satisfy all the desired requirements of management, and there is consequently a need to allocate the available resources in the best way possible. Typically, linear programming is used to solve problems involving the determination of production levels when there are limits on labour size, availability of materials and capital, and market demand.

The technique has three distinct steps:

1. A linear programming model has to be formulated mathematically. The objective and the constraints on the resources are written down in terms of the variables of interest. This is described in Sec. 19.1.

2. When the model has been formulated it is necessary to identify all the solutions that satisfy the constraints and then to find the solution that optimizes the objective. If we have only two variables then a graphical solution is possible, but for a problem with more variables an algebraic method, often requiring a computer package, has to be used. Section 19.2 describes the solution methods but concentrates on the graphical procedure for two variables.

3. When the optimum solution has been identified, we can extract from the solution relevant information which will be of use to the manager in the decision-making process. Section 19.3 describes this aspect of sensitivity analysis.

We now illustrate the approach to problem formulation by looking at some examples. The procedure for formulating all linear programmes is summarized in the following three stages:

(a) Identify the 'decision variables' in the problem.
(b) Identify the objective and write it mathematically in terms of the decision variables.
(c) Identify the constraints and write these in mathematical form.

Example 19.1.1 The Ultrasonic Technology Company makes and sells two models of stereo systems: the basic model, CD20, and the advanced model, CD90. Each CD20 model makes a contribution of £25 and each CD90 model £30. The output is limited because of the time required for the production and assembly of each system. It takes 150 minutes of production time and 30 minutes of assembly time for each CD20 and 120 minutes of production time and 40 minutes for assembly of CD90. Currently there is a maximum of 240 hours per week available in the production department and 60 hours in the assembly department. The company can sell all that it can produce but international quotas restrict the sales of CD20 to 80 per week and the sales of CD90 to 60 per week.

Ultrasonic Technology aims to maximize contribution. Formulate a linear programme to find the optimum production plan using the existing production and assembly time.

(ACCA Level 2: Dec. 1991)

ANSWER We answer this question in three steps.

(a) The problem facing the management of Ultrasonic Technology is to decide how many units of CD20 and CD90 to make per week. Let us suppose that the company each week makes and sells:

$$x \text{ of the basic model, CD20;}$$
$$y \text{ of the advanced model, CD90.}$$

In this problem x and y are the decision variables, the quantities of the products that should be made and sold.

(b) The objective is to maximize the weekly contribution. As the weekly contribution for a CD20 is £25 and the weekly contribution for a CD90 is £30 then the contribution from making x CD20s and y CD90s is

$$25x + 30y$$

This expression is known as the objective function. It is a linear mathematical function as it involves variables with powers no greater than 1.

The profit function can be used to find the weekly contribution for any combination of production levels. For example if the company makes and sells 100 CD20s and 50 CD90s then the weekly contribution would be

$$25(100) + 30(50) = £4000$$

However there may be limitations on the production process to prevent the company from making these amounts.

(c) The limitations that the company faces are more generally known as constraints. In this example restrictions may be described in terms of production time, assembly time, and the international quotas.

(i) Production time is the time to produce one CD20, which we know to be 2.5 hours so the total time to produce x of these products is $2.5x$. Similarly, to produce y CD90s requires $2y$ hours. Hence the total production time to make the x CD20s and y CD90s stated in step (a) is

$$2.5x + 2y$$

There is a maximum of 240 hours of production time available each week; therefore we have the expression (in mathematical terms)

$$2.5x + 2y \leqslant 240$$

Note that the symbol $\leqslant$ means 'less than or equal to'. Thus, for example, the inequality $2.5x + 2y \leqslant 240$ means that the production hours used, which amount to $2.5x + 2y$, must be less than or equal to the number available, i.e. 240.

(ii) Assembly time is the time required for x CD20s and y CD90s, i.e. $(1/2)x + (2/3)y$ hours. There is a maximum of 60 assembly hours each week, therefore the assembly time constraint can be expressed as

$$(1/2)x + (2/3)y \leqslant 60$$

(iii) International quotas restrict the number of CD20s per week, x, to no more than 80 and the number of CD90s per week, y, to no more than 60. These can be expressed by two mathematical constraints:

$$x \leqslant 80$$
$$y \leqslant 60$$

There are no more constraints on the production process but it is sensible to assume that the company cannot make a negative number of stereo systems. Therefore

$$x \geqslant 0$$
$$y \geqslant 0$$

We can now bring together the parts of our problem into a formal problem formulation.

The company's objective is to maximize profit (the objective function) subject to the various constraints faced. We have maximum profit $= 25x + 30y$ subject to:

$$2.5x + 2y \leqslant 240$$
$$0.5x + (2/3)y \leqslant 60$$
$$x \leqslant 80$$
$$y \leqslant 60$$
$$x \geqslant 0$$
$$y \geqslant 0$$

This is the standard way of presenting a linear programming formulation. It sets out clearly the objective function and the constraints. As with the objective function the constraints are linear in format.

Example 19.1.2 A company has an advertising budget for Brand X of £100 000. It must decide how much to spend on television advertising and how much on newspaper advertisements. From past experience each advertisement is expected to achieve extra sales of Brand X as follows:

> Newspaper advertisement   400 units
>
> Television spot   1000 units

The gross profit on sales is £10 a unit. For contractual reasons, the company can spend up to £70 000 on either form of advertising. For marketing balance, at least half as many newspaper advertisements as television spots are required. Each television spot and newspaper advertisement costs £5000 and £2000, respectively. The objective is to maximize expected contribution.

(a) Find the expected contributions for (i) a television spot, (ii) a newspaper advertisement.
(b) State the objective function and constraints in mathematical terms.

(CIMA Level 1: Nov. 1991)

ANSWER

(a) The expected contribution per television spot is the gross profit minus the advertising cost:

$$1000 \times £10 - £5000 = £5000$$

Similarly the expected contribution per newspaper advertisement is

$$400 \times £10 - £2000 = £2000$$

(b) We first need to define the decision variables by letting x be the number of television spots and y be the number of newspaper advertisements.

The objective is to maximize expected contribution, where the expected contribution per television spot is £5000 and per newspaper advert is £2000, giving an objective function

$$\text{Contribution} = 5000x + 2000y$$

The company has an advertising budget of £100 000. As the advertising costs are £5000 and £2000 for television and newspaper, respectively, the budgetary constraint is

$$5000x + 2000y \leqslant 100\,000$$

The contracts restrict the amount spent on either form of advertising to £70 000 so we have the constraints:

$$5000x \leqslant 70\,000$$

$$2000x \leqslant 70\,000$$

The marketing balance requires at least half as many newspaper adverts, y, as television spots, x, represented by

$$y \geqslant 0.5x$$

Finally, there cannot be a negative number of newspaper adverts or television spots.

$$x \geqslant 0$$
$$y \geqslant 0$$

In summary, the linear programming formulation is

$$\text{Max } 5000x + 2000y$$

subject to

$$5000x + 2000y \leqslant 100\,000$$
$$5000x \leqslant 70\,000$$
$$2000y \leqslant 70\,000$$
$$y \geqslant 0.5x$$
$$x \geqslant 0$$
$$y \geqslant 0$$

Examples 19.1.1 and 19.1.2 are classified as two-variable linear programming problems as there are only two decision variables. A more realistic business situation would include more than two variables.

Example 19.1.3 Apollo Products Limited is capable of manufacturing four products—alphas, betas, gammas, and deltas—and is currently drawing up its production plans for the forthcoming financial year.

Information about the sales price, unit costs and requirements, and maximum annual sales for each of these products is shown in the table below:

| | Product | | | |
	Alpha	Beta	Gamma	Delta
Sales price (£ per unit)	112	120	138	165
Cost of materials (£ per unit)	22	20	25	30
Variable overheads (£ per unit)	8	14	20	25
Assembly labour (hours per unit)	7	5	0	0
Packaging labour (hours per unit)	8	10	0	0
Machine time (hours per unit)	0	0	12	15
Maximum sales (units)	2500	1500	1000	1500

Fixed overheads of the firm amount to £25 000 per annum. Additional variable costs include assembly labour at £4 per hour, packaging labour at £3 per hour, and machine time at £4 per hour. Each year the resource availabilities are:

Resource	Hours available
Assembly labour	15 000
Packaging labour	21 000
Machine time	12 000

Formulate a linear programme from the above information.

(ACCA Level 2: Dec. 1988)

ANSWER Let us suppose that the annual production plan is a alphas, b betas, c gammas, and d deltas.

The contribution to profit for one alpha is:

Sales price − cost of materials − variable overheads − assembly cost − packaging cost − machine cost

$$= 112 - 22 - 8 - (7 \times 4) - (8 \times 3) - (0 \times 4) = £30$$

Similarly for

Betas	$= 120 - 20 - 14 - (5 \times 4) - (10 \times 3) - (0 \times 4) = £36$
Gammas	$= 138 - 25 - 20 - (0 \times 4) - (0 \times 3) - (12 \times 4) = £45$
Deltas	$= 165 - 30 - 25 - (0 \times 4) - (0 \times 3) - (15 \times 4) = £50$

The objective function for this problem is to maximize $30a + 36b + 45c + 50d$. (Note that we can ignore the fixed overheads of £25 000 per annum as this figure will be incurred no matter what production plan is implemented.)

The constraints are:

Assembly labour	$7a + 5b \leqslant 15\,000$
Packaging labour	$8a + 10b \leqslant 21\,000$
Machine time	$12c + 15d \leqslant 12\,000$
Maximum sales	$a \leqslant 2500$
	$b \leqslant 1500$
	$c \leqslant 1000$
	$d \leqslant 1500$
Non-negativity	$a, b, c, d \geqslant 0$

Exercise 19.1.1. A builder has purchased 21 000 square metres of land on which it is planned to build two types of houses, X (detached) and Y (a combination of town-house units), within an overall budget of £2 100 000.

A type X house costs £35 000 to build and requires 600 square metres of land.

A type Y house costs £60 000 to build and requires 300 square metres of land.

To comply with local planning regulations, not more than 40 buildings may be constructed on this land, but there must be at least five of each type.

From past experience the builder estimates the profit per type X house to be about £10 000 and per type Y house to be about £6000. Profit is to maximized.

(a) Write down the objective function.
(b) Write down the constraints (equations or inequalities).

(CIMA Level 1: May 1988)

19.2 GRAPHICAL SOLUTION

We are now at the stage where we can proceed to find the optimal solution to the formulated problem. In this section we introduce a solution method which is based on graphs. This solution method is often used to solve two-variable problems but also helps to increase understanding of more complex solution processes. To illustrate the graphical method of solution we look at two examples.

Example 19.2.1 In a machine shop a company manufactures two types of electronic component, X and Y, on which it aims to maximize the contribution to profit. The company wishes to know the ideal combination of X and Y to make. All the electronic components are produced in three main stages: assembly, inspection and testing, and packing.

In assembly each X takes one hour and each Y takes two hours. Inspection and testing takes 7.5 minutes for each X and 30 minutes for each Y, on average, which includes the time required for any faults to be rectified.

In total there are 600 hours available for assembly and 100 hours for inspection and testing each week. At all stages both components can be processed at the same time.

At the final stage the components require careful packing prior to delivery. Each X takes 3 minutes and each Y takes 20 minutes, on average, to mount, box, and pack properly. There is a total of 60 packing hours available each week.

The contribution on X is £10 per unit and on Y it is £15 per unit. For engineering reasons not more than 500 of X can be made each week. All production can be sold.

(a) State the objective function in mathematical terms.
(b) State the constraints as equalities.
(c) Graph these constraints on a suitable diagram, identifying the feasible region.
(d) Advise the company on the optimal product mix and contribution.

(CIMA Level 1: Nov. 1989)

ANSWER

(a) Let the company manufacture x of component X and y of component Y each week. The objective is to maximize contribution to profit

$$P = 10x + 15y$$

(b) The production constraints are

Assembly time	$x + 2y \leqslant 600$
Inspection time	$7.5x + 30y \leqslant 6000$
Packing time	$3x + 20y \leqslant 3600$
Engineering	$x \leqslant 500$
	$x \geqslant 0$
	$y \geqslant 0$

It is important to note that for both the inspection time constraint and the packing time constraint the units on each side of the inequality sign are the same. Here minutes have been used, but it would have been equally correct to have used constraints based on hours, e.g. the inspection time constraint could have been written as

$$(1/8)x + (1/2)y \leqslant 100$$

(c) We now need to graph the constraints for the problem. Let us examine the first constraint

$$x + 2y \leqslant 600$$

This is not an equation, but a region. Suppose we decided to produce no units of component X then the maximum possible production of Y is 300. Similarly if we produced no Y then the maximum X we would be able to produce is 600. We could represent this information by the two coordinates:

$$(0, 300) \quad \text{and} \quad (600, 0)$$

which we show on Fig. 19.1.

In order to identify all the other maximum production possibilities, we join the two points with a straight line and label appropriately. The result is shown in Fig. 19.2. We can therefore discard all points above this line as they violate this constraint. Figure 19.2 shows this region marked out.

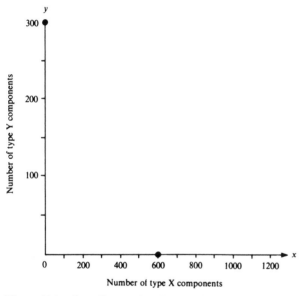

Figure 19.1 Coordinates showing maximum production limits given the assembly time constraint.

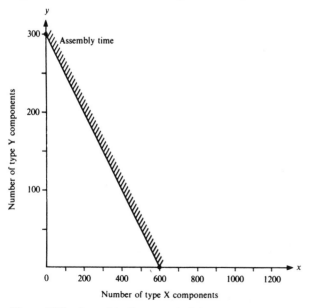

Figure 19.2 Assembly time constraint.

The other three constraints can be added to the diagram in the same way using the following procedure:

> Set $x=0$ and finding y.
>
> Set $y=0$ and finding x.
>
> Plot both points on the graph.
>
> Join the two points together.
>
> Label the constraint.
>
> Mark out the region that violates the constraint.

The final diagram is shown in Fig. 19.3. The region that satisfies all of the constraints is labelled the *feasible region*. Any combination of production which falls into the feasible region satisfies all of the constraints.

(d) We must now consider how to choose the production which will maximize the company's weekly contribution. We have seen that the objective function is

$$P = 10x + 15y \ (\pounds/\text{week})$$

If we let $P = \pounds 1500$ then we can illustrate the objective function graphically. If we then give P another value, the new line is parallel to the previous line. Figure 19.4 illustrates the objective function for contributions of £1500 and £3000, respectively. We note that we can generate a large number of possible contribution lines, all parallel and in such a way that the larger the contribution the further away from the origin the contribution line would be. As the objective is profit maximization, we need to move parallel to these lines away from the origin until we reach the last feasible solution, i.e. the last point before the line moves out of the feasible region. We see that point D is the last feasible solution in this example. The coordinates of point D give the optimum combination of production for the two components.

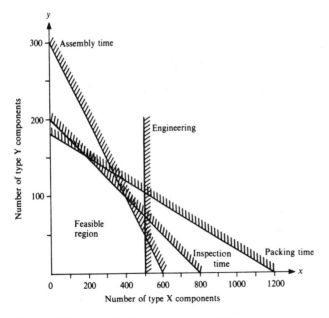

Figure 19.3 Graphical representation of the constraints.

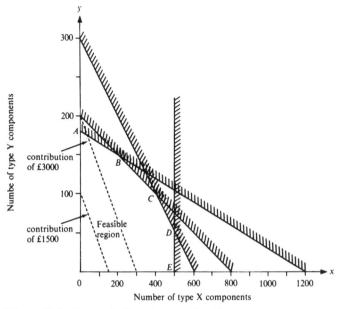

Figure 19.4 Iso-profit lines for $P = 10 \times 15y$.

The approximate coordinates of point D can be read from the graph, but for greater accuracy the optimum values can be obtained by solving simultaneously the two equations of the two constraints which form point D. Here the optimum solution occurs when

$$x = 500$$
$$x + 2y = 600$$

giving $x = 500$ and $y = 50$. Hence to maximize weekly contribution, the company should produce 500 type X components and 50 type Y components each week resulting in a maximum weekly contribution of

$$500(10) + 50(15) = £5750$$

Note that the solution of this problem has occurred at one of the corner points of the feasible region. This is typically where the optimal solution will be found. Hence the graphical solution to the problem can be found by evaluating $(10x + 15y)$ at each corner of the feasible region. The best production policy will be given by the values of x and y at the best corner and the maximum value of the objective function will be the value at that corner.

In our present example the feasible region has six corners (see Fig. 19.4).

The table below confirms that the maximum contribution is £5750 per week, obtained by manufacturing 500 of type X and 50 of type Y per week.

Corner	x	y	$P = 10x + 15y$
A	0	180	2700
B	200	150	4250
C	400	100	5500
D	500	50	5750*
E	500	0	5000
F	0	0	0

Example 19.2.2 The Bermuda Paint Company is a privately owned manufacturing firm, specializing in the production of industrial varnish. The selling prices and the associated unit variable costs for high gloss varnish and matt varnish are shown in the table below.

Product	Selling price (£) per gallon	Unit variable cost (£) per gallon
Matt	13.0	9.0
High gloss	16.0	10.0

Each gallon of matt varnish requires 6 minutes of skilled labour and each gallon of high gloss requires 12 minutes of skilled labour. In a given day there are 400 man-hours of skilled labour available. Also there are 100 ounces of an important blending chemical available each day, where each gallon of matt varnish needs 0.05 ounces of the blending chemical and each gallon of high gloss varnish needs 0.02 ounces of the chemical. The processing capacity at the plant is limited to 3000 gallons of varnish per day.

The company is committed to supplying a leading retailer with 5000 gallons of matt varnish and 2500 gallons of high gloss varnish each working week (consisting of five days). In addition, there is an agreement with the unions that at least 2000 gallons are produced each day. Bermuda management would like to determine the daily production volume of each of the two varnishes that will maximize total contribution.

(a) Develop a linear model of the production problem facing Bermuda Paint Company.
(b) Using a graphical approach, determine the optimum daily production plan and the consequent contribution.

(ACCA Level 2: June 1990)

ANSWER

(a) Let x and y represent the number of gallons of matt varnish and high gloss varnish, respectively, produced each day.

The objective is to maximize contribution, where the contribution from one gallon of matt is £$(13-9)=$£4 and from one gallon of high gloss is £$(16-10)=$£6. This results in an objective function:

$$P = 4x + 6y$$

which is to be maximized.

The constraints are as follows:

(i) In a given day there are 400 man-hours of skilled labour

$$0.1x + 0.2y \leqslant 400$$

(ii) There exists 100 ounces of an important blending chemical

$$0.05x + 0.02y \leqslant 100$$

(iii) The processing capacity is limited to 3000 gallons per day

$$x + y \leqslant 3000$$

(iv) The company supplies a minimum of 1000 gallons of matt and 500 gallons of high gloss each day (which is equivalent to 5000 gallons of matt and 2500 gallons of high gloss each working week)

$$x \geqslant 1000$$

$$y \geqslant 500$$

(v) There is an agreement with the unions that at least 2000 gallons are produced each day

$$x + y \geqslant 2000$$

The complete formulation is to maximize contribution $P = 4x + 6y$ subject to

$$0.1x + 0.2y \leqslant 400$$

$$0.05x + 0.02y \leqslant 100$$

$$x + y \leqslant 3000$$

$$x \geqslant 1000$$

$$y \geqslant 500$$

$$x + y \geqslant 2000$$

(b) The six constraint lines are shown in Fig. 19.5. You will note that, unlike the previous example, some of the constraints involve the $\geqslant$ sign. We need to be careful that we cross out the correct side of the constraint line. Figure 19.5 shows the feasible region with five corner points.

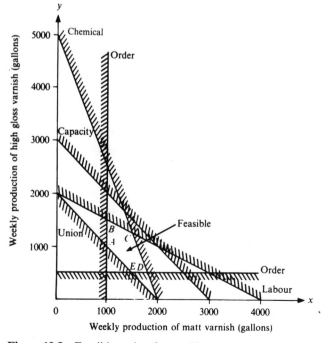

Figure 19.5 Feasible region for weekly production levels of matt and high gloss varnish.

Corner point	x	y	Contribution $= 4x + 6y$
A	1 000	1 000	10 000
B	1 000	1 500	13 000
C	1 500	1 250	13 500
D	1 800	500	10 200
E	1 500	500	9 000

The optimum point is at point C, which is at the intersection of the labour constraint and the chemical constraint. Solving the two equations gives

$$x = 1500 \text{ and } y = 1250$$

yielding a maximum contribution of £13 500 per day.

Nowadays linear programming problems tend to be solved via a computer package. Good packages would be able to display a graphical solution for a two-variable problem and be able to solve three- or higher-variable problems. QSB+ was used to solve Example 19.2.2, the Bermuda Paint Company problem. When the following data was entered into the package:

Input Data of The Problem Bermuda Paint		Page: 1

```
   Max    +4.00000MATT+6.00000GLOS
Subject to
(1)        +.100000MATT+.200000GLOS<  +400.000
(2)        +.050000MATT+.020000GLOS<  +100.000
(3)        +1.00000MATT+1.00000GLOS<  +3000.00
(4)        +1.00000MATT+0      GLOS>  +1000.00
(5)        +0      MATT+1.00000GLOS>  +500.000
(6)        +1.00000MATT+1.00000GLOS>  +2000.00
```

the output shown in Fig. 19.6 was produced.

Although decision problems with constraints usually involve the maximization of contribution, there may be a requirement to minimize costs. Such a graphical solution is very similar to a maximization problem, with the alteration that we need to find a corner point close to the origin rather than the one furthest away.

Exercise 19.2.1 A small company has just received an urgent order for its bathroom cabinets, which it makes in two styles, standard and de-luxe. The order is for 'at least 100 bathroom cabinets of either variety, including at least 30 of the de-luxe style'. The standard model takes two hours of assembly time and has variable costs of £40, whereas the de-luxe model takes five hours of assembly time and has variable costs of £60. There are 400 hours in total available for assembly. The equipment can be used to assemble either style of cabinet in any combination. Other reasons dictate that at least as many standard cabinets as de-luxe cabinets must be made. The company wishes to minimize its variable costs of production on this special order.

(a) Formulate this problem as a linear programme.
(b) Graph the constraints, shading the feasible region.
(c) Recommend the best product mix for the company and the variable costs incurred.

(CIMA Level 1: May 1990)

In this section we have seen how the graphical solution method can be used to find the optimal solution to a two-variable problem. Clearly, in a real business environment, we will

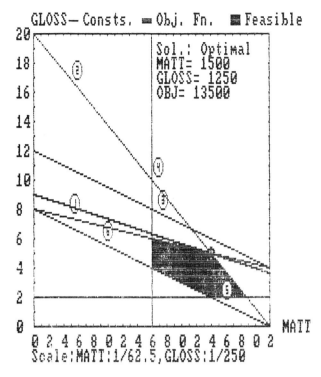

Figure 19.6 Graphical printout from QSB+package.

usually be faced with a more complex problem involving a large number of variables. One method of solving linear programming problems with a large number of variables is the simplex method. This is a fairly complex algebraic method of solution, which serves as a basis for most computer packages. As linear programming problems can be solved using a computer package this text does not describe the simplex method. We look briefly at an example where a computer has been used to solve a more complex problem.

Example 19.2.3 The Stonehouse Electronics Company manufactures four technical products, which it supplies to the computer industry. Each of the four products must pass through the following four processes: forming, wiring, assembly, and inspection. The time requirements (in hours) for each product together with the production time available (also in hours) for each process each month are summarized in the following table.

Product	Process			
	Forming	Wiring	Assembly	Inspection
XL35	1	2	4	0.5
RK27	2	3	2	0.5
RM93	2	1	3	1
TS15	1	3	2	0.5
Production time	2500	4000	4500	1200

The profit for each product together with the minimum monthly production requirement to fulfil contracts are as follows:

Product	Unit profit	Minimum production level
XL35	£25	200
RK27	£30	150
RM93	£20	300
TS15	£22	200

The production manager, a person with virtually no quantitative background, has the responsibility of specifying production levels for each product for the coming month.

(a) Help him by formulating the problem.
(b) A computer package produces an output that recommends a production level of

(XL35)425; (RK27)525; (RM93)300; (TS15)425.

Determine the optimum monthly profit time and the unused process time.

(ACCA Level 2: June 1991)

ANSWER

(a) If we let w, x, y, and z be the monthly production levels for XL35, RK27, RM93, and TS15 respectively, then the objective is to maximize the monthly profit

$$\text{Max } P = 25w + 30x + 20y + 22z$$

subject to the constraints of available production time:

Forming $w + 2x + 2y + z \leqslant 2500$
Wiring $2w + 3x + y + 3z \leqslant 4000$
Assembly $4w + 2x + 3y + 2z \leqslant 4500$
Inspection $0.5w + 0.5x + y + 0.5z \leqslant 1200$

and minimum production levels:

$$w \geqslant 200, \quad x \geqslant 150, \quad y \geqslant 300, \quad z \geqslant 200$$

(b) The proposed product mix results in a monthly profit figure of

$$425(25) + 525(30) + 300(20) + 425(22) = £41\ 725$$

Not all of the four processes will use up all the time available to them. In terms of forming

$$425(1) + 525(2) + 300(2) + 425(1) = 2500 \text{ hours}$$

will be required to make the required output. This in fact is the limit stated in the example. Similarly, for wiring

$$425(2) + 525(3) + 300(2) + 425(3) = 4000 \text{ hours}$$

For assembly 4500 hours and for inspection 987.5 hours are used up. Hence all process time is used up in forming, wiring, and assembly, but there is an excess of $1200 - 987.5 = 212.5$ hours of inspection. This time may be better utilized in other areas of the company. Most computer packages will supply this information on surplus resources together with other useful management information described in Sec. 19.3.

19.3 SENSITIVITY ANALYSIS

In Sec. 19.2 we investigated methods of solving linear programming problems. In this section we look at ways of extending the information available to the manager involved in the decision-making process. Consider the following example which we can solve using the methods described in this chapter.

Example 19.3.1 A small firm produces two qualities of a product—standard and de-luxe. The contribution per unit is £100 for the standard and £300 for the de-luxe.

Each model requires 1 hour per unit in the machine shop and 40 machining hours are available per week. The standard model can be assembled and finished in 2.5 hours per unit but the de-luxe takes 10 hours per unit. There are 200 hours per week available for assembly and finishing.

Market reseach suggests that the maximum weekly sales of the de-luxe model will be 18 units.

The products use a special component, of which only 1200 are currently available per week. Each standard unit uses 25 components and each de-luxe unit needs 50.

You are required to analyse the current position and recommend a weekly production plan, showing its contribution.

(CIMA Stage 2: May 1991)

ANSWER Let x be the number of standards produced and y the number of de-luxes each week. The objective of the small firm is to maximize contribution

$$\text{Max } P = 100x + 300y$$

subject to the constraints:

Machine shop time	$x + y \leqslant 40$
Assembly time	$2.5x + 10y \leqslant 200$
Market research	$y \leqslant 18$
Special component	$25x + 50y \leqslant 1200$

The constraints are shown graphically in Fig. 19.7. The feasible region contains six corner points as shown in the table below.

Corner point	x	y	$P = 100x + 300y$
A	0	18	5400
B	8	18	6200
C	16	16	6400*
D	32	8	5600
E	40	0	4000
F	0	0	0

The optimum weekly production plan is to manufacture 16 standard products and 16 de-luxe products, giving a weekly contribution of £6400.

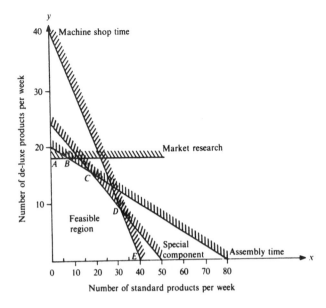

Figure 19.7 Graphical representation for problem given in Example 19.3.1.

It is likely that the firm would like to know what quantities of available resources are required at this optimum point.

The amount of machine shop time required is $16+16=32$ hours (with 40 available).

The amount of assembly time required is $16(2.5)+16(10)=200$ hours (with 200 available).

The number of special components required is $16(25)+16(50)=1200$ (with 1200 available).

We see that all the assembly time and special components are used up but that we do not require all of the machine shop time. In the context of linear programming we describe the assembly time constraint and special component constraint as *binding* constraints. They are the resources which are being fully utilized and therefore prevent the weekly contribution from increasing further. They are the two constraints that intersect at the optimum point. On the other hand the constraint relating to machine shop time is *non-binding*, i.e. there is spare capacity in terms of machine shop time at the optimum point. It is possible to determine directly from the graph which constraints are binding and which are non-binding. Those lines that intersect at the optimum point represent the binding constraints, the others are non-binding.

Sensitivity analysis is concerned with examining the sensitivity of the solution to changes in the problem formulation. There are two aspects of the problem that we need to consider:

1. The effect of changes to the constraints.
2. The effect of changes to the objective function.

We consider each of these situations in turn, but in all cases we assume that only one value is being changed at any one time.

In the above example we have seen that there is a fixed supply of certain resources that is restricting the company in terms of its production and hence its contribution. If we consider assembly time, we know that the resource is fully used at the optimum point. Suppose, however, that one more hour of assembly time becomes available, then the second constraint becomes

$$2.5x+10y \leqslant 201$$

This constraint is parallel to the original one but slightly further removed from the origin. The two binding constraints would then become

$$2.5x + 10y = 201$$
$$25x + 50y = 1200$$

The objective function and other constraints remain unchanged.

Using simultaneous equations we can determine the new optimum solution

$$x = 15.6 \qquad y = 16.2 \qquad \text{contribution} = £6420$$

We see that there is a marginal change to the solution, production of standards has gone down slightly and de-luxes have increased slightly and there has been a slight increase in contribution as a result. The manager knows that for every extra hour of assembly time then there is an increase of £20. We say that the *shadow price*, or *dual value*, of assembly time is £20 per hour. If one extra hour of assembly time can be obtained for less than £20 then it is worth while having that extra hour. If the additional cost of the extra hour is more than £20 then it is not worth while.

How many extra hours of assembly time is it worth buying? As the assembly constraint moves away from the origin, parallel to its current position, it moves towards the intersection of the special component and market research constraints. If the assembly time constraints were relaxed further it would then become non-binding and further additional assembly hours would not contribute further. The maximum number of assembly hours could be determined by solving

$$y = 18$$
$$25x + 50y = 1200$$

The solution is $x = 12$, $y = 18$ and the number of assembly hours used then is

$$2.5(12) + 10(18) = 210 \text{ hours per week}$$

This is an increase of 10 hours per week on the original 200 hours.

Providing that the additional assembly time is less than £20 per hour, then it is worth while increasing assembly time up to a maximum of 10 hours per week.

In the same way we could determine the dual value of the special components by first solving

$$2.5x + 10y = 200$$
$$15x + 50y = 1201$$

to give $x = 16.08$, $y = 15.98$, contribution $= £6402$. The dual value of special components is £2.

A manager might also wish to carry out sensitivity analysis into the objective function. If either of the profit contributions were to change, then it is quite possible that the optimum point would also change. Sensitivity analysis seeks to find the maximum change that can occur in one of the objective function parameters before the optimum solution changes.

Observing Fig. 19.8 we discover that point C remains optimal providing the slope of the contribution line lies between the slopes of the lines BC and CD:

$$\text{Slope } BC \text{ is } -0.25$$
$$\text{Slope } CD \text{ is } -0.5$$

The slope of the contribution line is $-(1/3)$, which satisfies the above condition. Now suppose we let the profit per unit of the de-luxe be $£a$, rather than £300, then the slope of the contribution line would be $(-100/a)$ and so the optimum point remains optimum providing

$$(-0.5) \leqslant (-100/a) \leqslant (-0.25)$$

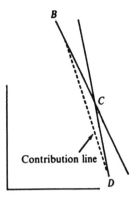

Figure 19.8 Slopes of binding constraints and the objective function.

Rearranging this expression gives

$$200 \leqslant a \leqslant 400$$

Providing the profit contribution of a de-luxe is between £200 and £400 the optimum point will not change. In the same way the range of contribution for a standard for which the optimum point remains optimal is obtained by rearranging.

$$-0.5 \leqslant -b/300 \leqslant -0.25$$

to get

$$75 \leqslant b \leqslant 150$$

These ranges indicate the sensitivity of the optimum point to changes in the objective function coefficients.

Exercise 19.3.1 A company makes two products, X and Y. Product X has a contribution of £124 per unit and product Y £80 per unit. Both products pass through the two departments for processing and the times in minutes per unit are shown in the table below.

	Product X	Product Y
Department 1	150	90
Department 2	100	120

Currently there is a maximum of 225 hours per week available in department 1 and 200 hours in department 2. The company can sell all it can produce of X but EC quotas restrict the sale of Y to a maximum of 75 units per week.

The company, which wishes to maximize contribution, currently makes and sells 30 units of X and 75 units of Y per week. It is considering several possibilities including the following:

1. Altering the production plan if it could be proved that there is a better plan than the current one.
2. Increasing the availability of hours in either department 1 or department 2. The extra costs involved in increasing capacity are £0.5 per hour for each department.

3. Transferring some of its allowed sales quota for product Y to another company. Because of commitments the company would always retain a minimum sales level of 30 units.

(a) Calculate the optimum production plan using the existing capacities and state the extra contribution that would be achieved compared with the existing plan.
(b) Advise management whether it should increase the capacity of either department 1 or department 2 and, if so, by how many hours and what the resulting increase in contribution would be over that calculated in the improved production plan.
(c) Calculate the minimum price per unit for which the company could sell the rights to its quota, down to the minimum level, given the plan in (a) as a starting point.

(CIMA Stage 2: May 1988)

19.4 TRANSPORTATION PROBLEM

In the previous sections of this chapter we looked at the linear programming model as a general purpose optimization model which can be applied to many different types of business situations. In this and the following section we look at certain special applications of linear programming problems. Both applications, transportation and assignment, can be formulated and solved as linear programming problems using a computer package but special-purpose algorithms are easier and more efficient to use. In this section we describe the transportation algorithm.

The transportation model was originally developed to provide optimal solutions to problems where items are to be transported from several suppliers (origins) to a number of customers (destinations) with the objective of minimizing total transportation costs.

Consider the problem faced by the transport department of a medium-sized company that has three factories (A, B, and C) and four regional warehouses (W, X, Y, and Z). Each month a list of requirements for each warehouse is available and the production capacities of the three factories are known. In addition, the cost of transporting a unit from each factory to each warehouse is known. Suppose that in one particular month the transportation costs, warehouse requirements, and factory capacities are as described in Table 19.1.

Table 19.1

	Unit transport costs				Capacity
	Warehouse W	Warehouse X	Warehouse Y	Warehouse Z	
Factory A	4	6	8	3	700
Factory B	5	5	7	4	900
Factory C	2	3	11	9	1600
Required	800	500	600	1300	3200

The problem is to determine which factories should supply which warehouses in such a way as to minimize the total transportation costs.

The basic format of the transportation algorithm is to find an allocation that is feasible (an allocation that works), then to make successive improvements until no further cost reductions can be made. Clearly, if we start with a good allocation, there will be fewer improvements to make. Table 19.2 summarizes the cost information and will form the basis of our solution process.

Table 19.2

Warehouse Factory		W	X	Y	Z	Capacity
A	4	6	8	3		700
B	5	5	7	4		900
C	2	3	11	9		1600
Required		800	500	600	1300	3200

We have a choice of routes that can be used to match requirements with availability. For example, factory A could supply warehouse W with 700 units but it could not supply all of the warehouse's requirements. We must decide how best to match the capacities to the requirements. As the objective is to minimize the total transportation costs it makes sense to use the cheapest route (factory C to warehouse W at a cost of 2). An initial feasible solution can therefore be produced in the following way:

1. Start with the route from C to W and allocate the maximum amount possible. This is 800 as that is the total requirement of warehouse W.
2. Factory C still has 800 units available and the next cheapest transport cost to a warehouse for this factory is warehouse X, so allocate the maximum possible, 500, to this route.
3. The final 300 units for factory C can be allocated to warehouse Z, as it is cheaper than allocating to Y. We have now distributed all of factory C's capacity.
4. As yet warehouse Z's requirements are only partly satisfied. The remaining 1000 units cannot be fully satisfied by either factory A or factory B. We allocate as much as possible from the factory with cheapest costs, A, and the remainder from factory B.
5. The last allocation to warehouse Y from factory B satisfies the remaining availabilities and requirements.

Hence our method for obtaining an initial feasible solution involves allocating as much as possible to the route with the minimum unit cost, then completing the unsatisfied rows and columns in the cheapest way possible. Table 19.3 shows the initial feasible solution.

Table 19.3

Warehouse Factory		W	X	Y	Z	Capacity
A	4	6	8	3 700		700
B	5	5	7 600	4 300		900
C	2 800	3 500	11	9 300		1600
Required		800	500	600	1300	3200

The transport cost (C) for this solution is

$$C = 700(3) + 600(7) + 300(4) + 800(2) + 500(3) + 300(9) = 13\ 300$$

As we set up this initial feasible solution by looking at warehouses and factories individually and not simultaneously, we do not know whether or not this solution is optimal. To find out, we calculate the shadow costs of routes *not currently used*. This is obtained by breaking down into two parts the total cost of transporting one unit from a factory to a warehouse for those routes used in the solution:

1. shadow cost of dispatch from the factory;
2. shadow cost of receipt at the warehouse.

To start the calculations we assume the shadow cost of dispatch from factory A to be 0. Other shadow costs can now be calculated. For example, A to Z is used in the initial solution and as the total unit cost is 3 and the dispatch cost from A is 0 then the receipt cost at Z must be $3 - 0 = 3$.

Similarly, the remaining shadow costs can be found:

$$
\begin{aligned}
\text{B dispatch cost} &= \text{BZ cost } - \text{Z receipt cost } = 4 - 3 = 1 \\
\text{Y receipt cost } &= \text{BY cost } - \text{B dispatch cost} = 7 - 1 = 6 \\
\text{C dispatch cost} &= \text{CZ cost } - \text{Z receipt cost } = 9 - 3 = 6 \\
\text{X receipt cost } &= \text{CX cost } - \text{C dispatch cost} = 3 - 6 = -3 \\
\text{W receipt cost } &= \text{CW cost} - \text{C dispatch cost} = 2 - 6 = -4
\end{aligned}
$$

These shadow costs are shown in Table 19.4.

Table 19.4

Factory \ Warehouse		W		X		Y		Z	Capacity	Shadow cost
A	4		6		8		3	700	700	0
B	5		5		7		4			1
						600		300	900	
C	2		3		11		9			6
		800		500				300	1600	
Required		800		500		600		1300	3200	
Shadow cost	-4		-3		6		3			

These dispatch and receipt costs for the used routes are now used to identify whether it would be cheaper to transport these items along any of the unused routes. It is now possible to calculate what is referred to as an improvement index for each route. This is calculated from the expression

$$\text{Cost of route} - (\text{Factory dispatch cost} + \text{Warehouse receipt cost})$$

For each of the unused routes the improvement index is as shown in Table 19.5.

Table 19.5

Route	Improvement index
AW	$4-(0+(-4))=8$
AX	$6-(0+(-3))=9$
AY	$8-(0+6)=2$
BW	$5-(1+(-4))=8$
BX	$5-(1+(-3))=7$
CY	$11-(6+6)=-1$

Looking at route CY the improvement index is negative, indicating that it is cheaper to use route CY than not to use it. Indeed, for every unit sent on this route, the cost will be reduced by 1. The improvement indices are shown circled in Table 19.6.

Table 19.6

Factory \ Warehouse	W	X	Y	Z	Capacity	Shadow cost
	4	6	8	3		0
A	⑧	⑨	②	700	700	
	5	5	7	4		1
B	⑧	⑦	600	300	900	
	2	3	11	9		6
C	800	500	⊖1	300	1600	
Required	800	500	600	1300	3200	
Shadow cost	-4	-3	6	3		

We now have to decide how many units to send along route CY. The more we send the more the cost will be reduced, but it is important that the row and column totals remain correct. We are unable to transfer items from routes CW and CX to CY without using further unused routes, hence the most we can transfer is the 300 units currently transported along CZ. The knock-on effect of this is to reduce route BY by 300 and increase BZ by 300. Table 19.7 shows an improved allocation.

Table 19.7

Factory \ Warehouse	W	X	Y	Z	Capacity
	4	6	8	3	
A				700	700
	5	5	7	4	
B			300	600	900
	2	3	11	9	
C	800	500	300		1600
Required	800	500	600	1300	3200

The total cost of employing this transportation plan is

$$C = 700(3) + 300(7) + 600(4) + 800(2) + 500(3) + 300(11) = 13\,000$$

This is cheaper than the initial feasible solution by 300. This could have been predicted because the improvement index for CY was -1 and 300 units were transported on this route, giving a saving of $300(1) = 300$.

We now need to find out if this transport plan is cheapest. Again we need to find the shadow costs for each factory and warehouse. Table 19.8 shows the new shadow costs and the new improvement index for each unused route.

Table 19.8

Warehouse / Factory	W	X	Y	Z	Capacity	Shadow cost
	4	6	8	3		0
A	⑦	⑧	②	700	700	
	5	5	7	4		1
B	⑦	⑥	300	600	900	
	2	3	11	9		5
C	800	500	300	①	1600	
Required	800	500	600	1300	3200	
Shadow cost	−3	−2	6	3		

The basic procedure for testing for a least cost plan involves calculating the improvement index for each unused route. If there is one or more negative improvement index, use the route that has the largest negative value and adjust remaining routes to agree with the row and column totals. If, as in Table 19.8, all improvement indices are zero or positive then an optimal transport plan has been found.

Hence the solution to the problem is:

1. Factory A sends 700 units to Warehouse Z.
2. Factory B sends 300 units to Y and 600 units to Z.
3. Factory C sends 800 units to W, 500 to X, and 300 to Y, costing 13 000.

Until now the transportation method has required that supply and demand be equal. In reality this is unlikely to be true. Most real problems are 'unbalanced', where supply and demand are unequal. In such cases, it is necessary to create a fictitious origin or destination to balance the problem. The following example illustrates the procedure.

Example 19.4.1 The Royal Wedgetown Pottery Company has orders to be completed next week for three of its products — mugs, cups, and bowls — as given in the table below.

Product	Order(units)
Mugs	4000
Cups	2400
Bowls	1000

There are three machines available for the manufacturing operations, and all three can produce each of the products at the same production rate. However the unit costs of these products vary depending upon the machine used. The unit costs (in £) of each machine are given in the following table.

Machine	Product		
	Mugs	Cups	Bowls
X	1.20	1.30	1.10
Y	1.40	1.30	1.50
Z	1.10	1.00	1.30

Furthermore, it is known that capacity for next week for machines Y and Z is 3000 units and for machine X is 2000 units.

Use the transportation model to find the minimum cost production schedule for the products nd machines. Determine this minimum cost.

(ACCA Level 2: June 1989)

ANSWER By comparing the others with the capacities we see there is a need for a 'dummy product' of 600 units. An initial feasible solution is shown in the table below.

Machine	Product				
	Mugs	Cups	Bowls	Dummy	Total
	1.2	1.3	1.1	0	
X	2000				2000
	1.4	1.3	1.5	0	
Y	1400		1000	600	3000
	1.1	1.0	1.3	0	
Z	600	2400			3000
Total	4000	2400	1000	600	8000

Assigning shadow costs to the rows and columns, improvement indices can be calculated for each unused machine/product combination. These are shown in the following table.

Machine	Product					Shadow cost
	Mugs	Cups	Bowls	Dummy	Total	
	1.2	1.3	1.1	0		0
X	2000	(0.2)	−0.2	(0.2)	2000	
	1.4	1.3	1.5	0		0.2
Y	1400	(0)	1000	600	3000	
	1.1	1.0	1.3	0		−0.1
Z	600	2400	(0.1)	(0.3)	3000	
Total	4000	2400			8000	
Shadow cost	1.2	1.1	1.3	−0.2		

This allocation is shown not to be optimal. There is a cost saving of £0.2 for every bowl that is allocated to machine X. Reallocating to this cell gives the following plan.

Machine	Product				
	Mugs	Cups	Bowls	Dummy	Total
A	1000		1000		2000
B	2400			600	3000
C	600	2400			3000
Total	4000	2400	1000	600	8000

The test for optimality shows that we have found the production plan that minimizes costs. The cost of the optimal production schedule is

$$1000(1.20) + 1000(1.0) + 2400(1.40) + 600(1.10) + 2400(1.00) = £8720$$

A further problem that can occur in the transportation problem is one called degeneracy. This occurs when the number of routes used by a proposed schedule is less than

$$\text{number of rows} + \text{number of columns} - 1$$

This makes it impossible to determine the shadow costs for the rows and columns. The difficulty is resolved by pretending to use a route, i.e. creating a dummy route where an infinitesimal quantity is transported so that its cost of transportation may be neglected.

19.5 ASSIGNMENT PROBLEM

In the last section we investigated a special type of optimization problem relating to transportation problems. In this section we look at another specialized type of optimization model relating to assignment problems. Consider the following example.

Example 19.5.1 The Midland Research Association has recently been notified that it has received government research grants to undertake four major projects. The managing director has to assign a research officer to each of these projects. Currently there are five research officers, Adams, Brown, Carr, Day, and Evans, who are available to carry out these duties. The amount of time required to complete each of the research projects is dependent on the experience and ability of the research officer who is assigned to the project. The managing director has been provided with an estimate of the project completion time (in days) for each officer and each project.

Research officer	Project			
	1	2	3	4
Adams	80	120	60	104
Brown	72	144	48	110
Carr	96	148	72	120
Day	60	108	52	92
Evans	64	140	60	96

As the four projects have equal priority, the managing director would like to assign research officers in a way that would minimize the total time (in officer-days) necessary to complete all four projects. Determine an optimal assignment of research officers to projects, and hence determine the total number of officer-days allocated to these four projects.

(ACCA Level 2: Dec. 1989)

This example provides a classic application of the assignment problem, where individuals are allocated to particular tasks in such a way as to minimize time or cost. In this section we only consider balanced assignment problems where the number of individuals is exactly the same as the number of tasks. This does not present a problem in the above example as Carr takes longer than each of the other four officers for each project. Consequently he can be disregarded from this problem, resulting in a 4×4 matrix of durations.

	Project			
	1	2	3	4
Adams	80	120	60	104
Brown	72	144	48	110
Day	60	108	52	92
Evans	64	140	60	96

This particular problem can be solved either using the general linear programming approach or the transportation algorithm; however, it is more usual to apply a specially-developed method called the Hungarian algorithm.

The following steps summarize this procedure which is illustrated by application to the above example.

1. Take the time (or cost) matrix, and for each row subtract the smallest value from the remaining values.

	1	2	3	4
A	20	60	0	44
B	24	96	0	62
D	8	56	0	40
E	4	80	0	36

2. For each column subtract the smallest value from the remaining values.

	1	2	3	4
A	16	4	0	8
B	20	40	0	26
D	4	0	0	4
E	0	24	0	0

3. We now test for optimality by drawing the minimum number of lines (horizontal or vertical) which cover all the zeros. If this is the same as the size of matrix (here 4) then the solution is optimal. If not, then the matrix needs to be further reduced.

	1	2	3	4
A	16	4	0̸	8
B	20	40	0̸	26
D	4	0	0̸	4
E	0	24	0̸	0

The minimum number of lines required for this matrix is three. Hence the matrix needs to be reduced.

4. The reduction takes place by observing the three classes of entry in the above matrix. Some of the entries have one line going through them (e.g. 24 in the 4th row, 2nd column), others have no lines through them (e.g. 16 in the 1st row, 1st column), and finally others have two lines through them (e.g. 0 in the 3rd row, 3rd column). For the 'no-line' entries we find the smallest value and reduce all the 'no-line' entries by this amount. 'One-line' entries are left unchanged but 'two-line' entries are increased by the smallest 'no-line' entry.

In our example the smallest 'no-line' entry is 4 (1st row, 2nd column). The reduced matrix becomes

	1	2	3	4
A	12	0	0	4
B	16	36	0	22
D	4	0	4	4
E	0	24	4	0

Again it is possible to draw three lines through the zeros, as follows:

	1	2	3	4
A	12	0̸	0̸	4
B	16	36	0̸	22
D	4	0	4	4
E	0	24	4	0

Repeating the above reduction procedure gives the matrix

	1	2	3	4
A	8	0	0	0
B	12	36	0	18
D	0	0	4	0
E	0	28	8	0

Four lines are now needed to cover the zeros. We have reached the optimal position.

5. We now allocate the jobs according to the zeros in this matrix. The only zero in row two is in column three. This indicates that Brown should be allocated to task 3. The remaining jobs can be allocated in a variety of ways, giving

(1) Evans; (2) Day;   (3) Brown; (4) Adams

or

> (1) Evans; (2) Adams; (3) Brown; (4) Day

or

> (1) Day; (2) Adams; (3) Brown; (4) Evans

Each of these allocations takes a total of 324 days.

TEST EXERCISES

19.1 A private hospital is reviewing its requirements for nursing care. It wishes to maintan a high quality service at the lowest cost, consistent with a variety of constraints.

Two categories of nurse are employed, 'qualified' and 'student'. Past experience has shown that at least 100 qualified nurses, or equivalent, are required. Because of knowledge, experience, and training, the work of one qualified nurse is deemed to be equivalent to that of two student nurses.

On average, a qualified nurse costs the hospital £13 000 a year and a student nurse £6000 (inclusive of pay, food, and accommodation). The student nurses' hall can accommodate 50 student nurses. For successful working practices there must be at least as many qualified nurses as student nurses. To meet the requirements of a local charity which donates substantial sums to the hospital, at least 30 student nurses must be under training. The hospital's personnel manager's assessment of the current job market is that a maximum of 140 qualified nurses could be recruited.

(a) State mathematically the hospital's objective function and its constraints.
(b) Draw a graph for this problem, shading the feasible region.
(c) Recommend the optimum combination of nurses to employ.
(d) Comment briefly on your recommendation.

(CIMA Stage 1: May 1989)

19.2 J Farms Ltd can buy two types of fertilizer which contain the following percentages of chemicals.

	Nitrates	Phosphates	Potash
Type X	18	5	2
Type Y	3	2	5

For a certain crop the following minimum quantities (kg) are required:

Nitrates 100; Phosphates 50; Potash 40

Type X costs £10 per kg and type Y costs £5 per kg. J Farms Ltd currently buys 1000 kg of each type and wishes to minimize its expenditure on fertilizers.

(a) Write down the objective function and constraints for J Farms Ltd.
(b) Draw a graph to illustrate all the constraints, shading the feasible region.
(c) Recommend the quantity of each type of fertilizer which should be bought and the cost of these amounts.
(d) Find the saving J Farms Ltd can make by switching from its current policy to your recommendation.
(e) State briefly any limitations of using this approach to problem solving in practice.

(CIMA Stage 1: Nov. 1987)

19.3 Princetown Paints Ltd manufactures three basic types of paint—emulsion, gloss, and undercoat—using the same mixing machines and direct labour for each of the three products. The management accountant of Princetown Paints was faced with the task of arranging the weekly production for his company. Information about the sales price and costs per 100 litres is given in the following table (in £).

	Emulsion	Gloss	Undercoat
Sales price (per 100 litres)	120	126	110
Variable costs (per 100 litres)			
Direct material costs	11	25	20
Direct labour costs	30	36	24
Mixing costs	32	20	36
Other variable costs	12	15	10

The cost of direct labour is £3 an hour and the variable cost of mixing is £4 an hour. In any one week, direct labour hours are restricted to 8000 hours and mixing machine hours are restricted to 5900 hours.

Due to contractual arrangements the company must produce exactly 25 000 litres of undercoat each week. There is a maximum weekly demand for emulsion paint of 35 000 litres and for gloss paint of 29 000 litres.

(a) Formulate the linear programming problem to determine the weekly production levels for emulsion and gloss paint that maximize contribution to profit.
(b) Solve the problem graphically. State the optimum weekly production levels and the corresponding contribution to profit.
(c) Calculate by how much the sales price of emulsion paint must change from its current level before the optimal solution will change.
(d) Suppose that the labour force is prepared to work overtime at a premium of £1 per overtime hour worked. Would it be profitable to work overtime? If so, how many hours would you recommend should be worked, and what would be the extra profit from these hours?

(ACCA Level 2: June 1988)

NETWORK ANALYSIS

20.1 NETWORK DIAGRAMS

Network analysis is a method used in the management of projects involving several (possibly hundreds) of activities related to each other in specified, and possibly complex, ways. The method is based on the drawing of a diagram to represent the activities and the relationships between them. In order to draw the diagram it is necessary also to have estimates of the durations of the constituent activities.

With modern computer facilities the drawing of the diagram can be eliminated by entering the data about durations of activities and relationships between them into a suitable piece of software and obtaining from it the various items of management information discussed in this chapter. In particular, reference will be made at various points in the chapter to the software QSB+ by Chang and Sullivan (see bibliograhy) which can be used to handle network analysis problems.

To understand what such software is doing it is important to go through the procedures for drawing diagrams as explained below. One of the benefits of using network analysis is the encouragement to clear thinking about the project which is required to set up the data in the form necessary for drawing a diagram, or delivering input to software which operates on the same principles as the diagram. In particular, it is necessary to identify the relationships between activities.

Network analysis allows the total time required to complete a project to be determined, and shows how much time to spare (or *float*) each activity has without completion in this time being prevented. Activities having no time to spare are called *critical activities* and any set of critical activities which must *all* be completed in order to finish the project constitute a *critical path*. The critical activities are of particular importance to decisions regarding the conduct of the project. Network analysis allows decisions to be made about use of resources. Such decisions might be made with a view to achieving as even a use of resources as possible over the life of the project, to minimizing the cost of the project, or to completing the project in the least possible time. Network analysis also allows a constant check to be maintained on the progress of the project and enables the updating of plans as the project proceeds and some activities take

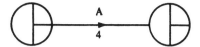

Figure 20.1 The arrow represents activity A. Its duration appears by the arrow.

times other than those estimated. It is also possible to take formal account of uncertainties about durations of activities through incorporation of probabilities into the construction of the network. The version involving probabilities is called *project evaluation and review technique* or *PERT*.

The range of applications of network analysis is very wide, including engineering, construction, manufacturing, and management of administrative systems. It is possible to have a computer terminal or PC on location at a building site, say, to enable the network to be constantly updated and a check kept on the current state of critical activities and expected completion time.

There are two main notations used in network diagrams. The first is the *arrow diagram* notation where each activity is represented by a line (or *arrow*) joining two circles (or *nodes*). The nodes represent transitions between activities, which are referred to as *events*. The duration of an activity is written by the arrow representing it. Figure 20.1 shows an event *A* in arrow diagram notation, the duration of *A* being four days. The reason for dividing the nodes in the manner shown will become clear as the discussion proceeds.

The other main notation is the *activity-on-node* (or *AON*) *diagram* notation. Here each activity is represented by a circle and the lines represent the events which are the transitions between activities. The duration of an activity is written by each of the arrows emerging from its node. Figure 20.2 shows activity *A* in AON notation, assuming it to have two successors. It will be noted that the name of the activity has been written in the left-hand section of the node in this case.

We consider now an example to illustrate the drawing and basic analysis of network diagrams.

Example 20.1.1 The following table gives data for a simple project:

Activity	Preceding activity	Duration (days)
A	—	3
B	—	3
C	—	7
D	A	1
E	D, J	2
F	B	2
G	C	1
J	B	1

(a) Draw a network diagram for the project.
(b) Draw up a table, with a list of activities, durations, earliest start and finish times, latest start and finish times, and total floats.

(CIMA Stage 1: Nov. 1991)

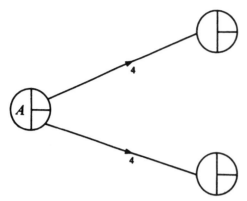

Figure 20.2 The node represents activity A. Its duration is on each emerging arrow.

ANSWER

(a) In order to illustrate the two notations we shall draw and analyse both the arrow diagram and the activity-on-node diagram for this network. For answering the question as posed, either one would be acceptable.

The arrow diagram is shown in Fig. 20.3.

(b) In order to answer this part of the question, we must number the nodes. (In some cases, as we shall see later, the activities in an arrow diagram are *defined* by the numbers of the nodes at their ends. In such cases the node numbering step is clearly unnecessary.) The numbering begins with the starting node as number 1 and then goes from left to right. At each step a node should be numbered only if it has no arrows coming into it from unnumbered nodes. The numbering in Fig. 20.4 is an acceptable one for this example but it is not unique. For instance nodes 2, 3, and 4 could be rearranged among themselves.

Having numbered the nodes, we can find the earliest starting times by performing a *forward pass* through the network. This involves working through the nodes in numerical order writing in the top right quadrant of each one the earliest time that activities beginning there can start. Figure 20.5 shows the arrow diagram with the earliest starting times inserted. Note that where there is more than one arrow coming into a node it is the *largest*

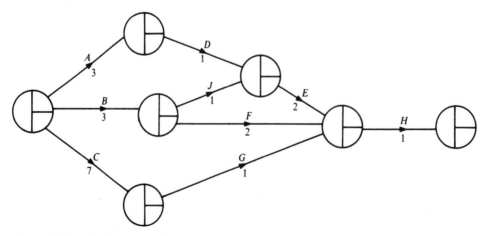

Figure 20.3 A basic arrow diagram.

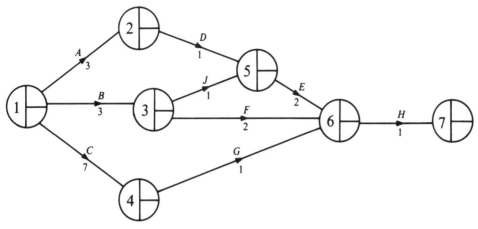

Figure 20.4 The nodes are numbered.

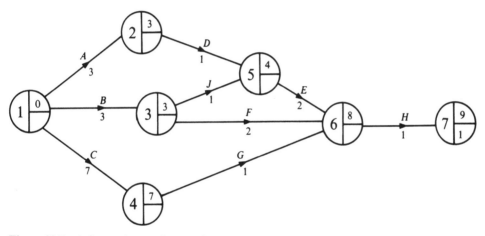

Figure 20.5 A forward pass gives earliest starting times.

accumulated value which must be entered, as *all* activities ending on the node must be completed before those beginning there can start.

Next, in order to find the latest finishing times, we perform a *backward pass* through the network. This involves working through the nodes in reverse numerical order writing in the bottom right quadrant of each one the latest time that activities terminating on that node can afford to finish if the whole project is not to be delayed beyond the completion time found on the forward pass. Figure 20.6 shows the arrow diagram with the latest finish times inserted. Note that where there is more than one arrow emerging from a node, as at nodes 1 and 3 in the example, it is the *smallest* number which is entered. Thus the latest finish time is decided by the most urgent of the activities beginning at that node.

From Fig. 20.6 we can deduce all the results required to answer part (b) of the question. Durations, earliest start times, and latest finish times can be read directly from the diagram. To obtain the earliest finish time of an activity we must add its duration to its earliest start time. To obtain latest start times we must subtract durations from latest finish times. To obtain floats we need to subtract duration and earliest start time from latest finish time.

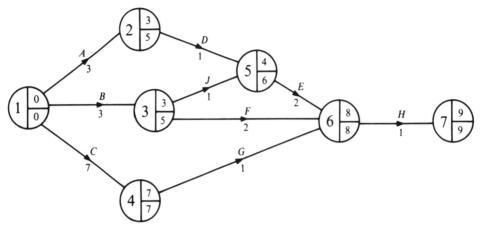

Figure 20.6   A backward pass gives latest finishing times.

Thus we obtain the following as the answer to part (b). The reader should check carefully to see that the values given follow from the procedures indicated above.

Activity	A	B	C	D	E	F	G	H	J
Duration	3	3	7	1	2	2	1	1	1
Earliest start	0	0	0	3	4	3	7	8	3
Earliest finish	3	3	3	4	6	5	8	9	4
Latest start	2	2	0	5	6	6	7	8	5
Latest finish	5	5	7	6	8	8	8	9	6
Float	2	2	0	2	2	3	0	0	2

The AON diagram for the example is shown in Fig. 20.7. In this type of diagram it is necessary to include an end node in order to show the duration of the concluding activity or activities. Also if, as in this example, there are several activities having no predecessors, it is usual to show a start node as well so that the network begins at a single node.

We can now go through a forward pass and a backward pass using a procedure which is from a computational point of view the same as for the arrow diagram. (It is not essential to

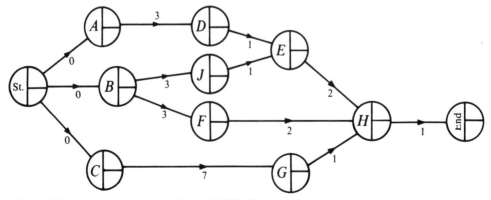

Figure 20.7   A basic Activity on Node (AON) diagram.

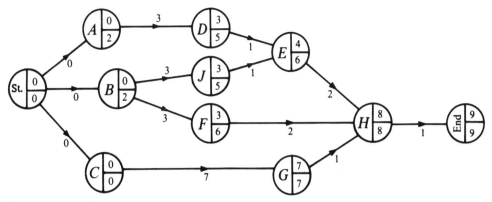

Figure 20.8 AON diagram showing earliest and latest starting times.

number the nodes in an AON diagram, but the order in which the nodes are dealt with in the forward pass must necessarily be such that no node can be given an earliest starting time if it has an arrow coming into it from an unnumbered node.) There is, however, an important point of difference in the interpretation of the number which appears in the bottom right quadrant after the backward pass. This number is now the latest starting time for the activity on that node. Figure 20.8 shows the AON diagram for the example after the forward pass and backward pass.

From this diagram we can read off directly the durations, earliest start times, and latest start times of the activities. The earliest finishing time for each activity can be found by adding its duration to its earliest start time, and the latest finishing time can be found by adding its duration to its latest start time. The float of an activity is found by subtracting its earliest start time from its latest start time, i.e. by finding the difference in the two numbers in its node.

The reader should check that these rules lead to the answer to part (b) given in the table above.

Exercise 20.1.1 Consider the project specified by the following table:

Activity	Predecessor(s)	Duration (days)
A	—	30
B	—	38
C	—	18
D	A	12
E	A	28
F	B, D	18
G	C	16

(a) Draw an arrow diagram and carry out a forward pass and a backward pass through the network.
(b) Draw an AON diagram and carry out a forward pass and a backward pass through the network.
(c) Draw up a table showing for each activity its earliest start time, latest start time, earliest finish time, latest finish time, and its float.

20.2 CRITICAL PATH ANALYSIS

In our answer to Example 20.1.1 we found that activities C, G, and H had floats of zero. This meant there was no time to spare in relation to these activities if completion of the project as a whole was not to be delayed. Such activities, as mentioned in the introduction to Sec. 20.1, are called critical activities and the path C–G–H through the network is called a critical path. The critical activities are important because if we want to complete the project faster than currently, then it is these activities which have to be carried out quicker. Obtaining faster completion will involve cost such as overtime payments to workers or hiring of extra equipment, so it is important to know into which activities such additional resources should be directed in order to receive maximum benefit. The purpose of speeding up the project could be to save money on project overheads, to avoid a penalty clause in the contract, or perhaps to earn a bonus for early completion.

This section concerns critical path analysis, where we consider speeding up a project in order to achieve some monetary benefit at each stage. The process is continued until the optimum situation from a financial point of view is reached. Complications arise in that as critical activities are speeded up more and more, then other activities also become critical and further speeding up of the project requires time to be saved on *all* critical paths.

The method is explained by means of an example.

Example 20.2.1 The table below represents a project to install a new computerized administrative system in an organization. The activities are described by their commencement and termination nodes in the network diagram corresponding to the table.

Activity	Estimated normal duration (days)	Normal cost (£)	Max. days savable	Extra cost (£) per day saved
1–2	9	600	2	80
1–3	5	1100	3	240
1–4	7	900	4	140
2–5	9	1600	4	220
3–4	8	1600	4	220
4–5	6	400	4	80
4–6	7	400	3	30
5–6	4	600	2	150
6–7	5	700	0	—

There is also a site overhead of £200 for each day the project is running.

(a) Draw the network diagram and show the earliest starting time and latest finishing time for each activity on it.
(b) State the normal duration and normal cost of the project and the critical path.
(c) Find the number of days in which the project should be completed in order to minimize total cost.
(d) State the duration and cost of each individual activity when the project is completed at minimum total cost, and state the minimum total cost.

Answer

(a) The way the activities are specified in this question makes the arrow diagram the more natural network to draw. (It would, however, be possible to deduce the relationships between the activities from the table and use an AON diagram.) The arrow diagram for normal completion of the project, including earliest start times and latest finishing times, and with the critical path emphasized by heavy print and double arrow heads, is shown in Fig. 20.9.

(b) The normal duration is 28 days. The normal cost is found by summing the normal costs of all the activities and adding a further £5600 for 28 days of overhead at £200 per day. The result is a figure of £13 500.

(c) Of the critical activities the cheapest to speed up is 4–5. First save *one* of the four available days on 4–5.

The reason for stopping at one is that 1–2 and 2–5 have a float of only one and become critical when this saving has been made, as shown in Fig. 20.10. There would therefore be no further saving on the project time from further reducing 4–5 alone. Cutting this one day costs £80 and saves a day of overhead costing £200. So the net saving is £120.

(Note that the float on activity 4–6 has been reduced from three days to two days. The project duration is now 27 days.)

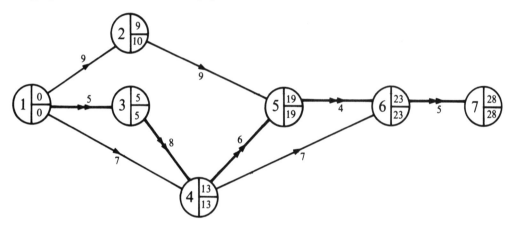

Figure 20.9 Arrow diagram showing the initial critical path.

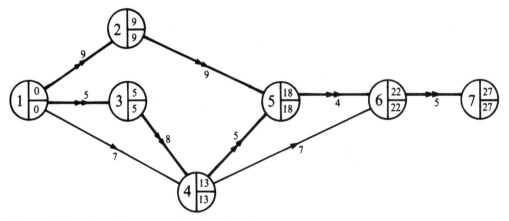

Figure 20.10 The critical path when duration is reduced to 27.

At the second step the cheapest speeding up that can be done is to save both the available days on 5–6. This costs $2 \times £150 = £300$ and saves $2 \times £200 = £400$. So the net saving is £100. The situation following this step is as shown in Fig. 20.11.

(Note that the float on activity 4–6 has now also disappeared. The project duration is 25 days.) Next save two days on 1–2, 4–5, and 4–6 all together. This reduces all three critical paths and costs $2 \times £(80 + 80 + 30) = £380$ while saving $2 \times £200 = £400$ and so giving a net saving of £20. We are restricted to two days because this is all that can be saved on 1–2 even though 4–5 and 4–6 both have a third day available. This results in a project time of 23 days as shown in Fig. 20.12.

No further saving is possible since on the critical path 1–2–5–6–7 the only activity not at its minimum (or *crash*) duration is 2–5 and this costs £220 per day to speed up. So the number of days required for minimum cost completion is 23.

(d) The required table is as follows:

Activity	1–2	1–3	1–4	2–5	3–4	4–5	4–6	5–6	6–7
Duration	7	5	7	9	8	3	5	2	5
Cost (£)	760	1100	900	1600	1600	640	460	900	700

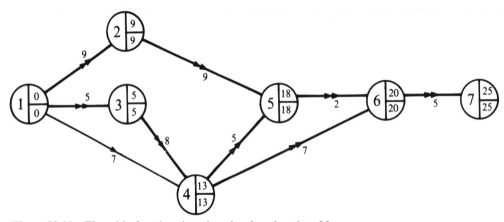

Figure 20.11 The critical paths when duration is reduced to 25.

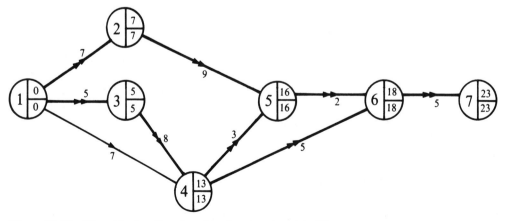

Figure 20.12 The critical paths when duration is reduced to 23.

Total cost is the sum of these plus 23 days of overhead at £200 which gives £8660 + £4600 = £13 260.

This agrees with subtracting the savings of £120, £100, and £20 from the normal total cost of £13 500.

Note that the solution to this example has been set out very fully for explanation purposes with a new diagram being drawn after each time reduction. This is an inefficient approach to answering such questions and the reader is advised to develop the facility to draw just one initial diagram and keep track of changes in floats and critical paths as savings are made, without further drawing.

Exercise 20.2.1 An on-line computer system has recently been installed in the accounts department of a television broadcasting company. The activities involved in introducing a computerized accounting function on this system are listed below together with their normal durations and costs. Since it would be possible to shorten the overall duration by crashing certain activities at extra cost, the relevant details are also included. In addition, there will be a weekly charge of £2500 to cover overheads.

Activity	immediate Predecessors	Normal Duration (weeks)	Cost (£)	Crash Duration (weeks)	Cost (£)
A	—	3	3000	2	4000
B	—	6	6000	—	—
C	A	4	8000	1	11 000
D	B	2	1500	—	—
E	A	8	4000	5	5500
F	B	4	3000	2	5000
G	C, D	2	2000	—	—
H	F	3	3000	1	6000

The crash time represents the shortest time in which the activity can be completed given the use of more costly methods of completion. Assume that it is possible to reduce the normal time to crash time in steps of one week and that the extra cost will be proportional to the time saved.

(a) Using the normal durations and costs construct an activity network for the introduction of a computerized accounts system. Determine the critical path and associated total cost.
(b) Activities E and F have to be supervised by the chief accountant who will not be available for the first seven weeks of the project period. Both activities however can be supervised simultaneously.

   Determine whether or not this will affect the completion date and, if so, state how it will be affected.
(c) Assuming that the chief accountant will be available whenever required and that all resources necessary to implement the crashing procedures will also be available, determine the minimum cost of undertaking this project.

(ACCA Level 2: Nov. 1987)

20.3 COMPLETING PROJECTS IN MINIMUM TIME

Sometimes the focus of interest when completing a project is to get it finished in the least possible time, even if this does not mean the least possible cost. This could be the case if, for example, equipment being used for the project were urgently needed for work elsewhere. The gain from having the equipment available for this other work could more than outweigh the loss from not completing the project in hand at minimum cost. Given that minimum time is the objective, it is, of course, necessary that this is achieved at the least possible associated cost. One way to find the minimum completion time for a project is to start with the normal completion and gradually speed up critical activities until the minimum time is reached. Thus in Example 20.2.1 we could have gone on reducing the times for critical activities, beyond the point where minimum cost completion had been achieved until the least possible time was achieved. In order to ensure least possible associated cost it would be necessary at each step to speed up in such a way that overall cost is increased as little as possible.

However, if minimum time is the focus of interest, there is another and more efficient way of proceeding. This is first to crash every activity to its minimum duration and consider the resulting network. This network will certainly show us the minimum duration for the project. It will, however, probably be a highly wasteful way of achieving this. So to complete the solution we need to consider the activities which are *not* critical and allow the ones which were most expensive to speed up to slow down as much as possible without the overall duration being increased above the minimum.

To illustrate the two approaches to the problem we return in Example 20.3.1 to the data in Example 20.2.1 and find by both methods the minimum duration with its least possible associated cost.

Example 20.3.1 The table below represents a project to install a new computerized administrative system in an organization. The activities are described by their commencement and termination nodes in the network diagram corresponding to the table.

Activity	Estimated normal duration (days)	Normal cost (£)	Max. days savable	Extra cost (£) per day saved
1–2	9	600	2	80
1–3	5	1100	3	240
1–4	7	900	4	140
2–5	9	1600	4	220
3–4	8	1600	4	220
4–5	6	400	4	80
4–6	7	400	3	30
5–6	4	600	2	150
6–7	5	700	0	—

There is also a site overhead of £200 for each day of the project.

(a) Find the minimum completion time for this project and its least possible associated cost by applying gradual time reductions from the normal completion situation.
(b) Find the minimum completion time for this project and its least possible associated cost by initially crashing all activities.

Answer
(a) Figure 20.13 repeats the minimum cost completion situation in 23 days as found in answer to Example 20.2.1.

The cheapest combination of critical activities that can usefully be speeded up is 2–5 with 4–5 and 4–6. There is one day available before 4–5 and 4–6 are reduced to their crash times.

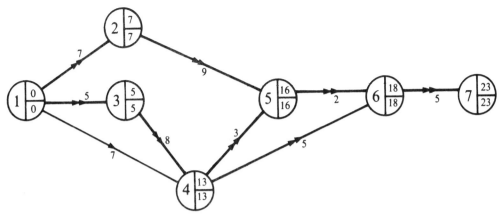

Figure 20.13 Arrow diagram for the minimum cost completion.

This reduces total time to 22 days and costs £330 while saving £200 in overheads, so net extra cost is £130. The situation is as shown in Fig. 20.14.

Next save three days on 2–5 in combination with 3–4. After this, 2–5 is reduced to its crash time, so no further time savings are possible on the critical path 1–2–5–6–7 and the project has reached its minimum duration of 19 days. This final time saving costs $3 \times (£220 + £220) = £1320$ while reducing overheads by £600 so the net increase in costs is £720. (Note in passing that the reduction in 3–4 has reduced the float on 1–4, the only non-critical activity, by three days to three days.) The situation is as shown in Fig. 20.15.

So the conclusion of the matter is that the minimum duration of this project is 19 days with a least possible associated cost of £13 260 + £130 + £720 = £14 110.

(b) We begin this method by crashing all activities to give the network shown in Fig. 20.16. It is immediately clear from this diagram that the minimum duration is 19 days. The only critical path is 1–2–5–6–7. The total cost is readily found from the table given in the question to be £11 810 + 19 × £200 = £11 810 + £3800 = £15 610.

Of the non-critical activities the most expensive to speed up was 1–2 at £240 per day. It has a float of four days so let it take its normal duration of five days. This reduces the cost by £720. The situation at this stage is shown in Fig. 20.17.

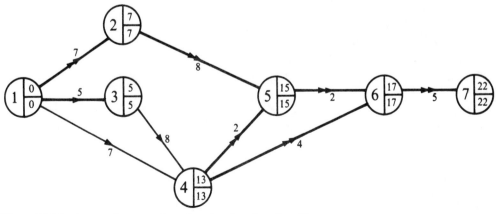

Figure 20.14 Arrow diagram when duration is reduced to 22.

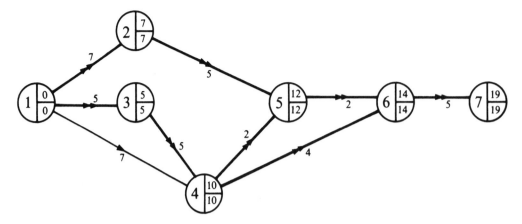

Figure 20.15   The minimum time completion.

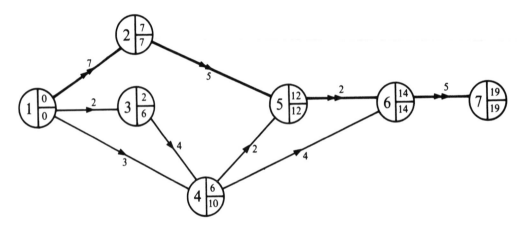

Figure 20.16   Instant determination of minimum time by crashing all activities.

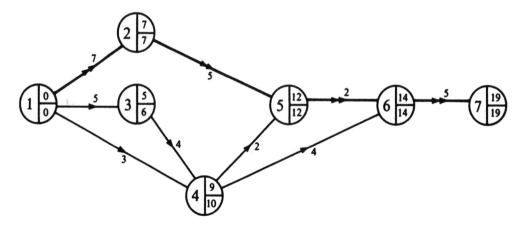

Figure 20.17   Saving on costs by allowing 1–3 a duration of 5.

The next most expensive to speed up was 3–4 at £220 per day. With 1–3 slowed down, there is now a float of only one day on 3–4 so allow 3–4 to take five days. This saves £220 and the paths 1–3–4–5 and 1–3–4–6 are now critical. The situation at this stage is shown in Fig. 20.18.

The only remaining non-critical activity is 1–4 which has a float of seven days. So let it take its normal duration of seven days giving a saving of £560.

As all activities are now critical except 1–4, which is at its minimum duration, no further slowing down is possible if the project is to be completed in 19 days. We are back to the situation seen already in Fig. 20.15.

The minimum duration is found to be 19 days with a least possible associated cost of £15 610 − £720 − £220 − £560 = £14 110.

Exercise 20.3.1 You are a management accountant responsible for the time and cost control of a site-based project. Activities have been specified and normal and 'crash' completion times and costs have been estimated as shown in the table below.

Activity code	Normal total activity cost (£)	Normal completion time (days)	Extra cost for crash completion (£)	Crash completion time (days)
10–20	100	10	20	8
10–30	160	15	10	14
10–40	90	7	—	7
10–50	220	8	30	6
20–100	110	9	12	8
30–60	—	—	—	—
30—90	200	15	40	13
40–60	300	21	70	19
50–70	270	17	80	16
100–120	130	9	15	8
60–80	90	10	20	9
60–90	160	18	30	15
70–90	100	8	—	8
80–90	—	—	—	—
70–110	70	9	20	8
90–120	300	12	60	10
110–120	200	6	40	5

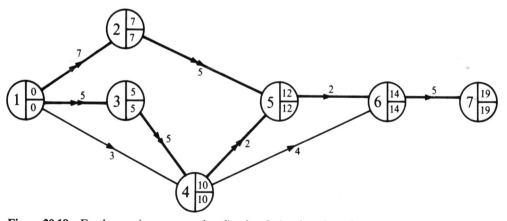

Figure 20.18 Further saving on costs by allowing 5–4 a duration of 5.

The project has a daily cost of £40 for site charges. An activity may only be undertaken at its normal or crash time.

(a) Draw an arrow diagram (network) and show the project duration and cost under its normal conditions.
(b) Show, with workings, the effect on project time, cost, and critical path (if any) of undertaking all tasks at fully crashed time.
(c) Show with workings and explanation how the project time in part (b) can be equalled and the cost reduced by crashing only some of the activities.

(CIMA Stage 3: Nov. 1988)

The software QSB+ is very well suited to dealing with problems of the type covered in this section. It is a menu-driven system, and having entered, the user should select the option listed as

Project Scheduling—CPM

The user is then invited to specify the activities in the network with their predecessors, normal durations, and crash durations. The output then takes the form of a listing of the activities with their earliest and latest times and floats for normal duration.

The opportunity to crash activities is then offered and revised tables of results are produced.

20.4 RESOURCE ALLOCATION

In this section we shall consider resource allocation within projects. The discussion will be in terms of manpower resources, but the principles apply to any other kinds of resource. Bar charts will be used to indicate which combinations of activities are in progress at various stages of the project. This is useful as it enables us to look at the possibility of delaying the start of some activities in order to vary the resource utilization over the life of the project. The explanation will once again be given by means of an example.

Example 20.4.1 The following table shows the activities involved in a particular project with, in each case, the duration of the activity, its predecessors, and the number of men needed to work on it each day it is in progress.

Activity	A	B	C	D	E	F	G	H	I	J
Duration (days)	9	10	4	10	5	9	7	8	7	8
Predecessor(s)	—	—	B	A	A	A	E	D	C, F	G, H, I
Men required	14	6	12	10	14	12	12	10	14	16

(a) Draw an AON diagram for the project and state which activities are on the critical path.
(b) Draw a bar chart showing the combinations of activities in progress on each day of the project, assuming all activities to begin at the earliest possible time.
(c) Draw a graph showing the number of men used each day over the life of the project.
(d) State the total number of man-days used in the project and the largest number of men needed on any single day. Indicate how this peak might be reduced by rescheduling the starts of some of the activities.

ANSWER

(a) The network diagram for the project is shown in Fig. 20.19.
    The critical path activities are seen to be A, D, H, and J.
(b) Figure 20.20 is the required bar chart showing the combinations of activities in progress on each day during the life of the project.

Using the bar chart in Fig. 20.20 and the information given in the question on manpower needs, we can draw up the following table showing the numbers of men needed on each of the 35 days of the project if we assume that each activity starts at the earliest possible time.

Days	Activities in progress	Number of men required
1–9	A, B	20
10	B, D, E, F	42
11–14	C, D, E, F	48
15–18	D, F, G	34
19	D, G, I	36
20–21	G, H, I	36
22–25	H, I	24
26–27	H	10
28–35	J	16

(c) The graph showing manpower requirements over the life of the project is given as Fig. 20.21.
(d) The total number of man-days used in the project is represented by the area under the graph in Fig. 20.21. It can be calculated directly from the information given in the question as

$$9 \times 14 + 10 \times 6 + 4 \times 12 + 10 \times 10 + 5 \times 14 + 9 \times 12 + 7 \times 12 + 8 \times 10 + 7 \times 14 + 8 \times 16$$
$$= 126 + 60 \quad + 48 \quad + 100 \quad + 70 \quad + 108 \quad + 84 \quad + 80 \quad + 98 \quad + 128$$
$$= 902.$$

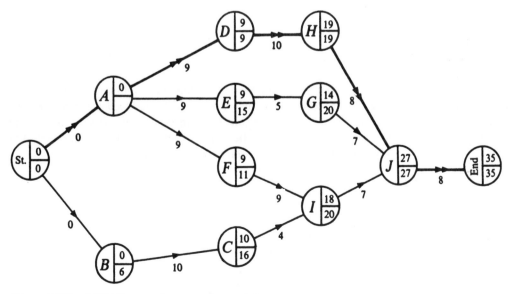

Figure 20.19 AON diagram for normal completion.

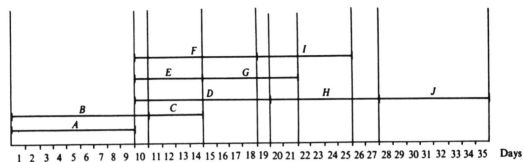

Figure 20.20 Diagram showing activities in progress on each day.

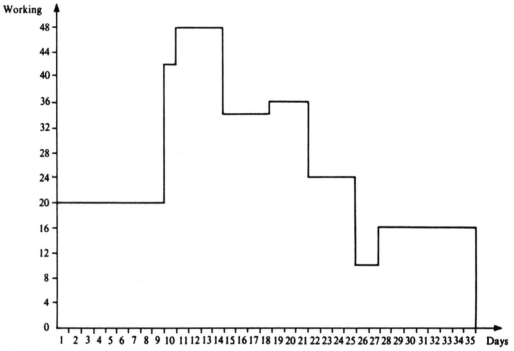

Figure 20.21 Graph showing number of men working on each day.

From Fig. 20.21 we see that the maximum manpower requirement is for 48 men on days 11–14.

From the bar chart in Fig. 20.20 we see that this peak could be reduced if we relaxed the requirement that each activity starts as early as possible. If, for instance, the starts of E and F are postponed until day 11, the start of C until day 16, the start of I until day 20, and the start of G until day 20, then we obtain a new table of manpower requirements as follows:

Days	Activities in progress	Number of men required
1–9	A, B	20
10	B, D	16
11–15	D, E, F	36
16–19	C, D, F	34
20–26	G, H, I	36
27	H	10
28–35	J	16

The peak manpower requirement is seen to have been reduced to 36 men on days 11–15 and 20–26.

Exercise 20.4.1 Saturnite plc is to initiate a project to study the feasibility of a new product. The end result of the feasibility project will be a report recommending the action to be taken for the new product. The activities to be carried out to complete the feasibility project are given in the table below.

Activity	Description	Immediate predecessors	Expected time (weeks)	Number of staff required
A	Preliminary design	—	5	3
B	Market research	—	3	2
C	Obtain engineering quotes	A	2	2
D	Construct prototype	A	5	5
E	Prepare marketing material	A	3	3
F	Costing	C	2	2
G	Product testing	D	4	5
H	Pilot testing	B, E	6	4
I	Pricing estimates	H	2	1
J	Final report	F, G, I	6	2

(a) Draw a network for the scheme of activities set out above. Determine the critical path and the shortest duration of the project.
(b) Assuming the project starts at time zero and that each activity commences at the earliest start date, construct a chart showing the number of staff required at any one time for this project.
(c) The management of Saturnite has decided that it does not want more than nine staff involved in this project at any one time. Describe how this can be achieved within the shortest duration time found in part (a). How many weeks of this project would require all nine members of staff.

(ACCA Level 2: Dec. 1988)

20.5 UNCERTAIN ACTIVITY TIMES

In all that has been done so far the estimates of activity durations have been used as if they were the known durations of the activities. In reality, there will almost always be some uncertainty associated with these estimates. In this final section we consider quantifying this uncertainty by means of probabilities. This brings us to the method known as project evaluation and review technique or PERT. Once again the explanation is given by using an example.

Example 20.5.1 A market research department plans a questionnaire survey. The following table shows the tasks involved, the immediately preceding tasks, and for each task duration the most likely estimate, the optimistic estimate, and the pessimistic estimate.

Task		Preceding tasks	Duration in days		
			Most likely (m)	Optimistic (a)	Pessimistic (b)
A	Design of questionnaire	—	3	2	4
B	Sampling design	—	12	10	20
C	Pilot survey	A	5	4	12
D	Interviewer recruitment	B	4	2	6
E	Interviewer training	D, A	3	3	3
F	Interviewer allocation	B	4	3	5
G	Interviews undertaken	C, E, F	10	8	18
H	Data entry on computer	G	3	2	4
I	Interviewer debriefing	G	2	2	2
J	Data analysis	H	5	4	6
K	Write report	I, J	4	2	12

Using the project evaluation and review technique (PERT) the mean time, μ, and standard deviation, σ, for the duration of each task are estimated from the most likely (m), optimistic (a), pessimistic (b) estimates by using the formulae:

$$\mu = (4m + a + b)/6$$
$$\sigma = (b - a)/6$$

(a) For each task, find the mean duration and standard deviation.
(b) Draw a network for this survey and use the mean times to find the critical path.
(c) Determine the mean and standard deviation of the critical path duration.
(d) What is the probability that the length of the critical path exceeds 50 days? State any assumptions you make.

(ACCA Level 2: Dec. 1990)

ANSWER
(a) Using the formulae given in the question, the means and standard deviations of the activity durations are seen to be as follows:

Activity	A	B	C	D	E	F	G	H	I	J	K
Mean (days)	3	13	6	4	3	4	11	3	2	5	5
Standard deviation	1/3	5/3	4/3	2/3	0	1/3	5/3	1/3	0	1/3	5/3

(b) The AON network diagram is shown in Fig. 20.22. The critical path is seen from Fig. 20.22 to comprise the activities B, D, E, G, H, J, and K.
(c) The mean value of the critical path duration is 44 days. To find the standard deviation of the critical path duration we must add the variances of the critical path activities and then find the square root of the result. The sum of the variances of B, D, E, G, H, J, and K is $25/9 + 4/9 + 25/9 + 1/9 + 25/9 = 80/9$. The square root of this is 2.98, so we can regard the standard deviation of the critical path duration as being three days.
(d) The calculation of standard deviation in part (c) is based on the assumption that the activity durations are independent of each other so that their variances are additive.
    In order to find the probability asked for in this part of the question we need to make the further assumption that the durations are normally distributed. On this assumption the

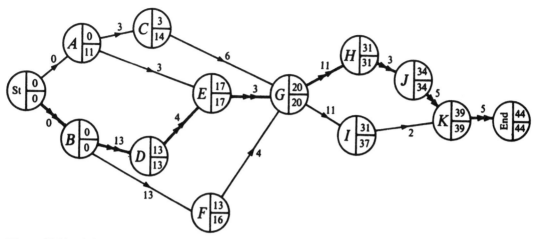

Figure 20.22 AON diagram for normal completion.

question is asking for the probability that a normal variable will exceed its mean by 2 standard deviations (since $(50-44)/3=2$) and this probability is found from the table of the normal distribution in Appendix 2 to be 0.022.

Exercise 20.5.1 A maufacturing company is planning to introduce a new product for sale in the market. The table below provides a list of the activities required to plan and control this marketing project effectively.

Activity		Immediate predecessors	Expected duration (days)
A	Initial discussions	—	6
B	Product design	A	22
C	Market survey	A	17
D	Market evaluation	C	3
E	Product costing	B	9
F	Sales plan	C	12
G	Product pricing	D, E	4
H	Prototype construction	F, G	22
I	Market information preparation	B	15
J	Prototype testing	H, I	17

(a) Draw a network to represent the various activities of the marketing project.
(b) Determine the critical path and minimum project time.
(c) It can be assumed that the expected durations of some of the activities are normally distributed, although the remaining activities are known with certainty. The standard deviation of those activities which are uncertain are as follows:

Activity	B	E	H	I	J
Standard deviation (days)	3	1	2.5	2.5	2

Determine a 90 per cent confidence interval for the duration of the critical path activities for the marketing project. State any assumption made.
(d) If the project takes longer than 84 days, the company will incur the loss of some potential income.
Determine the probability, to two significant figures, that this loss will take place.

(ACCA Level 2: Dec. 1989)

Problems of the type covered in this section can be dealt with by the software QSB+ if the user chooses the option

Project Scheduling—PERT

Opportunity is then given to input activity names and relationships along with optimistic, most likely, and pessimistic estimates of durations. The output is a listing of earliest and latest times for the activities, expected duration of the critical path, and its standard deviation.

TEST EXERCISES

20.1 The table below shows the activities involved in a project with their durations and their predecessors.

Activity	A	B	C	D	E	F	G	H	I	J
Predecessor(s)	—	A	A	B, C, E, G	A	A	F	F	F	D, H, I
Duration (weeks)	5	10	10	3	6	12	15	8	7	3

(a) Draw an arrow diagram and carry out a forward pass and a backward pass through the network.
(b) Draw an AON diagram and carry out a forward pass and a backward pass through the network.
(c) Draw up a table showing for each activity its earliest start time, latest start time, earliest finish time, latest finish time, and its float.

20.2 The Airdale Electronic Company has been awarded a contract to develop radar components for the armed forces of an overseas country. The development manager of the company has analysed the requirements of the contract and has split the overall project into eight separate activities. The following table gives the normal time to complete each activity, the normal cost of each activity, and each activity's immediate predecessors.

Activity	Immediate predecessors	Normal duration (months)	Normal cost (£000)
A	—	4	20
B	—	5	20
C	A	2	8
D	A	3	15
E	B, C	3	12
F	B, C	4	24
G	D, E	5	10
H	F	2	12

In addition to the above costs there is a penalty cost of £10 000 per month for each month that the overall project exceeds 12 months.

(a) Using the normal durations and costs construct an activity network for the project. Determine the critical path and the associated total cost.

(b) Determine the total float of each activity. Explain clearly what this means.
(c) The development manager is aware that six of the activities can be shortened by bringing in extra resources. The following table shows the minimum durations and the extra cost required to attain this minimum duration.

Activity	Minimum duration (months)	Extra cost (£000)
B	3	4
D	2	4
E	2	6
F	3	2
G	3	8
H	1	4

Assume that it is possible to reduce the normal to minimum time in steps of one month and that the extra cost is proportional to the time saved.
  (i) Find the minimum project time and the minimum cost of attaining this minimum project time.
  (ii) What is the minimum overall cost of the project? State the associated activity durations.

(ACCA Level 2: Dec. 1991)

20.3 The table below shows the activities involved in a construction project. It indicates the relationships between the activities, their estimated durations and also, in each case, the number of men required to work on the activity every day it is in progress.

Activity	Estimated duration (days)	Immediate predecessors	Men required
A	10	—	6
B	32	A	5
C	8	E	7
D	24	C	8
E	14	A	6
F	28	E	7
G	8	I, D, F	5
H	12	E	6
I	4	E	3
J	12	H, I	7
K	8	A	4
L	8	B, K	5
M	9	L, J, G	7

(a) Draw a network diagram and show on it the earliest starting times and latest finishing times of the activities.
(b) State which path is the critical path.
(c) State the total duration of the project.
(d) Draw a bar chart showing which activities are in progress during each day of the project, on the assumption that every activity begins at the earliest possible moment.
(e) Making the same assumption as in part (d), draw a graph showing the number of men being used on each day of the project.

20.4 The production manager at Gemini Machines Limited has been asked to present information about the times and costs for the development of a new machine that the company may choose to manufacture. The managing director requires accurate time and cost estimates since the project will involve a fixed-fee contract offering no provisions for later renegotiation, even in the event of modifications.

Activity		Preceding activities	Duration (weeks)	Cost (£000)
A	Obtain engineering quotes	I	1	4
B	Sub-contract specifications	A, J	4	8
C	Purchase of raw materials	—	3	24
D	Construct prototype	I	5	15
E	Final drawings	I	2	6
F	Fabrication	H	6	30
G	Special machine study	—	4	12
H	Sub-contract work	B, E	8	40
I	Preliminary design	G	2	8
J	Vendor evaluation	C, D	3	3

The production manager has been asked to identify the critical activities, to determine the shortest project duration, and to provide a week-by-week cost schedule.

(a) Draw a network to represent the interrelationships between the activities indicated, and insert earliest and latest event times throughout.
(b) Determine the critical path and the shortest possible duration of the project.
(c) Assuming each activity commences at the earliest start data, and that for each activity the cost is incurred evenly over its duration, construct a week-by-week schedule of cash flows.

The project is to be financed by £50 000 available initially, a further £50 000 available at the start of week 9, and the final £50 000 available from week 20.

Identify any particular problems and suggest solutions.

(ACCA Level 2: June 1991)

20.5 An engineering firm is tendering for a contract to supply a steel fabrication with a target duration of 60 days. The tasks have been analysed as shown in the table.

Task	Immediate predecessors	Duration (days)
A	—	10
B	—	12
C	A	10
D	A	9
E	A	13
F	A, B	17
G	C	12
H	C, D	14
I	E	13
J	G, H	12
K	H	10
L	H, I	14
M	H, I, F	13

(a) You are required to calculate the expected project duration and identify the critical path.

The firm is awarded the contract and starts work with all activities commencing on their earliest start times but after work on the 23rd day there is a fire which destroys all the work done on task C and the work in progress on tasks G and H. Fortunately no other completed tasks are affected but it is estimated that task M will now need 15 days. The project manager thinks that after the fire there will be variability in the task times and has made some uncertainty estimates which are shown as task standard deviations in days.

Task	Standard deviation (days)
C	0.33
F	0.82
G	0.17
H	1.33
I	2.17
J	0.50
K	2.17
L	1.33
M	0.33

Required:

(b) Calculate the new expected project duration and the critical path through the remaining activities after the fire.

(c) Calculate the probability of the project being completed on time after the fire.

(CIMA Stage 3: Nov. 1990)

21

STOCK CONTROL

21.1 COSTS ASSOCIATED WITH STOCK CONTROL

Proper control of stock costs, which are an important part of working capital for many firms, is a vital aspect of financial control. Stock can take the form of raw materials, of work-in-progress, or of finished items to be dispatched.

In this chapter we consider stock control situations of varying degrees of complexity, beginning with a very simple model in Sec. 21.2 and then moving on to situations involving discounts, lead times and variable demand patterns. The model considered in Sec. 21.2, despite its gross simplifications, is seen to be a useful starting point because it provides the basis for the more realistic models considered later. An efficient stock control system is important for the following reasons:

1. It ensures that raw material is available for the production processes.
2. It ensures that there are adequate quantities of finished goods available for dispatch to customers.
3. It enables work-in-progress to be valued.
4. It helps keep to a minimum the resources tied up in stock.
5. It helps to control wastage and pilferage of material.

The relative importance of these will vary from business to business.

At the most basic level the two areas of cost associated with stock control are, on the one hand, those resulting from ordering too often, and, on the other hand, those resulting from having individual orders which are too large. Having a lot of small orders means that less capital is tied up in stock, less storage space is needed, insurance costs are less, and there is less danger of deterioration or of obsolescence. However, having larger orders less frequently means that ordering costs are smaller, there is less vulnerability to any problems affecting the supplier, and it becomes possible to take advantage of price increases affecting the item. Also if the matters of discounts and variability in demand are taken into account, these both encourage larger orders.

Reference will be made at various points in the chapter to the software QSB+ by Chang and Sullivan (see bibliography) which can be used to handle stock control problems.

21.2 ECONOMIC ORDER QUANTITY

The economic order quantity (EOQ) model for stock control makes a number of simplifying assumptions, as specified below:

1. Demand rate is constant.
2. Orders are delivered immediately they are requested.
3. No time is (by choice) spent out of stock.
4. No discounts are available for large orders.
5. The whole of an order arrives at one moment.
6. The delivery cost for every order is the same.
7. Stock holding cost is constant (either in monetary terms or as a proportion of stock value).
8. No account is taken of the time value of money.

The formula for order size which emerges from these assumptions is what is called the EOQ. Despite the very simplistic nature of the assumptions, this order size provides a useful first approximation even for cases where they do not all apply. Moreover, an understanding of this model is helpful to the understanding of models considered in later sections where various of the assumptions are relaxed.

If the above assumptions hold, maximum stock level will occur immediately after orders are received. Figure 21.1 is the graph of stock level against time under the assumptions.

The only thing we are left to find is how many items are to be ordered in each batch. If too few items are ordered each time, there will be high ordering and delivery costs. If too many are ordered in each batch, there will be high stock holding costs. The EOQ is the quantity to order each time in order to minimize the *sum* of stock holding costs and delivery costs.

Derivation of the formula for the EOQ will be carried out as part of the following example.

Example 21.2.1 The cost of ordering stock, OC, is given by

$$OC = \frac{D \times c1}{q}$$

where D is the demand per period, $c1$ is the cost of placing an order, and q is the size of an order.

The cost of holding stock, HC, is given by

$$HC = \frac{q \times c2}{2}$$

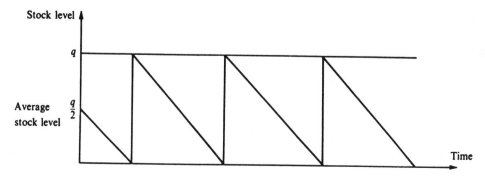

Figure 21.1 Graph of stock level against time.

where c_2 is the cost of holding a unit of stock for one period. The equation for the total cost, T, of a stock control policy is given by

$$T = \text{stock holding cost} + \text{stock ordering cost}$$

(a) Using the techniques of differentiation find the equation for the order quantity which minimizes total cost.

A firm demands 400 units of an input per period, has an order cost of £10 per order and it costs £20 to hold a unit of stock for one period.

Required:

(b) Find the order quantity which minimizes the total cost.
(c) What is the minimum total cost?
(d) Plot graphs of the stock holding cost, the stock ordering cost, and the total cost for the interval 0 to 40 at points 5 units apart.

(ACCA Level 1: June 1989)

ANSWER

(a) In order to obtain q items per period in batches of size q, the number of batches needed will be D/q.

Since each delivery costs c_1, it follows that the total delivery cost per period is $OC = D \times c_1/q$ as stated in Example 21.2.1. It is clear from Fig. 21.1 that the average stock level through the period on the assumptions given is $q/2$ items.

Since each item costs c_2 to hold it through a period, it follows that the stock holding cost for a period is $HC = q \times c_2/2$ as stated.

The minimization can be carried out as follows:

$$T = HC + OC$$

$$\frac{dT}{dq} = \frac{c_2}{2} - \frac{D \times c_1}{q^2}$$

Then $\dfrac{dT}{dq} = 0$ gives $\dfrac{c_2}{2} = \dfrac{D \times c_1}{q^2}$ so $q^2 = \dfrac{2 \times D \times c_1}{c_2}$

Hence

$$q = \sqrt{\frac{2 \times D \times c_1}{c_2}}$$

$$\frac{d^2 T}{dq^2} = \frac{2 \times D \times c_1}{q^3}$$

which is positive for any positive q. So,

$$q = \sqrt{\frac{2 \times D \times c_1}{c_2}}$$

gives the required minimum value for T and we can say that

$$q = \sqrt{\frac{2 \times D \times c_1}{c_2}} \text{ is the economic order quantity, EOQ}$$

(b) For the figures given, the order quantity which minimizes total cost is

$$q = \sqrt{\frac{2 \times 400 \times 10}{20}} = \sqrt{400} = 20$$

i.e. The best number of items to order each time is 20.

(c) In this situation $HC = 20 \times 20/2 = 200$
and $OC = 400 \times 10/20 = 200$

So total cost of stock holding and ordering is £400.

It is left as an exercise for the reader to confirm that the equality of HC and OC is not just a coincidence which has occurred for these figures. If the EOQ expression for q is substituted into both the HC formula and the OC formula, it will be found that both expressions reduce to $\sqrt{c1 \times c2 \times D/2}$. Thus

$$T = HC + OC = \sqrt{2 \times c1 \times c2 \times D}$$

(d) To plot the graphs we draw up a table of values as follows:

q	0	5	10	15	20	25	30	35	40
$OC = 4000/q$	—	800	400	267	200	160	133	114	100
$HC = 10q$	0	50	100	150	200	250	300	350	400
$T = OC + HC$	—	850	500	417	400	410	433	464	500

Figure 21.2 is the graph drawn from this table showing holding cost, ordering cost, and total cost. Note that the minimum point of the total cost curve is above the intersection of the holding cost and ordering cost curves. This corresponds to the fact that these two elements of cost are equal for the quantity that minimizes total cost.

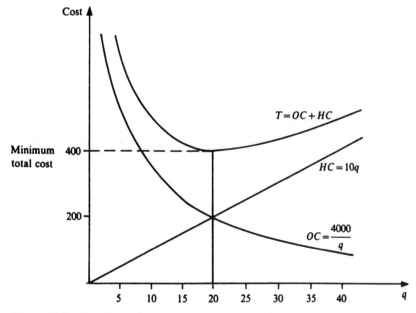

Figure 21.2 Graph showing ordering cost (OC), holding cost (HC) and total cost (T) for different re-order quantities (q).

Exercise 21.2.1 A statistician from office services estimates that a typist types at a rate of 20 words per minute for two hours a day. It is also estimated that there are on average five characters to a word. The working year has 250 days. The ribbons currently in use have a life of 200 000 characters.

(a) How many ribbons will the typist use, on average, in a year?
(b) The cost of ordering a ribbon, $c1$, is £2.50 and the cost of holding a ribbon in stock, $c2$, is £0.50 per year. If the economic order quantity (EOQ) is given by

$$EOQ = \sqrt{(2 \times c1 \times D/c2)}$$

where D is the number of ribbons used per year, find the EOQ.
(c) For an order of size q the total ordering cost, TOC, is given by

$$TOC = £D \times c1/q$$

and the total stock holding cost, TSH, is given by

$$TSH = £q \times c2/2$$

Plot TOC and TSH against order size for orders of size 6, 8, 10, and so on up to an order size of 18.
(d) On the same scale and axes as used for part (c) plot the total cost of orders against size.
(e) On your graph indicate the EOQ.

(ACCA Level 1: Dec. 1988)

The software QSB+ can be used to deal with problems of the type covered in this section. It is a menu-driven system, and having entered, the user should select the option listed as

Inventory theory

The user is invited to specify the demand, the delivery cost and the storage cost, and the program will then give the EOQ. It will also give a drawing of the delivery cost, stock holding cost, and total cost graphs.

21.2 QUANTITY DISCOUNTS

In this section assumption 4 of Sec. 21.2 is relaxed and we take into account discounts for larger orders. The effect of this change will be to encourage larger orders so that advantage can be taken of the resulting lower unit price. Larger orders will also mean lower ordering costs, but the penalty is that stock holding costs will be higher. Thus a way to assess the best policy in this case is to look for the order quantity which minimizes the *average value per item* of

purchase cost + ordering cost + stock holding cost

The situation can be represented graphically by the extension of Fig. 21.2 shown in Fig. 21.3.
The graph in Fig. 21.3 is like the total cost curve in Fig. 21.2 but with kinks inserted at the values of q where discounts take effect. The curve will also be higher above the axis than in Fig. 21.3 as the cost now includes the unit cost of the item, and the changes in value of this element at the discount points also means some 'flattening out' in the shape of the curve.
The following example illustrates the principles involved in solving stock control problems with discounts.

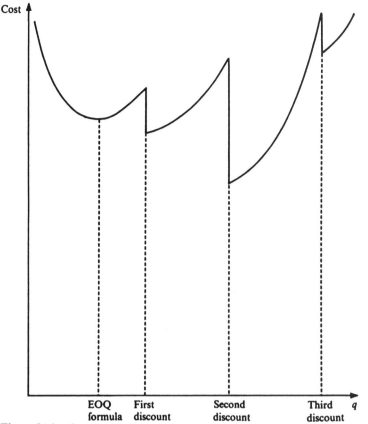

Figure 21.3 Graph of cost against order quantity when there are discounts.

Example 21.3.1 The manager of a large sports shop, open for 50 weeks each year, holds a regular stock of quality golf balls. Although the manager has to purchase boxes of these golf balls at £9.60 per box containing 12 balls, he is prepared to sell these balls as single items. Over the past year he has sold, on average, 12 boxes of golf balls each week and it is likely that this level of sales will continue into the future.

Due to telephone, secretarial, and transport costs it is estimated that the cost of receiving each order is £16. The annual cost of storage is estimated at 20 per cent of the stock item value and is based on the cost of storage space and the company's cost of capital. The manager of the shop sets a price for his goods by taking the sum of the purchase cost and the appropriately allocated stock holding cost (storage and delivery) and then applying a mark-up of 50 per cent.

(a) Determine the optimum number of boxes of golf balls the sports shop manager should order at a time and the number of orders per year.

Show that the selling price per ball that results from this optimum policy is £1.24.

(b) The supplier offers a discount of 4 per cent on the price of each box of golf balls if the manager is prepared to purchase 500 boxes at a time. (It can be assumed that there are no price effects on demand.)

Show whether or not this discount, assuming it is passed on, is advantageous to the customer in terms of shop price.

(c) What percentage discount is required for the order quantity of 500 boxes to be beneficial to the shop customer?

(ACCA Level 2: June 1990)

ANSWER Answers to questions of this kind can usually be set out most efficiently using a table. We do this below and derive from the table the answers to the three specific questions posed. Part (a) does not involve any discounts and is just asking for the normal EOQ calculation explained in Sec. 21.2. Even if this is not specifically requested in a discounts question, it is always worth finding because the lowest point of the curve shown in Fig. 21.3 could well still be the EOQ point.

For this problem, working in terms of boxes of golf balls, we have throughout the question $D = 50 \times 12 = 600$ boxes and $c1 = £16$. Also $c2 = 0.2p$ where p is the cost of a box to the shop manager.

In part (a) we have $p = £9.60$.

In part (b) $p = £9.60 \times 0.96 = £9.216$.

In part (c) $p = £9.60 \times (1 - d)$ where d is the proportional discount rate.

So for part (a)

$$q = \text{EOQ} = \sqrt{\frac{2 \times D \times c1}{c2}} = \sqrt{\frac{2 \times 600 \times 16}{0.2 \times 9.6}} = \sqrt{\frac{19\,200}{1.92}} = 100$$

This answers the first part of question (i).

We can now draw up a table showing

purchase cost + ordering cost + stock holding cost

per box of 12 balls for the conditions of the three parts.

The total ordering cost for the year is $£16 \times 600/q$. Allocating this over the 600 boxes sold per year leads to an allocated ordering cost per box of $£16/q$.

Total holding cost for the year is $£0.2p \times q/2 = £pq/10$. Allocating this over the 600 boxes sold per year leads to an allocated stock holding cost per box of $£pq/6000$.

Boxes purchased, q	Purchase cost per box, $£p$	Ordering cost per box, $£16/q$	Holding cost per box, $£pq/6000$
(a) 100	9.60	0.16	0.16
(b) 500	9.216	0.032	0.768
(c) 500	$9.6 \times (1-d)$	0.032	$0.8 \times (1-d)$

To complete the answer to part (a) we note that the total cost per box is £9.92 when the stock costs have been allocated. Applying the 50 per cent mark-up to this gives a selling price of £14.88. Then dividing by 12 gives a price per ball of £1.24.

For part (b) the total cost per box is £10.016 after allocation of the stock costs. Since this exceeds £9.92, the discount cannot be advantageous to the customer.

For part (c) the total cost per box is $10.4 \times (1-d) + 0.032$. In order for the discount to be advantageous to the customer we need

$$10.4(1-d) + 0.032 < 9.92$$

Hence

$$10.4d > 10.4 + 0.032 - 9.92 = 0.512$$

i.e.

$$d > 0.049\,23$$

In order for the discount for buying batches of 500 boxes to be beneficial to the customer it would need to exceed 4.923 per cent.

Exercise 21.3.1 A company requires 400 000 tonnes of raw material each year at a cost of £800 per tonne. The cost incurred for each delivery is also £800. Stock holding costs are 20 per cent per year of the value of stock held. Further storage costs arise because special containers, each capable of holding 280 tonnes, have to be hired at a cost of £5000 each per year in order to store the raw material.

Find the number of tonnes that should be ordered in each batch.

(*Note* This exercise involves the same issues that arise with quantity discounts but the situation is in a sense 'reversed'. The reader is advised to sketch a graph of the nature of Fig. 21.3 before embarking on the calculations. The table format is again helpful in solving this problem. Each time a further container is introduced there will be an additional line in the table. For discount problems the software QSB+ can again be used to obtain solutions. In addition to the data required for the simple EOQ model it is necessary to supply information on the discount points and the size of discount allowed. On the basis of this information the program will output the optimum batch size.)

21.4 LEAD TIME AND REORDER LEVELS

Assumption 2 in the list given in Sec. 21.2 was that orders are delivered immediately they are requested. That is to say there is no *lead time* on orders. Relaxing this assumption has hardly any effect on the model so long as assumptions 1 and 3 of constant demand and no time out of stock, respectively, remain in force. The only change is that the next batch needs to be requested when the stock level falls to the amount that it is known will be used during a lead time (assumed constant). This quantity, which when reached signals that it is time to order another batch, is called the *reorder level*. Thus, for example, if usage is at a constant rate of 20 items per day and the lead time on orders is two days, then the reorder level is 40 items. The situation where assumption 1 is relaxed as well as assumption 2 is the subject of Sec. 21.5 on stochastic demand.

However, another situation of interest is where assumption 3 is relaxed as well as assumption 2. Thus, in addition to lead time being non-zero, it is permissible to choose to spend time out of stock. This could be a worthwhile thing to do if the penalties arising from being out of stock are of similar size to the cost of carrying stock. The diagram representing this situation is a variation on Fig. 21.1 and is shown as Fig. 21.4.

Let the batch size be q and let the acceptable backlog of orders when the batch arrives be b. Let the cost of an order be $c1$, the cost of carrying an item of stock through a year be $c2$, and the cost of carrying a backlogged order through a year be $c3$. Then minimizing the sum of the costs of ordering, stock holding, and backlogs for a year leads to the following formulae for batch size and for backlog when order is received:

$$q = \sqrt{\frac{2 \times c1 \times D}{c2}} \times \sqrt{1 + \left(\frac{c2}{c3}\right)}$$

$$b = \sqrt{\frac{2 \times c1 \times D}{c3 \times (1 + c3/c2)}}$$

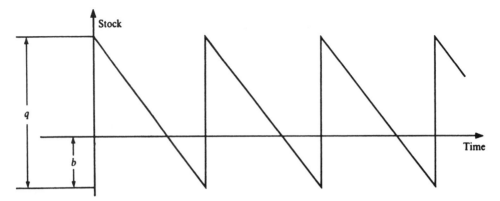

Figure 21.4 Graph of stock level against time when backlogging is permitted.

The formula for q is seen to be the same as for the simple model except for a multiplicative adjustment. This multiplier will be close to 1 if $c3$ is large relative to $c2$, so having a backlog of orders becomes unattractive in this situation.

We see also from the formula for b that if $c3$ is large then b will be small, while a small $c3$ will lead to a large b.

Example 21.4.1 Demand for a particular item is at a constant rate of 39 000 units per 52-week year. The cost associated with each order is £180, the cost of carrying an item of stock through a year is £4.50 and the cost of carrying a backlogged order for an item through a year is £2. If the lead time on an order is four weeks, find the quantity which should be ordered each time and the reorder level.

ANSWER

$$Q = \sqrt{\frac{2 \times c1 \times D}{c2}} \times \sqrt{1 + \left(\frac{c2}{c3}\right)} = \sqrt{\frac{2 \times 180 \times 39\,000}{4}} \times \sqrt{1 + \left(\frac{4}{2}\right)}$$

$$= 1873.5 \times 1.732 = 3245$$

$$b = \sqrt{\frac{2 \times c1 \times D}{c3 \times (1 + c3/c2)}} = \sqrt{\frac{2 \times 180 \times 39\,000}{2 \times (1 + 2/4)}} = 2163$$

The usage in a four-week lead time will be $4 \times (39\,000/52) = 3000$. Hence the time to order is when the stock level has fallen to $3000 - 2163 = 837$. Then usage of 3000 items during the lead time will mean that 2163 orders have been accumulated when the batch arrives and makes the stock level up to $3245 - 2163 = 1082$.

Exercise 21.4.1 Demand for items of a certain type is constant at a rate of 6500 items per year (to be regarded as 52 weeks). The lead time on each order is two weeks, the cost associated with each order is £40, the cost of carrying an item of stock through a year is to be taken as 80p, and that of carrying an accumulated order through a year as £1.00.

Find the optimum order size and the reorder level.

The idea of lead times is also important to an alternative approach to stock control called *just in time* (*JIT*). This is really an approach to production, of which the stock control aspect is just one of the implications. The underlying principle as far as stock is concerned is that *stock is evil*. The reasons for holding stock given in Sec. 21.1 are seen as symptoms of a reductionist approach to business, where parts of the operation are concerned with optimizing their own element without due regard for the overall good of the business. Thus, for example, the purchasing department likes stock because it is a buffer against unreliability of supply, the production department is happy to produce output for stock because it helps utilization of the production facilities, and the sales department favours stock so that it can respond to unexpected orders. For the business as a whole, however, stock in all its forms is an undesirable cost.

The principle behind the JIT approach to production is that it is a 'pull' strategy as opposed to the traditional approach which is a 'push' strategy. In the traditional approach the purchasing department buys a quantity of material which goes into stock. The production department draws from this stock, carries its own stock of work-in-progress, and outputs stock of finished goods which it is then the role of the sales department to move on to customers. On the JIT approach the sales department determines how much it wants and communicates this to the production department. Similar communication then takes place through all the stages of production with each stage telling its predecessor how much it requires. This communication takes place through the medium of so called Kanban cards. The idea then is that the production communicates to the supplier what material it needs and receives this as required.

The ideal being aimed at is processing on the basis of a batch size of one with no stock being held at all and no order lead time. In reality batch sizes can rarely be quite as small as one and material has to be received once a day. This, however, represents significant reductions in stock levels as compared with traditional approaches and the method has been used to very good effect both in Japan, where the Toyota experience was seminal, and in the United States, where Hewlett-Packard has embraced it. In addition to its benefits from the stock point of view JIT is seen as having benefits in saving production space, reducing the amount of production needing to be reworked, reducing time lost through breakdowns, reducing the time spent by each item in the production process, and increasing employee motivation. It is also found that this approach improves the scope for using robotics in the process.

Idle time is introduced into the production line as a stoppage at one point means that preceding processes must stop. In order for JIT to work in respect of obtaining materials from suppliers, it is necessary to have a supplier who is willing to cooperate in such a system and be able to produce orders of the required size and quantity when needed and at acceptable prices. As further reading on the subject of JIT the reader is referred to the book by Browne, Harhen, and Shivnan called *Production Management Systems*, referred to in the bibliography.

21.5 STOCHASTIC DEMAND

In this section we consider the situation where there is simultaneous relaxation of the assumptions 1 and 2 set out in Sec. 21.1. That is to say we consider variable (or stochastic) demand and also a non-zero lead time. As in the situation considered in Sec. 21.4 we have to order in advance to cover the lead time, but because demand is now variable we do not know exactly how much will be demanded during the lead time. Hence involuntary stock-outs may occur as there may be more than the anticipated number of orders during the lead time.

It should be noted that the expression *stock-out* has a very specific meaning. A stock-out occurs every time a request for an item cannot be met from stock. Thus there could be several stock-outs during one period out of stock, or there might be no stock-outs during such a period, if no requests are received.

In problems involving stochastic demand the EOQ formula can still be used to find the optimum batch size, with the expected annual demand being used as D. The expected usage can also be used as a first step towards obtaining the reorder level as in Sec. 21.4. However, the possibility now arises of the actual usage during a lead time being greater than the average usage, and so it may be considered desirable to set a reorder level such that the anticipated stock level when the batch arrives is actually greater than zero. Thus we can imagine a 'saw tooth' diagram like Fig. 21.1 or Fig. 21.4 where the bottom points are *above* the horizontal axis. However, the downward sloping lines in this case will not be straight lines and they will not all finish at the same level. As the batch size is still constant, the vertical jumps will continue to be equal. The number of units by which the reorder level exceeds the expected usage in a lead time is called the *buffer stock*.

Example 21.5.1 DB plc operates a conventional stock control system based on reorder levels and economic ordering quantities. The various control levels were set originally based on estimates which did not allow for any uncertainty and this has caused difficulties because, in practice, lead times, demands, and other factors do vary.

As part of a review of the system, a typical stock item, Part No. X206, has been studied in detail as follows:

Data for Part No. X206 Lead times	Probability
15 working days	0.2
20 working days	0.5
25 working days	0.3

Demand per working day	Probability
5000 units	0.5
7000 units	0.5

(*Note* It can be assumed that the demands would apply for the whole of the appropriate lead time.)

DB plc works for 240 days per year and it costs £0.15 pa to carry a unit of X206 in stock. The reorder level for this part is currently 150 000 units and the reorder cost is £1000.

(a) Calculate the level of buffer stock implicit in a reorder level of 150 000 units.
(b) Calculate the probability of a stock-out.
(c) Calculate the expected annual stock-outs in units.
(d) Calculate the stock-out cost per unit at which it would be worth while raising the reorder level to 175 000 units.
(e) Discuss the possible alternatives to a reorder level EOQ system and their advantages and disadvantages.

(CIMA Stage 3: May 1990)

ANSWER

(a) To answer this part of the question we need to find the expected usage during a lead time. The buffer stock is then the amount by which 150 000 units exceeds this expected figure. The expected usage is found by calculating the different numbers of units which might be used, V, and their respective probabilities, p, in order to obtain ΣpV.

Usage, V (units)	Probability, p, of this usage	pV
$15 \times 5000 = 75\,000$	$0.2 \times 0.5 = 0.1$	7 500
$15 \times 7000 = 105\,000$	$0.2 \times 0.5 = 0.1$	10 500
$20 \times 5000 = 100\,000$	$0.5 \times 0.5 = 0.25$	25 000
$20 \times 7000 = 140\,000$	$0.5 \times 0.5 = 0.25$	35 000
$25 \times 5000 = 125\,000$	$0.3 \times 0.5 = 0.15$	18 750
$25 \times 7000 = 175\,000$	$0.3 \times 0.5 = 0.15$	26 250
		$\Sigma pV = 123\,000$

Hence buffer stock $= 150\,000 - 123\,000 = 27\,000$ items.

(b) If the lead time were 25 days and the daily usage were 7000 units, then the usage during the lead time would be 175 000 units. This is the only circumstance which leads to stock-outs. So the probability of a stock-out is the probability of this combination, which is seen from the above table to be 0.15.

(c) The expected number of stock-outs in a single lead time is

$$0.15 \times (175\,000 - 150\,000) = 0.15 \times 25\,000 = 3750$$

In order to find the expected annual number this must be multiplied by the number of lead times in a year.

Expected daily usage is $0.5 \times 5000 + 0.5 \times 7000 = 6000$ units. So the EOQ batch size is

$$\sqrt{\frac{2 \times c1 \times D}{c2}} = \sqrt{\frac{2 \times 1000 \times (240 \times 6000)}{0.15}}$$

$$= 138\,564 \text{ units}$$

Thus the number of deliveries, and hence lead times, in a year is

$$\frac{240 \times 6000}{138\,564} = 10.392$$

So expected annual stock-outs $= 3750 \times 10.392 = 38\,970$.

(d) Raising the reorder level to 175 000 units would increase the annual stock holding cost by £$0.15 \times 25\,000 =$ £3750.

The expected annual saving from reduced stock-outs would be $38\,970 \times S$ where S is the cost per stock-out. Thus increasing the reorder level is worth while if $38\,970 \times S >$ £3750 and hence $S >$ £3750/38 970 $=$ £0.096, i.e. it is worth while if the cost per stock-out exceeds 9.6p.

(e) In answering this part of the question reference should be made to the JIT system discussed in Sec. 21.4.

Consideration should also be given to the *periodic review system*. Under this system stock levels are inspected at regular intervals and if, at inspection, an item's level is found to have fallen below a specified level, an order is placed to bring it up to a predetermined level. Thus the quantities ordered will in general be different each time. This system has the advantage that orders for several different items can all be placed at the same time. It would, for example, be the system used by a small retailer who would normally want to place an order with his wholesaler once a week rather than order each type of item separately. There are savings on administrative costs and suppliers may well offer concessions for regular orders. Disadvantages are that it could lead to more stock-outs if demand is very variable, and in order to seek to compensate for this possibility, there are likely to be larger buffer stocks required than under a reorder level EOQ system.

Exercise 12.5.1 The Oxygon Office Supplies Company Limited is a well-established firm of paper merchants and stationers, which is open for 50 weeks each year and specializes in the retailing of general office supplies. Its many customers include financial institutions, legal establishments and insurance companies. However, steadily increasing operating costs have diminished the company's financial reserves which has prompted the chief accountant to recommend a reduction in overall stock levels. Whereas in previous times it was common for the company to hold over 12 months' stock for many stock items in order to guarantee availability, pressures on liquidity seemed to demand a reduction in inventory levels.

The company's main selling item was a high quality typing paper which tended to have erratic demand but can be assumed to have a normal distribution with a mean of 800 boxes each week and a standard deviation of 250 boxes per week. This paper is supplied by the Tiara Paper Company at a cost of £2.50 per box. It was found that the lead time of supply of this paper recently had been very consistent at three weeks.

The annual cost of stock holding was estimated at 15 per cent of stock item value and is based on the cost of storage and the company's cost of capital. In order to estimate the cost of a delivery of paper from Tiara, the cost of making and receiving the order together with the associated accounting and stock control tasks requires a total effort of approximately 12 man-hours, where the average wage rate is £160 per week for a 40-hour week.

(a) Outline the basic principles of inventory control policy and explain why a good inventory control policy is of value to Oxygon.
(b) Calculate the economic order quantity for this stock item, together with the average length of time between replenishments.
(c) Determine the recommended reorder level if there is to be no more than a 1 per cent chance that a stock-out will occur in any one replenishment period.
(d) Determine the total stock holding cost (storage and delivery costs) per annum using the calculated values of the economic order quantity and reorder level.

(ACCA Level 2: Dec. 1987)

QSB + can be used to handle problems of stochastic demand so long as the demand pattern can be taken as either normally distributed or involving discrete probabilities. Given this information along with all relevant costs, the program will output the optimum batch size and reorder level.

TEST EXERCISES

21.1 A company sells units of a particular item at a constant rate of 125 000 per year. The order cost for a batch is £1600 and the cost of holding an item in stock for a year is £1. Find the economic order quantity EOQ.

21.2 Your departmental manager has asked for help in the design of a stock control system for a client. The following data is available for the system. The rate at which the client uses the stock is 1000 units per year. His order cost is £10 per order. The cost of storing one unit of the stock for a year is £2.

(a) The cost, £C, of an ordering policy is given by

$$C = D \times c1/q + q \times c2/2$$

where D is the demand per period, q is the quantity ordered, $c1$ is the cost (£) of placing an order, and $c2$ is the cost (£) of holding a unit of stock for a period.
   Derive the formula for the order quantity which minimizes the cost of the ordering policy.
(b) For a batch delivery system determine the order quantity which minimizes cost.
(c) Draw a schedule of order size against ordering cost, stock holding cost, and total cost for order sizes of 0, 20, 40,..., 160.

(d) Use the schedule of part (c) to construct a graph of ordering cost, holding cost, and total cost against order size.
(e) What assumptions are made in this model of stock control?

(ACCA Level 1: Dec. 1991)

21.3 Neptune Builder's Merchants supplies a number of products for the building industry. Of particular importance to the company is the supply of bags of cement, valued at £4 per bag, which are purchased from a manufacturer who guarantees immediate availability of goods. Demand for these bags can be considered to be spread evenly throughout the year (which you may assume consists of 300 working days) at a rate of 200 bags per day. The company's purchasing department estimates that the cost of placing an order is £20 but, in addition, labour is involved in the transportation and loading of the cement bags. These costs consist of a fixed £17.50 transportation cost per order and a loading cost at the rate of £25 per 1000 bags ordered.

   On arrival at the company, all bags of cement have to go into stock in a special warehouse unit. Warehouse units suitable for Neptune are available in one size only; these have indefinitely long lives and are capable of holding 2000 bags of cement. Neptune currently owns one such warehouse unit but is considering the purchase of a further one. The company's accountant has extracted certain further information from the accounts which he considers may be relevant in deciding whether it is financially worth while to purchase a second warehouse unit.

Cost of capital	11.5 per cent per annum
New warehouse cost	£4000
Contents insurance	£100 per annum fixed, covering all warehouse stock
Buildings insurance	£25 per annum per warehouse unit
Product deterioration	1 per cent of stock value per annum
Warehouse maintenance cost	£50 per warehouse unit

(a) Determine
   (i) the unit stock holding cost for one year;
   (ii) the replenishment costs per order, necessary for the calculation of the economic order quantity.
(b) Calculate the optimum order size and the number of replenishments per annum if the company owns
   (i) two warehouses units;
   (ii) one warehouse unit.
(c) Advise the company on whether the additional warehouse unit should be purchased.
(d) If the demand rate per day was to increase to 360 bags, would the decision concerning the additional warehouse unit be changed? Hence comment on the sensitivity of the demand rate to your original decision.

(ACCA Level 2: June 1989)

21.4 A construction company uses sand and gravel at an average rate of 3000 tonnes per year. The lead time on orders from the company's regular suppliers is five days and usage during this period has been found to conform to the following pattern.

Usage in tonnes	Frequency
0	0
1	0.01
2	0.05
3	0.15
4	0.25
5	0.30
6	0.10
7	0.09
8	0.05

The cost per tonne is £20 and stock holding costs are 25 per cent per month of stock value. Delivery cost is £4 per batch.
   If a stock-out occurs, a rush order can be arranged, and the cost of such a stock-out can be taken as being £4.

(a) Find the economic order quantity (EOQ) for sand and gravel.
(b) By calculating the expected total annual cost from stock holding and stock-outs for different possible reorder levels, determine the reorder level that should be used.

21.5 SPB Ltd is a small engineering company, which is open for 50 weeks each year and specializes in the assembly of one component used in the motor industry. This component, for which there is an annual demand of 20 000 components, is assembled from two types of bought-in part, A and B. The numbers of parts used in each component and their associated costs and lead times are given in the following table.

Part	Number per component	Unit cost (£)	Lead times (weeks)
A	3	5	1
B	8	1	3

Currently SPB retains fairly high stock levels to ensure continuous production, but liquidity difficulties seem to demand a reduction in stock levels. SPB's current stock control policy for these parts is outlined in the table below.

Part	Reorder quantity	Reorder level
A	5 000	5 000
B	20 000	15 000

It is estimated that each time an order is placed for any part there is a cost of £100 per order plus £0.02 per item ordered. Also it is estimated that the storage costs of parts in stock is 20 per cent per annum of the value of the parts in addition to a fixed annual holding cost of £5000.

(a) Describe briefly the basic principles of stock control and explain why a good stock control policy is of value to the management of SPB Ltd.
(b) Determine the total annual cost incurred by SPB Ltd for production of these components, using the current stock control policy.
(c) Assuming the given lead times are constant:
   (i) show that the optimum reorder quantities for parts A and B are 3464 and 12 649 respectively;
   (ii) find the optimum reorder levels for each part.
   Determine the annual saving, both in value and percentage terms, that can be obtained by implementing this optimum stock control policy.
(d) Describe the advantages of the current stock control policy compared with the optimum one if the given lead times are stochastic.

(ACCA Level 2: June 1991)

22

SIMULATION

22.1 PRINCIPLES OF SIMULATION

In the previous three chapters we have looked at a variety of quantitative techniques that make various major assumptions and hence can be considered of limited use. For example, in linear programming, it is assumed that all constraints within the model are linear. Such quantitative techniques cannot usually be applied to models involving more complicated situations.

Simulation is not a quantitative technique in the same way as the methods described in these previous chapters. It is rather a method of approach to problems which involves building a model of the system to be investigated, observing the behaviour of the system, and gathering useful data about the model. It is thus a 'try it and see what happens' method which is cheaper than direct experimentation.

Simulation can be regarded as a procedure to which we are forced if the system is extremely complicated and hence not susceptible to mathematical analysis. However, even to build a simulation model would require considerable simplification of the real system and great ability is needed to make these simplifications in the correct way. However the real disciples of the art of simulation object to this 'last resort' view and argue that even if rigorous mathematical treatment is possible, simulation might still be a preferable way of investigating the system. The main reason given is that if we have a simulation model, then it is possible to introduce changes into the system much more easily than with mathematical procedures, where recalculation would be required.

To illustrate both the principles and mechanics of simulation modelling we will use a detailed example.

Example 22.1.1 A flower trader, who currently works on his own, establishes himself at a site in a lay-by off a busy main road. The lay-by can accommodate a maximum of two cars, including any car that is being served, and local traffic laws prohibit cars from waiting on the road. Consequently any potential customer arriving when the lay-by is full will be lost. The interarrival time distribution of service times is provided in the following table.

Time (min)	Interarrival times (%)	Service times (%)
0–2	15	10
2–4	50	25
4–6	20	30
6–8	5	25
8–10	5	10
10–12	5	0
Total	100	100

(a) Estimate the mean number of potential customers per hour.
(b) Use the random numbers below to simulate the operation of the trader for the service of 10 potential customers and hence estimate the number of potential customers lost per hour, explaining how you generated the interarrival and service times.

Customer	1	2	3	4	5	6	7	8	9	10
Random interarrival	87	69	19	21	62	07	31	30	60	88
Number service time	90	67	83	32	65	18	74	08	18	38

(c) Why is your estimate, found in part (b), not very reliable and how would you improve upon it?
(d) The flower trader is considering the employment of an assistant. Assuming that the assistant will serve customers with the same service distribution as the trader, simulate the operation with the two servers for the service of 10 potential customers using the same random numbers as above.

Estimate the number of potential customers lost per hour for the new service system.

Explain why it is more sensible to use the same random numbers than different random numbers when comparing two simulation models.

(ACCA Level 2: June 1990)

ANSWER
(a) The mean interarrival time is

$$\frac{15(1) + 50(3) + 20(5) + 5(7) + 5(9) + 5(11)}{100}$$

$$= 4 \text{ minutes}$$

Hence the mean number of potential customers per hour is 15. In the same way the mean service time per customer is 5 minutes.

As the mean service time is greater than the interarrival time it seems inevitable that queues would result if traffic laws allowed traffic to build up on the road. In this case the restriction on queue length indicates that some customers will be lost.

(b) The information provided by averages is of some interest but by using averages alone we are failing to use the information provided about the variability around these averages.

We need a process to develop a suitable simulation model for the problem. We need to generate data representing actual passers-by. The simulation is performed by sampling motorist interrarrival times in a way that corresponds with their real-life distribution. In order to do this, we use a sequence of random numbers between 00 and 99 and select interarrival times according to the following rules.

Interarrival time	Midpoint	Random number range
0–2	1	00–14
2–4	3	15–64
4–6	5	65–84
6–8	7	85–89
8–10	9	90–94
10–12	11	95–99

It can be seen that the random numbers are allocated to the distribution to reflect the likelihood of each possible interarrival time. Also, to simplify the system, the intervals of time are reduced to their midpoints to provide discrete values for the simulation.

We could now use printed tables of random numbers (in pairs) to generate the interarrival times for potential customers. For example, if the number 87 is generated first from the random number tables it would indicate that the first motorist arrives after 7 minutes.

In the same way, a table representing the random number ranges for the possible simulated service times is shown below.

Service time	Midpoint	Random number range
0–2	1	00–09
2–4	3	10–34
4–6	5	35–64
6–8	7	65–89
8–10	9	90–99

In this example we do not need to use a printed table of random numbers as a selection of such numbers is produced as part of the question.

Consider the first motorist:

interarrival time random number	87
interarrival time (min)	7

As this is the first motorist and we assume that the starting time of the system is 0 then the arrival time of this motorist is 7.

service time random number	90
service time (min)	9

Hence the first motorist will complete his service at time $7 + 9 = 16$ minutes.

Moving on to the second motorist:

interarrival time random number	69
interarrival time (min)	5
arrival time (min)	$7 + 5 = 12$

As the first motorist does not finish being served until time 16, the second motorist must join the queue until this time.

service time random number	67
service time (min)	7

The second motorist completes his service at time $16 + 7 = 23$ minutes.
Considering the third motorist:

interarrival random number	19
interarrival time (min)	3
arrival time (min)	$12 + 3 = 15$

At this time the first motorist is still being served and has not left the lay-by and the second motorist is waiting to be served. As the lay-by only holds two cars this third motorist is unable to stop and hence a potential customer is lost.

For the fourth motorist:

interarrival time random number	21
interarrival time (min)	3
arrival time (min)	$15 + 3 = 18$

By this time the first motorist has completed his service and has left, allowing the second motorist to be served. The fourth motorist waits in the lay-by to be served. This will start when motorist 2 leaves, at time 23.

service time random number	32
service time (min)	3
service completed	$23 + 3 = 26$ minutes

It is usual to represent the information provided by a simulation in table form. For this system the following table represents the data for the first 10 potential customers.

Potential customer	Interarrival time	Arrival time	Start of service	Service time	End of service
1	7	7	7	9	16
2	5	12	16	7	23
3	3	15	Leaves		
4	3	18	23	3	26
5	3	21	Leaves		
6	1	22	Leaves		
7	3	25	26	7	33
8	3	28	33	1	34
9	3	31	Leaves		
10	7	38	38	5	43

Of the 10 potential customers, 4 (or 40 per cent) were lost because there was no room on the lay-by. This might be a cause for concern for the flower trader. Given that the mean number of potential customers arriving per hour is 15 then we would estimate that $0.4 \times 15 = 6$ of these would be lost.

Input Data of The Problem flower trader page 1

Svr £1 Mean time: 5.0000 Dstn: Dscrt

Qu. £1 Qu. limit: 1 Dspch: FIFO

Mean interarrival time = 4.0000 Dstn: Dscrt Random seed = 113

Discrete Values of Service Time for flower trader Page 2

No.	Value	Prob.	C. Prob.	No.	Value	Prob.	C. Prob.
1	1.0000	0.1000	0.1000	4	7.0000	0.2500	0.9000
2	3.0000	0.2500	0.3500	5	9.0000	0.1000	1.0000
3	5.0000	0.3000	0.6500				

Mean = 5   Variance = 5.200001

Discrete Values of Interarrival Time for flower trader Page 3

No.	Value	Prob.	C. Prob.	No.	Value	Prob.	C. Prob.
1	1.0000	0.1500	0.1500	4	7.0000	0.0500	0.9000
2	3.0000	0.5000	0.6500	5	9.0000	0.0500	0.9500
3	5.0000	0.2000	0.8500	6	11.00	0.0500	1.0000

Mean = 4   Variance = 6.200003

Figure 22.1 Input data for QSB + package for flower trader example.

(c) Naturally we would be extremely cautious about these results given the 'sample' size of only 10 motorists. In practice we would want a much larger sample, perhaps several hundred or several thousand potential customers, to allow the averaging process to stabilize.

In practice, simulation is undertaken using appropriate computer technology. As well as writing specialist programs for particular programs in languages like BASIC or PASCAL, there are also general-purpose simulation packages available on both mainframe computers and PCs. With this technology it becomes possible to generate a large amount of data, which should increase accuracy.

One such easy-to-use PC package is QSB + (Quantitative Systems for Business Plus). For this flower trader example the data in Fig. 22.1 is entered into the package. The package will then carry out a simulation of 1000 potential customers in about two minutes. The printout shown in Fig. 22.2 is produced from the package.

In particular, we make the following observations:

1. The number of lost customers (out of 1000) is 301.
2. The server is busy for 89.25 per cent of the time.
3. The average number of motorists in the lay-by is 1.38.
4. The average number in the queue is 0.49.
5. The average system time is 7.80 minutes.
6. The average queuing time is 2.76 minutes.

We see that the package produces a lot of detailed information, all of which may be relevant to the flower trader.

Summary Results for Servers in flower trader				Page 1		
Servers	Util.	Wq.	Var. (Wq)	W.	Var. (W)	Obsvtn.
1	0.8925	2.7611	6.0960	7.7954	10.31	699

Data collection period: 0 to 3943 (in min)

Summary Results for Queues in flower trader				Page 2		
Queues	Qmax.	Qmin.	Current Q	Lq.	Var. (Lq)	L.
1	1	0	0	0.4895	0.2499	1.3819

Data collection period: 0 to 3943 (in min.)

Figure 22.2 Summary results from QSB + package for flower trader example.

(d) Carrying out the simulation manually assuming two servers results in the following table of results. Note that the same random numbers were used as before. Each customer is served immediately, providing there is space in the lay-by.

Potential customer	Interarrival time	Arrival time	Start of service	Service time	End of service
1	7	7	7	9	16
2	5	12	12	7	19
3	3	15	Leaves		
4	3	18	18	3	21
5	3	21	21	7	28
6	1	22	22	3	25
7	3	25	25	7	32
8	3	28	28	1	29
9	3	31	31	3	34
10	7	38	38	5	43

From the simulation we would now expect to lose one out of ten customers; that is, $0.1(15) = 1.5$ customers per hour.

It is important to note that it is more sensible to use the same random numbers when comparing two models so that any difference in the results is due to the difference in the models rather than the difference between the random numbers.

In this section we have introduced the general principles of simulation via an example. We have seen that uncertainty makes the application of some of the more formal quantitative techniques difficult to operate in practice. Simulation offers the decision maker the opportunity to alter key parameters of a problem involving variability. The process of applying simulation requires a clear and concise description of the problem under investigation.

To conclude this section we list some reasons why analysts would use simulation to solve management problems:

1. It provides a method of solving problems where other methods are not possible.
2. Actual observation of the system is too expensive.

3. The simplifying assumptions are not so great in simulation exercises as they are with other quantitative models.

However the use of simulation in place of other techniques involves a trade-off and we should be mindful of the disadvantages of using the simulation approach:

1. Unlike most other quantitative techniques, simulation is non-optimizing. We are only able to select what appears to be the best policy after testing several possible policies.
2. Simulation is not precise. To obtain great accuracy a substantial amount of calculation is required (and hence the need for a computer package).

Exercise 22.1.1 The AB Travel Agency deals with numerous personal callers each day and prides itself on its level of service. The time to deal with each caller depends on the client's requirements which range from, say, a request for a brochure to booking a round-the-world cruise. If clients have to wait more than 10 minutes for attention it is AB's policy for the manager to see them personally and to give them a £5 holiday voucher.

Observations have shown that the time taken to deal with clients and their arrival patterns follow the distributions below.

Time to deal with clients	
Minutes	Probability
2	0.05
4	0.10
6	0.15
10	0.30
14	0.25
20	0.10
30	0.05

Time between arrivals	
Minutes	Probability
1	0.2
8	0.4
15	0.3
25	0.1

(a) Describe how you would simulate the operation of AB Travel Agency based on the use of random number tables.
(b) Simulate the arrival and serving of 12 clients and show the number of customers who receive a voucher (use line 1 of the random numbers below to derive the arrival pattern and line 2 for the serving times).

					Random numbers							
Line 1	03	47	43	73	86	36	96	47	36	61	46	98
Line 2	63	71	62	33	26	16	80	45	60	11	14	10

(c) Calculate the weekly cost of vouchers, assuming the proportion receiving vouchers derived from part (b) applies throughout a week of 50 opening hours.

(CIMA Level 2: Nov. 1989)

22.2 APPLICATIONS

Simulation has been extensively applied to decision making. In the management area, simulation has been applied to inventory control, plant location, transportation systems, queuing problems, and numerous other areas. Some examples of where simulation has been used are given below.

1. *Replacement problems*: determining the optimum time to replace electronic components when downtime is expensive.
2. *Manpower problems*: modelling the progression of staff through a company in order to predict the future recruiting requirements and to evaluate the effect of different recruiting and promotion schemes.
3. *Queuing problems:* problems where people or objects arrive at a point where further progress is restricted. Some particular queuing problems can be solved using analytical methods, but simulation is more generally applicable and easier to use.
4. *Inventory problems:* where demand and lead time for a product is uncertain. A suitable order policy can be derived.
5. *Transport problems:* finding how many road tankers are required to provide a satisfactory service between a number of depots.

In this section we apply manual simulation techniques to two of these areas. The first is in the area of inventory control and the second is a queuing problem. Exercise 22.2.1 describes a manpower planning situation which can be investigated using simulation.

Example 22.2.1 A large garage, open for 50 weeks each year, is examining its inventory policy in relation to one type of tyre it stocks. Weekly demand for the tyre is distributed according to the following table.

Weekly demand	Probability
20	0.1
30	0.6
40	0.3

The garage uses a reorder level of 100 for this tyre and the lead time is fixed at three weeks. The cost of placing each order for tyres is estimated to be £12. For any tyre in stock it is estimated that the annual storage cost is equal to 15 per cent of its cost. A tyre costs £10.

(a) Determine the expected annual demand and hence use the simple EOQ formula to show that the optimum order quantity for this tyre is 160.
(b) Use the random digits below to simulate the inventory operation for a period of 10 weeks in order to estimate the total weekly stock holding costs of this garage. Start with an initial stock of 150, use the order quantity found in part (a) and assume that the cost of being out

of stock is £0.25 per tyre. State any further assumptions made and explain how the demand data is generated.

Random digits: 6 9 1 4 7 1 8 9 3 0

(c) Explain how this simulation method might be used to determine the optimum order quantity and reorder level.

(ACCA Level 2: Dec. 1990)

ANSWER

(a) The expected weekly demand is given by

$$20(0.1) + 30(0.6) + 40(0.3) = 32$$

As there are 50 working weeks each year the expected annual demand for tyres is $50(32) = 1600$. We use the simple EOQ model (see Sec. 21.2) to obtain

$$q = \sqrt{\frac{2 \times D \times c1}{c2}} = \sqrt{\frac{2 \times 1600 \times 12}{1.50}} = 160 \text{ tyres}$$

(b) The following table shows how the demand data is generated

Weekly demand	Probability	Random digits
20	0.1	0
30	0.6	1–6
40	0.3	7–9

You will note that the size of block of random digits is in proportion to the probabilities for the demand data, and that only one random digit is required to represent the probabilities. Before we perform the calculations we need to consider any assumptions for the system. These assumptions are needed to simplify the model.

1. It is assumed that orders are placed at the end of the week in which the stock goes below 100.
2. Shortfalls are assumed to be satisfied out of the next delivery.

The simulation then proceeds as follows:

Week number	Opening stock	Demand	Shortfall	Delivery	Closing stock	Order
1	150	30			120	
2	120	40			80	
3	80	30			50	
4	50	30			20	
5	20	40	20	160	140	
6	140	30			110	
7	110	40			70	
8	70	40			30	
9	30	30			0	
10	0	20	20	160	140	

The total cost of running out of cost during this 10-week period is

$$(20+20)0.25=£10$$

The total cost of ordering over the 10 weeks is

$$2(12)=£24$$

The total storage costs can be calculated in a variety of ways, each giving a slightly different value. The most straightforward is to use the average closing stock level of 76 for the 10-week period. As the annual unit storage cost is £1.50, then the cost of storing 76 items over a 10-week period (or one-fifth of a year) is

$$76(1.50)/5=£22.80$$

An estimate of the total weekly stock holding costs is

$$(10.00+24.00+22.80)/10=£5.68$$

(c) The simulation model could be represented over many weeks (possibly using a computer) with various combinations of Q (order quantity) and R (reorder level) in order to identify the combination with lowest costs.

Example 22.2.2 Brightside Chemicals, a firm that manufactures non-hazardous chemicals, distributes its product in barrels from its main depot. The premises, having a congested inner-city location, have only one loading bay. If further vehicles arrive while the loading bay is being utilized then they have to form a queue. This queue takes place on the local road system and often causes traffic congestion.

The effective utilization of the loading bay and the queuing up of vehicles waiting to be loaded has been a consistent problem for some time. In August 1991 the transport manager decided to examine the queuing problem more closely. He knew from past observation that large queues tended to form in the morning period, so on two consecutive Mondays in August he recorded the arrival times and service times of the vehicles to be loaded.

The distribution of interarrival times and service times is shown in the table below.

Time (min)	Interarrival times (%)	Service times (%)
0–10	18	12
10–20	25	20
20–30	36	45
30–40	13	23
40–50	5	0
50–60	3	0

(a) Assume initial conditions at 9.00 a.m. with no customers in the system. Simulate, using the following random numbers, the arrival and service sequences until 1.00 p.m. State clearly, for each vehicle, the arrival time at the firm's premises, together with the start and finish time at the loading bay.

Interarrival times	57	23	85	03	48	28	89	44	37	76	15	98	12
Service times	42	01	67	34	63	21	80	11	83	89	58	16	51

(b) Use your simulation results to estimate:
    (i) the level of utilization of the loading bay between 9.00 a.m. and 1.00 p.m. (that is, the time for which the loading bay is in use as a percentage of the total time).
    (ii) the average queuing time for each of the vehicles arriving between 9.00 a.m. and 1.00 p.m.
    (iii) The average queue length between 9.00 a.m. and 1.00 p.m.
    Briefly explain why it may have been more sensible to base these three estimates on the simulation results for the time period between 10.00 a.m. and 1.00 p.m. only.

(ACCA Level 2: Dec. 1991)

ANSWER

(a) The random numbers can be allocated to the interarrival times and the service times in a variety of ways. Here we allocate in the same way as before using the so-called 'top-hat' method.

Interarrival	Times (min)	Service	Times (min)
5	00–17	5	00–11
15	18–42	15	12–31
25	43–78	25	32–76
35	79–91	35	77–99
45	92–96		
55	97–99		

In the following simulation the arrival time of one vehicle is obtained by adding the interarrival time to the arrival time of the previous vehicle. Service is started as soon as the previous lorry leaves and is ended at the time obtained by adding the service start time to the randomly-generated service time.

Customer	Interarrival	Arrival	Service	In	Out
1	25	9.25	25	9.25	9.50
2	15	9.40	5	9.50	9.55
3	35	10.15	25	10.15	10.40
4	5	10.20	25	10.40	11.05
5	25	10.45	25	11.05	11.30
6	15	11.00	15	11.30	11.45
7	35	11.35	35	11.45	12.20
8	25	12.00	5	12.20	12.25
9	15	12.15	35	12.25	1.00
10	25	12.40	35	1.00	1.35
11	5	12.45	25	1.35	
12	55	1.40	15		

(b)   (i) During the four-hour morning period of the simulation the loading bay was free between 9.00 and 9.25 and between 9.55 and 10.15, a total time of 45 minutes (and therefore the loading bay was occupied for 3 hours 15 minutes).

The level of utilization of the loading bay is

$$\frac{3.25 \times 100}{4} = 81.25 \text{ per cent}$$

that is, the loading bay is being occupied for 81.25 per cent of the time.

(ii) The queuing time of the first 11 vehicles is obtained by subtracting the arrival time from the 'In' column. The waiting time for the first vehicle is clearly zero and for the second vehicle it is the 10 minutes between 9.40 a.m. and 9.50 a.m. The queuing times of the 11 vehicles are (in minutes)

$$0, \quad 10, \quad 0, \quad 20, \quad 20, \quad 30, \quad 10, \quad 20, \quad 10, \quad 20, \quad 50$$

giving a mean queuing time of just over 17 minutes per vehicle.

(iii) By observing the simulation results we can determine the queue length over the four-hour period:

Time	Queue length
9.00 to 9.40	0
9.40 to 9.50	1
9.50 to 10.20	0
10.20 to 10.40	1
10.40 to 10.45	0
10.45 to 11.00	1
11.00 to 11.05	2
11.05 to 11.30	1
11.30 to 11.35	0
11.35 to 11.45	1
11.45 to 12.00	0
12.00 to 12.15	1
12.15 to 12.20	2
12.20 to 12.25	1
12.25 to 12.40	0
12.40 to 12.45	1
12.45 to 1.00	2

If we only consider between 9.00 a.m. and 1.00 p.m., the size of the queue is

0 vehicles for 110 minutes

1 vehicle for 105 minutes

2 vehicles for 25 minutes

The mean queue length is

$$\frac{0(110) + 1(105) + 2(25)}{240} = 0.646 \text{ vehicles}$$

The simulation over such a short period of four hours is highly dependent on the initial conditions of no customers in the system. If the simulation is meant to reflect the situation over a longer period of time then it would be wise to consider a period where the initial conditions did not have this influence.

Exercise 22.2.1 The personnel manager of the Orpheus Life Assurance Company has recently been analysing the turnover of secretarial and clerical staff at the company's head office. Currently there are three grades of secretarial and clerical staff (SC1, SC2, and SC3) and it is the company's policy to recruit new staff only into the lowest grade SC1. To maintan appropriate numbers of staff in the two higher grades, promotions are made on a basis of strict seniority (i.e. length of service) from the grade immediately below. In the past, a reasonably high turnover of staff has meant that most employees have been able to progress to the highest grade (SC3) within a few years. More recently, however, the turnover of staff has fallen and, as a consequence, there have been fewer vacancies in the two higher grades which has slowed down the rate of promotion. The number of employees currently required in each of the three grades is

SC1:54   SC2:48   SC3:32

and, on the basis of present figures, the distributions of 'wastage' due to number of employees leaving the company per year are as follows:

Grade SC1	Probability	Grade SC2	Probability	Grade SC3	Probability
0–4	0.1	0–4	0.2	0–4	0.4
5–9	0.3	5–9	0.5	5–9	0.4
10–14	0.4	10–14	0.3	10–14	0.2
15–19	0.2				

Use the random numbers below to simulate wastage and recruitment over a five-year period assuming that there is no change in the number of employees required in each grade.

Random numbers   SC1:3 2 8 8 2   SC2:5 4 1 6 3   SC3:9 5 2 2 1

In all of our examples the random values (such as interarrival time, service time, and demand) that we have generated have been based explicitly on the available sample data. However our sample is typically a sample from some population distribution—possibly normal or negative exponential. It is possible to generate random numbers from known probability distributions but it is beyond the needs of the professional accountancy examinations for which this text is appropriate.

TEST EXERCISES

22.1 (a) Describe the advantages and disadvantages of using simulation to investigate business problems compared with the use of mathematical formulae.

(b) The time between arrivals at a complaints counter in a large department store has been observed to follow the distribution shown below.

Time between arrivals (minutes)	Probability
0–4	0.25
4–8	0.45
8–12	0.20
12–16	0.10

Customers' complaints are handled by a single complaints officer, but all customers who consider their complaints to be 'serious' or who have to wait five minutes or more before being seen by the complaints officer demand to see the store manager, who deals with them separately. The time to deal with complaints by the complaints officer had a normal distribution with a mean of seven minutes and a standard deviation of two minutes. It is estimated that 20 per cent of customers with complaints consider that their complaint is 'serious'.

(i) Describe how you would simulate the arrival and service flows of this system using the above information, a table of random digits, and the following table derived from the standard normal distribution table.

Random number	Number of deviations from mean	Random number	Number of deviations from mean
00–01	−2.5	61–77	+0.5
02–04	−2.0	78–88	+1.0
05–10	−1.5	89–94	+1.5
11–21	−1.0	95–97	+2.0
22–38	−0.5	98–99	+2.5
39–60	0		

(ii) Use the following random digits to simulate the handling of 10 complaining customers, some of whom may have 'serious' complaints.

Interarrival time	09	06	51	62	83	61	59	20	82	68
Serious complaint	5	0	7	3	8	2	9	8	1	6
Service time	39	60	50	31	02	02	83	90	71	16

(iii) Use your simulation to estimate the proportion of customers who eventually see the store manager. Hence estimate the total amount of time that the store manager spends dealing with complaints, assuming an eight-hour day and that the time he spends on each complaint has the same distribution as that of the complaints officer.
(iv) Explain briefly how to use simulation to decide if it would be worth while employing an additional complaints officer.

(ACCA Level 2: June 1988)

22.2 The development of appropriate models and the process of simulation are important aspects of the work of the modern manager accountant.

(a) Explain the terms 'appropriate model' and 'simulation'.
(b) Describe how model development and simulation assist the management accountant and help to assess uncertainty.
(c) Give three specific examples, with a brief description of each, where simulation can be of value in management accounting.
(d) Give the steps necessary to construct a simulation model for a management accounting application of your choice.

(CIMA Level 2: Nov. 1988)

1

SOLUTIONS TO EXERCISES

CHAPTER 1

1.4.1 (a) £80 000 ∓ £5500 (6.88 per cent)
(b) £120 000 ∓ £3504 (2.92 per cent)
(c) £40 000 ∓ £9004 (22.51 per cent)
(d) £13.33 ∓ £3.22 (24.18 per cent)

Test exercises

1.1 £4 501 920 ∓ £70 580
1.3 −27 per cent to +33 per cent

CHAPTER 2

2.1.3 $a = -3$
2.2.1 (E) $X = 12$, $Y = 52$
2.2.2 $P = 7.5$, $Q = 4.5$
2.2.3 2400 units per month
2.3.1 (b) $x = 3$, $x = 6$
2.3.2 $x = 0.5$, $x = 2.75$
2.3.3 (B) $x = 1.5$
2.3.4 $x = -1.0986$, $x = 0.5602$
2.3.5 40 chairs or 80 chairs

Test exercises

2.1 $P = 12$, $Q = 76$
2.2 (b) 4000 units per month
2.3 (i) Hire method (b) (ii) Hire method (a) (iii) Buy
2.4 (b) $P = 5$, $Q = 2.5$
2.5 (b) $P = 11$, $Q = \ln 9 = 2.20$

CHAPTER 3

3.1.1 £3650
3.1.2 11.24 per cent
3.1.3 £18 603
3.1.4 (a) £4517 (b) £4665 (c) 5.04 years (d) 5.31 years
3.2.1 (A) £38 500
3.2.2 (a) Yes (NPV = £381 > 0); (b) No (NPV = −£5973 < 0)
3.2.3 (a) 20.13 per cent (b) 20 per cent
3.3.1 £27 237
3.3.2 £98 147
3.3.3 Repayment size is £2040; effective annual rate is 16.986 per cent
3.3.4 £6492

Test exercises

3.1 £87 022
3.2 (B) 19 per cent
3.3 (A) £10 000
3.4 (B) £31 623
3.5 (D) £11 260
3.6 (C) 10.80 per cent
3.7 The internal rate of return is 13 per cent

CHAPTER 4

4.1.1 $\begin{pmatrix} 200 & 150 \\ 50 & 80 \\ 100 & 120 \end{pmatrix}$

4.2.1 $\begin{pmatrix} 3 & 7 \\ 3 & 5 \end{pmatrix}$

4.2.2 $\begin{pmatrix} 1 & 3 \\ -2 & -1 \end{pmatrix}$

4.2.3 $\begin{pmatrix} 6 & 18 \\ 12 & 10 \\ 4 & 8 \end{pmatrix}$

4.2.4 $\begin{pmatrix} 1.2 & 1.8 & 0.8 & 1.1 \\ 0.5 & 2.5 & 0.7 & 0.8 \\ 1.3 & 1.3 & 0.7 & 1.3 \end{pmatrix}$

4.2.5 $\begin{pmatrix} 5 & 13 \\ 18 & 14 \end{pmatrix}$

4.2.6 $\begin{pmatrix} 12 \\ 20 \end{pmatrix}$

4.2.7 $\begin{pmatrix} 10 & 12 \\ 14 & 16 \end{pmatrix}$

4.4.1 $\begin{pmatrix} 0.5 & -1.5 \\ -0.25 & 1 \end{pmatrix}$

4.4.2 $x=0,\ y=4$

Test exercises

4.1

$$(100 \quad 50 \quad 75 \quad 25) \begin{pmatrix} 1.2 \\ 2.0 \\ 1.0 \\ 0.8 \end{pmatrix} = £315$$

4.2

$$(6 \quad 2 \quad 7) \begin{pmatrix} 2 & 6 \\ 3 & 1 \\ 1 & 2 \end{pmatrix} = (25 \quad 52)$$

$$(25 \quad 52) \begin{pmatrix} 2 \\ 3 \end{pmatrix} = £206$$

4.3 (a) $\begin{pmatrix} 2 & -5 \\ -3 & 8 \end{pmatrix}$ (b) $\begin{pmatrix} -0.5 & 1.5 \\ -0.5 & 1 \end{pmatrix}$

CHAPTER 5

5.1.1 $dy/dx = 35x^4$
5.1.2 $dy/dx = 72x^7$
5.1.3 $dy/dx = 36x^3 + 12x^2 + 16x + 12$
5.1.4 $dy/dx = 50x^4 + 24x^3 + 4x$
5.1.5 (a) $dy/dx = 10x - 3 = 17$ when $x = 2$
   (b) $dy/dx = 4 - 2/x^2 = 2$ when $x = -1$
   (c) $dy/dx = -14/x^3 = -14$ when $x = 1$
   (d) $dy/dx = 5/x = 5$ when $x = 1$
5.1.6 $x^9/3 + c$ where c is an arbitrary constant
5.1.7 (B) The value is $3\frac{1}{3}$
5.2.1 $dy/dx = 12x^2 + 6x - 36 = 0$ when $x = -2$ or $x = 3/2$
5.3.1 (a) $TC = x^3/3 - 14x^2 + 211x + 10$
   (b) $TR = 200x - 8x^2$
   (c) $x = 1$ is a minimum point; $x = 11$ is a maximum point
   (d) $MR = 200 - 16x$
5.3.2 (a) $\pi = -10x^2 + 100x - 140$
   (b) $x = 5$ gives maximum profit
   (c) $MR = 100 - 10x$
   (e) Price elasticity of demand is 3

Test exercises

5.1 (B) 16
5.2 (B) 11
5.3 (A) (a) only
5.4 $x = -5$ is a maximum point; $x = 1$ is a minimum point
5.5 (a) $MR = 50$ (b) $MC = 4x$ (c) Marginal profit $= 50 - 4x$
    (d) $x = 12\,500$ units (e) £112.50 (f) $5000 < x < 20\,000$
5.6 (a) Profit $= -x^3 + 6.5x^2 + 14x - 65$
    (d) 523 screws (e) £43 (f) £8.50
5.7 (a) $TC = x^2 + 4$ (b) $TR = 30x - 2x^2$
    (c) $x = 5$ gives maximum profit (d) $AR = 30 - 2x$

CHAPTER 6

Test exercises

6.2 (a) is true, (b) is false, (c) is true
6.3 (b) and (c) only

CHAPTER 8

8.2.1 5
8.2.2 £239
8.3.1 48
8.3.2 £222
8.4.1 19
8.4.2 £162
8.5.1 (a) mean $=$ £140.20; (b) median $=$ £132.31; (c) mode $=$ £116.15
8.6.1 1.67
8.6.2 2
8.6.3 2
8.6.4 variance $= 9491.50$ pounds squared; s.d. $=$ £97.42
8.7.1 (b) mean $=$ £2505; standard deviation $=$ £1190
    (c) median $=$ £2270; semi-interquartile range $=$ £776

Test exercises

8.1 (c) mean $= 35.75$ microseconds; s.d. $= 11.62$ microseconds
    (e) median $= 36.25$ microseconds; $QD = 7.92$ microseconds
8.2 (a) median $= 4.3$ days; $QD = 4$ days; top decile $= 17.6$ days
    (c) £520 200
8.3 (a) mean $=$ £148.71; median $=$ £148.50; mode $=$ £148.70
    (c) $MD =$ £61.49; s.d. $=$ £76.50; $QD =$ £61.55
8.4 mean $= 1420$ gallons; s.d. $= 272$ gallons
8.5 (a) mean age $= 36.4$ years
    (b) s.d. $= 22.6$ years
    (e) median age $= 34.2$ years

CHAPTER 9

9.1.1 (a) Profit $= -9.2367 + 0.04777 \times$ Sales; predict £38.5 million profit
9.2.1 (a) $y = 14.5352 + 2.1221x$
     (c) $r = 0.9338$
9.3.1 $VR = 54.49$
9.3.2 (c) 95 per cent interval is from 53 to 63 (inclusive) applications
9.4.1 (a) $a = 748$; $b = 1.053$
     (b) 1314; 1195; 1259
     (d) Optimistic: 188; 201; 214. Pessimistic: 186; 196; 206
9.5.1 (E) Rank correlation coefficient is 0.79

Test exercises

9.1 (b) Price $= 129.54 - 11.72 \times$ Distance
    (c) £76 800
9.2 (a) Contribution $= 2.22 + 1.012 \times$ Sales, giving £265 340
    (b) 95 per cent interval from £328 000 to £203 000
9.3 (b) Predicted turnover for multiples is £1151.5 million
       Predicted turnover for cooperatives is £357.73 million
9.5 (b) $y = 18.5 + 8.5x$; $r = 0.9113$
    (c) $y = 22.2052 + 52.4119z$; $r = 0.9809$

CHAPTER 10

10.2.1 (a) Trend: 114.000, 114.875, 115.625, 116.625, 118.000, 119.125, 119.875, 120.250,
             120.125, 120.125
      (b) Seasonals: $Q1 -10.81$, $Q2$ 11.01, $Q3$ 12.57, $Q4 -12.77$
      (c) Product with summer sales peak, e.g. ice cream
      (d) Deseasonalized: 111, 114, 114, 115, 115, 117, 117, 120, 121, 120, 120, 120, 120, 121
      (e) 0.93
10.3.1 (a) Deseasonalized forecasts: 205, 210, 215
        Actual forecasts: 164, 294, 172
      (b) Revenue forecasts: £167 280, £305 878, £182 528

Test exercises

10.1 (a) Trend: 16.875, 16.375, 15.750, 15.375, 14.625, 13.500, 12.750, 12.000, 11.125, 10.375, 9.375, 8.375, 7.875,
            7.750, 7.500, 7.000, 6.875, 7.000, 6.875, 6.875
    (b) Seasonals: $Q1 -2.4875$, $Q2 -1.9625$, $Q3$ 4.2875, $Q4$ 0.1625
    (c) Deseasonalized: 17, 18, 17, 16, 16, 15, 15, 15, 11, 11, 13, 11, 8, 8, 8, 8, 7, 8, 6, 6, 8, 8, 5, 7
10.2 Deseasonalized: 50, 55, 60.8, 66.7, 71.1, 82.5, 80.8, 100, 100
10.3 (a) Trend: 24.667, 26.667, 29.000, 29.333, 29.500, 28.833, 27.833, 28.000, 29.333, 31.333
    (b) Seasonals: JFMA: 5.4400, MJJA: -7.0462, SOND: 1.6063
    (c) Forecasts: 38.3, 26.5, 35.9
10.4 (A) 510
10.5 (a) Trend: 331.8844, 349.2236, 366.5628, 383.9020, 401.2412, 418.5804, 435.9196, 453.2588, 470.5980, 487.9373,
            505.2764, 522.6156
    (b) Seasonals: $Q1 -4.9079$, $Q2$ 36.0863, $Q3 -9.2529$, $Q4 -21.9255$
    (c) Forecasts: 535, 593, 565, 570

CHAPTER 11

11.1.1 (a) 122.2 (b) 128.25
11.1.2 120.7
11.1.3 125.8
11.1.4 105.0
11.1.5 107.9
11.1.6 120.7
11.1.7 127.0
11.1.8 110.4
11.1.9 (a) Year 2 Laspeyres = 135.8; Year 3 Laspeyres = 142.0
　　　　(b) Year 2 Paasche = 129.7; Year 3 Paasche = 141.9
11.3.1 (a) 100, 102, 107, 110, 113, 116
　　　　(b) 85, 90, 91, 95, 98, 100, 102, 107, 110, 113, 116
　　　　(c) 115, 117, 121, 123, 123, 125, 126, 124, 124, 124, 131

Test exercises

11.1 (D) 94
11.2 (b) 123.7
　　　(d) 120.6
　　　(e) It is a Laspeyres price index
11.3 (E) Sales value index
11.4 (a) 121.20
　　　(b) 104.37
　　　(c) 104.05
　　　(d) 130.39
11.5 (C) (c) only

CHAPTER 12

12.1.1 (a) 0.40 (b) 0.31 (c) 0.06 (d) 0.20
12.3.1 (b) 0.804 (c) 0.182
12.4.1 (a) 0.1977 (b) 0.0971
12.4.2 (a) $5/9 = 0.556$ (b) $5/73 = 0.0685$

Test exercises

12.1 (D) 0.4
12.2 (E) 0.9
12.3 $8/11 = 0.727$
12.4 (a) 0.79 (b) 0.833 (c) 0.036 (d) 127
12.5 $5/6 = 0.833$

CHAPTER 13

13.2.1 Average cost = 37.5 p
　　　　Use 200 000 leaflets
13.2.2 Respective expected profits in pounds:
　　　　1100, 1301.50, 1405, 1386, 1244.50

13.3.1 (b) £102 637 for no market research and high demand
£41 392 for no market research and low demand
£126 159 for market research and high demand
£53 153 for market research and low demand
£40 581 for market research followed by old range

(c) (i) £84 264 (ii) £40 581 (iii) £87 547

(d) Carry out the market research and act on it as specified in the question

(e) Yes. The expected return from market research followed by appropriate action reduces to £79 720, and it is better to proceed with the new range without market research

13.4.1 £107.80 per match

13.4.2 (a) Hold 14 cars (b) Hold 16 cars

Test exercises

13.1 (b) (i) 3 units, giving expected profit £63
(ii) £46.67
(c) 1 unit
(e) (i) leads to £74 maximum from 4 units and
(ii) leads to £69 maximum from 3 units
Both are worth while and (i) is to be recommended

13.2 (c) 70 garments, giving expected profit £4120

13.3 Method C, giving expected contribution £44 000

13.4 (a) Recommend giving a high limit
(b) £2 per customer
(c) £10 per customer

13.5 (b) Attempt in-house production. If it fails, sub-contract. Expected return is £53 000

CHAPTER 14

14.1.1 60 480

14.1.2 924

14.1.3 (a) 0.3932 (b) 0.3446

14.1.4 Between 40 and 60

14.2.1 No, because expected increase in daily profit is only £1430

14.3.1 No, since expected cost per box is currently only 2.8 p

14.5.1 (a) 0.8413 (b) 45.3 grams

14.6.1 0.0968

14.6.2 0.5717

Test exercises

14.1 (D) 350

14.2 Mean $= 0.24$, $p = 0.048$
Probabilities are 0.78, 0.20, 0.02, 0.00, 0.00, 0.00
Expected numbers are 78, 20, 2, 0, 0, 0

14.3 0.879

14.4 (E) 0.78

14.5 (E) 4.6

14.6 (B) 0.0228

14.7 (B) 0.80

14.8 1244

CHAPTER 15

15.1.1   (a) 502 g, 0.9375 g   (b) 0.017
15.2.1   £150; £11 613 to £12 387
15.2.2   0.146 to 0.174
15.3.1   11.75 to 17.25

Test exercises

15.1   (a) £2.83   (b) £82.70, £97.30
          (d) 0.058, 0.142   (e) 800
15.2   £5.82
15.3   86 minutes, 12.54 minutes
15.4   £150, £35

CHAPTER 16

16.2.1 $T = -3$ (< -1.645); reject H_0
16.2.2 $T = 0.9$ (< 1.645); accept H_0
16.2.3 $T = 0.897$ (< 1.96); accept H_0
16.3.1 $T = 1.91$ (< 2.26); accept H_0

Test exercises

16.1   Using independent sample t-test, $T = 0.84$ (< 2.14); accept H_0
16.2   (b) Using matched t-test, $T = 1.94$ (< 2.57); accept H_0
16.3 $T = -2.60$ (< -2.58); reject H_0

CHAPTER 17

17.1.1 $\chi^2 = 6.88$ (< 7.81); accept H_0
17.2.1 $\chi^2 = 1.05$ (< 9.49); accept H_0
17.3.1 $\chi^2 = 2.16$ (< 16.92); accept H_0

Test exercises

17.1   (a) $\chi^2 = 2.18$ (< 7.81); accept H_0
17.2 $\chi^2 = 7.574$ (> 5.99); reject H_0
17.3 $\chi^2 = 11.1$ (> 3.84); reject H_0

CHAPTER 18

Test exercises

18.1   (a)   17.461 to 17.359
          (c)   Fault rectified after sample 6

18.2   (a)   0.0342

(b)   Inner limit $= 0.0470$; outer limit $= 0.0599$

(c)   No

CHAPTER 19

19.1.1   (a)   Max $P = 10x + 6y$

(b) $600x + 300y \leqslant 21\,000$

$35x + 60y \leqslant 2100$

$x + y \leqslant 40$

$x \geqslant 5$

$y \geqslant 5$

19.2.1   (a)   Min $P = 40x + 60y$

subject to $x + y \geqslant 100$

$y \geqslant 30$

$2x + 5y \geqslant 400$

$x \geqslant y$

(c) $x = 70$, $y = 30$, $C = 4600$

19.3.1   (a)   Max $P = 124x + 80y$

subject to $150x + 90y \leqslant 13\,500$

$100x + 120y \leqslant 12\,000$

$y \leqslant 75$

$x = 60$, $y = 50$ Increase contribution $= £1720$

(b)   Increased contribution $+ £3402.50$

(c)   Minimum price $+ £5.60$ per unit

Test exercises

19.1   Min $C = 13x + 6y$ (in £'000s)

subject to $x + 0.5y \geqslant 100$

$y \leqslant 50$

$y \geqslant 30$

$y \leqslant x$

$x \leqslant 140$

$x = 75$, $y = 50$, minimum cost $= £1\,275\,000$

19.2   Min $C = 10x + 5y$

subject to $0.18x + 0.03y \geqslant 100$

$0.05x + 0.02y \geqslant 50$

$0.02x + 0.05y \geqslant 40$

$x = 809.5$, $y = 476.2$, giving a total cost of £10 476

19.3   (a)   Max $P = 35a + 30b + 20c$

subject to $10a + 12b + 8c \leqslant 8000$

$8a + 5b + 9c \leqslant 5900$

$c = 250$

$a \leqslant 350$

$b \leqslant 290$

(b) $a = 300$, $b = 250$, $c = 250$, $P = £23\,000$

(c)   £110 − £123

(d)   £1.41 up to 230 hours

CHAPTER 20

20.1.1 (c)

Activity	A	B	C	D	E	F	G
Earliest start	0	0	0	30	30	42	18
Latest start	0	4	26	30	32	42	44
Earliest finish	30	38	18	32	58	60	34
Latest finish	30	42	44	42	60	60	60
Float	0	4	26	0	2	0	26

20.2.1 (a) Critical path is B–F–H. Associated cost is £63 000
(b) Completion time is extended from 13 weeks to 15 weeks
(c) Minimum cost is £59 500
20.3.1 (a) Normal duration is 58 days. Normal cost is £4820
(b) Crash duration is 51 days. Crash cost is £4987
Critical path is unchanged at 10–40–60–90–120
(c) Least cost for 51 days is £4700, obtained by crashing 40–60, 60–90, and 90–120 while doing everything else at normal speed
20.4.1 (a) A–E–H–I–J is critical path. Duration is 22 weeks.
20.5.1 (b) A–B–E–G–H–J is critical path. Duration is 80 days.
(c) 72.6 days to 87.4 days. Independence is assumed.
(d) 0.19

Test exercises

20.1 (c)

Activity	A	B	C	D	E	F	G	H	J
Earliest start	0	0	0	3	4	3	7	8	3
Latest start	3	3	3	4	6	5	8	9	4
Earliest finish	2	2	0	5	6	6	7	8	5
Latest finish	5	5	7	6	8	8	8	9	6
Float	2	2	0	2	2	3	0	0	2

20.2 (a) Critical path is A–C–E–G. Associated cost is £141 000
(b) Floats (in months) are:

A	B	C	D	E	F	G	H
0	1	0	2	0	2	0	2

(c) (i) Minimum time is 11 months. Least cost is £137 000
(ii) Minimum cost is £129 000. Durations (months) are:

A	B	C	D	E	F	G	H
4	5	2	3	3	4	3	2

20.3 (b) A–E–C–D–G–M is critical
(c) Duration is 73 days
20.4 (b) Critical path is G–I–D–J–B–H–F. Duration is 32 weeks
20.5 (a) Expected duration is 50 days. A–E–I–L is critical path
(b) Expected duration is 62 days. C–H–M is critical path
(c) Probability of completion on time is 0.0778

CHAPTER 21

21.2.1 (a) 15 ribbons
(b) 12.5 ribbons
21.3.1 1680 tonnes

21.4.1   Order size is 1082 items

      Reorder when 231 orders have been accumulated

21.5.1   (b) EOQ is 3200 boxes

           Average time between replenishments is four weeks

Test exercises

21.1   20 000 units

21.2   (b) 100 units

21.3   (a) (i) £0.50   (ii) £37.50

      (b) (i) 3000 bags with 20 replenishments

            (ii) 2000 bags with 30 replenishments

      (c) No

      (d) No

21.4   (a) 20 tonnes

      (b)   7 tonnes

21.5   (b) £480 780

      (c) (ii) 1200 of part *A* and 9600 of part *B*

           The saving is £5386 or 1.12 per cent

STATISTICAL TABLES

Percentage points of the normal distribution

$Z = \dfrac{X-\mu}{\sigma}$	0	1	2	3	4	5	6	7	8	9
0.0	0.5000	0.4960	0.4920	0.4880	0.4840	0.4801	0.4761	0.4721	0.4681	0.4641
0.1	0.4602	0.4562	0.4522	0.4483	0.4443	0.4404	0.4364	0.4325	0.4286	0.4247
0.2	0.4207	0.4168	0.4129	0.4090	0.4052	0.4013	0.3974	0.3936	0.3897	0.3859
0.3	0.3821	0.3783	0.3745	0.3707	0.3669	0.3632	0.3594	0.3557	0.3520	0.3483
0.4	0.3446	0.3409	0.3372	0.3336	0.3300	0.3264	0.3228	0.3192	0.3156	0.3121
0.5	0.3085	0.3050	0.3015	0.2981	0.2946	0.2912	0.2877	0.2843	0.2810	0.2776
0.6	0.2743	0.2709	0.2676	0.2643	0.2611	0.2578	0.2546	0.2514	0.2483	0.2451
0.7	0.2420	0.2398	0.2358	0.2327	0.2296	0.2266	0.2236	0.2206	0.2177	0.2148
0.8	0.2119	0.2090	0.2061	0.2033	0.2005	0.1977	0.1949	0.1922	0.1894	0.1867
0.9	0.1841	0.1814	0.1788	0.1762	0.1736	0.1711	0.1685	0.1660	0.1635	0.1611
1.0	0.1587	0.1562	0.1539	0.1515	0.1492	0.1469	0.1446	0.1423	0.1401	0.1379
1.1	0.1357	0.1335	0.1314	0.1292	0.1271	0.1251	0.1230	0.1210	0.1190	0.1170
1.2	0.1151	0.1131	0.1112	0.1093	0.1075	0.1056	0.1038	0.1020	0.1003	0.0985
1.3	0.0968	0.0951	0.0934	0.0918	0.0901	0.0885	0.0869	0.0853	0.0838	0.0823
1.4	0.0808	0.0793	0.0778	0.0764	0.0749	0.0735	0.0721	0.0708	0.0694	0.0681
1.5	0.0668	0.0655	0.0643	0.0630	0.0618	0.0606	0.0594	0.0582	0.0571	0.0559
1.6	0.0548	0.0537	0.0526	0.0516	0.0505	0.0495	0.0485	0.0475	0.0465	0.0455
1.7	0.0446	0.0436	0.0427	0.0418	0.0409	0.0401	0.0392	0.0384	0.0375	0.0367
1.8	0.0359	0.0351	0.0344	0.0336	0.0329	0.0322	0.0314	0.0307	0.0301	0.0294
1.9	0.0287	0.0281	0.0274	0.0268	0.0262	0.0256	0.0250	0.0244	0.0239	0.0233
2.0	0.02275	0.02222	0.02169	0.02118	0.02068	0.02018	0.01970	0.01923	0.01876	0.01831
2.1	0.01786	0.01743	0.01700	0.01659	0.01618	0.01578	0.01539	0.01500	0.01463	0.01426
2.2	0.01390	0.01355	0.01321	0.01287	0.01255	0.01222	0.01191	0.01160	0.01130	0.01101
2.3	0.01072	0.01044	0.01017	0.00990	0.00964	0.00939	0.00914	0.00889	0.00866	0.00842
2.4	0.00820	0.00798	0.00776	0.00755	0.00734	0.00714	0.00695	0.00676	0.00657	0.00639
2.5	0.00621	0.00604	0.00587	0.00570	0.00554	0.00539	0.00523	0.00508	0.00494	0.00480
2.6	0.00466	0.00453	0.00440	0.00427	0.00415	0.00402	0.00391	0.00379	0.00368	0.00357
2.7	0.00347	0.00336	0.00326	0.00317	0.00307	0.00298	0.00289	0.00280	0.00272	0.00264
2.8	0.00256	0.00248	0.00240	0.00233	0.00226	0.00219	0.00212	0.00205	0.00199	0.00193
2.9	0.00187	0.00181	0.00175	0.00169	0.00164	0.00159	0.00154	0.00149	0.00144	0.00139

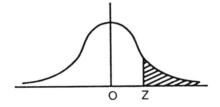

Tail Area	10%	5%	2.5%	2%	1%	0.1%	0.01%	0.001%
$\dfrac{x-\mu}{\sigma}$	1.2816	1.6449	1.9600	2.0537	2.3263	3.0902	3.7190	4.2649

Percentage points of the *t*-distribution

v	5%	2.5%	1%	0.5%	0.05%
			P%		
1	6.31	12.7	31.8	63.7	637
2	2.92	4.30	6.96	9.92	31.6
3	2.35	3.18	4.54	5.84	12.9
4	2.13	2.78	3.75	4.60	8.61
5	2.01	2.57	3.36	4.03	6.87
6	1.94	2.45	3.14	3.71	5.96
7	1.89	2.36	3.00	3.50	5.41
8	1.86	2.31	2.90	3.36	5.04
9	1.83	2.26	2.82	3.25	4.78
10	1.81	2.23	2.76	3.17	4.59
11	1.80	2.20	2.72	3.11	4.44
12	1.78	2.18	2.68	3.05	4.32
13	1.77	2.16	2.65	3.01	4.22
14	1.76	2.14	2.62	2.98	4.14
15	1.75	2.13	2.60	2.95	4.07
16	1.75	2.12	2.58	2.92	4.01
17	1.74	2.11	2.57	2.90	3.96
18	1.73	2.10	2.55	2.88	3.92
19	1.73	2.09	2.54	2.86	3.88
20	1.72	2.09	2.53	2.85	3.85
21	1.72	2.08	2.52	2.83	3.82
22	1.72	2.07	2.51	2.82	3.79
23	1.71	2.07	2.50	2.81	3.77
24	1.71	2.06	2.49	2.80	3.74
25	1.71	2.06	2.48	2.79	3.72
26	1.71	2.06	2.48	2.78	3.71
27	1.70	2.05	2.47	2.77	3.69
28	1.70	2.05	2.47	2.76	3.67
29	1.70	2.05	2.46	2.76	3.66
30	1.70	2.04	2.46	2.75	3.65
40	1.68	2.02	2.42	2.70	3.55
60	1.67	2.00	2.39	2.66	3.46
120	1.66	1.98	2.36	2.62	3.37
∞	1.64	1.96	2.33	2.58	3.29

v is the number of degrees of freedom

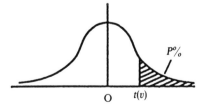

Percentage points of the χ^2 distribution

					$P(\%)$							
v	99.5	99	97.5	95	90	10	5	2.5	1	0.5	0.1	v
1	0.0000	0.0002	0.0098	0.0039	0.016	2.71	3.84	5.02	6.63	7.88	10.8	1
2	0.010	0.020	0.051	0.103	0.211	4.61	5.99	7.38	9.21	10.6	13.8	2
3	0.02	0.115	0.216	0.352	0.584	6.25	7.81	9.35	11.3	12.8	16.3	3
4	0.207	0.297	0.484	0.711	1.06	7.78	9.49	11.1	13.3	14.9	18.5	4
5	0.412	0.554	0.831	1.15	1.61	9.24	11.1	12.8	15.1	16.7	20.5	5
6	0.676	0.872	1.24	1.64	2.20	10.6	12.6	14.4	16.8	18.5	22.5	6
7	0.989	1.24	1.69	2.17	2.83	12.0	14.1	16.0	18.5	20.3	24.3	7
8	1.34	1.65	2.18	2.73	3.49	13.4	15.5	17.5	20.1	22.0	26.1	8
9	1.73	2.09	2.70	3.33	4.17	14.7	16.9	19.0	21.7	23.6	27.9	9
10	2.16	2.56	3.25	3.94	4.87	16.0	18.3	20.5	23.2	25.2	29.6	10
11	2.60	3.05	3.82	4.57	5.58	17.3	19.7	21.9	24.7	26.8	31.3	11
12	3.07	3.57	4.40	5.23	6.30	18.5	21.0	23.3	26.2	28.3	32.9	12
13	3.57	4.11	5.01	5.89	7.04	19.8	22.4	24.7	27.7	29.8	34.5	13
14	4.07	4.66	5.63	6.57	7.79	21.1	23.7	26.1	29.1	31.3	36.1	14
15	4.60	5.23	6.26	7.26	8.55	22.3	25.0	27.5	30.6	32.8	37.7	15
16	5.14	5.81	6.91	7.96	9.31	23.5	26.3	28.8	32.0	34.3	39.3	16
17	5.70	6.41	7.56	8.67	10.1	24.8	27.6	30.2	33.4	35.7	40.8	17
18	6.26	7.01	8.23	9.39	10.9	26.0	28.9	31.5	34.8	37.2	42.3	18
19	6.84	7.63	8.91	10.1	11.7	27.2	30.1	32.9	36.2	38.6	43.8	19
20	7.43	8.26	9.59	10.9	12.4	28.4	31.4	34.2	37.6	40.0	45.3	20
21	8.03	8.90	10.3	11.6	13.2	29.6	32.7	35.5	38.9	41.4	46.8	21
22	8.64	9.54	11.0	12.3	14.0	30.8	33.9	36.8	40.3	42.8	48.3	22
23	9.26	10.2	11.7	13.1	14.8	32.0	35.2	38.1	41.6	44.2	49.7	23
24	9.89	10.9	12.4	13.8	15.7	33.2	36.4	39.4	43.0	45.6	51.2	24
25	10.5	11.5	13.1	14.6	16.5	34.4	37.7	40.6	44.3	46.9	52.6	25
26	11.2	12.2	13.8	15.4	17.3	35.6	38.9	41.9	45.6	48.3	54.1	26
27	11.8	12.9	14.6	16.2	18.1	36.7	40.1	43.2	47.0	49.6	55.5	27
28	12.5	13.6	15.3	16.9	18.9	37.9	41.3	44.5	48.3	51.0	56.9	28
29	13.1	14.3	16.0	17.7	19.8	39.1	42.6	46.7	49.6	52.3	58.3	29
30	13.8	15.0	16.8	18.5	20.6	40.3	43.8	47.0	50.9	53.7	59.7	30

v is the number of degrees of freedom

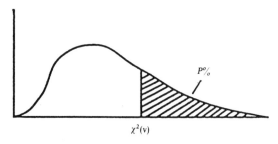

$P\%$

$\chi^2(v)$

Table of compound interest factors

Interest rate (%)

Yrs.	1	2	3	4	5	6	7	8	9	10	11	12	13	14	15	16	17	18	19	20	21	22	23	24	25
1	1.01	1.02	1.03	1.04	1.05	1.06	1.07	1.08	1.09	1.10	1.11	1.12	1.13	1.14	1.15	1.16	1.17	1.18	1.19	1.20	1.21	1.22	1.23	1.24	1.25
2	1.02	1.04	1.06	1.08	1.10	1.12	1.14	1.17	1.19	1.21	1.23	1.25	1.28	1.30	1.32	1.35	1.37	1.39	1.42	1.44	1.46	1.49	1.51	1.54	1.56
3	1.03	1.06	1.09	1.12	1.16	1.19	1.23	1.26	1.30	1.33	1.37	1.40	1.44	1.48	1.52	1.56	1.60	1.64	1.69	1.73	1.77	1.82	1.86	1.91	1.95
4	1.04	1.08	1.13	1.17	1.22	1.26	1.31	1.36	1.41	1.46	1.52	1.57	1.63	1.69	1.75	1.81	1.87	1.94	2.01	2.07	2.14	2.22	2.29	2.36	2.44
5	1.05	1.10	1.16	1.22	1.28	1.34	1.40	1.47	1.54	1.61	1.69	1.76	1.84	1.93	2.01	2.10	2.19	2.29	2.39	2.49	2.59	2.70	2.82	2.93	3.05
6	1.06	1.13	1.19	1.27	1.34	1.42	1.50	1.59	1.68	1.77	1.87	1.97	2.08	2.19	2.31	2.44	2.57	2.70	2.84	2.99	3.14	3.30	3.46	3.64	3.81
7	1.07	1.15	1.23	1.31	1.41	1.50	1.61	1.71	1.83	1.95	2.08	2.21	2.35	2.50	2.66	2.83	3.00	3.19	3.38	3.58	3.80	4.02	4.26	4.51	4.77
8	1.08	1.17	1.27	1.34	1.48	1.59	1.72	1.85	1.99	2.14	2.30	2.48	2.66	2.85	3.06	3.28	3.51	3.76	4.02	4.30	4.59	4.91	5.24	5.59	5.96
9	1.09	1.20	1.30	1.42	1.55	1.69	1.84	2.00	2.17	2.36	2.56	2.77	3.00	3.25	3.52	3.80	4.11	4.44	4.79	5.16	5.56	5.99	6.44	6.93	7.45
10	1.10	1.22	1.34	1.48	1.63	1.79	1.97	2.16	2.37	2.59	2.84	3.11	3.39	3.71	4.05	4.41	4.81	5.23	5.69	6.19	6.73	7.30	7.93	8.59	9.31
11	1.12	1.24	1.38	1.54	1.71	1.90	2.10	2.33	2.58	2.85	3.15	3.48	3.84	4.23	4.65	5.12	5.62	6.18	6.78	7.43	8.14	8.91	9.75	10.66	11.64
12	1.13	1.27	1.43	1.60	1.80	2.01	2.25	2.52	2.81	3.14	3.50	3.90	4.33	4.82	5.35	5.94	6.58	7.29	8.06	8.92	9.85	10.87	11.99	13.21	14.55
13	1.14	1.29	1.47	1.67	1.89	2.13	2.41	2.72	3.07	3.45	3.88	4.36	4.90	5.49	6.15	6.89	7.70	8.60	9.60	10.70	11.92	13.26	14.75	16.39	18.19
14	1.15	1.32	1.51	1.73	1.98	2.26	2.58	2.94	3.34	3.80	4.31	4.89	5.53	6.26	7.08	7.99	9.01	10.15	11.42	12.84	14.42	16.18	18.14	20.32	22.74
15	1.16	1.35	1.56	1.80	2.08	2.40	2.76	3.17	3.64	4.18	4.78	5.47	6.25	7.14	8.14	9.27	10.54	11.97	13.59	15.41	17.45	19.74	22.31	25.20	28.42
16	1.17	1.37	1.60	1.87	2.18	2.54	2.95	3.43	3.97	4.59	5.31	6.13	7.07	8.14	9.36	10.75	12.33	14.13	16.17	18.49	21.11	24.09	27.45	31.24	35.53
17	1.18	1.40	1.65	1.95	2.29	2.69	3.166	3.70	4.33	5.05	5.90	6.87	7.99	9.28	10.76	12.47	14.43	16.67	19.24	22.19	25.55	29.38	33.76	38.74	44.41
18	1.20	1.43	1.70	2.03	2.41	2.85	3.38	4.00	4.72	5.56	6.54	7.69	9.02	10.58	12.38	14.46	16.88	19.67	22.90	26.62	30.91	35.85	41.52	48.04	55.51
19	1.21	1.46	1.75	2.11	2.53	3.03	3.62	4.32	5.14	6.12	7.26	8.61	10.20	12.06	14.23	16.78	19.75	23.21	27.25	31.95	37.40	43.74	51.07	59.57	69.39
20	1.22	1.49	1.81	2.19	2.65	3.21	3.87	4.66	5.60	6.73	8.06	9.65	11.52	13.74	16.37	19.46	23.11	27.39	32.43	38.34	45.36	53.36	62.82	73.86	86.74
21	1.23	1.52	1.86	2.28	2.79	3.40	4.14	5.03	6.11	7.40	8.95	10.80	13.02	15.67	18.82	22.57	27.03	32.32	38.59	46.01	54.76	65.10	77.27	91.59	108.42
22	1.24	1.55	1.92	2.37	2.93	3.60	4.43	5.44	6.66	8.14	9.93	12.10	14.71	17.86	21.64	26.19	31.63	38.14	45.92	55.21	66.26	79.42	95.04	113.57	135.53
23	1.26	1.58	1.97	2.46	3.07	3.82	4.74	5.87	7.26	8.95	11.03	13.55	16.63	20.36	24.89	30.38	37.01	45.01	54.65	66.25	80.18	96.89	116.90	140.83	169.41
24	1.27	1.61	2.03	2.56	3.23	4.05	5.07	6.34	7.91	9.85	12.24	15.18	18.79	23.21	28.63	35.24	43.30	53.11	65.03	79.50	97.02	118.21	143.79	174.63	211.76
25	1.28	1.64	2.09	2.67	3.39	4.29	5.43	6.85	8.62	10.83	13.59	17.00	21.23	26.46	32.92	40.87	50.66	62.67	77.39	95.40	117.39	144.21	176.86	216.54	264.70
26	1.30	1.67	2.16	2.77	3.56	4.55	5.81	7.40	9.40	11.92	15.08	19.04	23.99	30.17	37.86	47.41	59.27	73.95	92.09	114.48	142.04	175.94	217.54	268.51	330.87
27	1.31	1.71	2.22	2.88	3.73	4.82	6.21	7.99	10.25	13.11	16.74	21.32	27.11	34.39	43.54	55.00	69.35	87.26	109.59	137.37	171.87	214.64	267.57	332.95	413.59
28	1.32	1.74	2.29	3.00	3.92	5.11	6.65	8.63	11.17	14.42	18.58	23.88	30.63	39.20	50.07	63.80	81.13	102.97	130.41	164.84	207.97	261.86	329.11	412.86	516.99
29	1.33	1.78	2.36	3.12	4.12	5.42	7.11	9.32	12.17	15.86	20.62	26.75	34.62	44.69	57.58	74.01	94.93	121.50	155.19	197.81	251.64	319.47	404.81	511.95	646.23
30	1.35	1.81	2.43	3.24	4.32	5.74	7.61	10.06	13.27	17.45	22.89	29.96	39.12	50.95	66.21	85.85	111.06	143.37	184.68	237.38	304.48	389.76	497.91	634.82	807.79
31	1.36	1.85	2.50	3.37	4.54	6.09	8.15	10.87	14.46	19.19	25.41	33.56	44.20	58.08	76.14	99.59	129.95	169.18	219.76	284.85	368.42	475.50	612.43	787.18	1009.74
32	1.37	1.88	2.58	3.51	4.76	6.45	8.72	11.74	15.76	21.11	28.21	37.58	49.95	66.21	87.57	115.52	152.04	199.63	261.52	341.82	445.79	580.12	753.29	976.10	1262.18
33	1.39	1.92	2.65	3.65	5.00	6.84	9.33	12.68	17.18	23.23	31.31	42.09	56.44	75.48	100.70	134.00	177.88	235.56	311.21	410.19	539.41	707.74	926.55	1210.36	1577.72
34	1.40	1.96	2.73	3.79	5.25	7.25	9.98	13.69	18.73	25.55	34.75	47.14	63.78	86.05	115.80	155.44	208.12	277.96	370.34	492.22	652.68	863.44	1139.66	1500.85	1972.15
35	1.42	2.00	2.81	3.95	5.52	7.69	10.68	14.79	20.41	28.10	38.57	52.80	72.07	98.10	133.18	180.31	243.50	328.00	440.70	590.67	789.75	1053.40	1401.78	1861.05	2465.19
36	1.43	2.04	2.90	4.10	5.79	8.15	11.42	15.97	22.25	30.91	42.82	59.14	81.44	111.83	153.15	209.16	284.90	387.04	524.43	708.80	955.59	1285.15	1724.19	2307.71	3081.49
37	1.45	2.08	2.99	4.27	6.08	8.64	12.22	17.25	24.55	34.00	47.53	66.23	92.02	127.49	176.12	242.63	333.33	456.70	624.08	850.56	1156.27	1567.88	2120.75	2861.56	3851.86
38	1.46	2.12	3.07	4.44	6.39	9.15	13.08	18.63	26.44	37.40	52.76	74.18	103.99	145.34	202.54	281.45	390.00	538.91	742.65	1020.67	1399.08	1912.82	2608.52	3548.33	4814.82
39	1.47	2.16	3.17	4.62	6.70	9.70	13.99	20.12	28.82	41.14	56.56	83.08	117.51	165.69	232.92	326.48	456.30	636.91	883.75	1224.81	1692.89	2333.64	3208.48	4399.93	6018.53
40	1.49	2.21	3.26	4.80	7.04	10.29	14.97	21.72	31.41	45.26	65.00	93.05	132.78	188.88	267.86	378.72	533.87	750.38	1051.67	1469.77	2048.40	2847.04	3946.43	5455.91	7523.16

Table of present value factors

Interest rate (%)

Yrs.	1	2	3	4	5	6	7	8	9	10	11	12	13	14	15	16	17	18	19	20	21	22	23	24	25
1	0.9901	0.9804	0.9709	0.9615	0.9524	0.9434	0.9346	0.9259	0.9174	0.9091	0.9009	0.8929	0.8850	0.8772	0.8696	0.8621	0.8547	0.8475	0.8403	0.8333	0.8264	0.8197	0.8130	0.8065	0.8000
2	0.9803	0.9612	0.9426	0.9246	0.9070	0.8900	0.8734	0.8573	0.8417	0.8264	0.8116	0.7972	0.7831	0.7695	0.7561	0.7432	0.7305	0.7182	0.7062	0.6944	0.6830	0.6719	0.6610	0.6504	0.6400
3	0.9706	0.9423	0.9151	0.8890	0.8638	0.8396	0.8163	0.7938	0.7722	0.7513	0.7312	0.7118	0.6931	0.6750	0.6575	0.6407	0.6244	0.6086	0.5934	0.5787	0.5645	0.5507	0.5374	0.5245	0.5120
4	0.9610	0.9238	0.8885	0.8548	0.8227	0.7921	0.7629	0.7350	0.7084	0.6830	0.6587	0.6355	0.6133	0.5921	0.5718	0.5523	0.5337	0.5158	0.4987	0.4823	0.4665	0.4514	0.4369	0.4230	0.4096
5	0.9515	0.9057	0.8626	0.8219	0.7835	0.7473	0.7130	0.6806	0.6499	0.6209	0.5935	0.5674	0.5428	0.5194	0.4972	0.4761	0.4561	0.4371	0.4190	0.4019	0.3855	0.3700	0.3552	0.3411	0.3277
6	0.9420	0.8880	0.8375	0.7903	0.7462	0.7050	0.6663	0.6302	0.5963	0.5645	0.5346	0.5066	0.4803	0.4556	0.4323	0.4104	0.3898	0.3704	0.3521	0.3349	0.3186	0.3033	0.2888	0.2751	0.2621
7	0.9327	0.8706	0.8131	0.7599	0.7107	0.6651	0.6227	0.5835	0.5470	0.5132	0.4817	0.4523	0.4251	0.3996	0.3759	0.3538	0.3332	0.3139	0.2959	0.2791	0.2633	0.2486	0.2348	0.2218	0.2097
8	0.9235	0.8535	0.7894	0.7307	0.6768	0.6274	0.5820	0.5403	0.5019	0.4665	0.4339	0.4039	0.3762	0.3506	0.3269	0.3050	0.2848	0.2660	0.2487	0.2326	0.2176	0.2038	0.1909	0.1789	0.1678
9	0.9143	0.8368	0.7664	0.7026	0.6446	0.5919	0.5439	0.5002	0.4604	0.4241	0.3909	0.3606	0.3329	0.3075	0.2843	0.2630	0.2434	0.2255	0.2090	0.1938	0.1799	0.1670	0.1552	0.1443	0.1342
10	0.9053	0.8203	0.7441	0.6756	0.6139	0.5584	0.5083	0.4632	0.4224	0.3855	0.3522	0.3220	0.2946	0.2697	0.2472	0.2267	0.2080	0.1911	0.1756	0.1615	0.1486	0.1369	0.1262	0.1164	0.1074
11	0.8963	0.8043	0.7224	0.6496	0.5847	0.5268	0.4751	0.4289	0.3875	0.3505	0.3173	0.2875	0.2607	0.2366	0.2149	0.1954	0.1778	0.1619	0.1476	0.1346	0.1228	0.1122	0.1026	0.0938	0.0859
12	0.8874	0.7885	0.7014	0.6246	0.5568	0.4970	0.4440	0.3971	0.3555	0.3186	0.2858	0.2567	0.2307	0.2076	0.1869	0.1685	0.1520	0.1372	0.1240	0.1122	0.1015	0.0920	0.0834	0.0757	0.0687
13	0.8787	0.7730	0.6810	0.6006	0.5303	0.4688	0.4150	0.3677	0.3262	0.2897	0.2575	0.2292	0.2042	0.1821	0.1625	0.1452	0.1299	0.1163	0.1042	0.0935	0.0839	0.0754	0.0678	0.0610	0.0550
14	0.8700	0.7579	0.6611	0.5775	0.5051	0.4423	0.3878	0.3405	0.2992	0.2633	0.2320	0.2046	0.1807	0.1597	0.1413	0.1252	0.1110	0.0985	0.0876	0.0779	0.0693	0.0618	0.0551	0.0492	0.0440
15	0.8613	0.7430	0.6419	0.5553	0.4810	0.4173	0.3624	0.3152	0.2745	0.2394	0.2090	0.1827	0.1599	0.1401	0.1229	0.1079	0.0949	0.0835	0.0736	0.0649	0.0573	0.0507	0.0448	0.0397	0.0352
16	0.8528	0.7284	0.6232	0.5339	0.4581	0.3936	0.3387	0.2919	0.2519	0.2176	0.1883	0.1631	0.1415	0.1229	0.1069	0.0930	0.0811	0.0708	0.0618	0.0541	0.0474	0.0415	0.0364	0.0320	0.0281
17	0.8444	0.7142	0.6050	0.5134	0.4363	0.3714	0.3166	0.2703	0.2311	0.1978	0.1696	0.1456	0.1252	0.1078	0.0929	0.0802	0.0693	0.0600	0.0520	0.0451	0.0391	0.0340	0.0296	0.0258	0.0225
18	0.8360	0.7002	0.5874	0.4936	0.4155	0.3503	0.2959	0.2502	0.2120	0.1799	0.1528	0.1300	0.1108	0.0946	0.0808	0.0691	0.0592	0.0508	0.0437	0.0376	0.0323	0.0279	0.0241	0.0208	0.0180
19	0.8277	0.6864	0.5703	0.4746	0.3957	0.3305	0.2765	0.2317	0.1945	0.1635	0.1377	0.1161	0.0981	0.0829	0.0703	0.0596	0.0506	0.0431	0.0367	0.0313	0.0267	0.0229	0.0196	0.0168	0.0144
20	0.8195	0.6730	0.5537	0.4564	0.3769	0.3118	0.2584	0.2145	0.1784	0.1486	0.1240	0.1037	0.0868	0.0728	0.0611	0.0514	0.0433	0.0365	0.0308	0.0261	0.0221	0.0187	0.0159	0.0135	0.0115
21	0.8114	0.6598	0.5375	0.4388	0.3589	0.2942	0.2415	0.1987	0.1637	0.1351	0.1117	0.0926	0.0768	0.0638	0.0531	0.0443	0.0370	0.0309	0.0259	0.0217	0.0183	0.0154	0.0129	0.0109	0.0092
22	0.8034	0.6468	0.5219	0.4220	0.3418	0.2775	0.2257	0.1839	0.1502	0.1228	0.1007	0.0826	0.0680	0.0560	0.0462	0.0382	0.0316	0.0262	0.0218	0.0181	0.0151	0.0126	0.0105	0.0088	0.0074
23	0.7954	0.6342	0.5067	0.4057	0.3256	0.2618	0.2109	0.1703	0.1378	0.1117	0.0907	0.0738	0.0601	0.0491	0.0402	0.0329	0.0270	0.0222	0.0183	0.0151	0.0125	0.0103	0.0086	0.0071	0.0059
24	0.7876	0.6217	0.4919	0.3901	0.3101	0.2470	0.1971	0.1577	0.1264	0.1015	0.0817	0.0659	0.0532	0.0431	0.0349	0.0284	0.0231	0.0188	0.0154	0.0126	0.0103	0.0085	0.0070	0.0057	0.0047
25	0.7798	0.6095	0.4776	0.3751	0.2953	0.2330	0.1842	0.1460	0.1160	0.0923	0.0736	0.0588	0.0471	0.0378	0.0304	0.0245	0.0197	0.0160	0.0129	0.0105	0.0085	0.0069	0.0057	0.0046	0.0038
26	0.7720	0.5976	0.4637	0.3607	0.2812	0.2198	0.1722	0.1352	0.1064	0.0839	0.0663	0.0525	0.0417	0.0331	0.0264	0.0211	0.0169	0.0135	0.0109	0.0087	0.0070	0.0057	0.0046	0.0037	0.0030
27	0.7644	0.5859	0.4502	0.3468	0.2678	0.2074	0.1609	0.1252	0.0976	0.0763	0.0597	0.0469	0.0369	0.0291	0.0230	0.0182	0.0144	0.0115	0.0091	0.0073	0.0058	0.0047	0.0037	0.0030	0.0024
28	0.7568	0.5744	0.4371	0.3335	0.2551	0.1956	0.1504	0.1159	0.0895	0.0693	0.0538	0.0419	0.0326	0.0255	0.0200	0.0157	0.0123	0.0097	0.0077	0.0061	0.0048	0.0038	0.0030	0.0024	0.0019
29	0.7493	0.5631	0.4243	0.3207	0.2429	0.1846	0.1406	0.1073	0.0822	0.0630	0.0485	0.0374	0.0289	0.0224	0.0174	0.0135	0.0105	0.0082	0.0064	0.0051	0.0040	0.0031	0.0025	0.0020	0.0015
30	0.7419	0.5521	0.4120	0.3083	0.2314	0.1741	0.1314	0.0994	0.0754	0.0573	0.0437	0.0334	0.0256	0.0196	0.0151	0.0116	0.0090	0.0070	0.0054	0.0042	0.0033	0.0026	0.0020	0.0016	0.0012
31	0.7346	0.5412	0.4000	0.2965	0.2204	0.1643	0.1228	0.0920	0.0691	0.0521	0.0394	0.0298	0.0226	0.0172	0.0131	0.0100	0.0077	0.0059	0.0046	0.0035	0.0027	0.0021	0.0016	0.0013	0.0010
32	0.7273	0.5306	0.3883	0.2851	0.2099	0.1550	0.1147	0.0852	0.0634	0.0474	0.0355	0.0266	0.0200	0.0151	0.0114	0.0087	0.0066	0.0050	0.0038	0.0029	0.0022	0.0017	0.0013	0.0010	0.0008
33	0.7201	0.5202	0.3770	0.2741	0.1999	0.1462	0.1072	0.0789	0.0582	0.0431	0.0319	0.0238	0.0177	0.0132	0.0099	0.0075	0.0056	0.0042	0.0032	0.0024	0.0019	0.0014	0.0011	0.0008	0.0006
34	0.7130	0.5100	0.3660	0.2636	0.1904	0.1379	0.1002	0.0730	0.0534	0.0391	0.0288	0.0212	0.0157	0.0116	0.0086	0.0064	0.0048	0.0036	0.0027	0.0020	0.0015	0.0012	0.0009	0.0007	0.0005
35	0.7059	0.5000	0.3554	0.2534	0.1813	0.1301	0.0937	0.0676	0.0490	0.0356	0.0259	0.0189	0.0139	0.0102	0.0075	0.0055	0.0041	0.0030	0.0023	0.0017	0.0013	0.0009	0.0007	0.0005	0.0004
36	0.6989	0.4902	0.3450	0.2437	0.1727	0.1227	0.0875	0.0626	0.0449	0.0323	0.0234	0.0169	0.0123	0.0089	0.0065	0.0048	0.0035	0.0026	0.0019	0.0014	0.0010	0.0008	0.0006	0.0004	0.0003
37	0.6920	0.4806	0.3350	0.2343	0.1644	0.1158	0.0818	0.0580	0.0412	0.0294	0.0210	0.0151	0.0109	0.0078	0.0057	0.0041	0.0030	0.0022	0.0016	0.0012	0.0009	0.0006	0.0005	0.0003	0.0003
38	0.6852	0.4712	0.3252	0.2253	0.1566	0.1092	0.0765	0.0537	0.0378	0.0267	0.0190	0.0135	0.0096	0.0069	0.0049	0.0036	0.0026	0.0019	0.0013	0.0010	0.0007	0.0005	0.0004	0.0003	0.0002
39	0.6784	0.4619	0.3158	0.2166	0.1491	0.1031	0.0715	0.0497	0.0347	0.0243	0.0171	0.0120	0.0085	0.0060	0.0043	0.0031	0.0022	0.0016	0.0011	0.0008	0.0006	0.0004	0.0003	0.0002	0.0002
40	0.6717	0.4529	0.3066	0.2083	0.1420	0.0972	0.0668	0.0460	0.0318	0.0221	0.0154	0.0107	0.0075	0.0053	0.0037	0.0026	0.0019	0.0013	0.0010	0.0007	0.0005	0.0004	0.0003	0.0002	0.0001

Table of depreciation factors

Interest rate (%)

Yrs.	1	2	3	4	5	6	7	8	9	10	11	12	13	14	15	16	17	18	19	20	21	22	23	24	25
1	0.9900	0.9800	0.9700	0.9600	0.9500	0.9400	0.9300	0.9200	0.9100	0.9000	0.8900	0.8800	0.8700	0.8600	0.8500	0.8400	0.8300	0.8200	0.8100	0.8000	0.7900	0.7800	0.7700	0.7600	0.7500
2	0.9801	0.9604	0.9409	0.9216	0.9025	0.8836	0.8649	0.8464	0.8281	0.8100	0.7921	0.7744	0.7569	0.7396	0.7225	0.7056	0.6889	0.6724	0.6561	0.6400	0.6241	0.6084	0.5929	0.5776	0.5625
3	0.9703	0.9412	0.9127	0.8847	0.8574	0.8306	0.8044	0.7787	0.7536	0.7290	0.7050	0.6815	0.6585	0.6361	0.6141	0.5927	0.5718	0.5514	0.5314	0.5120	0.4930	0.4746	0.4565	0.4390	0.4219
4	0.9606	0.9224	0.8853	0.8493	0.8145	0.7807	0.7481	0.7164	0.6857	0.6561	0.6274	0.5997	0.5729	0.5470	0.5220	0.4979	0.4756	0.4521	0.4305	0.4096	0.3895	0.3702	0.3515	0.3336	0.3164
5	0.9510	0.9039	0.8587	0.8154	0.7738	0.7339	0.6957	0.6591	0.6240	0.5905	0.5584	0.5277	0.4984	0.4704	0.4437	0.4182	0.3939	0.3707	0.3487	0.3277	0.3077	0.2887	0.2707	0.2536	0.2373
6	0.9415	0.8858	0.8330	0.7828	0.7351	0.6899	0.6470	0.6064	0.5679	0.5314	0.4970	0.4644	0.4336	0.4046	0.3771	0.3513	0.3269	0.3040	0.2824	0.2621	0.2431	0.2252	0.2084	0.1927	0.1780
7	0.9321	0.8681	0.8080	0.7514	0.6983	0.6485	0.6017	0.5578	0.5168	0.4783	0.4423	0.4087	0.3773	0.3479	0.3206	0.2951	0.2714	0.2493	0.2288	0.2097	0.1920	0.1757	0.1605	0.1465	0.1335
8	0.9227	0.8508	0.7837	0.7214	0.6634	0.6096	0.5596	0.5132	0.4703	0.4305	0.3937	0.3596	0.3282	0.2992	0.2725	0.2479	0.2252	0.2044	0.1853	0.1678	0.1517	0.1370	0.1236	0.1113	0.1001
9	0.9135	0.8337	0.7602	0.6925	0.6302	0.5730	0.5204	0.4722	0.4279	0.3874	0.3504	0.3165	0.2855	0.2573	0.2316	0.2082	0.1869	0.1676	0.1501	0.1342	0.1199	0.1069	0.0952	0.0846	0.0751
10	0.9044	0.8171	0.7374	0.6648	0.5987	0.5386	0.4840	0.4344	0.3894	0.3487	0.3118	0.2785	0.2484	0.2213	0.1969	0.1749	0.1552	0.1374	0.1216	0.1074	0.0947	0.0834	0.0733	0.0643	0.0563
11	0.8953	0.8007	0.7153	0.6382	0.5688	0.5063	0.4501	0.3996	0.3544	0.3138	0.2775	0.2451	0.2161	0.1903	0.1673	0.1469	0.1288	0.1127	0.0985	0.0859	0.0748	0.0650	0.0564	0.0489	0.0422
12	0.8864	0.7847	0.6938	0.6127	0.5404	0.4759	0.4186	0.3677	0.3225	0.2824	0.2470	0.2157	0.1880	0.1637	0.1422	0.1234	0.1069	0.0924	0.0798	0.0687	0.0591	0.0507	0.0434	0.0371	0.0317
13	0.8775	0.7690	0.6730	0.5882	0.5133	0.4474	0.3893	0.3383	0.2935	0.2542	0.2198	0.1898	0.1636	0.1408	0.1209	0.1037	0.0887	0.0758	0.0646	0.0550	0.0467	0.0396	0.0334	0.0282	0.0238
14	0.8687	0.7536	0.6528	0.5647	0.4877	0.4205	0.3620	0.3112	0.2670	0.2288	0.1956	0.1670	0.1423	0.1211	0.1028	0.0871	0.0736	0.0621	0.0523	0.0440	0.0369	0.0309	0.0258	0.0214	0.0178
15	0.8601	0.7386	0.6333	0.5421	0.4633	0.3953	0.3367	0.2863	0.2430	0.2059	0.1741	0.1470	0.1238	0.1041	0.0874	0.0731	0.0611	0.0510	0.0424	0.0352	0.0291	0.0241	0.0198	0.0163	0.0134
16	0.8515	0.7238	0.6143	0.5204	0.4401	0.3716	0.3131	0.2634	0.2211	0.1853	0.1550	0.1293	0.1077	0.0895	0.0743	0.0614	0.0507	0.0418	0.0343	0.0281	0.0230	0.0188	0.0153	0.0124	0.0100
17	0.8429	0.7093	0.5958	0.4996	0.4181	0.3493	0.2912	0.2423	0.2012	0.1668	0.1379	0.1138	0.0937	0.0770	0.0631	0.0516	0.0421	0.0343	0.0278	0.0225	0.0182	0.0146	0.0118	0.0094	0.0075
18	0.8345	0.6951	0.5780	0.4796	0.3972	0.3283	0.2708	0.2229	0.1831	0.1501	0.1227	0.1002	0.0815	0.0662	0.0536	0.0434	0.0349	0.0281	0.0225	0.0180	0.0144	0.0114	0.0091	0.0072	0.0056
19	0.8262	0.6812	0.5606	0.4604	0.3774	0.3086	0.2519	0.2051	0.1666	0.1351	0.1092	0.0881	0.0709	0.0569	0.0456	0.0364	0.0290	0.0230	0.0182	0.0144	0.0113	0.0089	0.0070	0.0054	0.0042
20	0.8179	0.6676	0.5438	0.4420	0.3585	0.2901	0.2342	0.1887	0.1516	0.1216	0.0972	0.0776	0.0617	0.0490	0.0388	0.0306	0.0241	0.0189	0.0148	0.0115	0.0090	0.0069	0.0054	0.0041	0.0032
21	0.8097	0.6543	0.5275	0.4243	0.3406	0.2727	0.2178	0.1736	0.1380	0.1094	0.0865	0.0683	0.0537	0.0421	0.0329	0.0257	0.0200	0.0155	0.0120	0.0092	0.0071	0.0054	0.0041	0.0031	0.0024
22	0.8016	0.6412	0.5117	0.4073	0.3235	0.2563	0.2026	0.1597	0.1256	0.0985	0.0770	0.0601	0.0467	0.0362	0.0280	0.0216	0.0166	0.0127	0.0097	0.0074	0.0056	0.0042	0.0032	0.0024	0.0018
23	0.7936	0.6283	0.4963	0.3911	0.3074	0.2410	0.1884	0.1469	0.1143	0.0886	0.0685	0.0529	0.0406	0.0312	0.0238	0.0181	0.0138	0.0104	0.0079	0.0059	0.0044	0.0033	0.0025	0.0018	0.0013
24	0.7857	0.6158	0.4814	0.3754	0.2920	0.2265	0.1752	0.1352	0.1040	0.0798	0.0610	0.0465	0.0354	0.0268	0.0202	0.0152	0.0114	0.0085	0.0064	0.0047	0.0035	0.0026	0.0019	0.0014	0.0010
25	0.7778	0.6035	0.4670	0.3604	0.2774	0.2129	0.1630	0.1244	0.0946	0.0718	0.0543	0.0409	0.0308	0.0230	0.0172	0.0128	0.0095	0.0070	0.0052	0.0038	0.0028	0.0020	0.0015	0.0010	0.0008
26	0.7700	0.5914	0.4530	0.3460	0.2635	0.2001	0.1516	0.1144	0.0861	0.0646	0.0483	0.0360	0.0268	0.0198	0.0146	0.0107	0.0079	0.0057	0.0042	0.0030	0.0022	0.0016	0.0011	0.0008	0.0006
27	0.7623	0.5796	0.4394	0.3321	0.2503	0.1881	0.1409	0.1053	0.0784	0.0581	0.0430	0.0317	0.0233	0.0170	0.0124	0.0090	0.0065	0.0047	0.0034	0.0024	0.0017	0.0012	0.0009	0.0006	0.0004
28	0.7547	0.5680	0.4262	0.3189	0.2378	0.1768	0.1311	0.0968	0.0713	0.0523	0.0383	0.0279	0.0203	0.0147	0.0106	0.0076	0.0054	0.0039	0.0027	0.0019	0.0014	0.0010	0.0007	0.0005	0.0003
29	0.7472	0.5566	0.4134	0.3061	0.2259	0.1662	0.1219	0.0891	0.0649	0.0471	0.0341	0.0245	0.0176	0.0126	0.0090	0.0064	0.0045	0.0032	0.0022	0.0015	0.0011	0.0007	0.0005	0.0003	0.0002
30	0.7397	0.5455	0.4010	0.2939	0.2146	0.1563	0.1134	0.0820	0.0591	0.0424	0.0303	0.0216	0.0153	0.0108	0.0076	0.0054	0.0037	0.0026	0.0018	0.0012	0.0008	0.0006	0.0004	0.0003	0.0002
31	0.7323	0.5346	0.3890	0.2821	0.2039	0.1469	0.1054	0.0754	0.0537	0.0382	0.0270	0.0190	0.0133	0.0093	0.0065	0.0045	0.0031	0.0021	0.0015	0.0010	0.0007	0.0005	0.0003	0.0002	0.0001
32	0.7250	0.5239	0.3773	0.2708	0.1937	0.1381	0.0981	0.0694	0.0489	0.0343	0.0240	0.0167	0.0116	0.0080	0.0055	0.0038	0.0026	0.0017	0.0012	0.0008	0.0005	0.0003	0.0002	0.0002	0.0001
33	0.7177	0.5134	0.3660	0.2600	0.1840	0.1298	0.0912	0.0638	0.0445	0.0309	0.0214	0.0147	0.0101	0.0069	0.0047	0.0032	0.0021	0.0014	0.0010	0.0006	0.0004	0.0002	0.0002	0.0001	0.0001
34	0.7106	0.5031	0.3550	0.2496	0.1748	0.1220	0.0848	0.0587	0.0405	0.0278	0.0190	0.0130	0.0088	0.0059	0.0040	0.0027	0.0018	0.0012	0.0008	0.0005	0.0003	0.0002	0.0001	0.0001	0.0001
35	0.7034	0.4931	0.3444	0.2396	0.1661	0.1147	0.0789	0.0540	0.0369	0.0250	0.0169	0.0114	0.0076	0.0051	0.0034	0.0022	0.0015	0.0010	0.0007	0.0004	0.0003	0.0002	0.0001	0.0001	0.0000
36	0.6964	0.4832	0.3340	0.2300	0.1578	0.1078	0.0733	0.0497	0.0335	0.0225	0.0151	0.0100	0.0066	0.0044	0.0029	0.0019	0.0012	0.0008	0.0005	0.0003	0.0002	0.0001	0.0001	0.0000	0.0000
37	0.6894	0.4735	0.3240	0.2208	0.1499	0.1013	0.0682	0.0457	0.0305	0.0203	0.0134	0.0088	0.0058	0.0038	0.0024	0.0016	0.0010	0.0006	0.0004	0.0003	0.0002	0.0001	0.0001	0.0000	0.0000
38	0.6826	0.4641	0.3143	0.2120	0.1424	0.0952	0.0634	0.0421	0.0278	0.0182	0.0119	0.0078	0.0050	0.0032	0.0021	0.0013	0.0008	0.0005	0.0003	0.0002	0.0001	0.0001	0.0000	0.0000	0.0000
39	0.6757	0.4548	0.3049	0.2035	0.1353	0.0895	0.0590	0.0387	0.0253	0.0164	0.0106	0.0068	0.0044	0.0028	0.0018	0.0011	0.0007	0.0004	0.0003	0.0002	0.0001	0.0000	0.0000	0.0000	0.0000
40	0.6690	0.4457	0.2957	0.1954	0.1285	0.0842	0.0549	0.0356	0.0230	0.0148	0.0095	0.0060	0.0038	0.0024	0.0015	0.0009	0.0006	0.0004	0.0002	0.0001	0.0001	0.0000	0.0000	0.0000	0.0000

Table of capital recovery factors

Yrs.	Interest rate (%) 1	2	3	4	5	6	7	8	9	10	11	12	13	14	15	16	17	18	19	20	21	22	23	24	25
1	1.0100	1.0200	1.0300	1.0400	1.0500	1.0600	1.0700	1.0800	1.0900	1.1000	1.1100	1.1200	1.1300	1.1400	1.1500	1.1600	1.1700	1.1800	1.1900	1.2000	1.2100	1.2200	1.2300	1.2400	1.2500
2	0.5075	0.5150	0.5226	0.5302	0.5378	0.5454	0.5531	0.5608	0.5685	0.5762	0.5839	0.5917	0.5995	0.6073	0.6151	0.6230	0.6308	0.6387	0.6466	0.6545	0.6625	0.6705	0.6784	0.6864	0.6944
3	0.3400	0.3468	0.3535	0.3603	0.3672	0.3741	0.3811	0.3880	0.3951	0.4021	0.4092	0.4163	0.4235	0.4307	0.4380	0.4453	0.4526	0.4599	0.4673	0.4747	0.4822	0.4897	0.4972	0.5047	0.5123
4	0.2563	0.2626	0.2690	0.2755	0.2820	0.2886	0.2952	0.3019	0.3087	0.3155	0.3223	0.3292	0.3362	0.3432	0.3503	0.3574	0.3645	0.3717	0.3790	0.3863	0.3936	0.4010	0.4085	0.4159	0.4234
5	0.2060	0.2122	0.2184	0.2246	0.2310	0.2374	0.2439	0.2505	0.2571	0.2638	0.2706	0.2774	0.2843	0.2913	0.2983	0.3054	0.3126	0.3198	0.3271	0.3344	0.3418	0.3492	0.3567	0.3642	0.3718
6	0.1725	0.1785	0.1846	0.1908	0.1970	0.2034	0.2098	0.2163	0.2229	0.2296	0.2364	0.2432	0.2502	0.2572	0.2642	0.2714	0.2786	0.2859	0.2933	0.3007	0.3082	0.3158	0.3234	0.3311	0.3388
7	0.1486	0.1545	0.1605	0.1666	0.1728	0.1791	0.1856	0.1921	0.1987	0.2054	0.2122	0.2191	0.2261	0.2332	0.2404	0.2476	0.2549	0.2624	0.2699	0.2774	0.2851	0.2928	0.3006	0.3084	0.3163
8	0.1307	0.1365	0.1425	0.1485	0.1547	0.1610	0.1675	0.1740	0.1807	0.1874	0.1943	0.2013	0.2084	0.2156	0.2229	0.2302	0.2377	0.2452	0.2529	0.2606	0.2684	0.2763	0.2843	0.2923	0.3004
9	0.1167	0.1225	0.1284	0.1345	0.1407	0.1470	0.1535	0.1601	0.1668	0.1736	0.1806	0.1877	0.1949	0.2022	0.2096	0.2171	0.2247	0.2324	0.2402	0.2481	0.2561	0.2641	0.2722	0.2805	0.2888
10	0.1056	0.1113	0.1172	0.1233	0.1295	0.1359	0.1424	0.1490	0.1558	0.1627	0.1698	0.1770	0.1843	0.1917	0.1993	0.2069	0.2147	0.2225	0.2305	0.2385	0.2467	0.2549	0.2632	0.2716	0.2801
11	0.0965	0.1022	0.1081	0.1141	0.1204	0.1268	0.1334	0.1401	0.1469	0.1540	0.1611	0.1684	0.1758	0.1834	0.1911	0.1989	0.2068	0.2148	0.2229	0.2311	0.2394	0.2478	0.2563	0.2649	0.2735
12	0.0888	0.0946	0.1005	0.1066	0.1128	0.1193	0.1259	0.1327	0.1397	0.1468	0.1540	0.1614	0.1690	0.1767	0.1845	0.1924	0.2005	0.2086	0.2169	0.2253	0.2337	0.2423	0.2509	0.2596	0.2684
13	0.0824	0.0881	0.0940	0.1001	0.1065	0.1130	0.1197	0.1265	0.1336	0.1408	0.1482	0.1557	0.1634	0.1712	0.1791	0.1872	0.1954	0.2037	0.2121	0.2206	0.2292	0.2379	0.2467	0.2556	0.2645
14	0.0769	0.0826	0.0885	0.0947	0.1010	0.1076	0.1143	0.1213	0.1284	0.1357	0.1432	0.1509	0.1587	0.1666	0.1747	0.1829	0.1912	0.1997	0.2082	0.2169	0.2256	0.2345	0.2434	0.2524	0.2615
15	0.0721	0.0778	0.0838	0.0899	0.0963	0.1030	0.1098	0.1168	0.1241	0.1315	0.1391	0.1468	0.1547	0.1628	0.1710	0.1794	0.1878	0.1964	0.2051	0.2139	0.2228	0.2317	0.2408	0.2499	0.2591
16	0.0679	0.0737	0.0796	0.0858	0.0923	0.0990	0.1059	0.1130	0.1203	0.1278	0.1355	0.1434	0.1514	0.1596	0.1679	0.1764	0.1850	0.1937	0.2025	0.2114	0.2204	0.2295	0.2387	0.2479	0.2572
17	0.0643	0.0700	0.0760	0.0822	0.0887	0.0954	0.1024	0.1096	0.1170	0.1247	0.1325	0.1405	0.1486	0.1569	0.1654	0.1740	0.1827	0.1915	0.2004	0.2094	0.2186	0.2278	0.2370	0.2464	0.2558
18	0.0610	0.0667	0.0727	0.0790	0.0855	0.0924	0.0994	0.1067	0.1142	0.1219	0.1298	0.1379	0.1462	0.1546	0.1632	0.1719	0.1807	0.1896	0.1987	0.2078	0.2170	0.2263	0.2357	0.2451	0.2546
19	0.0581	0.0638	0.0698	0.0761	0.0827	0.0896	0.0968	0.1041	0.1117	0.1195	0.1276	0.1358	0.1441	0.1527	0.1613	0.1701	0.1791	0.1881	0.1972	0.2065	0.2158	0.2251	0.2346	0.2441	0.2537
20	0.0554	0.0612	0.0672	0.0736	0.0802	0.0872	0.0944	0.1019	0.1095	0.1175	0.1256	0.1339	0.1424	0.1510	0.1598	0.1687	0.1777	0.1868	0.1960	0.2054	0.2147	0.2242	0.2337	0.2433	0.2529
21	0.0530	0.0588	0.0649	0.0713	0.0780	0.0850	0.0923	0.0998	0.1076	0.1156	0.1238	0.1322	0.1408	0.1495	0.1584	0.1674	0.1765	0.1857	0.1951	0.2044	0.2139	0.2234	0.2330	0.2426	0.2523
22	0.0509	0.0566	0.0627	0.0692	0.0760	0.0830	0.0904	0.0980	0.1059	0.1140	0.1223	0.1308	0.1395	0.1483	0.1573	0.1664	0.1756	0.1848	0.1942	0.2037	0.2132	0.2228	0.2324	0.2421	0.2519
23	0.0489	0.0547	0.0608	0.0673	0.0741	0.0813	0.0887	0.0964	0.1044	0.1126	0.1210	0.1296	0.1383	0.1472	0.1563	0.1654	0.1747	0.1841	0.1935	0.2031	0.2127	0.2223	0.2320	0.2417	0.2515
24	0.0471	0.0529	0.0590	0.0656	0.0725	0.0797	0.0872	0.0950	0.1030	0.1113	0.1198	0.1285	0.1373	0.1463	0.1554	0.1647	0.1740	0.1835	0.1930	0.2025	0.2122	0.2219	0.2316	0.2414	0.2512
25	0.0454	0.0512	0.0574	0.0640	0.0710	0.0782	0.0858	0.0937	0.1018	0.1102	0.1187	0.1275	0.1364	0.1455	0.1547	0.1640	0.1734	0.1829	0.1925	0.2021	0.2118	0.2215	0.2313	0.2411	0.2509
26	0.0439	0.0497	0.0559	0.0626	0.0696	0.0769	0.0846	0.0925	0.1007	0.1092	0.1178	0.1267	0.1357	0.1448	0.1541	0.1634	0.1729	0.1825	0.1921	0.2018	0.2115	0.2213	0.2311	0.2409	0.2508
27	0.0424	0.0483	0.0546	0.0612	0.0683	0.0757	0.0834	0.0914	0.0997	0.1083	0.1170	0.1259	0.1350	0.1442	0.1535	0.1630	0.1725	0.1821	0.1917	0.2015	0.2112	0.2210	0.2309	0.2407	0.1506
28	0.0411	0.0470	0.0533	0.0600	0.0671	0.0746	0.0824	0.0905	0.0989	0.1075	0.1163	0.1252	0.1344	0.1437	0.1531	0.1625	0.1721	0.1818	0.1915	0.2012	0.2110	0.2208	0.2307	0.2406	0.2505
29	0.0399	0.0458	0.0521	0.0589	0.0660	0.0736	0.0814	0.0896	0.0981	0.1067	0.1156	0.1247	0.1339	0.1432	0.1527	0.1622	0.1718	0.1815	0.1912	0.2010	0.2108	0.2207	0.2306	0.2405	0.2504
30	0.0387	0.0446	0.0510	0.0578	0.0651	0.0726	0.0806	0.0888	0.0973	0.1061	0.1150	0.1241	0.1334	0.1428	0.1523	0.1619	0.1715	0.1813	0.1910	0.2008	0.2107	0.2206	0.2305	0.2404	0.2503
31	0.0377	0.0436	0.0500	0.0569	0.0641	0.0718	0.0798	0.0881	0.0967	0.1055	0.1145	0.1237	0.1330	0.1425	0.1520	0.1616	0.1713	0.1811	0.1909	0.2007	0.2106	0.2205	0.2304	0.2403	0.2502
32	0.0367	0.0426	0.0490	0.0559	0.0633	0.0710	0.0791	0.0875	0.0961	0.1050	0.1140	0.1233	0.1327	0.1421	0.1517	0.1614	0.1711	0.1809	0.1907	0.2006	0.2105	0.2204	0.2303	0.2402	0.2502
33	0.0357	0.0417	0.0482	0.0551	0.0625	0.0703	0.0784	0.0869	0.0956	0.1045	0.1136	0.1229	0.1323	0.1419	0.1515	0.1612	0.1710	0.1808	0.1906	0.2005	0.2104	0.2203	0.2302	0.2402	0.2502
34	0.0348	0.0408	0.0473	0.0543	0.0618	0.0696	0.0778	0.0863	0.0951	0.1041	0.1133	0.1226	0.1321	0.1416	0.1513	0.1610	0.1708	0.1806	0.1905	0.2004	0.2103	0.2203	0.2302	0.2402	0.2501
35	0.0340	0.0400	0.0465	0.0536	0.0611	0.0690	0.0772	0.0858	0.0946	0.1037	0.1129	0.1223	0.1318	0.1414	0.1511	0.1609	0.1707	0.1806	0.1904	0.2003	0.2103	0.2202	0.2302	0.2401	0.2501
36	0.0332	0.0392	0.0458	0.0529	0.0604	0.0684	0.0767	0.0853	0.0942	0.1033	0.1126	0.1221	0.1316	0.1413	0.1510	0.1608	0.1706	0.1805	0.1904	0.2003	0.2102	0.2202	0.2301	0.2401	0.2501
37	0.0325	0.0385	0.0451	0.0522	0.0598	0.0679	0.0762	0.0849	0.0939	0.1030	0.1124	0.1218	0.1314	0.1411	0.1509	0.1607	0.1705	0.1804	0.1903	0.2002	0.2102	0.2201	0.2301	0.2401	0.2501
38	0.0318	0.0378	0.0445	0.0516	0.0593	0.0674	0.0758	0.0845	0.0935	0.1027	0.1121	0.1216	0.1313	0.1410	0.1507	0.1606	0.1704	0.1803	0.1903	0.2002	0.2101	0.2201	0.2301	0.2401	0.2501
39	0.0311	0.0372	0.0438	0.0511	0.0588	0.0669	0.0754	0.0842	0.0932	0.1025	0.1119	0.1215	0.1311	0.1409	0.1506	0.1605	0.1704	0.1803	0.1902	0.2002	0.2101	0.2201	0.2301	0.2401	0.2500
40	0.0305	0.0366	0.0433	0.0505	0.0583	0.0665	0.0750	0.0839	0.0930	0.1023	0.1117	0.1213	0.1310	0.1407	0.1506	0.1604	0.1703	0.1802	0.1902	0.2001	0.2101	0.2201	0.2301	0.2400	0.2500

LIST OF FORMULAE

Here we provide a summary of the more important formulae and concepts that have appeared in this text.

CHAPTER 2

General equation of straight line: $y = a + bx$

where a is the intercept with the y-axis

b is the gradient.

General equation of quadratic curve: $y = ax^2 + bx + c$

The solutions of $ax^2 + bx + c = 0$ are $x = \dfrac{-b \pm \sqrt{b^2 - 4ac}}{2a}$

CHAPTER 3

Compound interest:	$P_n = P_0(1 + i)^n$
Present value:	$P_0 = P_n(1 + i)^{-n}$
Annuity:	$V = A[1 - (1 + i)^{-n}]/i$
Repayment:	$w = M\{i/[1 - (1 + i)^{-n}]\}$
Sinking fund:	$S = w(1 + i)[(1 + i)^n - 1]/i$
Depreciation:	$P_n = P_0(1 - i)^n$

CHAPTER 8

Mean for ungrouped data: $\bar{x} = \dfrac{\Sigma x}{n}$

Mean for grouped data: $\bar{x} = \dfrac{\Sigma x f}{\Sigma f}$

Standard deviation for ungrouped data: $s = \sqrt{\dfrac{\Sigma(x - \bar{x})^2}{n}} = \sqrt{\dfrac{\Sigma x^2}{n} - \left(\dfrac{\Sigma x}{n}\right)^2}$

Standard deviation for grouped data:

$$s = \sqrt{\frac{\Sigma x^2 f}{\Sigma f} - \left(\frac{\Sigma xf}{\Sigma f}\right)^2}$$

Mean deviation:

$$MD = \frac{\Sigma |x - \bar{x}|}{n}$$

Quartile deviation:

$$QD = \frac{Q3 - Q1}{2}$$

Coefficient of variation:

$$CV = \frac{s}{\bar{x}} \times 100$$

CHAPTER 9

Least squares regression line:

$$y = a + bx$$

where

$$b = \frac{\Sigma xy - (\Sigma x)(\Sigma y)/n}{\Sigma x^2 - (\Sigma x)^2/n}, \quad a = \frac{\Sigma y - b\Sigma x}{n}$$

Correlation coefficient:

$$r = \frac{\Sigma xy - (\Sigma x)(\Sigma y)/n}{\sqrt{\left[\Sigma x^2 - \frac{(\Sigma x)^2}{n}\right]\left[\Sigma y^2 - \frac{(\Sigma y)^2}{n}\right]}}$$

Spearman's coefficient of rank correlation: $\quad r' = 1 - \frac{6\Sigma d^2}{n(n^2 - 1)}$

CHAPTER 11

Simple aggregative price index:

$$\frac{\Sigma P_n}{\Sigma P_0} \times 100$$

Simple mean of price relatives:

$$\frac{1}{k} \Sigma \left(\frac{P_n}{P_0}\right) \times 100$$

Laspeyres price index:

$$\frac{\Sigma P_n Q_0}{\Sigma P_0 Q_0} \times 100$$

Paasche price index:

$$\frac{\Sigma P_n Q_n}{\Sigma P_0 Q_n} \times 100$$

CHAPTER 12

Addition rule:

$$P(A \cup B) = P(A) + P(B) - P(A \cap B)$$

Multiplication rule:

$$P(A \cap B) = P(A)P(B|A)$$

Bayes' Theorem:

$$P(A_i|B) = \frac{P(B|A_i)P(A_i)}{\displaystyle\sum_{j=1}^{n} P(B|A_j)P(A_j)} \quad (i = 1, \ldots, n)$$

CHAPTER 13

Expected value:

$$\sum_{\text{all outcomes}} (\text{value associated with outcome}) \times (\text{probability of outcome})$$

CHAPTER 14

Binomial distribution:

$$P(r \text{ successes}) = {_nC_r}\, p^r(1-p)^{n-r}$$

$$\text{Mean} = np \quad \text{s.d.} = \sqrt{np(1-p)}$$

Poisson distribution:

$$P(r \text{ occurrences}) = \frac{m^r e^{-m}}{r!}$$

$$\text{Mean} = m \qquad \text{s.d.} = \sqrt{m}$$

Normal distribution:

$$f(x) = \frac{1}{\sqrt{2\pi\sigma^2}}\, e^{-[(x-\mu)^2/2\sigma^2]}$$

$$\text{Mean} = \mu \qquad \text{s.d.} = \sigma$$

CHAPTER 15

Standard error of the mean:

$$\frac{\sigma}{\sqrt{n}}$$

Standard error of a proportion:

$$\sqrt{\frac{\pi(1-\pi)}{n}}$$

Unbiased estimate of population variance: $\hat{\sigma}^2 = \dfrac{1}{n-1} \displaystyle\sum_{i=1}^{n}(x_i - \bar{x})^2$

CHAPTER 16

Test of one mean:

$$T = \frac{\bar{x} - \mu}{\sigma/\sqrt{n}}$$

which has a normal distribution when n is large and σ known.

Standard error of the difference between means: $\sqrt{(\sigma_1^2/n_1) + (\sigma_2^2/n_2)}$

Standard error of the difference between proportions: $\sqrt{\dfrac{\pi_1(1-\pi_1)}{n_1} + \dfrac{\pi_2(1-\pi_2)}{n_2}}$

Test of one mean:

$$T = \frac{\bar{x} - \mu}{\hat{\sigma}/\sqrt{n}}$$

which has a t-distribution with $v = n-1$ degrees of freedom when the underlying population is normal.

Test for no correlation:
$$T = \frac{r}{\sqrt{(1-r^2)/(n-2)}}$$

which has a t-distribution with $v = n - 2$ degrees of freedom.

CHAPTER 17

Chi-squared statistic:
$$\chi^2 = \sum \frac{(O_i - E_i)^2}{E_i}$$

CHAPTER 20

PERT formulae
$$\mu = (4m + a + b)/6$$
$$\sigma = (b - a)/6$$

CHAPTER 21

Economic order quantity (EOQ)
$$q = \sqrt{\frac{2 \times D \times c1}{c2}}$$

BIBLIOGRAPHY

It is intended that the books listed in this appendix should help readers to obtain a wider perspective on the topics covered by enlarging the range of examples and exercises to be found on these topics and by expanding on aspects which space considerations have allowed us to deal with only briefly. In the latter respect we are mindful of the great importance of computers in statistics, operational research, and mathematics. We have, therefore, sought to give very specific references to enable the reader to follow up this area.

We have tried to provide a genuinely *useful* bibliography by deliberately avoiding giving a mere list of books. Instead we have endeavoured to indicate readings relevant to particular chapters of our text, and also, where appropriate, to indicate which parts of the suggested readings relate to the chapter concerned.

Chapter 1

Ryan, B. F., B. L. Joiner and T. A. Ryan, *MINITAB Handbook*, Wadsworth, Boston, Massachusetts, 1985.

Chapter 2

Francis, A., *Business Mathematics and Statistics*, DPP, Winchester, 1988 (esp. units 30, 31, 32, pp. 226–47).
Jacques, I., *Mathematics for Economics and Business*, Addison-Wesley, Wokingham, 1991 (esp. chapters 1 and 2).
Owen, F. and R. Jones, *Modern Analytical Techniques*, Polytech, Stockport, 1984 (esp. chapter 1).

Chapter 3

Ayres, F. J., *Mathematics of Finance*, McGraw-Hill, New York, 1963.
Jacques, I., *Mathematics for Economics and Business*, Addison-Wesley, Wokingham, 1991 (esp. chapter 3).
Lucey, T., *Quantitative Techniques*, DPP, Winchester, 1982.

Chapter 4

Jacques, I., *Mathematics for Economics and Business*, Addison-Wesley, Wokingham, 1991 (esp. chapter 8).
Owen, F. and R. Jones, *Modern Analytical Techniques*, Polytech, Stockport, 1984 (esp. chapter 5).

Chapter 5

Jacques, I., *Mathematics for Economics and Business*, Addison-Wesley, Wokingham, 1991 (esp. chapters 4 and 6).
Mendelson, E., *Beginning Calculus*, McGraw-Hill, New York, 1985.
Weber, J. E., *Mathematical Analysis—Business and Economic Applications*, Harper & Rowe, New York, 1976.

Chapter 6

Moser, C. A. and G. Kalton, *Survey Methods in Social Investigation*, Heinemann, London, 1971.
Reeves, T. K. and D. Harper, *Surveys at Work*, McGraw-Hill, London, 1981.
Rendell, F. J. and D. M. Wolf, *Statistical Sources and Techniques*, McGraw-Hill, Maidenhead, 1983.

Chapters 7–17

There are various books that cover the statistical topics in these chapters. Those the reader may find helpful, particularly from the point of view of finding numbers of examples and exercises are:

Freund, J. E. and F. J. Williams, *Elementary Business Statistics: The Modern Approach*, Prentice-Hall, London, 1977.
Gregory, D. and H. Ward, *Statistics for Business*, McGraw-Hill, London, 1978.
Kazmier, L. J., *Theory and Problems of Business Statistics*, 'Schaum Outline Series', McGraw-Hill, New York, 1976.
Whitehead, P. and G. Whitehead, *Statistics for Business*, Pitman, London, 1986.

Other books to which the reader is referred in respect of the computer aspects of the work in these chapters are:

Judge, G., *Quantitative Analysis for Economics and Business Using LOTUS 1-2-3*, Harvester Wheatsheaf, Hemel Hempstead, 1990.
Ryan, B. F., B. L. Joiner and T. A. Ryan, *MINITAB Handbook*, Wadsworth, Boston, Massachusetts, 1985.

Judge is very good at showing the application of spreadsheets to statistical work and references are given to specific chapters in our text. It is essential further reading for anybody wanting to use spreadsheets for these purposes.

Chapter 18

Arkin, H., *Handbook of Sampling for Auditing and Accounting*, McGraw-Hill, New York, 1974.
McRae, T. W., *Statistical Sampling for Audit and Control*, Wiley, London, 1974.
Smith, T. M., *Statistical Sampling for Accountants*, Haymarket, London, 1976.

Chapter 19

Chang, Y-L and R. S. Sullivan, *Quantitative Systems for Business +*, Prentice-Hall, Englewood Cliffs, 1990.
Wilkes, F. M., *Elements of Operational Research*, McGraw-Hill, London, 1980.

Chapter 20

Chang, Y-L and R. S. Sullivan, *Quantitative Systems for Business +*, Prentice-Hall, Englewood Cliffs, 1990.
Moore, P. G., *Basic Operational Research*, Pitman, London, 1976.
Tafler, R. J., *Using Operational Research*, Prentice-Hall, London, 1979.

Chapter 21

Browne, J., J. Harhen and J. Shivnan, *Production Management Systems*, Addison-Wesley, New York, 1988.
Chang, Y-L and R. S. Sullivan, *Quantitative Systems for Business +*, Prentice-Hall, Englewood Cliffs, 1990.

Chapter 22

Chang, Y-L and R. S. Sullivan, *Quantitative Systems for Business +*, Prentice-Hall, Englewood Cliffs, 1990.

INDEX